Translated Texts for Historians

This series is designed to meet the needs of students of ancient and medieval history and others who wish to broaden their study by reading source material, but whose knowledge of  hem to do so in the original languag rk Age texts are currently unavailab H will help to fill this gap and to co nglish which already exists. The se 0–800 AD and includes Late Imper ; well as source books illustrating a e is a self-contained scholarly trans ... ... introductory essay on the text and its author and notes on the text indicating major problems of interpretation, including textual difficulties.

Editorial Committee
Sebastian Brock, Oriental Institute, University of Oxford
Averil Cameron, Keble College, Oxford
Henry Chadwick, Oxford
John Davies, University of Liverpool
Carlotta Dionisotti, King's College, London
Peter Heather, University College, London
Robert Hoyland, University of St Andrews
William E. Klingshirn, The Catholic University of America
Michael Lapidge, Clare College, Cambridge
Robert Markus, University of Nottingham
John Matthews, Yale University
Claudia Rapp, University of California, Los Angeles
Raymond Van Dam, University of Michigan
Michael Whitby, University of Warwick
Ian Wood, University of Leeds

General Editors
Gillian Clark, University of Bristol
Mark Humphries, National University of Ireland, Maynooth
Mary Whitby, University of Liverpool

A full list of published titles in the Translated Texts for Historians series is available on request. The most recently published are shown below.

A Christian's Guide to Greek Culture: The Pseudo-Nonnus *Commentaries* on *Sermons* 4, 5, 39 and 43 of Gregory of Nazianzus
Translated with an introduction and notes by JENNIFER NIMMO SMITH
Volume 37: 208pp., 2001, ISBN 0-85323-917-7

Avitus of Vienne: Letters and Selected Prose
Translated with introduction and notes by DANUTA SHANZER and IAN WOOD
Volume 38: 472pp., 2002, ISBN 0-85323-588-0

Constantine and Christendom: The Oration to the Saints, The Greek and Latin Accounts of the Discovery of the Cross, The Edict of Constantine to Pope Silvester
Translated with introduction and notes by MARK EDWARDS
Volume 39: 192pp., 2003, ISBN 0-85323-648-8

Lactantius: Divine Institutes
Translated with introduction and notes by ANTHONY BOWEN and PETER GARNSEY
Volume 40: 488pp., 2003, ISBN 0-85323-988-6

Selected Letters of Libanius from the Age of Constantius and Julian
Translated with introduction and notes by SCOT BRADBURY
Volume 41: 308pp., 2004, ISBN 0-85323-509-0

Cassiodorus: Institutions of Divine and Secular Learning and On the Soul
Translated and notes by JAMES W. HALPORN; Introduction by MARK VESSEY
Volume 42: 316 pp., 2004, ISBN 0-85323-998-3

Ambrose of Milan: Political Letters and Speeches
Translated with an introduction and notes by J. H. W. G. LIEBESCHUETZ and CAROLE HILL
Volume 43: 432pp., 2005, ISBN 0-85323-829-4

The Chronicle of Ireland
Translated with an introduction and notes by T. M. CHARLES-EDWARDS
Volume 44: 2 vols., 349pp. + 186pp., 2006, ISBN 0-85323-959-2

The Acts of the Council of Chalcedon
Translated with an introduction and notes by RICHARD PRICE and MICHAEL GADDIS
Volume 45: 3 vols., 365pp. + 312pp. + 312pp., 2005, ISBN 0-85323-039-0

For full details of Translated Texts for Historians, including prices and ordering information, please write to the following:
All countries, except the USA and Canada: Liverpool University Press, 4 Cambridge Street, Liverpool, L69 7ZU, UK (*Tel* +44-[0]151-794 2233, *Fax* +44-[0]151-794 2235, Email J.M. Smith@liv.ac.uk, http://www.liverpool-unipress.co.uk). **USA and Canada:** University of Chicago Press, 1427 E. 60th Street, Chicago, IL, 60637, US (*Tel* 773-702-7700, *Fax* 773-702-9756, www.press.uchicago.edu)

Translated Texts for Historians
Volume 13

The Lives of the Eighth-Century Popes
(Liber Pontificalis)

The Ancient Biographies of Nine Popes
from AD 715 to AD 817

Translated with introduction and notes by
RAYMOND DAVIS

Liverpool
University
Press

First published 1992
Liverpool University Press
4 Cambridge Street
Liverpool, L69 7ZU

Revised edition 2007

Copyright © 1992, 2007 Raymond Davis

The right of Raymond Davis to be identified as the author
of this work has been asserted by him in accordance
with the Copyright, Designs and Patents Act, 1988

All rights reserved. No part of this book may be reproduced
stored in a retrieval system, or transmitted, in any form or
by any means, electronic, mechanical, photocopying, recording,
or otherwise, without the prior written permission of the publisher.

British Library Cataloguing-in-Publication Data
A British Library CIP Record is available.

ISBN 978-1-84631-154-3

Set in Times by
Koinonia, Manchester
Printed in the European Union by
Bell and Bain Ltd, Glasgow

CONTENTS

Preface	vii
Introduction	xi
The Manuscripts of the Liber Pontificalis for the Lives from AD 715 onwards	xvii
Texts and Commentaries	xxii
Abbreviations	xxiv

The Lives of the Eighth-Century Popes

91 Gregory II (715–731):	introduction	1
	translation	3
92 Gregory III (731–741):	introduction	17
	translation	19
93 Zacharias (741–752):	introduction	29
	Domuscultae	30
	translation	34
94 Stephen II (752–757):	introduction	50
	translation	52
95 Paul (757–767):	introduction	76
	translation	79
96 Stephen III (768–772):	introduction	84
	translation	87
97 Hadrian I (772–795):	introduction	106
	translation	120
98 Leo III (795–816):	introduction	170
	The Chronology of the Life of Leo III	171
	The Catalogue of Donations in 807	172
	Omissions from the Catalogue of 807	173
	translation	176
99 Stephen IV (816–817):	introduction	228
	translation	231

Glossary	234
Bibliography	242
Index of Persons and Places	250
Maps of Italy and of Rome	262

PREFACE

When the General Editors of this series approached me to undertake a continuation of *The Book of Pontiffs* I accepted with trepidation. The text of the lives of the popes in the Liber Pontificalis from A.D. 715 to A.D. 891 is some three times the length of that translated in the earlier volume, and the material is such that a translation would serve little purpose without a running commentary. It was a daunting prospect, and the present volume, first published in 1992, which carries the lives of the popes from 715 down to 817 (the 'eighth century', roughly) represents one half of the undertaking; the third volume, covering the remaining lives of the ninth century, was published in this series in 1995.

I am conscious that this volume appears in the centenary of the completion of Duchesne's magisterial edition of the Latin text and commentary. My commentary is intended to retain in as brief a compass as possible all that Duchesne had to say which is still useful and valid; inevitably his extensive quotations of other literary sources and of inscriptions have suffered excision in the interests of space. Updating has been necessary most particularly for chapters in the text which concern the political history of the period. I doubt if the task could have been attempted by one whose historical training is in a rather earlier period had T. F. X. Noble's *The Republic of St Peter* not been available; to this work I willingly acknowledge my indebtedness, and to it I refer readers for fuller discussion.

The text translated is that of Duchesne entire and unaltered. Mommsen's edition of the lives after 715 was planned but never appeared. In fact the textual problems for these later lives are far less complicated than for the earlier period.

There are conflicting systems of reference to the text of the Liber Pontificalis. I have chosen the chapter numbers of Vignoli's edition as given (not always quite accurately) in Duchesne's edition; each of these is about half the length of the sections in the Bianchini edition and about a quarter of the length of Duchesne's own pages. The Bianchini sections, even though this is the edition reprinted (as 'Anastasius') in the *Patrologia Latina*, seem now to be used by no one; and Duchesne himself expressed a preference for Vignoli (though he used Bianchini in his commentary when referring to parts of the text he had not yet reached). Duchesne's pages are simply too long to be convenient for purposes of reference or indexing.

The paragraphing of the translation follows Duchesne as far as possible; the main modifications occur where the analysis by H. Geertman (*More Veterum*) of material on donations and repairs to churches requires a different arrangement. In lives 97 and 98 I have inserted chronological headings, following Geertman.

The rendering of proper names is a problem for every translator. Where familiar English forms do not exist I have generally preferred Latin for persons, Latin for those geographical features which are of uncertain location or whose modern name does not reflect the old form, and Italian for other place-names; this may be inconsistent, but I was not prepared to write of king Desiderio, to return to the older Ticinum where the text employs the later form Pavia, or to disguise Centumcellae as Civitavecchia. For the orthography of Italian names I have followed the *Atlante Automobilistico* of the Touring Club Italiano, and in a number of instances I have retained the antepenultimate accents used there. If Italian readers find it useful to be warned against false stresses in names like Céccano and Césena, I trust non-Italians will not object.

In the preparation of this work by far my greatest debt was to the late Dr Margaret Gibson of St Peter's College Oxford, who not merely showed enthusiasm for this work at every stage but checked the translation word by word and reviewed the introductions and commentary in detail when, as I am sure, she had much more worthwhile projects in hand. My deepest gratitude is due to her and also to Mrs Christa Mee whose cartographic skills have turned scrawl into usable maps, and to Mr Robin Bloxsidge and his colleagues at the Liverpool University Press who have worked to a tight schedule. I owe thanks also to my colleagues in the Queen's University of Belfast, many of whom I have pestered for their opinions and expertise, be it on the niceties of Latin vocabulary – particularly Dr Brian Campbell and Dr Brian Scott; or on points of Byzantine history – particularly Dr Margaret Mullett; nor can I omit to thank Miss Janis Boyd, Secretary to the School of Greek, Roman and Semitic Studies, and the late Professor Alan Astin, Director of the same School and Professor of Ancient History. Even in his last weeks he maintained interest in the progress of this work and offered me his encouragement: *iustitia eius manet in saeculum saeculi.*

PREFACE

In preparing this revised (2007) edition the opportunity has been take to correct a few errors or misprints and to clarify a good number of points in the translation and the notes.

PARENTIBUS BENE MERENTIBUS
REGINALDO IOHANNI (1908–1977)
ET ELEANORAE ALICIAE (1909–2002)

INTRODUCTION

The individual lives have their own introductions, but it is convenient here to consider some general points.

1. The nature of the *Liber Pontificalis* of the Roman Church

The origins of the work in episcopal lists maintained from the third century, the development of these into biographies in the early sixth century, the production from these of a 'second edition' and the early continuations of this in the sixth and seventh centuries have been discussed in my *Book of Pontiffs*, and there is little to be gained by rehearsing material which has no direct bearing on the biographies contained in this volume. It is enough to recall that during most of the seventh century the LP was being updated spasmodically, and by the beginning of the eighth century on a life by life basis.

As for the lives in this volume, which are serially numbered in the manuscripts 91 through to 99, it is clear from Bede's use of material in the life of Gregory II (see introduction to life 91) that the continuators no longer thought it necessary to wait until the pope whose reign they were chronicling had died; and the increasing length of most of the successive lives is itself a sign of compilation by contemporary writers who knew at first hand of the events they were recording.

The various continuators, all anonymous in this period, were probably clerks in the Lateran *vestiarium*. Politically they were all loyal to the church in whose service they worked and to the policies of the regime at Rome; as contemporaries, their comments on the defects of that regime are guarded or non-existent: one would search life 97 in vain for anything on Hadrian I's nepotistic tendencies. The authors were not members of any literary élite; their Latinity is usually, though by no means always, transparent in meaning, but their style, their grammar and their vocabulary are not such as would pass muster with the scholars of the Carolingian Renaissance. Many of the continuators were liable to fall back on register material preserved in their own office as a substitute for political history.

A single life need not have had a single author, and in the case of the lengthy pontificate of Hadrian (97) it is virtually certain that there were at least two authors. On the other hand I suspect a single author was responsible for lives 95, 96 and 97 cc. 1–44. His bible-influenced Latin style suggests that the author of life 93 was not the same as that of 92 or 94. The author of 91 is fond of military details, whereas the author of 92 shows no interest in Lombard activities. Peculiarities of vocabulary help to isolate authors: the author of 91 is fond of the words *praepedire* (six times) and *consilium* (six times in the original text, and *consiliator* once), whereas neither word occurs in 92. Life 93 contains words seldom or not at all used earlier in the LP: *spondere* (and *sponsio*), *conspicere*, *advenire*, *conviare*, *redonare*. Life 94 uses superlative epithets tediously (*christianissimus, sanctissimus* etc.), repeats royal titles every time Pepin or Aistulf are mentioned, likes to begin sentences with *ad haec* (four times), and favours the word *imminere* (seven times, in the sense 'press upon'). The lengthy life 98 never employs the verb *properare* (a word which unless qualified seems by this date to have lost any sense of haste), though it occurs 14 times in 96 and 20 times in 97. Other examples could be selected from these and later lives.

2. The text's importance for the history of the eighth century.

Little familiarity with the source material for eighth-century Europe is needed before it is realised that the bulk of it originates from the Frankish kingdom. Constantinople was immersed in a dark age from the historiographical point of view. Italian material is hardly plentiful. Yet these were the very years when with Frankish help the Roman church eased itself out of the orbit of the eastern empire and accepted a degree of Frankish protection. They were the years that saw the collapse of the Lombard kingdom in Italy, and in the last year of the century occurred the coronation of Charlemagne at Rome. For these events, each in its way critical in the development of Europe, the LP provides the most detailed surviving account. Among Italian sources therefore, the details preserved in these biographies are of paramount importance – if they are trustworthy.

The life of Hadrian I, with its information on Charles' donation in 774 of territories to the Roman church, and its reference back to the donation made by Pepin at Quierzy twenty years earlier, has caused the greatest controversy about the sincerity of the LP. The matter is fully discussed in the introduction to life 97, where it is argued that the account of both promised donations is reliable.

INTRODUCTION

Even the register material which seems to loom so large in parts of the text has its importance. Though this was hardly the intention of the compilers, it shows the effectiveness of the papal management of the patrimonies whose revenues made the donations and restorations on such an opulent scale possible. Equally the writers show no awareness of the tensions between Rome and the east resulting from the main religious dispute of the century, that over iconoclasm; but our authors make it abundantly clear how the Roman church went overboard on providing more and more images to decorate churches while the imperial regime was pursuing the opposite line. For the art historian the material preserved by the LP is fascinating. A treatise on the nature and manufacture of the various cloths and silks recorded in the LP is invited!

For a long time the issue of papal sovereignty has bedevilled studies of the history of this period. In what sense, and precisely when, did the papal state come into existence as a separate political entity from the eastern Roman empire? To what extent and with what effect was the new state constitutionally subject to or dependent on the Frankish kingdom and, later, empire, rather than Constantinople? The narrative of events given in the LP is crucial and must be taken into account in any view on these questions; but the compilers were not constitutional theorists.

If an ancient historian may interject a view in such controversial ground, it is that the issue should not be approached in terms of territorial sovereignty: such a concept is not one that men whose outlook was based on the ancient world and in no way on medieval or modern political systems could readily have understood. The fact that christian theology had provided a new ultimate source of authority does not affect the matter. Sovereignty, if the word must be used, is to be seen in personal terms, for individuals or for groups.

In some sense the Roman people, even in the eighth century, had *imperium* and were conscious that they had it, and the pope was their representative (*vicarius*), the man they had elected much as their ancestors had elected other holders of *imperium*. But he was more than that; he was the Vicar of St Peter. And they, as christian Romans, were more than just the Roman people; their outlook, and that of the popes, consciously or otherwise, is that of Leo the Great: Rome is a christian city founded by Peter and Paul, replacing the pagan city founded by Romulus and Remus, but not thereby losing any of the imperial prerogatives of the Roman people, rather gaining added spiritual ones. For *imperium* is not equivalent to 'empire' in the territorial sense the word now bears. It is a personal right to expect one's instructions to be fulfilled. There were, of course, still Roman emperors who held *imperium*, even if they resided on the Bosphorus, and even if, after Constans II in 667, none of them visited Rome. But had one of them done so in the eighth or the ninth century, he would still have been recognized as the personal holder of an *imperium* somehow conferred on him by the Roman people; and no doubt he would have resided, as Constans II had done, in the imperial palace on the Palatine, probably still intact at this date. From the Roman point of view – and there is nothing new about this in the eighth century – the *imperium* he held, while real, was not coextensive or identical with that of the Roman and christian people; but neither for him nor for them was the distinction territorial.

When Pepin promised to give 'back' to St Peter former Roman territory recently occupied by the Lombards, neither Pepin nor even the eastern Roman emperor saw matters as they would be seen in the modern world: it was not a matter of reducing the size of the Roman empire. The inherited conceptual framework was one of the *auctoritas*, sometimes of the *potestas* or *potentia*, of individuals, not of territorial sovereignty. To be sure, one can consider the constitutional position of the popes and of the Frankish and Lombard kings vis-à-vis the Basileus at Constantinople. But if the issue is reduced to territorial terms the results are meaningless or contradictory.

The concept of imperium was not merely metaphysical: it needed a *provincia* for its exercise; but even a *provincia* in older thought was not primarily territorial. The word survives in eighth-century usage at Rome: thus in the LP, apart from less specific uses, Italy is described as a province at 92:4, 93:2, 94:9, 15, 96:17, 97:41, the province of the Ravennates occurs at 93:12, 15, that of the Romans at 92:14 (in an insertion dating from the 750s, 'the province under Roman control', more literally 'subject to the *dicio* of the Romans'), 94:15–16 (where it is apparently synonymous with Italy), that of the Romans and the exarchate of Ravenna at 96:22, that of France at 94:30, and those of Venetiae and Istria at 97:42; while at 94:6, the *provincia* is what is coveted by Aistulf. But most telling of all is the expression in 94:13, where Stephen II institutes a litany for 'the safety of the province and of all Christians': these are not alternatives, they are the same thing. In ninth-century lives, 'province' is used under Nicholas I (107:29,55) for the spheres of jurisdiction of bishops, in practice their territorial dioceses as we would say; but as late as the life of Hadrian II (108:30) we are told, in a speech directed against Photius, how *comprovinciales* go up to Constantinople as to a *regia civitas*. Thus it is that in the period with which we are dealing, as in the days when the Roman empire was intact, *provincia* is the sphere in which power is exercised. The insistence by the popes that the authority of the emperor did not extend to spiritual matters – that church and state had separate *provinciae* – served to restrain the word province from coming to be seen in purely territorial terms; and as long as that was the case the concept of *imperium*, as that which was exercised within a province, could not be seen as merely geographical.

Of course the reality of territorial control is a different matter. Since the fifth century areas of what had been the (geographical) Roman empire had come under the control of barbarian kings, and in the eighth century the Lombards controlled parts of Italy. Liutprand, Aistulf and Desiderius are kings (of the Lombards rather than of territories), just as Pepin and his sons are kings (of the Franks rather than of France). They are not emperors, though they have little truck with the emperor; but equally their own Lombard dukes in practice come to control territories such as Benevento and Spoleto with little reservation of real power to the Lombard king. For the pope in eighth-century Rome this means that as Vicar of St Peter he was like the Vicar of a Praetorian Prefect (who had once in a given territory, called a diocese, exercised certain aspects of power on behalf of his senior who had a sphere of authority throughout the empire). St Peter's Vicar held certain aspects of authority among the christian people (more particularly those of Rome, but the Roman people saw itself as the christian people), just as the Basileus, the kings and the dukes had other aspects of authority. There was no simple hierarchy in this: it was more a matter of wheels within wheels. But above all it was personal, not territorial. *Respublica* comes in the eighth century to be used of what we call the papal state; and 'State' has been used to render the word throughout this volume, rather than 'Republic', in the belief both that the word has marginally less of a territorial connotation and that it does not imply a contrast with 'empire' or 'kingdom'.

I will not pursue this matter further, but leave it to experts in the field. Suffice it to say that I believe that much talk of the creation at some precise moment in the eighth century of a territorially-bounded politically independent papal state is a reflection of modern concepts of nationhood. It is probably no coincidence that the modern discussion began at much the same time as the struggle was occurring to turn Germany and Italy into nation-states and when, in the latter case, the survival of the States of the Church (which could all too easily be seen as originating in the eighth century) was viewed as an obstacle to national unity and independence. In the 'Roman Question' as it existed down to 1929 it suited both sides to perceive the origins and development of the Papal States in modern terms.

3. The manuscript tradition and variant recensions.

The later the life, the fewer the manuscripts. This results from the fact that our surviving MSS are all copies of on-going texts which left Rome at different dates and therefore ended at different points. The earlier the text left Rome, the longer the opportunities for its diffusion. By life 98 (that of Leo III) we are dealing with only six manuscripts of the full text, and the situation deteriorates even further in the ninth century. Lives 109 to 111 are missing entirely (if they were ever written), while the last paragraph of life 112, the last in the series, is known from only one manuscript, itself incomplete.

Apart from normal textual variants, the manuscripts bear witness to different recensions; the text did not have the sacrosanctity of a literary work, and the very fact of its anonymity may even have encouraged interpolations in and modifications to the existing text. In some cases later manuscripts show a strong tendency to regularize spelling and grammar to accord with classical norms. But for lives 91 to 99, the most serious textual variants are in 91, which exists both in its original form and in a much revised version, produced perhaps 20 years later.

Until the 11th century editorial activity only occasionally took the form of deliberate excision of material: an exception here is life 94 which exists also in what is known as the Lombard recension, designed to remove opprobrious comments about the Lombards to suit the taste of Lombard readers; this change was presumably made before the fall of the Lombard kingdom in 774. But from the 11th century on, new recensions were produced which treated the ancient text in a much more cavalier fashion. For example, the earliest of these, that of Adhémar of Chabannes, has a text down to life 105 showing many alterations to the text and heavily abbreviating longer lives like that of Leo III by excising most of the register-type material on donations and repairs to churches as no longer of interest. The same can be said of other medieval recensions. In the twelfth century Cardinal Pandulf produced what is called the 'third edition' of the LP (known from the *Codex Dertusensis* and from Petrus Gulielmus' manuscript, *Vaticanus* 3762, see Přerovský's edition), designed as a preliminary to newly composed lives beginning with Gregory VII. Medieval recensions are not much help for the text of the earlier lives; at the most they reflect the readings of one manuscript of the standard text which was used to produce a new edition. The recensions provide, in Duchesne's view, no help in any of the difficult passages.

INTRODUCTION

THE MANUSCRIPTS OF THE LIBER PONTIFICALIS FOR THE LIVES FROM A.D. 715 ONWARDS

Group A:

A^1: *Lucensis* 490; in a hand not later than the early 9th century it has lives 91–97 (with the earlier version of 91), but abbreviates occasionally, e. g. 93:24–28, 97:54–55, 97:86, 97:90, omits 97:73–85, and duplicates part of 96:21–22. It has the Lombard recension of 94. A 12th-century scribe made various corrections, not based on another MS; seven direct descendants can aid the decipherment of what he obliterated:

a Florentine Group:
Vaticanus 629, end of 11th century, down to life 97; its twin,
Florentinus I, iii, 17, 12th century, down to life 97, itself the parent of
Laurentianus XXIII, 4, written about 1515, and of
Urbinas 395, end of 15th century (except that the latter from life 95 is a copy of the 'third edition');

a French Group:
Vat. Reg. 1852, 11th century, down to life 97 but abridged;
Pictaviensis 6, 11th–12th century, very like the last; and
Parisinus 4999A, 14th century, down to life 97, abridged, a twin or copy of the last.
A^3: *Parisinus* 317, 12th century, has only the first 6 words of 91.
A^5: *Vaticanus* 5269, written between 1237 and 1261, also breaks off in the first chapter of 91, of which it has the later text.

Group B:

B^2: *Parisinus* 13729, perhaps written 824–827, goes down to life 97 but omits 92:11–13; its twin,
Laudunensis 342 (ignored in Duchesne's apparatus to avoid duplication), may have been copied by the same scribe. To judge from a list of popes they both contain, which breaks off after giving Hadrian I a pontificate of only 20 years, their common original was written in 792. It is perhaps no coincidence that Geertman's analysis has shown that the register material in Hadrian's life stops at 792, though another explanation can be offered for this (see p. 171).
B^3: *Coloniensis* 164, 9th century, ends at 96:17.
B^4: *Leydensis Vossianus* 41, end of 9th century. This MS alone has the lists of names in 96:17, and it continues to the end of that life.
Bernensis 412, 13th century, has 91:17 to 92:15 and 93:27 to 96.
Trevirensis 1341, 12th–13th century, has the lives down to 96.
Trevirensis 1344, 14th century, and

Trevirensis 1348, 15th century, are copies of 1341. Duchesne rejects these four MSS as useless in a class well represented by older MSS.

B⁵: *Bruxellensis* 8380, 9th–10th century, goes down to life 94;

Audomarensis 188, 11th century, is a copy of it.

B⁶: *Vindobonensis* 473, end of 9th century, has down to life 94. A copy or twin of it is *Ambrosianus* M, 77, 9th–10th century (called B⁷ by Duchesne but not collated to avoid duplication).

Parisinus, nouv. acq. 2252, 11th century, has 92:17 to 94, is generally ignored by Duchesne, largely because of its numerous corrections of spelling.

All of group B have the later text of 91; like D they have the insertions in lives 92–94, and (unlike D) those that continue that far have the insertions in 95.

Group C:

C¹: *Leydensis Vossianus* 60, 8th–9th century, has the Lombard version of 94 and goes no further; various correctors, none very long after the original scribe, have revised the spelling, added in omitted passages, and added some marginal notes.

Parisinus 16897, 12th century, also goes down to life 94, and

Parisinus 5141, 14th century, is a copy of it; while

Tolosanus 365, end of 11th century, and

Arsenaliensis 679, 14th century, have the same contents.

Gratianopolitanus 473, 12th century, also goes down to life 94. All these have a text close to C¹, though not derived from it.

C²: *Guelferbytanus* 10–11, 9th century, goes down to 94 (of which it gives the Lombard recension), and a second hand has added 95 and 96:1–17 as well as supplying from a MS of group B some missing passages.

Vindobonensis 388, 11th–12th century, descends from a copy of C² made before that MS had been modified.

C³: *Bernensis* 408, 9th century, breaks off after 94:46.

For lives 91–94, C¹²³ are very similar. They have the earlier version of 91. C³ is the best of the class; Duchesne gives all its readings, but for C¹² he gives only variants affecting the sense.

C⁴: *Parisinus* 5140, 11th century, down to 105:109, followed by 107 and 108; the text is a combination of C³ and E¹, and it thoroughly reworks the style and grammar; Duchesne found it difficult to record its readings but gave them where he considers them important. It has the later version of 91.

Group D:

D: *Parisinus* 5516, from Tours, written before mid-871; Duchesne preferred its readings to those of other MSS for lives 98ff. It lacks 102 and ends at 105:66. It has the later version of 91 (with a text very like E). For 91 and 95 onwards, Duchesne gives all its readings other than spelling variants. It is not cited in Duchesne's ap-

THE MANUSCRIPTS OF THE LIBER PONTIFICALIS xix

paratus for lives 92–94 (where its text is very like B, especially B^{567}), except for the inserted passages in those lives, which it shares with group B. Its importance resumes at life 95 (where it lacks the additions of group B), given the dearth of other MSS. It seems that its original at one time ended with life 94 and that 95ff were an addition.

Parisinus 2769, 9th century, perhaps older than the last, has 90:6 to 94.

Leydensis Vulcanii 58, 12th century, is probably a copy of it, made when it was complete; this MS now lacks 88:6 to 94:19.

Bituricensis 97, 13th century, is a heavy abridgment made from a text like the last two MSS. This group is like B (especially B^{567}) for lives 91 to 94 and is therefore ignored by Duchesne.

Group E:

E^1: *Vaticanus* 3764, from Cava or Farfa, end of 11th century; this is the only manuscript which continues through to the last known paragraph of life 112. It has the later version of 91. Five copies, made in the 16th and 17th centuries, are known, and it was the basis of all the pre-Duchesne editions. Duchesne gives its readings in full, even the very frequent grammatical improvements, and also the corrections made in the MS, which he thinks represent a collation with its original.

E^2: *Parisinus* 5143, 14th century, is much the same as E^1 but, though not derived from it, is less valuable; it stops at 112:18.

E^4: *Estensis* VI F 5, end of 11th century, goes down to 97:56.

E^5 (lost): *Farnesianus*, an uncial 9th-century MS; some folios were already missing when the existing collations by Holstein and Bianchini were made; the MS then contained 60 to 93:2 (except 91:5–7), 93:28 to 96:3, 96:12–17, 96:25–97:4 and also part of 104 (in a startlingly different recension). It had the later version of 91. Duchesne gives all known details of its readings (some only in his note in I, CCII). Its text was close to E^{126}; its loss is unfortunate given the late date of MSS of this class.

E^6: *Laurentianus* LXVI, 35, 15th century (closest to E^{12} but full of faults, gaps, and arbitrary changes); it stops at 112:15.

Parisinus 9768 + *Vat. Reg.* 1964, 10th–11th century, has lives 94–97 only.

G: *Vaticanus* 3761, 10th–11th century, has the earlier version of 91, omits 91:21–92:3, has the Lombard version of 94, and ends at 97:47.

V: the Vatican fragments, 10th–11th century, were reconstructed by Duchesne (I, CCI) and later scholars (Duchesne III, 67). As far as these lives are concerned there survive 91:1–23, 97:95–98:5, 17–33, 52–113 and the first few lines of 99.

E^4 and G are close to each other, and for the 8th century their text is that of group C; but in life 97 G is very close to E^1. Duchesne saw no point in regularly giving the readings of E^{26}. Thus, the MSS of the original text of lives 98 and 99 are DVCE^{126}; so for these lives he gives the variants of DVCE^1 virtually in full. But where all others fail in the last part of 105 and all of 106 and 112, rather than follow E^1 alone he does consider E^{26}, even though all three are members of the same group.

The later recensions are represented by the following MSS.

Similar to group B is the recension compiled c. 1030 by Adhémar of Chabannes, represented by:

Alentianus 18, 11th century (has the lives down to 105:84; the manuscript was used by Orderic Vitalis as source for his own brief lives of the popes, appended to Book II of his *Ecclesiastical History*);
Rotomagensis 31, 11th century (probably a copy of the last, but with alterations and abridgments);
Parisinus 5094, 11th century, with a text identical to the *Alentianus*; and
Ottobonianus 2629, 15th century, which has the same text but with some contamination from a different recension, and also has the Scholia on the LP of Peter, bishop of Orvieto in the 14th century.
Parisinus 5145, 15th century, has a similar text, though now down to 104:24 only, and the Scholia.

It seems that Adhémar himself produced an abridgment of his own recension, with a version of life 108 not found elsewhere; it is represented by:

Parisinus 2400, 11th century, which goes down to life 107;
Parisinus 2268, 11th century has the same text, as does
Parisinus 5517, end of 11th century.

The text from which Adhémar worked seems to have been closer to B^2 than to any other MS of group B, and from life 98 to life 107 he seems to have used a MS similar to, but not identical with, D. Duchesne considers the recension has nothing to offer for the text of the lives before the 9th century.

Around 1120, Lambert, canon of St Omer, produced his *Liber Floridus* (the original MS survives, *Gandavensis* 92), basing himself on B^5, then for the lives after 94 on the *Annals of St Bertin* down to 882, and then on nothing more than a papal list down to 1085, concluding with short contemporary lives of the next four popes. At least 10 descendants of the surviving MS are known.

The English recension of the time of William of Malmesbury:
Cantabrigiensis 2021 (KK IV 6) has a version of the LP partly abridged and partly with much interpolated material; from 91 on it follows type E to life 96 and then continues with a list of popes only, with brief notices resuming with Gregory VII down to 1119;
Harleianus 633, 12th century, has a similar arrangement but its LP text, which runs to life 94 only, is closer to type B.

The Recension of St Denis:
Mazarinaeus 2013, 12th century, down to life 94, and
Arsinaliensis 998, 13th century, Vat. Reg. 1896, 13th century, are very similar though the latter lacks 91 and 92:1–5. For lives 91–94 the recension follows type B.

From the above listing one can quantify the decline in the number of available MSS as the text proceeds. For lives 91–94 there are (excluding the later recensions) about 40 MSS of the full text with all or most of each of these lives (Duchesne uses about 17); lives 95–96 have about 26 (Duchesne uses 13); life 97 has 18 (Duchesne uses 9); 98 has 6; 99–101 and 103 have 5; 102, 105, 107–108 have 4; and 106 and 112 have merely 3.

TEXTS AND COMMENTARIES

Le Liber Pontificalis, Texte, introduction et commentaire, ed. L. Duchesne, 2 volumes, 1886–1892; reissued by Cyrille Vogel, 1955–57, with a third volume in part updating the commentary and with useful bibliography and full indexes. The three volumes are cited as Duchesne, I, II and III; the text of lives 91–97 is in Duchesne, I; the text of lives 98–99 is in Duchesne, II.

Monseigneur Duchesne et son temps, Actes du Colloque organisé par l'école française de Rome (23–25 mai 1973), Collection de l'école française de Rome 23 (Rome, 1975) has various articles including C. Pietri, 'Duchesne et la topographie romaine', 23–48, and C. Vogel, 'Le *Liber Pontificalis* dans l'édition de Louis Duchesne. État de la question', 99–127.

Anastasii abbatis opera omnia : *Patrologia Latina*, volumes 127–8, ed. J.-P. Migne, Paris, 1852. This reprints the Bianchini edition of 1718 with the pre-Duchesne text of the LP, along with commentaries (in Latin), down to the life of Paul only.

Liber Pontificalis nella recensione di Pietro Guglielmo O.S.B. et del card. Pandolfo, glossato da Pietro Bohler, ed. Ulderico Přerovský, (3 vols., Studia Gratiana 21–23, Rome, 1978), contains the 'Third edition' of the LP, which shortened the texts, especially of lives 97–98; but Přerovský prints Duchesne's text for comparison.

H. Geertman (ed.), *Atti del colloquio internazionale: Il Liber Pontificalis e la storia materiale, Roma, 21–22 febbraio 2002*, Papers of the Netherlands Institute in Rome (Antiquity), vol. 60/61, 2004; contains several useful papers on this period.

The Turin and other medieval catalogues of churches are in C. Hülsen (1927) and Valentini-Zucchetti vol. 3.

Some translations of primary sources appear in:

S. Allott, *Alcuin of York* (York, 1974).

A. Cabaniss, *Son of Charlemagne: a contemporary life of Louis the Pious* (Syracuse, N.Y., 1961).

D. Mauskopf Deliyannis (trans.), *Agnellus of Ravenna, The Book of Pontiffs of the Church of Ravenna* (2004).

M. Edwards, *Constantine and Christendom*, Translated Texts for Historians 39 (Liverpool 2003), contains 'The Edict of Constantine to Pope Silvester'.

E. Emerton, *The letters of St Boniface* (New York, 1940).
W. D. Foulke, *Paul the Deacon* (Philadelphia, 1907).
H. R. Loyn and J. Percival, *The reign of Charlemagne* (London, 1975).
J. L. Nelson, The Annals of St-Bertin, Ninth-Century Histories, Volume I, Manchester Medieval Sources Series (Manchester, 1991).
B. W. Scholz and Barbara Rogers, edd., *Carolingian Chronicles* (Ann Arbor 1970).
R. E. Sullivan, *The coronation of Charlemagne* (Boston, 1959).
C. H. Talbot, ed., *The Anglo-Saxon missionaries in Germany* (London, 1954).
L. Thorpe, *Two lives of Charlemagne* (Harmondsworth, 1969).

ABBREVIATIONS

Most of these are standard; below are listed those which may mystify.

BP *The Book of Pontiffs (Liber Pontificalis), the ancient biographies of the first ninety Roman bishops to AD 715,* Revised edition, translated with an introduction by Raymond Davis (Liverpool University Press, Translated Texts for Historians 6, 2000).

CC The *Codex Carolinus,* ed. W. Gundlach, *MGH Epistolarum Tomus III, Merowingici et Karolini Aevi* I (Berlin, 1892).

J P. Jaffé, *Regesta Pontificum Romanorum ab condita ecclesia ad a. 1198,* 2ª edit. cur. S. Loewenfeld, F. Kaltenbrunner, P. Ewald, 2 vols. (Berlin 1885–88, repr. Graz, 1958).

LNCP *The Lives of the Ninth-Century Popes (Liber Pontificalis),* translated with an introduction and commentary by Raymond Davis, Liverpool University Press, Translated Texts for Historians 20, 1995.

MGH *Monumenta Germaniae Historica:*
    Conc *Concilia Aevi Karolini*
    DK *Diplomata Karolinorum*
    EKA *Epistolae Merowingici et Karolini Aevi*
    SS *Scriptores*
    SSrL *Scriptores rerum Langobardicarum et Italicarum*

VZ Valentini, R., G. Zucchetti, *Codice Topografico della città di Roma,* R. Istituto storico italiano per il medio evo, 4 vols. (Rome, 1940–53).

The lexica are referred to as follows:

Niermeyer *Mediae Latinitatis Lexicon minus,* ed. J. F. Niermeyer, Leiden, 1976.

NGML *Novum Glossarium Mediae Latinitatis,* edd. F. Blatt and others, Copenhagen, 1957ff.

MLW *Mittellateinisches Wörterbuch,* Munich, 1959ff.

91. GREGORY II (715–731)

There are two recensions of this life: the earlier, which was being compiled even during Gregory's life, is represented by MSS ACG; the later, an adaptation made (to judge from its attitude to the Lombards) in the 750s, is found in MSS BDE. Duchesne (I, CCXX –CCXXIII) discusses the matter in detail. He prints the text in two columns, but the importance of the changes is made clearer by a single translation, with the ACG tradition in ordinary type (the parts omitted by BDE are in curly brackets) and the additions of BDE in italics; changes merely of word order or grammar are ignored.

The contemporary author of this life presents Gregory II as a consummate politician. The author's loyalties naturally lay with Rome, not with Byzantium or the Lombards, and he stresses Gregory's efforts to contain Lombard expansion in Italy and his loyalty to the empire, despite imperial plans to have him deposed or murdered. He makes it equally clear what effects the iconoclastic policy had on Italy's loyalty to the empire. But he was honest enough to note that papal obstructionism to heavy imperial taxation (Gregory was heading Italian opposition to it), not merely opposition to iconoclasm, caused the breach with Constantinople. These were the years when economic motives as much as theological differences caused the de facto secession of much of Italy from the empire. How far Gregory should be seen as a revolutionary or as a loyal subject is controversial (Noble, 33 n. 90). Noble sees him as a man trying to secure Italian interests against both Byzantines and Lombards, and as no more revolutionary that any of his predecessors since 685. The breach with the empire was not caused by Gregory, even if the role he played was decisive. The various actions of the empire in recent years and its inability to provide defence against the Lombards were not likely to convince Italy, Rome or the pope of the merits of Byzantine rule. There was at the time no clear alternative. Eutychius' interventions (c. 19) would lead to a new papal policy that tended 'in the direction of full autonomy for central Italy'. The Lombard dukes would protect Gregory from Byzantine emperor and Lombard king, and the pope would decide how far the imperial writ would run.

The author of the life was fond of military detail, and less concerned with details on church repairs and endowments. The later adapter tried to redress the balance and so preserves valuable information on churches. He also inserted portents and chronological notes (he may have had access to local annals). The latter are enough to show that the original compiler followed a generally chronological order. The only serious problem is the placing of the reference to bishop Boniface in c. 3, where it should refer to events around 716, though his first visit to Rome was not until 719 and he was not made a bishop until 722; so even the 'earlier' recension may have been subject to interpolations. The events in c. 13 are commonly referred to 717 or 718; the chapter may be a misplaced interpolation, but equally the life may be right to place them around 722. Events in Italy, particularly in the latter half of the 720s, moved very fast, and in its ordering of these, from c. 14 on, the life can nowhere be proved at fault. The original author, in a back reference to explain the events of 721, implied in c. 11 that the Saracen invasion of Spain in 711 fell in this pontificate. The second editor removed the implication, but was led into a major geographical error: he thought that Eudes' campaign at Toulouse in 721 took place *east* of the Rhone. The later adapter also regularized the life's closing formulae.

The life is a valuable record, but its selection of facts is not that which a present-day historian might make. It is the best available source for Italian events of this period, and for some events it is the only source. Its testimony is creditworthy. However inadequate it may be in stating the motives of the principal actors, it is 'not palpably tendentious' and it 'is a valid perception of the course of events as they were seen through Italian eyes' (Noble, 28–9).

This was the last life in the LP available to Bede, who for his Chronicle (which stops at the year 724) took from it the accounts of Liutprand's restoration of the Cottian Alps to the pope, of the defeat of the emperor Anastasius by Theodosius III, and of the flooding of the Tiber (*Chron.* anno 720); but his account of the Saracen siege of Constantinople came from a different source. It is crucial for understanding the dissemination of the LP to realize that Bede had access to part of the text of this life before its subject was dead. A manuscript must have been brought back to Northumbria by one of the numerous parties of Englishmen who visited Rome at this time; the most distinguished of these, not mentioned in the LP, was to be Ine, ex-king of Wessex, in 726. We know of a party led by Bede's own abbot, Ceolfrid; the abbot died before reaching Rome, but the party reached Rome with their gift, the *Codex Amiatinus* of the Latin Bible; Duchesne suggested that they returned home with a copy of the LP. Bede must have had the ACG recension in front of him, though his selection of material does not prove this. Paul the Deacon certainly used this recension in his *History of the Lombards* (see n. 33), though by his time the BDE version would also have been available.

91. 1. GREGORY [II; 19 May 715–11 February 731], of Roman origin, son of Marcellus, held the see 15 years 8 months 24 days. *He was bishop in the time of the emperors Anastasius [II], Theodosius [III], Leo [III] and Constantine [V].* From early youth he was brought up in the patriarchate;[1] *in the time of lord pope Sergius of sacred memory he was made subdeacon and sacellarius,*[2] *and given charge of the library*[3]. Next he was advanced to the order of the diaconate and set out with the holy pontiff Constantine for the imperial city.[4] *When the prince Justinian [II] inquired of him about certain chapters*[5] *his excellent reply solved every disputed point.* He was chaste, learned in divine Scripture, eloquent and of resolute mind, a defender of the church establishment and a strenuous adversary of its assailants.

2. *At the start of his pontificate he ordered the burning of lime;*[6] he had issued a decree to restore this city's walls, commencing at St Laurence's portico. He made some progress, but was prevented when various inconvenient tumults arose.

In his time John, bishop of Constantinople, sent his synodic letter[7], and the pontiff adopted the same terms in his reply.[8]

At St Paul's {he replaced the roofbeams which had broken through age,} *he had roofbeams brought from Calabria*[9] and he roofed the greater

---

1 This term begins to replace *episcopium* at the end of the 7th century (BP 86:2) and gives way in turn to *palatium* in the ninth century. For the idea of a school there, cf. 98:1 where Leo III is stated to have learnt psalmody and scripture in the *vestiarium*, and 104:2 where Sergius II learnt chant and ordinary letters in the choir school.

2 Gregory is the first recorded holder of this post in the papal court since he evidently preceded Cosmas (BP 90:3; Halphen, 1907, 115, 135).

3 Gregory would also be the earliest known papal librarian, if the job was really separate. Noble, 221, holds that the first man entrusted with the library on a full-time basis was Zacharias in 773 (J 2401); others reckon no such office existed until 829.

4 5 October 710, cf. BP 90:3. Gregory thus added diplomatic to his pastoral and bureaucratic experience. Current or former *sacellarii* were appropriate envoys; as financial officials they will have been trusted. Cosmas was on this same mission.

5 i.e. the Canons of the Quinisext Council *in Trullo* of 692.

6 Cf. Sisinnius in 708, BP 89:1.

7 Letter with a profession of faith sent by a new pope or patriarch to his colleagues.

8 John, patriarch from 711, was monothelite until the accession of Anastasius (4 June 713) when he became orthodox and then sent a long-winded synodic letter (which survives) to Gregory's predecessor, who died too soon to answer it. John died 11 August 715 and may never have seen Gregory's reply, which is not extant.

9 Calabria was the usual source of timber, cf. Gregory the Great, *Ep.* 12. 20–22, and BP 86:12. Duchesne thought that the second recension combined what the first recension intended to be two separate sets of repairs to St Paul's; but as the life is chronological the two occasions would be so close as to count as one anyway.

part[10] of the basilica which had fallen down, and rebuilt the altar and the silver canopy which had been broken by the collapse. He also repaired St Laurence's outside the wall*s*, which with its roofbeams broken was near to collapse, and he restored the long-failed water supply[11] to the same church by joining up the pipes. He renewed various {basilicas} *churches* which were collapsing, which would take too long to list.

3. Through bishop Boniface[12] he preached the message of salvation in Germany, and by teaching light to a people that sat in darkness he converted them to Christ {and he bathed the greater part of that people with the water of holy baptism}.

{The holy pope} *He* renewed the deserted monasteries alongside St Paul's and by installing monks as God's servants he established the long failed community, so that {three times} by day and night they should {recite matins} *render praise to God there.*[13]

He also established the old people's home {close to the church} *behind the apse* of God's holy mother ad praesepe *as a monastery*, and restored the {nearby} monastery of St Andrew's called Barbara's, which had {both} been abandoned without a single monk;[14] he admitted monks and arranged

---

10 Perhaps merely the transept, in view of the repairs to the nave roof not long after (92:13; Krautheimer, *Corpus* 5, 100).

11 For the provision of the water supply here see BP Hilarus 48:12.

12 Wynfrith of Crediton, Devonshire (680–754; it was Gregory who renamed him Boniface), first visited Rome in 719 and went to evangelize Frisia with a letter of commission from Gregory dated 15 May 719 (J 2157, Boniface, *Ep.* 12, ed. Tangl, *MGH,* 17–18). His episcopal consecration took place only during his second visit, on 30 November 722, following the success of his work, when Gregory gave him letters of recommendation to Charles Martel and others (J 2162). There was frequent correspondence later between Gregory and Boniface; thus Gregory II, though his plan to visit the north in person was never fulfilled, got much the same credit for Boniface's work in Germany that Gregory I got for Augustine's work in England (cf. BP 66:3). See Schiefer, 1980. The last part of the sentence was deleted in the second recension perhaps for its hyperbole.

13 At any rate by Leo III's time there were two monasteries at S. Paolo, dedicated to St Caesarius and St Stephen (98:77 with nn. 140–41).

14 No traces of the *gerocomium* survive. It is implied that at this date there were but two monasteries in this area, but by 807 (98:77, cf. 98:91) there were at least three around S. Maria Maggiore and by 998–9 there were certainly four (see Duchesne, 1907, Ferrari, 51–57):

1) SS Cosmas and Damian (cf. the oratory of that name built here by Symmachus (BP 53:9); this may be the *gerocomium*). SS Cosmas and Damian survived as a church dedicated to St Luke till its destruction by Sixtus V (Ferrari, 100–102).

2) St Andrew cata Barbara. The name Barbara (elsewhere *cata Barbara patricia*) occurs also for a monastery at St Peter's (St Stephen Major's, where her name is joined with Galla patricia) and presumably originates from Barbara, the orphaned daughter of the patrician Venantius, a friend of Gregory I.

for {them to perform terce, sext, none and matins on weekdays} *both monasteries to chant praise to God every day and night* in the church of God's holy mother {and his pious arrangement survives even now}.[15]

4. Then on this great man's advice {and reproof} king Liutprand confirmed the restoration of the patrimony of the Cottian Alps; king Aribert had made this donation and he had repeated it.[16]

{In his time} *Then in the 14th indiction* [715/6] there occurred a sign in the moon: it was bloody until midnight.[17]

Theodo, duke of the Bavarian people, {with others of his people} was the first of that people to come and pray at the home of St Peter.[18]

A (different?) foundation to St Andrew certainly existed in the same area – that of Valila; if separate, it need not have been a monastery at this date. On Valila's basilica, originally the *schola domestica* of the consul Junius Bassus, see Simplicius c. 1 (BP 49:1 with xlii), *ILCV* 1785 (Simplicius' dedicatory inscription to St Andrew), G. Lugli, 'La basilica di Giunio Basso sull'Esquilino', *RAC*, 1932, 221–5, Krautheimer, *Corpus* 1, 64–5. Valila's foundation seems to be the one later called St Andrew *in Exaiolo* or *in Assaio*; later still it was called St Andrew in Piscinula or in Piscina; from about 1260 it was a hospital under the control of a French order, who rededicated it to their patron, St Antony; the site is that of the present Pontifical Oriental Institute.

3) St Andrew in Massa Juliana, named presumably from an estate on the Esquiline on which it was founded; not all of the estate need have belonged to the monastery or church; the name lasted until the 15th century. It may be the same as the later S. Andrea de fractis a (re)foundation of c. 1270, near S. Vito and S. Giuliano, with a community of nuns; the site may be that of the modern church of the Conception (Hülsen, 184–5, 187).

The LP donation list of 807 has St Andrew's church iuxta praesepe and St Andrew's monastery Massa Juliana; in the same life (98:91) occurs St Andrew's basilica cata Barbara. Hülsen, 187, has three dedications to St Andrew in the area, which seems excessive. Probably Valila's is identical with that called iuxta praesepe, and cata Barbara is an alternative name; Massa Juliana may be a foundation after the time of Gregory II. But other permutations are possible.

4) St Hadrian (apparently located between St Andrew and S. Vito, and since apparently not mentioned here perhaps founded later in the 8th century; see further 97:86 with n. 185). It survived till the 15th century (Hülsen, 261).

15 The last words need not imply a long interval before the ACG version of this life was written; their omission in BDE may imply that the arrangements did not in fact last very long.

16 Cf. Paul the Deacon, *HL* 6.44, *Codice Diplomatico Langobardo* 3.1 (ed. Brühl, *Fonti per la storia d'Italia* vol. 64, Rome, 1973, no. 4, p. 299). Liutprand had been king of the Lombards since 712, and early in his reign while consolidating his position in northern Italy was anxious to establish good relations with the pope; by 717/8 his attitude would have changed (c. 13). The Cottian Alps patrimony had been seized by Rotharis about 640. Its donation by Aripert to John VII about 706 (BP 88:3) had, it seems, not taken effect. The area would later be reconquered, and reconceded, by Liutprand.

17 The total eclipse of 13 January 716 ended a little before 9.30 p.m. mean time in Rome (Schove and Fletcher, 1984, 187).

18 Theodo was father- (or grandfather-)in-law of Liutprand; he came to Rome on his own initiative, wanting Gregory's help to set up a regular hierarchy in Bavaria. Gregory's

5. In his time[19] the emperor Anastasius made ready a fleet of ships and sent them to the districts of Alexandria against the Agareni (whom God destroy!). But before they arrived at their intended destination, they changed their plan and in mid journey[20] returned to the imperial city; seeking out the orthodox Theodosius, they elected him emperor and after compelling him to accept the imperial throne they confirmed him as such. So Anastasius made his way to the fortified city of Nicaea with those citizens and such of the army as he could; there[21] he battled with the fleet on board which the emperor Theodosius had been, and about 7000 of the army were cut down. Anastasius' faction was defeated and asked for a safe-conduct and when he had been given it on oath he was made a cleric and consecrated as a priest. The moment Theodosius entered the imperial city, he set up on its original {monument and} place the venerable image on which the six holy synods were depicted and which had been taken down by the unspeakable Philippicus.[22] So it was that by the fervour of his faith all dispute in the church ended.

6. The river called Tiber then left its channel and spread itself over the plains; it swelled in *great* spate and entered the Gate called Flaminia. Meanwhile in some places it even lapped over the *city* walls and it extended itself through the streets beyond St Mark's basilica, so that on the Via Lata the riverwater rose up to one and a half times a man's height. The waters dispersed themselves from St Peter's Gate to the Milvian Bridge, and the force of the river took it as far as near the Remissa.[23] It overturned houses and desolated fields, uprooting trees and crops {and sweeping them away}. At that time the greater part of the Romans could not even sow; which

---

instructions to three legates he sent to Bavaria survive, dated 15 May 716 (J 2153, *MGH Leges* 4, 451); perhaps these legates returned with Theodo. Gregory may also have been thinking of wider diplomacy, hoping to secure alliances in northern Italy and Bavaria, and seeing Bavaria as a potential restraint on the Lombards; but his plans for Bavaria were not fulfilled for many years (Noble, 26).

19 Theodosius was proclaimed late in 715. Verbal parallels in this paragraph suggest that the LP is using the same source as Nicephorus and Theophanes.

20 In fact at Rhodes. The Byzantine chroniclers make Theodosius' unwillingness clear.

21 In the Bosphorus (not at Nicaea); the battles lasted some six months.

22 Agatho the deacon clarifies this: Theodosius removed the images of Philippicus and his monothelite patriarch Sergius, and replaced the image of the anti-monothelite 6th Ecumenical Council of 681 alongside those of the five earlier councils which had not been removed. This has nothing to do with iconoclasm; though in fact 'images' of councils can be aniconic: the best known examples are those in the church of the Nativity at Bethlehem; see Walter, 1970, 16, 75–7, citing Grabar, 1957, 55.

23 Duchesne, I, 411 n. 14, shows that this was probably a place on the right bank of the Tiber, on rising ground close to where the Vatican obelisk now stands.

meant that great trouble was in store. For seven days the water held Rome in its grip. So litanies were held repeatedly by the lord pope, and when he continued in prayer and litanies, on the eighth day God showed his mercy and removed the water; and the river returned to its own channel *in the 15th indiction* [716/7].[24]

7. At that time too the Lombards,[25] though pretending peace, seized the Castrum of Cumae; at this news all were {utterly} dismayed {at the loss of the Castrum}.[26] The holy pontiff urged and advised the Lombards to return it – he declared in his writings that if they would not do so their treachery would incur God's wrath; he was even willing to give them many gifts to get them to restore it. But in their haughtiness they would endure neither to hear his advice nor to return it. This made the holy pontiff smart greatly; he entrusted himself to his hope in God and supplied leadership by devoting himself to advising the duke and people of Naples, writing to them every day how they were to act. Obeying his instruction they adopted a plan and entered the walls of that Castrum by force in the quiet of the night – that is to say, the duke John,[27] with Theodimus the subdeacon and rector,[28] and the army; they killed about 300 Lombards including their gastald, and they captured more than 500 and took them to Naples. In this way they managed to get the Castrum back; even so the holy pope paid[29] the 70 lb of gold he had promised for its ransom.

24 So presumably in autumn 716 – but the date may belong to the next paragraph.

25 Under Romuald II, who had succeeded Gisulf (BP 87:2) as duke of Benevento, on the southern side of the duchy of Rome; cf. Paul, *HL* 6.40. Noble, 25, takes this event as strikingly simultaneous with the events of c. 13; it is to be seen as opportunism rather than as part of a concerted plan, given the vulnerability of Byzantine Italy, with the Arabs at the walls of Constantinople.

26 Since the loss of Capua to the Lombards the Via Domitiana had been the only surviving land route from Rome to Naples; the loss of Cumae put this out of action. Cumae was in the duchy of Rome and as a castrum was public (not church) property (Noble, 26). This is the first occasion that a pope arranged for the defence of the Roman duchy.

27 John is called *magister militum* in the account of these events in the *Gesta epp. Neapol.* c. 36 (*MGH SSrL,* 424). He was duke of Naples, not of Rome, and was the nearest available public official.

28 Theodimus was the nearest available official of the Roman church. As his tombstone (now lost, but known to Baronius in the 16th century, *ad ann.* 715) recorded, he was simultaneously a regionary subdeacon of Rome, rector of the Roman patrimony at Naples (in which capacity he will have dealt with the leases of property such as are recorded there under Gregory II, J 2216–2218), and *dispensator* of the Neapolitan deaconry of St Andrew *ad Nilum*, in which church he was buried.

29 To Romuald, evidently. The recovered public land was now treated by the pope as part of the patrimony of the church.

8. The holy Jerusalem church[30] had for a long time been roofless and all the porticos around were broken through age; he brought roofbeams, and roofed and repaired it. In the same church he provided a marble ambo, and enriched it with various linens and services.

11.[31] Then the unspeakable race of the Agareni {crossed the strait from the place called Ceuta, entered Spain, and slaughtered most of it along with their king; they subdued all the rest with their property, and in this way occupied that province for 10 years; but in the eleventh[32] year [721]}, *who had now seized the province of the Spains for 10 years, in the eleventh year were attempting the crossing of the river Rhone*[33] *so as to occupy the Franciae, where Eudes was in command; and they, in* a general campaign of the Franks against the Saracens surrounded them and cut them down: the letter *of Eudes duke* of the Franks to the pontiff mentioned that 375000 were killed on one day; they said that only 1500 Franks had died in the war; *he added* that, as for the three sponges the pontiff had sent them as a blessing the previous year from those provided for use on his own table, at the time the war was beginning Eudes prince of Aquitania had given them to his people to consume in small amounts, and of those who had shared in them not one had been injured or killed.

Then in a certain place in the districts of Campania burnt wheat, barley and legumes fell from the sky just like rain.

9. He instituted that on the Thursdays in Lent there should be *a fast and* a celebration of mass in churches;[34] this used not to occur. He built a new

---

30 Sta Croce in Gerusalemme, Helena's palace-chapel (BP 34:22). For the portico, Krautheimer, *Corpus* 1, 186.

31 The chapter number was assigned by Vignoli following the pre-Duchesne text.

32 The *Chronicon Moissiacense* (*MGH SS* I, 290) puts Sema's capture of Narbonne and failure at Toulouse at the hands of Eudes *princeps Aquitaniae* in the 9th year; cf. Isidorus Pacensis c. 11 (ed. Tailhan, p. 32).

33 The geographical error may have been caused by confusion with the last serious pre-Carolingian encounters between Franks and Saracens in 737-9, which must have made a great impression in Italy, especially as Liutprand came to help the Franks. Paul the Deacon's use of the early recension of this paragraph (*HL* 6. 46) results in a different error: he brings Charles Martel into the story by confusing this campaign of 721 with that of 732 which culminated in the Battle of Poitiers.

34 The second recension is in error: it was a liturgy, not a fast, which Lent Thursdays (except Maundy Thursday) had lacked. This is clear from the absence of any mass texts for these days in the surviving Roman Sacramentary from c. 700 wrongly attributed to Gelasius, from the subsequent variations in the lessons assigned to these masses, from the borrowing of most of the chants from elsewhere, and even from the fact that the antiphons sung at the communion on other Lent weekdays down to the present day are from the psalms in order with the Thursdays

oratory indeed[35] in the patriarchate in the name of St Peter and adorned it with various metals *and coated the walls all around the altar with silver and depicted the 12 apostles, weighing 180 lb.*

12. Meanwhile in that same period the unspeakable Agareni besieged Constantinople for two years,[36] but God was against them and the greater number there were cut down by famine and war, and they fell back in confusion,[37] Leo then being emperor; it is said that of that city's population 300000 of *both sexes and* all ages were destroyed by scarcity and plague.

10. *Now at that time, the pontiff's mother, whose name Honesta truly reflected her character, was taken from this life.* After his mother's death he reconstructed his own house[38] in honour of Christ's martyr St Agatha from the ground up, inserting chambers and all that was needed for a monastery; and there he presented city and country estates for the monks' needs; and in this church of St Agatha he built {anew} a canopy *of silver weighing 720 lb, 6 silver arches each weighing 15 lb, 10 canisters each weighing 12 lb; he also presented many other gifts.*

13. Then the Lombards seized the Castrum of Narni.[39] Liutprand king of the Lombards in a general campaign proceeded to Ravenna and besieged it for some days, and seizing the Castrum of Classe they took many captives and removed untold wealth.[40]

---

omitted from the sequence. The absence of a fast would have been too remarkable to be overlooked by those, e.g. at the Quinisext Council, searching for abuses in Roman customs.

35 Otherwise unknown. Except for C³, the MSS of the early recension turn the word *sane* ('indeed') into Hosanna (or similar), as if this were the name of the chapel, and as such it was listed in reference works down to the late 19th century; Hülsen, 520.

36 One year – though following a previous year's campaigning in Asia Minor.

37 15 August 718.

38 There are several dedications to St Agatha in Rome which might represent Gregory II's monastery. In Duchesne's view (followed by Hülsen, 166–7, Ferrari, 20) it was close to Sant'Agata dei Goti in the Subura (BP 66:4). Cecchelli identified it with St Agatha in Caput Africae (C. Hülsen, C. Cecchelli et al., *S. Agata dei Goti, Monografie sulle chiese di Roma* I (1924), 47–50. Krautheimer (*Corpus* 1, 3 and 13) doubts between S. Agata dei Goti and Sant'Agata in Trastevere. The latter is not mentioned in literary sources till 1121, but the brickwork is in part 5th-century; it was not built originally as a church, but it could well have become a monastery long before the 12th century. Local tradition, for what it is worth, supports the identification.

39 Duke Faraold of Spoleto seized Narni from the duchy of Rome (Paul, *HL* 6.48). It was apparently returned by Liutprand to Zacharias along with other cities (Noble, 50, citing *Codice Diplomatico Langobardo* 3.1, ed. Brühl, no. 5, pp. 299–300); but by February 756 it had been seized by Aistulf; it was returned after Pepin's expeditions to Italy (94:41, 47).

40 On this campaign, Paul the Deacon, *HL* 6. 44; Paul says Faraold captured Classe, but returned it on Liutprand's orders; but then (6.49) Liutprand besieged Ravenna and captured

14. Some time later[41] the duke Basil, the cartularius Jordanes and the subdeacon John surnamed Lurion, adopted a plan to kill the pontiff. Marinus the imperial spatharius who held the duchy of Rome – he had been sent from the imperial city with the emperor's order for this – gave them his consent,[42] but they could find no opportunity. By God's judgment he was weakened by arthritis[43] and so withdrew from Rome. **15.** Afterwards Paul the patrician[44] was sent to Italy as exarch and again they were thinking of carrying out the crime. But their plan was made clear to the Romans. They *all rose up and killed Jordanes and John Lurion, while Basil was made a monk and his life came to an end in confinement somewhere.* **16.** {In those days} on the order of the emperors Paul the {patrician who had been} exarch was attempting to kill the pontiff for the reason that he was preventing the imposition of tax in the province,[45] strip the churches of their wealth as had been done elsewhere, and ordain someone else in his place.

After him another spatharius[46] was sent with mandates to remove the

---

Classe; Agnellus, life of John V (c. 151), has Liutprand capturing (apparently) Classe. Perhaps Faraold took Classe, and Liutprand took it from him to prevent Spoleto becoming too powerful (Bertolini, 1955[a], 10–12, 17–18); and perhaps Liutprand feared the emperor's reprisals, now that the latter had his hands free of the Arabs. Liutprand's capture of Ravenna itself apparently occurred only after Gregory's death, otherwise this life would have mentioned it, but the date is controversial (brief discussion of the evidence in Noble, 41–2 n. 131, arguing for 738).

41 Perhaps not long after Gregory's refusal to pay the taxes demanded in 722/3 (cf. n. 45); it is important that the plots against Gregory began before the emperor Leo III issued the first of the iconoclast edicts – Gregory's resistance to Constantinople began on economic, not theological, grounds.

42 i.e. though he was duke of Rome, Marinus did not show open support. Noble, 29, interprets this plot as 'an effort by some zealous local officials and a disgruntled cleric to curry favour with the Byzantines. What is, however, most significant and interesting is the powerlessness of the duke of Rome and the continued willingness of the Romans to protect the pope'.

43 *contractus*: articular rheumatism (Niermeyer); but perhaps an attack of paralysis is meant.

44 Possibly the same Paul who put down the Sicilian rebellion in 718 (Nicephorus p. 54, Theophanes a. 6210), now exarch, but standing in also as duke of Rome for Marinus; the second recension may be right to delete 'had been' in the next paragraph; it seems that like Marinus he gave no open support to the scheme.

45 Cf. Theophanes, a. 6217; the dispute was still about taxation, not iconoclasm, and the churches are to be stripped of their wealth, not their images. Leo's intention, after defeating the Arabs, was to shore up his rule in Italy and make Italy contribute more to the cost of its own defence. The tax increased was one levied on all land, including that of the church. Gregory's resistance may have been economically motivated, but it was tantamount to political rebellion. Paul now had imperial authority for action for which he had previously not shown open support: at the very least, to punish Gregory's rebellion. The decree on tax may have been passed in 722 or 723; the events of the present chapter almost certainly belong to 725.

46 i.e. a new duke to replace Marinus; identity unknown.

pontiff from his see; again, Paul the patrician sent from Ravenna some men he was able to pervert, along with his count and some men from the castra, to carry out this crime.[47] But the Romans rose up, and the Lombards on every side – the Spoletines and the dukes of the Lombards from all areas[48] surrounding the borders of the Romans – came to defend the pontiff at the Milvian Bridge and prevented it.[49]

17. In the mandates he later sent, the emperor had decreed that no *church image* of any saint, martyr or angel should be kept, as he declared them all accursed;[50] if the pontiff would agree he would have the emperor's favour; if he prevented this being carried out as well he would be degraded from his office. So the *pious* man despised the prince's profane mandate, and now he armed himself against the emperor as against an enemy, denouncing his heresy and writing that Christians everywhere must guard against the impiety that had arisen. So all the Pentapolitans and the armies of the Venetiae[51] rose in resistance to the emperor's mandate – never would they stoop to killing this pontiff; rather they would manfully strive to defend him and to subject Paul the exarch, the one who had sent him, and his adherents to an anathema. Throughout Italy, scorning {the exarch's} *his* arrangement, they all elected their own dukes, and in this way they all tried to achieve freedom for the pontiff and themselves. Once the emperor's wickedness was known, the whole of Italy adopted a plan: they would elect themselves an emperor[52]

47 The text seems to reflect Paul's difficulties in finding accomplices who were both willing and competent.

48 Or, on each side (*hinc inde*); Paul the Deacon, *HL* 6.49, interprets the expression to refer to dukes of the Lombards in Tuscany, not the two dukes of Spoleto and Benevento. But Noble, 29, thinks the Beneventans may have been involved, and remarks, 34, that for the next decade solidarity with the two duchies would be a cornerstone of papal policy, whether against the emperor or the Lombard king.

49 'Paul had to return abjectly to Ravenna... Neither Paul nor the new duke of Rome was able to impose the imperial will in the city. The taxes, as far as is known, were never collected' (Noble, 29).

50 This is the first of Leo III's iconoclast edicts, after the catastrophe of Thera and Therasia; its immediate result was the revolt of Greece and the islands, whose fleet attacked Constantinople and was defeated 18 April 727. No other contemporary source deals with the implementation of these edicts in Italy; Leo evidently contacted the pope and ordered Paul to fulfil his orders. The traditional view rejected a formal decree on iconoclasm at this time (Ostrogorsky, 160 ff), but see Anastos, 1968, 5–41.

51 i.e. the areas of Italy still under Byzantine control. The effect was to trap the exarch in Ravenna; John, *Chronicon Venetum*, *MGH SS* 7, 11; Paul, *HL* 6.49.

52 Duchesne doubted this, suspecting a misplaced reminiscence either of the attempt to make Basilius (Tiberius) emperor in 718, or of the usurpation of Tiberius Petasius (c. 23). But the account is given in the contemporary recension of this life and merits credence. The Italians

and take him to Constantinople; but the pontiff restrained this plan as he hoped for the prince's conversion.

18. In this same period the duke Exhilaratus, taken in and prompted by the devil, was, along with his son Hadrian,[53] holding the districts of Campania; they were leading the people astray to obey the emperor and kill the pontiff. Then all the Romans pursued, caught and killed him with his son {saying they had written to the emperor against the pontiff}; and after him they also blinded the duke Peter[54] *saying he had written to the emperor against the pontiff.*

There was dispute in the districts of Ravenna. Some agreed with the emperor's iniquity, others sided with the pontiff and those who kept the faith. There was strife[55] between them and they killed Paul the patrician. The castra in Emilia – Ferronianum,[56] Monteveglio and Verabulum,[57] with

---

went a stage beyond electing their own dukes; they 'were openly declaring an end to Byzantine rule' (Noble, 30). A yearning for autonomy in Ravenna and Venice coincided with defending orthodoxy and the pope. Gregory opposed the usurper as he realized that the resulting anarchy would be worse than the existing disruption and, with the eastern emperor powerless, an emperor in Ravenna would be a major danger. Ravenna had long been hostile to Roman influence and recent popes had been keen to exert influence there. Even worse, the collapse of Byzantine rule in Italy would give control of the whole country to the Lombards. But Gregory was in a dilemma – he could not give in on iconoclasm to get Greek support against Liutprand. So he remained loyal (c. 20) to the heretical and oppressive government, opposed the usurper, and stated he hoped for Leo's conversion.

53 Father and son were both mentioned at the Roman Council of 5 April 721 (canons 14–16): Hadrian was excommunicated for marrying one Epiphania, a deaconess. Exhilaratus, with a grudge against Gregory, gathered support and was now trying to hold Campania for the empire – Rome lay to the north, and Naples (still apparently loyal to the emperor) to the south. The incident shows that even in Rome Gregory's position was insecure and his leadership was not unanimously acknowledged.

54 Duchesne presumed Peter was Exhilaratus' successor, but Peter was evidently duke of Rome while Exhilaratus had not as far as we know held that position. Peter's fate showed that imperial control of Rome was effectively at an end.

55 Duchesne suggested this was the battle between Greeks and Ravennates in Agnellus (John V, no. 153); Noble, 30, regards it as an otherwise unrecorded struggle between papal and imperial factions in Ravenna in which the exarch was killed.

56 Zenzano, near Vignola. This and the next cities may have seen Liutprand as their orthodox liberator. The king now saw himself as the pope's ally: if this fitted his own sense of devotion it did not stop him conquering Sutri soon after (c. 21); Gregory was cool in the face of a zeal which might cause the dismemberment of Italy and even reduce the papacy to the status of a glorified Lombard bishopric (Noble, 31).

57 Unknown, even to Paul the Deacon who (*HL* 6.49) substitutes for it Bologna – probably wrongly, since all 5 places mentioned seem small ones west of Bologna, and Liutprand's capture of Bologna took place later (so Duchesne; Noble, 41, disagrees).

their towns Buxum[58] and Persiceto – and in the Pentapolis the city of Osimo, surrendered to the Lombards.[59]

19. Some time after, the emperor sent Eutychius the patrician and eunuch *who had formerly been exarch* to Naples[60] to achieve what the exarch Paul, the spatharii and the other schemers of evil could not do. But even so, it was God's bidding that the miserable treachery did not remain secret: the appalling plan was evident to everyone, that they were attempting to violate Christ's churches, put everyone to death and lay waste everybody's property. When he sent his own man to Rome with his written instructions for the death of the pontiff[61] and the chief men in Rome, and when his cruel madness became known, they straightaway wanted to kill this envoy of the patrician, only the pontiff's vigorous defence prevented this. But they anathematized the exarch Eutychius: great and small, they bound themselves under oath never to permit a pontiff who was a zealot for the christian faith and a defender of the churches to be harmed or removed; instead they were all ready to die for his safety. Then the patrician used his envoys to promise numerous gifts to the dukes of the Lombards in all areas[62] and to the king, to persuade them to give up helping the pontiff. They wrote back scorning the man's detestable treachery; and Romans and Lombards bound themselves together like brothers in the tie of faith, all of them willing to undergo a glorious death in the pontiff's defence – they would not tolerate his having to endure any vexation as {he} *they* fought for the true faith and the safety of Christians. **20.** In this situation the father chose as a greater safeguard to distribute whatever he could find to the poor with a bountiful hand. He devoted himself to prayers and fasting, and implored God in litanies every day; he always continued to rely more on this hope than on men, though he thanked the people for their goodwill and intention. In persuasive language he asked them all to gain credit with God by good works and be steadfast in the faith, but he urged them not to abandon their love for and loyalty to the Roman empire. In this way he soothed everyone's hearts

58 A place called El Bus, near Bazzano.
59 These losses reduced the Pentapolitan duchy to the coast and the military road from Rimini to Rome; by 741 even Ancona and Numana belonged to the Lombards.
60 Ravenna was evidently no longer safe for the emperor's representative.
61 Gregory's own letters to the emperor somewhat later (c. 24 with n. 73) refer to the threat against his life. The translation of the next few words follows Duchesne's punctuation, but perhaps it should be '... death of the pontiff, and when his cruel madness became known to the chief men of Rome, they straightway...'
62 Or, 'on each side' (the two dukes of Spoleto and Benevento); but see c. 16 and n. 48. Eutychius is presumably trying to forestall the papal alliance (not explicitly mentioned, but cf. c. 16) with the two duchies.

and lessened their unremitting suffering.

21. Then *in the 11th indiction* [727/8] *the castellum of Sutri*[63] *was treacherously seized by the Lombards, who occupied it for 140 days. But the pontiff wrote unremittingly to the king of the Lombards to urge him – though he also had to give many gifts and all but strip himself of his entire wealth. So the king restored it and presented it by issuing a donation to the blessed apostles Peter and Paul.*[64]

Then in January of the 12th indiction [729] *the star called Antifer appeared with rays in the western sky for 10 days and more; its rays looked northwards and spread themselves to the centre of the sky.*[65]

22. {After some time the king, in a general campaign to subdue the dukes of Spoleto and Benevento,[66]} *Then the patrician Eutychius and king Liutprand adopted a wicked plan that with an assembled army the king should subdue the dukes of Spoleto and Benevento, and the exarch should subdue Rome and carry out what he had long been ordered to do to the pontiff's person. The king came to Spoleto,* received oaths and hostages from {these} *both dukes, and came with his entire army to the Campus Neronis.*[67] The pontiff came out

---

63 On the border between Lombard and Roman territory. Gregory's alliance with the dukes (c. 19) and his attitude over the occupation of Sutri seem to have provoked the king into concluding his alliance with the exarch (c. 22): in return for Eutychius' help in subduing the duchies, the king would help restore imperial authority in Rome. He could then make himself ruler of Italy while presenting himself as an ally of the empire, and neither Eutychius nor Gregory would be able to stop him.

64 Liutprand handed it back without its surrounding territory and much booty (Noble, 32). This is the second case (after Cumae) of public property being given to the pope, but Gregory in some sense still recognized imperial authority.

65 Bede, *HE* 5. 23, has two comets in this month; Schove and Fletcher, 1984, xxxii, 294 and 329, prefer Chinese sources giving June/July 730 and suppose Bede antedated to presage the deaths of two famous men. Either the LP's interpolator copied Bede (unlikely: 'Antifer' is not in Bede), or the phenomenon of January 729 was real.

66 Romuald II (who lived till *ca.* 731); on Spoleto, cf. Paul, *HL* 6.55; Transamund (who had succeeded his father Faraold when the latter was expelled by his own people, *id.* 6. 44) now fled from Liutprand to Rome and was replaced by Hilderic.

67 The area on the right of the Tiber extending beyond Castel S. Angelo; the name is first recorded by Procopius (*BG* 1. 19, 28–29; 2, 1–2). It was probably this visit to Rome to which Liutprand alluded in inscriptions at the church of St Anastasia which he founded near Pavia. The second editor supposes (c. 23) that Eutychius was present during the negotiations. The result must have been an agreement that Eutychius was not to harm Rome or the pope, Leo's iconoclastic decrees were not to be imposed, and (probably) Gregory was to give up his alliance with the duchies, while Liutprand would give up his alliance with Eutychius. On some such terms, Liutprand laid down his insignia and received them back from the pope as an ally. Gregory had no choice but to accept him as arbiter of Italy. But (cf. next chapter) there was

91. GREGORY II

to him, was presented to him, and was able to soothe the king's spirit with his pious urging, so that he prostrated himself at his feet and promised he would cause no one any trouble and so {would withdraw; for} he was steered by his pious advice to such remorse that he removed what he had been wearing and laid it before the apostle's body – *his cloak, corslet, sword-belt, broad-sword and pointed sword, all gilded, and a gold crown and a silver cross.* Afterwards a prayer was said and *he begged the pontiff to receive the exarch in concord and peace. Which is what happened. And so* he withdrew, {for he had come to Rome mainly to carry out what the emperor had ordered with the exarch; but urged by the pontiff's persuasive language that it was inexpedient, he was then steered to the side of safety, did what he was instructed, and did not go along with the iniquitous plans – fiercely had he come, mildly he withdrew. Thus was the wickedness of adversaries put down,} the king drawing back from the evil plans in which {they} *he and the exarch* were involved.

23. *While the exarch was still in Rome, there came to the Castrum of Monterano*[68] *in the districts of Tuscia a certain seducer, Tiberius named Petasius, who was attempting to usurp the rule of the Roman empire for himself. He deceived those who were more fickle, so that the people of Monterano, Luna*[69] *and Blera swore him fealty. When the exarch heard this he was troubled, but the holy pope comforted him, sending the church dignitaries and the army with him.*[70] *They set out and reached the castellum of Monterano; Petasius was struck down and his head was cut off and sent to the prince in Constantinople. Yet not even this made the emperor bestow full favour on the Romans.*

{A few days} later the emperor's wickedness that made him persecute the pontiff became clear: to force his way on everyone living in Constantinople by both compulsion and persuasion to take down the images, wherever they were, of the Saviour, his holy mother and all the saints, and, what is painful to mention, to burn them in the middle of the city *and to whitewash all the painted churches.* **24.** Since many of that city's population were preventing

---

some rapprochement between Gregory and Eutychius, even if the latter's authority in Rome was subject to the pope's pleasure – Gregory was an ally, rather than a subject.

68 In Roman-controlled Tuscia, a bishopric (probably originally located at Forum Clodii). This paragraph is an addition of the second recension, made some 25 years after the event, but there is no need to identify this Tiberius with the usurper of 718 (even if he too had his head sent to Constantinople). The incident shows, again, the weakness of the emperor and the insecurity of papal control even close to Rome.

69 An unknown locality (clearly not Luni near La Spezia and Carrara).

70 Note how the pope controls the army of Rome. As in c. 17, Gregory will not countenance a rival emperor.

this crime, some were beheaded and others paid the price by mutilation.

{Then[71] the patriarch Germanus was expelled from his see through the emperor's wickedness.} *For this reason, since Germanus, bishop of the holy church of Constantinople, would not give him his assent, the emperor deprived him of his pontificate.* He set up in his place one of his own followers, the priest Anastasius.[72] He sent his synodic letter, but when the {apostolic} *holy* man realized he gave his consent to such error, he did not accept him *in the normal way* as a brother or fellow sacerdos, but in the admonishments he wrote *back* he commanded that if he would not {declare for} *convert to* the catholic faith he should be driven out of his sacerdotal office. As for the emperor, in his writings[73] he *commanded and* tried to persuade him what was advantageous and warned him to draw back from such execrable wretchedness.

25. *He provided an excellent gold chalice adorned with various precious stones, weighing 30 lb; also a gold paten weighing 29½ lb. To all the clergy, to the monasteries that served the poor, and to the mansionarii,[74] he left 2160 solidi, and to provide for the lights of St Peter's 1000 solidi.*

He performed five ordinations, *four in September and one in June*, 35 priests, 4 deacons; for various places {149} *150* bishops. {The bishopric was vacant 35 days.} He was buried in St Peter's on the 11th day of February in the 14th indiction [731] *when Leo and Constantine were emperors. The bishopric was vacant 35 days.*

---

71 7 January 730; much more detail on all this is given by Nicephorus and Theophanes. It is surprising how long Leo had tolerated patriarchal opposition. On 17 January followed another decree against images, issued in an imperial Silentium or council meeting (Ostrogorsky, 164; Christophilopulu, 1951, 79-85).

72 22 January 730.

73 Two letters purportedly from Gregory II to Leo III head the Acts of the 7th Ecumenical Council (787) (J 2180, 2182; critical text with French translation in Gouillard, 1968, 276-297 and 298-307). Their genuineness is much disputed; see Caspar, 1933; Ostrogorsky, 151 and n. 5; Gouillard, 1968; Grotz, 1980, 9-40; Noble, 33 and n. 89; Herrin, 1987, 336 n. 87. The letters present Gregory as uncompromising: he condemns iconoclasm and the treatment of Germanus; dogma is for pontiffs not emperors, and each must keep to his own sphere (Leo had evidently told Gregory he was both priest and king). He refuses to agree to a general Council; western kings have rejected Leo's letters on iconoclasm; the Lombards and Sarmatians have attacked the Decapolis, occupied Ravenna, sent Leo's officials packing and set up their own, and intend to do the same to Rome itself, as the emperor cannot defend it. Leo should not threaten him but remember that once he was 24 stades outside Rome into Campania Gregory was safe, as all the west revered St Peter's successor. In the second letter he repeats the arguments on the different spheres of church and state and says he is departing to answer those in the far west who want baptism.

74 Keepers of a church, sextons.

92. GREGORY III (731-741)

Two themes only were of interest to the compiler of this life: Gregory III's dealings with Constantinople in the iconoclast dispute, and the improvements the pope made, materially and liturgically, to churches in Rome, with which may be classed his support for monasticism.

The account of relations with the imperial court is adequate down to 733 only; the compiler then turns his attention entirely to internal matters and never returns to the earlier theme or to any other political matter (except the affair of Gallese). So we are told nothing of Leo III's attempt to invade Italy, of the confiscation of the papal patrimonies in Illyricum, Calabria and Sicily (a crippling financial blow to the papacy), of the transfer of these areas by the emperor to the ecclesiastical jurisdiction of his own patriarch, of the unspoken truce between emperor and pope, or of the help given by Gregory in the recovery of Ravenna when it was occupied, about 738, by the Lombards. But the compiler provides a fine account of the remarkable beautification of Roman churches in the next years; and it becomes clear, even if the compiler does not note the point, that this is in fact Gregory's initiative in reaction against iconoclasm while it was at its most influential in the east. We cannot be quite certain whether these details belong, like the political history given, only to the earliest years of this pontificate, or whether they span the rest of Gregory III's life.

The most obvious political gap in this life is the total silence on the dealings of Gregory with the Lombards and their king Liutprand. Perhaps as a result of his deal with Gregory II, for most of this pontificate the king avoided any attack on Rome or provocation of Gregory III. But in or after 735 Agatho duke of Perugia tried and failed to reconquer Bologna from Liutprand. This provoked the king's coregent Hildeprand and Peredeo duke of Vicenza to capture Ravenna: the exarch Eutychius fled to Venice. Gregory wrote to Ursus, the doge of Venice, and Antoninus, patriarch of Grado, asking them to help the exarch regain Ravenna for 'the holy State and the imperial service of our sons Leo and Constantine' (the emperors; J 2177, *Epp. Lang.* 11, 12, *MGH EKA* 3, 702). This they did, Ravenna was retaken, Peredeo killed, and Hildeprand captured. Gregory was acting almost more as an ally than as a subject of Byzantium. His motive was clear: he did not want to accept a disruption of the delicate balance of power between the empire, the Lombard kingdom, and the papacy itself, which had kept the peace of Italy for some 10 years. But to Liutprand his intervention seemed uncalled for. A general resumption of hostilities occurred; in this context Transamund duke of Spoleto attacked Gallese (c. 15). The details which belong to the last two years of Gregory's pontificate (especially his alliance with Transamund and with Godescalc duke of Benevento against their king, on the motives for which see Noble, 44, 50) are largely supplied by the compiler of the next life. But one later interpolator, probably in the 750s (see below), found a particular omission which had not been made good even there to be too glaring: with the hindsight of later events, he felt he had to record (c. 14) the significant decision Gregory III took to call on the Franks to defend the duchy of Rome against Liutprand's attacks, even if Charles Martel failed to respond to Gregory's appeals. This interpolated chapter may be misplaced chronologically (see note ad loc.).

Another gap in this life is the story of Rome's relations with Boniface and the young German church, briefly touched on in the previous life, but equally ignored in the life of Gregory III's successor Zacharias. Noble (46) suggests it was Boniface, in Rome during 737, who inspired Gregory to appeal to the Franks – he certainly suggested that Zacharias should do so in 745 (Boniface, *Ep.* 60, ed. Tangl, *MGH* p. 122).

The original text of this life is that given in MSS ACEG; after what has been said already, it comes as no surprise to find that it lacks the regular concluding formulas of the life. The later interpolator already mentioned, whose work underlies MSS BD, supplied these details.

92. GREGORY III

92. 1. GREGORY [III; 18 March 731–28 November 741], of Syrian origin, son of John, held the see 10 years 8 months 24 days. He was gentle[1] and exceptionally wise, competently versed in holy scripture, proficient in Greek and Latin, knowing by heart all the psalms in order and interpreting them elegantly and with the most sensitive and subtle touches. In speech too he was refined through his reading. He gave encouragement to all good works, and among the people he flourishingly preached salvation, preaching his salutary warnings about preserving unmutilated the catholic and apostolic faith for ever, invigorating the hearts of the faithful. He was a zealot for the orthodox faith and its most strenuous defender. He loved the poor, and was concerned to look after the destitute not merely with dutiful attention but through his own hard work and toil. He ransomed captives and bountifully gave orphans and widows what they needed. He was a lover of religious life by the christian rule, and had affection for those who wanted to live the religious life and have the fear of God in their hearts. By God's favour he reached the sacred order of the priesthood.[2] It was when his predecessor departed from this world and he was noticed in front of the bier at the funeral, that the men of Rome and the whole people from greatest to least by God's inspiration suddenly took him away by force and elected him to the order of the pontificate.

2. He was bishop in the time of the emperors Leo [III] and Constantine [V], while there was raging the persecution they started for the removal and destruction of the sacred images of our Lord Jesus Christ, God's holy mother, the holy apostles and all the saints and confessors. On behalf of these, just as his predecessor of sacred memory had done, this holy man sent written warnings, with the authority of the apostolic see's teaching, for them to change their minds and quit their error. The priest George[3] carried these writings, but he was moved by human fear and did not hand them to the emperor. On his return he brought them back with him here to Rome and exhibited them to the holy pontiff, confessing the fault of which he was guilty. The pontiff threatened him greatly and meant to deprive him of his sacerdotal office. But when a council[4] was in session, and both council and chief men begged that this

---

1 The eulogy which follows is a padded out version of that for Leo II (BP 82:1), itself based on two passages in Gennadius, *de viris illustribus* 70, 81.

2 Duchesne suggested he was priest of the *titulus* of St Chrysogonus, which received more attention from him as pontiff than any other parish church; if so, he was not one of the two priests named Gregory at the Roman Council of 721, but since the attendance there was not complete we cannot assume he had not yet been ordained.

3 Perhaps the same George who attended the Roman Council of 721. It was the last time a pope formally notified Constantinople of his accession.

4 The pope and prominent Romans are again acting together to oppose Leo's will. Duchesne

priest be not deposed but subjected to a penance, a just penance was laid on him. He sent him again to the imperial city with the same writings expanded. But the emperors' demonstrably wicked arrangement saw to the detention of these venerable writings in Sicily: they did not let this letter-carrier cross over to the imperial city, but exiled him for almost a full year.[5]

3. So[6] spurred with a greater enthusiasm for the faith, the supreme and venerable pope [held] a sacerdotal synod in front of the most holy confessio of St Peter's most sacred body. With him in session were the archbishops Antoninus of Grado[7] and John of Ravenna,[8] with other bishops of this Hesperian district, *93* in number,[9] and priests of this holy apostolic see; the deacons and all the clergy were in attendance, and the noble consuls and the rest of the christian people assisted.[10] The synod decreed that if anyone thenceforth, despising the faithful use of those who held the ancient custom of the apostolic church, should remove, destroy, profane and blaspheme against this veneration of the sacred images, viz. of our God and Lord Jesus Christ, of his mother the ever-virgin immaculate and glorious Mary, of the blessed apostles and of all the saints, let him be driven forth from the body and blood of our Lord Jesus Christ and from the unity and membership of the entire church. They also confirmed this by their signatures and sanctioned that it be attached to the other teachings of the previous approved orthodox pontiffs.

4. So when this synodal decree was passed, he again sent Constantine the *defensor* with other similar warnings in writing for setting up the sacred

---

suggested this was a 'regular' council, perhaps meeting in late June, citing Agnellus c. 124 (*MGH SSrL,* 360) on the year 683.

5 From summer 731; hence George's absence from Gregory's third council, held in April 732 (n. 23). Imperial policy was to delay, since Gregory's opposition could no more be broken than his predecessor's.

6 Diplomacy had failed, so Gregory responded more directly with a council.

7 Grado was the location of the bishopric originally at Aquileia, though in the early 7th century (when Grado had returned to communion with Rome) a separate line of schismatic bishops had been set up at Aquileia (by this date these also were in communion with Rome). The summons to Antoninus survives (J 2232; *Epp. Lang.* 13, *MGH EKA* 3, 703): it was issued before the change of indiction in 731; the council was to meet at Rome on 1 November 731. The *Chronica patriarcharum Gradensium* c. 12 (*MGH SSrL,* 396) confirm the attendance of Antoninus and John at this council. The Acts are lost; the LP shows they contained an impassioned defence of images; Gregory undid in the west what Leo had done in the east (Noble, 38–9).

8 John V (on whom Agnellus c. 151–153). The political significance of the chief archbishop of the exarchate taking the Roman line on iconoclasm against Constantinople is crucial.

9 The figure, omitted by ACE, is supplied by BD.

10 'Gregory was turning the Roman synod into a focal point of Italian national life' (Noble, 39; Llewellyn, 1971, 129).

images. But these were detained like the previous ones; and they constrained their bearer in the most strenuous confinement for almost an entire year. Afterwards they forcibly removed the actual writings from him, and threatening him with violence after a such a lengthy confinement they sent him back. The whole commonalty of this province of Italy similarly and singlemindedly sent writings of supplication to the princes for the setting up of the images; these writings, like the previous ones, were stolen by Sergius[11] the patrician and *strategus* of the same island of Sicily; and the carriers were held almost eight months and likewise sent back with outrageous dishonour. Once more he composed a letter[12] urging the setting up of these sacred images and reinforcing the orthodox faith, and sent it with Peter the *defensor* to the imperial city, both to Anastasius the intruder into the see of Constantinople and to the princes Leo and Constantine.[13]

5. The exarch Eutychius[14] granted him six twisted onyx columns; these

11 Perhaps the same Sergius who had put up Basil (Tiberius) as pretender to the throne in 718; as he had been pardoned (Nicephorus p. 55, Theophanes a. 6210) he could still have held the same post.
12 Lost, like all Gregory III's correspondence on images.
13 The author now abandons the topic of relations with the empire. Theophanes, a. 6234 (= 732–3), gives the sequel: Leo replied by sending a fleet to punish Italy (particularly Ravenna?) but when this was shipwrecked in the Adriatic he instead confiscated the Roman patrimonies in Sicily, which brought in 3½ gold talents, and imposed heavy taxes on the island; also lost were the patrimonies in Calabria and Illyricum. Probably at this date (but Grumel, 1952, 191–200, and Ostrogorsky, 170 and n. 1, prefer the 750s) all three areas were transferred to the ecclesiastical jurisdiction of the patriarch of Constantinople, apparently with ease (no papal objection is recorded for two generations); see Anastos, 1957, 14–31. Illyricum was no great loss to Rome (Mandic, 1964), being beyond effective papal control, but to the emperor it was strategically important for the defence of the Balkans. Southern Italy and Sicily had been loyal to the empire, were thoroughly hellenized by this date, and were strategically important against the Arabs. On Leo's motivation, see Ewig, 1969, 7 (to 'condemn Rome to insignificance' and/or to 'abandon old Rome, fallen from its former height, to its own fate'); Llewellyn, 1971, 168–9; and, above all, Noble, 40: Leo cut his losses in the west by tightly securing what he could hold, and casting the rest adrift. Eutychius remained as exarch de jure, but he was powerless in central Italy; when Ravenna fell to Liutprand about 738, he fled to Venice. The duchy of Rome was now de facto under papal rule. 'The creation of a papal Republic may be dated to the years between 729 and 733. The pope, with the Italian nobility arrayed behind him, had thrown off almost every vestige of imperial authority, and the Basileus had recognized the new ordering of affairs by reorganizing the territories where his power was still effective'. Problems remained: how large would the state be, could it defend itself against a Lombard threat, and what would its relations be with the empire?
14 His motivation depends in part on the date of the gift. Was he trying to shore up the 'false peace' of 729–32 (91:22–3)? Or to show that the intended removal of icons from St Peter's could be substituted by other adornment? Was he simply being neutral as between Rome and

he brought into St Peter's and set them over against the *presbyterium*, in front of the confessio, three on the right and three on the left, close to the other six ancient ones uniform in design.[15] On top of them he placed beams and coated them with fine silver on which were depicted in relief, on one side, the Saviour and apostles and, on the other side, God's mother and holy virgins. On top[16] of these he placed lilies and lights of silver, weighing altogether 700 lb.

6. He built an oratory within the same basilica, close to the principal arch, on the men's side;[17] in it, to honour the Saviour and his holy mother, he placed in safety relics of the holy apostles and 'all the holy martyrs and confessors, perfect and righteous'[18] resting in peace throughout the world. It was his institution that their feasts should consist of vigils[19] held every day in turn by the monks of the three[20] monasteries which ministered there, that the masses of their *natalicia*[21] should be celebrated[22] in the same place, and that in the Canon the *sacerdos* should say: 'Whose solemnity is this day celebrated throughout the world in the sight of thy majesty, O Lord our God'. This institution he had inscribed on stone panels[23] in the same oratory. **7.** In it he built a

---

Constantinople? Or, if after 738, might the gift be his thank-offering for papal help in regaining Ravenna from the Lombards? Note how Gregory immediately mounts fresh icons on to the exarch's gift!

15 On the twelve twisted columns see Ward Perkins, 1952. All six of Constantine's columns, moved in Gregory I's rearrangements (BP 66:4), were again moved in 1592 and still survive in St Peter's; of Eutychius' columns, dismantled in 1507, five survive in St Peter's, but the sixth is missing. The original six are clearly a set; the survivors of Eutychius' group consist of two sets, of which one set of three is very similar to the Constantinian group, the other, of two, slightly less so. The origin of all eleven survivors is certainly eastern – from 'Greece' as the LP says of the first group (BP Silvester 34:16). Artistically they provided the model for the four enormous bronze columns on which Bernini supported his canopy in St Peter's.

16 There were still candelabra on the entablature over the columns when in the mid 16th century Giulio Romano painted 'The Donation of Constantine' in the stanze di Raffaello in the Vatican (see, e.g., Ward Perkins, 1952, plate 1, 3).

17 The south, or left hand side (when entering). In 1495 the chapel was provided with a reliquary for the Holy Lance given to Innocent VIII by sultan Bajazet II, but was then demolished in the rebuilding of St Peter's.

18 A quotation both from Gregory III's speech on the panels mentioned below, and from the 'proper *Communicantes*' of which part is quoted below.

19 A service of three psalms and the morning gospel to be chanted after vespers.

20 The inscription (n. 23) names these as SS John and Paul (for which, 98:77 with n. 138), St Stephen (97:53 n. 91) and St Martin (98:77 n. 139).

21 (Heavenly) birthdays; death-anniversaries. Unlike the daily vigils, the mass is held only on feasts of saints whose relics were there.

22 The inscription clarifies this: the priest on weekly duty is to say a second mass here after the one said at St Peter's body.

23 These four panels survived long enough (and fragments of three still survive) for the

pergola[24] and conferred gifts of various kinds: 2 gold bowls and 5 other Saxon ones; 4 hanging crosses; 10 other similar crosses; 2 pairs of hanging gilded vessels; 5 clasped-garments; a gold crown with a cross, hanging, with jewels, over the altar; a gold paten and chalice, one pair, with jewels; silver handbasins, one pair; and on the image[25] of God's holy mother, a gold jewelled diadem and a gold jewelled necklace, with jewels hanging from it, the earrings with 6 jacinths;[26] and he coated with silver the front of the altar and the confessio with its gates;[27] and on the three sides of the altar he placed 3 silver crosses, weighing altogether 36 lb; 2 silver canisters; 1 everyday chalice of silver; 5 silver circlets; 1 silver chalice which hangs in this oratory's apse;[28] at the top of this apse, 3 silver crosses; and the other things which are assigned for the pergola's adornment and as altarcloths.

8. In the church of God's holy mother *ad praesepe* he built round over the columns a tringle candelabrum[29] just like that at St Peter's. He also provided in the holy oratory there called *praesepe*[30] a gold image of God's mother embracing our Lord God and Saviour, with various jewels, weighing 5 lb. He renewed the roof, the apse-vault and the murals at St Chrysogonus the martyr's;[31] also a

---

entire text to be copied in manuscript (full text in Duchesne, I, 422, with III, 101); three of the panels gave the acts of the Council at which the chapel was dedicated; the date was 12 April 732; 7 bishops, 19 priests and 5 deacons are named as present; despite anathemas against any who break the new ordinance, there is no trace in any later document of this cult in this chapel. The fourth panel gave the text of the mass for the repose of Gregory III who was buried here.

24 An arch or cross-beam in front of the altar to hold the sacred objects.

25 The location of this is not clear; it was probably a half-length painted image, covered by metal except for the face. This picture (or its replacement) was later described (by Mallius) as having a cavity above it for a relic (the arm of St Stephen); it was therefore on a wall – perhaps the pilaster corresponding to the first colonnade of the nave (on the left), which bounded Gregory III's oratory on the south.

26 *hyacinthus* may be a sapphire or a dark-coloured amethyst.

27 *regiolae*: a small two-leafed door, which pierced the front of the altar and opened over the confessio, i. e. over the inside of the altar itself, where the relics were.

28 The apse itself has a hanging decoration, different from the crosses and vessels suspended in the chapel and also (apparently) from the gold crown over the altar.

29 *regulare candelabrum*; a tringle is a connecting-rod. The object is a cross-beam or entablature over or round the altar, carrying lamps, much as at St Peter's.

30 This is the earliest direct reference to the 'manger' at S. Maria Maggiore, though *ad praesepe* is regularly used as part of the basilica's name from the 640s (BP 75:2, 76:6, 77:2, 81:18); for this to have happened by then, the manger-relic can have appeared no later than 600. There are no references to the church in the LP between the 520s and 640s. A 9th century inscription copies a 6th-century deed of gift by one Flavia Xanthippe to the basilica *ad praesepem*, but the last two words might be interpolated.

31 The ancient church is beneath its successor (the present left aisle is vertically over the ancient right aisle). The walls of the lower church, one of the oldest in Rome, are adorned with

silver canopy and 5 arches, weighing in all 210 lb. He presented there: 4 silver crowns; 2 chandeliers; 1 silver paten; 1 silver chalice; also altar-cloths and white silk veils adorned with purple and hanging all round.

9. In connexion with this *titulus* he constructed a monastery of the martyrs SS Stephen, Laurence and Chrysogonus;[32] he established there an abbot and community of monks to perform God's praises, as arranged for daytime and nighttime, just like the offices at St Peter's, in this *titulus*; and he exempted them from the jurisdiction of the priest of the *titulus*. To support the monastery there this holy man bestowed estates, gifts and dependants; various others of the faithful and lovers of our Lord Jesus Christ devoutly conferred estates and gifts on this monastery of SS Stephen, Laurence and Chrysogonus.

10. He likewise renewed the monastery[33] of SS John the Evangelist, John the Baptist and Pancras, founded of old alongside the Saviour's church; through excessive neglect it had been abandoned by every monastic order. On this monastery he conferred estates and gifts, and he restored to this place, paying the price for it, whatever he had found to be alienated from it. He established there a community of monks and an abbot to perform every day the sacred offices of divine praise, as arranged for daytime and nighttime, just like the offices at St Peter's, in the Saviour our Lord Jesus Christ's basilica, called the Constantinian, close to the Lateran.

He silvered the ancient image[34] of God's holy mother and covered it with fine silver weighing 50 lb; he provided a large gold paten with various stones, weighing 26 lb; also a chalice with jewels, weighing 29 lb; also gold gospels with jewels, weighing 15 lb. **11.** He built a fresh roof and apse-vault, which he painted, for St Andrew the Apostle's at St Peter's; in the same basilica he provided a gold image with jewels of St Andrew, weighing 8 lb; and he coated the inside of the confessio with silver, which he gilded with fine gold. The basilica of St Callistus,[35] pontiff and martyr, had been destroyed almost

---

paintings, including some attributable to the time of Gregory III. Krautheimer, *Corpus* 1, 159, 163 dates the annular crypt to this pontificate.

32 Later known just as St Stephen; the future Stephen III (96:1) was a founder member. Krautheimer (*Corpus* 1, 145) suggests the monks were Greek; but Gregory would hardly have forced Greeks to copy the (Latin) office chanted in St Peter's (Ferrari, 92–95). The church was in the hands of the Benedictines by the 12th century.

33 On this and the other Lateran monasteries see 98:76 with nn. 134–6; by 807 the monastery here mentioned was known simply as S. Pancras.

34 Location not given; Duchesne withdrew his suggestion of S. Maria Antiqua.

35 As the next item is outside the walls, this will be S. Callisto on the Via Aurelia, not S. Maria in Trastevere (the *titulus Callisti*); but Hülsen, 234, takes it as the small shrine to Callistus recorded in the medieval catalogues, just south of S. Maria.

down to ground level; he reconstructed the fabric and roof, and painted it all; there he conferred a silver paten and chalice, and an altarcloth. He constructed afresh the roof of SS Processus and Martinian's basilica;[36] he placed piles underneath the very strong fabric behind these saints' venerable bodies to strengthen the holy basilica's walls. **12.** In St Genesius the martyr's church[37] he freshly restored the roof; there too he set up an altar in the name of the Saviour our Lord God. On it he conferred a silver paten and a chalice, and a silver crown with 6 dolphins, and also a gold circlet, with a cross, hanging over the altar. In God's holy mother's basilica called *ad martyres* the roof was damaged[38] by longterm decay; he had it cleaned spotless and freshly restored with a great quantity of limestone and lead sheets, and he constructed with fresh splendour everything spread over this roof's circumference. As for God's holy mother's basilica called *Aquiro*,[39] in which there had previously been a deaconry and a small oratory, he constructed it longer and wider from the ground up and painted it. **13.** As for SS Sergius and Bacchus' deaconry at St Peter's,[40] in which there was long since a small oratory, he much extended the fabric from the ground up. He granted everything that a deaconry uses and laid down that it should be at the service of the deaconry's ministry to support the poor for all time. It was his institution that a *statio* should be held annually in St Petronilla's cemetery;[41] there he presented a gold crown, a silver

36 This dated at least from the time of Theodosius (Duchesne, I, 222 n. 2), and was 1½ miles out on the Via Aurelia, not far from St Pancras'; undiscovered.

37 Near St Hippolytus' on the Via Tiburtina.

38 *demolitum*; but the building (the Pantheon) had suffered at the hands of Constans II (BP Vitalian 78:3) in 663 the loss of only the bronze from its cupola; in fact, the second-century roof still survives. Perhaps Gregory was responsible for some patching.

39 This is the earliest mention of this church, located in the former temple precinct of Matidia and Marciana in the Campus Martius, but the LP makes it clear that the site already had a deaconry with an oratory. In its place Gregory III built a basilica bigger than the old oratory. 'Nothing is known as to when and by whom the diaconia was established, whether or not it was installed inside a Roman building, and if so what building it was' (Krautheimer, *Corpus* 2, 275). Despite Gregory III's work, the smallness of gifts in the 9th century (98:45, 70, 103:17, 105:62) hints at its insignificance. Gregory's church was rebuilt in the 12th century, while now there is nothing visible from earlier than 1590. Aquiro may be from Equirria, festivals once held nearby.

40 To be distinguished from its homonym near the Arch of Septimius Severus; not otherwise known unless it is the later church of S. Sergius palatii Caruli; Alfarano placed it on his plan of old St Peter's at the north transept of the basilica.

41 The cemetery of SS Nereus and Achilleus (cf. BP 55:7). Since the LP does not here give the other saints as part of the name, and since Gregory I delivered his 28th Homily at a *statio* here on 12 May, the LP apparently means that Gregory III instituted a feast and *statio* for Petronilla herself; her name begins to appear in Roman calendars (on 31 May) during this

chalice and paten, and various other things pertaining to the church's adornment. He freshly restored from the ground up and painted the chambers[42] at St Peter's which had collapsed. He rebuilt anew the destroyed roof of St Mark's basilica outside the walls of this city of Rome on the Via Appia. At St Paul's he replaced 5 roofbeams, and he checked over and restored the whole of the basilica's roof from the arch over the altar to the main doors.[43] He replaced 5 roofbeams at God's holy mother *ad praesepe*. He rebuilt SS Marcellinus and Peter's church[44] close to the Lateran. As for the cemeteries[45] of the martyrs SS Januarius, Urban, Tiburtius, Valerian and Maximus, he completely rebuilt their roof which had collapsed.

14. In his time *And[46] the province under Roman control was subjugated*

---

century. On Petronilla, cf. 95:3 with n. 6.

42 *accubita*; the *cubicula* mentioned at BP Sergius I 86:11, and Leo III 98:89 (beginning), probably identifiable with the *pauperibus habitacula* (accommodation for the poor) at BP Symmachus 53:10; not 'dining couches' as in 98:39, 89 (near end).

43 Gregory II's work (91:2) may have been on the transept roof, since the present activity evidently concerns the roof of the nave.

44 The first certain reference to this church (as opposed to its namesake on the Via Labicana) occurs only in 595, when it is named as a *titulus* among the subscriptions to the Council of that year. Duchesne, 1887, 228–9, speculated that the *titulus Matthaei* listed at the Council of 499 was identical with the *titulus Nicomedis* listed at the same council, and that in the 6th century it lost its titular status to SS Marcellinus and Peter. After 595 SS Marcellinus and Peter does not recur as a *titulus* until the 12th century – the present passage vaguely calls it *ecclesia*; almost certainly it was not a *titulus* in the 8th and 9th centuries (cf. 98: n. 100).

45 The main sanctuary at the Catacomb of Praetextatus on the Via Appia, cf. BP 63:5.

46 The faulty grammatical link betrays this passage (found only in the BD recension) as an interpolation; Duchesne, I, CCXXIII, argues from its failure to distinguish between good and bad Lombards (they are all 'unspeakable', *nefandi*, an attitude not shown to them in lives 92 and 93) and from its concern with the Franks that it was written under Stephen II (752–7). The LP is the only source for Liutprand's expedition to the Campus Neronis under the walls of Rome itself, but there is no reason to doubt it (it is not a doublet of 91:22); whether he intended to conquer Rome is uncertain. The appeal to the Franks is certainly historical; in fact Gregory appealed twice, and two letters to Charles, dated several months apart from each other, survive (*CC* 1, 2). In the first of these Gregory states that the Lombards have stolen all the lights from St Peter's; in the second he writes of the damage done to Roman church property by Liutprand both at Rome and at Ravenna and refers to his alliance with Transamund and Godescalc, the Lombard dukes of Spoleto and Benevento, in revolt against their king. The main problem is the relationship of this interpolated chapter with other events. In Duchesne's view, Liutprand had not long before (738) sent troops to help Charles Martel get the Saracens out of Provence (Paul, *HL* 6.54). On his chronology, the present passage is correctly placed in the LP: Gregory, determined to force Liutprand to return the four cities he had captured in the summer of 739 (93:2; in neither of his letters to Charles does Gregory mention these cities) went on to make the alliances with Transamund and Godescalc. But on the chronology preferred by Fröhlich, 1980, I, 193, Bertolini, 1972, 467, and Noble, the campaign in Provence was in 739, and

by the unspeakable Lombards and their king Liutprand. Coming to Rome he pitched his tents in the Campus Neronis; he plundered Campania, and shaved and clothed many noble Romans Lombard-fashion. At this the man of God was racked with pain on every side, and taking the holy keys from St Peter's confessio, he sent his envoys, the holy bishop Anastasius and the priest Sergius,[47] on a journey by ship to the districts of France and to His Excellency Charles, the shrewd man who then ruled the kingdom of the Franks, to request[48] him to deliver them from such oppression by the Lombards.[49] **15. Then as he was forced by necessity** the greater part of the walls of this city of Rome were restored;[50] at his own expense he gave the workers their rations and met the cost of purchasing the limestone. Finally in his time when the duchy of Rome was under daily attack by the duchy of Spoleto for possession of the Castrum of Gallese,[51] he succeeded in ending the affair by giving much money to their duke Transamund to end the wars and the points in dispute; and he ordered its annexation to the structure of the Holy State[52] and to Christ's

---

Liutprand broke off the siege of Rome in order to help Charles. On this ordering of events Liutprand's move against Rome came after Gregory made his alliance with the two dukes, and was, specifically, a punishment for Gregory's harbouring of Transamund (Noble, 44, cf. n. 178; Hallenbeck, 1982, 34–5): 'A papal-ducal alliance, in 738–9 as in 728, posed a dire threat to the integrity of the Lombard kingdom'. If so, the present passage was inserted at the wrong point in the LP: the context is the events mentioned in 93:2 as occurring late in the pontificate of Gregory III – but there was nowhere else it could be placed in this life.

47 There were three priests of this name at the Roman Council of 732.

48 Presumably *CC* 1, though in Duchesne's view it was an earlier, not surviving, letter.

49 Whatever the chronology, Gregory received no help from Charles, though he did send an envoy to Rome (Anthat, who returned to France bearing *CC* 2). Charles' view was probably that Gregory had caused the problem himself by intervening in Lombard quarrels, and he was not prepared to break with Liutprand to assist the pope.

50 This chapter is not necessarily in the right chronological relationship with the interpolated c. 14 or with 93:2; the quarrel over Gallese can hardly belong after Gregory's alliance with Transamund. Gregory II (91:2) had already begun to repair the walls of Rome. Gregory III's move was significant in the context of imminent trouble with Transamund, all the more so if Liutprand had just made an attempt on Rome (or was likely to, if c. 14 is placed later). Civitavecchia was also now refortified (c. 16).

51 Gallese was in the duchy of Rome and commanded the road to Ravenna. Noble, 43, and others write as if Transamund actually captured Gallese. Duchesne's text does not say this, but note that Jaffé (ad ann. 738) quotes the LP with the addition *recuperatum est* which implies it. Noble also has Transamund selling it to the pope; the LP says, rather, that Gregory bribed him to go away. In any case Transamund was showing independence of the king, who would clearly take offence. Benevento at about this time elected Godescalc, a duke with separatist leanings. If c. 14 is wrongly placed, Gregory's alliance with the dukes now produced a direct conflict with Liutprand.

52 To Duchesne, the Holy State still means the empire (as opposed to the Lombard prin-

beloved Roman army's body.[53] **16.** He provided altarcloths in the Saviour's, God's mother's, St Peter's, St Paul's, and St Andrew's churches, and others in various churches. In the city of Centumcellae, he had the destroyed walls stoutly constructed almost from the ground up.

17. As for the decree that had been passed by the college of *sacerdotes* when it met in front of St Peter's holy body, on celebrating the ceremonies of vigils and mass of Christ our Lord God, his holy mother, the holy apostles and all the holy martyrs and confessors, perfect and righteous resting in peace throughout the world – to maintain it he decreed that, in the oratory dedicated to their name inside St Peter's under the principal arch, the vigils should be celebrated by the monks and the ceremonies of mass by the priests in their weekly turns. In these instructions he laid down that for holding the vigils in the cemeteries all round Rome on the day of their *natalicia* the lights and the offering should be brought from the patriarchate by the *oblationarius*,[54] for mass to be celebrated by the *sacerdos* whom the pontiff for the time being[55] would appoint. **18.** *He performed three December ordinations, 24 priests, 3 deacons; for various places 80 bishops. By giving him the pallium*[56] *he constituted the venerable Wilchar*[57] *as archbishop in the districts of France in the city of Vienne. He was buried in St Peter's on 28 November in the 10th indiction* [741]. *The bishopric was vacant 8 days.*

---

cipalities); to Noble, 43, it means instead the duchy of Rome, even if at much the same time Gregory was helping in the recovery of Ravenna on behalf of the Holy State = the empire. If so, by the late 730s the pope regards, as yet only half consciously, his new state as constitutionally equal to the empire; cf. 93:11 and n. 38.

53 Not the imperial army but the local militia of Rome and, in effect, the leading citizens. Gregory deals with the matter on his own, acting as the sole authority over Rome and its army. The Gallese incident was almost certainly the first occasion when a pope deployed troops; it would happen again in 742 against Transamund (93:5), during Aistulf's siege in 756, and in support of Desiderius' claim to the Lombard throne in 756–7. For the remaining political events of this pontificate see 93:2–4.

54 One in charge of the offerings (*oblationes*, the bread and wine for the Eucharist).

55 *qui pro tempore fuerit* qualifies 'pontiff' grammatically, but *sacerdos* logically.

56 Rome had given the *pallium* for Gaul to the see of Arles from the time of St Caesarius to that of Florianus (613), and had specifically denied it to Vienne in 599 as unprecedented (Gregory I, *Ep.* 9.112).

57 Ado, archbishop of Vienne in the 9th century, makes (*Chron.*, PL 123, 121–123) Wilchar a contemporary of Charles Martel (who died in the same year as Gregory III), but says that he gave up his see, went to Rome for the first time and met Stephen II (an error?), and subsequently became abbot of Agaunum. He was still alive in 771.

93. ZACHARIAS (741–752)

The author of this life, that of the last Greek pope, fills in the gaps on Lombard–Roman relations in the last years of Gregory III's pontificate. But despite the space devoted to the Lombards, this life too gives up short at the abdication of Ratchis in 749, so there is nothing on Aistulf's restoration of royal power at Spoleto and Benevento and, most glaringly, nothing on that king's capture of Ravenna, Comácchio, Ferrara and (perhaps) Istria in 751. The LP thus manages to ignore the extinction of the exarchate and the end of Byzantine rule in northern Italy. Unfortunately the compiler of the next life (Stephen II) did not make the inadequacies good in the way that this life's compiler did for that of Gregory III; Stephen's life treats Aistulf's attack on the Roman duchy in 752 without explaining the preliminaries.

Another fault is that relations with the Franks are simply ignored. Although Carloman's abdication is dealt with (but only because he came to Rome), it is startling that not a word is said about Zacharias' momentous ruling that the royal title should belong to him who had the power, the consequent deposition of the last Merovingian king, Childeric III, in November 751, and the anointing of Pepin as first king of the Carolingian dynasty (Noble, 67–71). The absence of any reference to these events in the other contemporary papal source, the letters preserved in the *Codex Carolinus*, led Noble to conclude that at Rome no particular significance was seen in them, and that no sort of bargain was struck between Zacharias and Pepin. But in so far as this conclusion rests on the LP's silence, it is unsafe, given the nature of the LP. Lack of interest in the Franks may also account for the author's failure to refer to Boniface, the reform he inspired in the Frankish church, and Zacharias' dealings with him.

These omissions are perhaps merely signs that the life was never completed by its original compiler. There is one certain sign: the concluding formula on the pope's ordinations, his burial and the length of the vacancy is given only in MSS BD, and is clearly a late addition to the basic text as preserved by MSS ACEG (compare how the same MSS BD provided the concluding formulas and one additional passage in the life of Gregory III). It seems that the biographer of Zacharias effectively gave up his task nearly two years before his subject's death.

But the author was a contemporary and even an eyewitness of what he describes. His account of the pontiff's visit to Liutprand even mentions the days of the week: rather pointless when he does not reveal the months concerned. As far as can be seen the life is chronological, though for the church restorations (there are no new foundations) this cannot be proved; and the placing of chapter 20 on events at Constantinople (the chronology of which is controversial) may be governed by the date of events at the end of the chapter.

The most remarkable feature of the text, however, is its style; that it is generally more fluent than that of earlier lives in the LP is due in large measure to the influence of the Latin Bible. So pervasive is this that the translator has tried to reflect the author's mannerisms by the vocabulary of the English RSV Bible where possible and appropriate. The author's main purpose in this was to stress the pontiff's character as the father of his people and the good shepherd of his flock. Noble (51) draws attention to the connexion between this 'pastoral' terminology and the concept of the Romans as the pope's 'peculiar people' (where Latin *pecus* = 'herd'). And the moment the people of Ravenna realized that only the pope could save them from Liutprand's invasion, the idea is extended to cover the people of that area as well: Zacharias heads towards Ravenna to liberate the 'sheep' who would have been lost (c. 13; Noble, 53). The conceit was taken to its extreme by the interpolator of two short passages (c.13; though found in ACEG which usually reflect the earlier text, their absence from BD must in this case show they are not original – the matter is discussed by Duchesne, I, CCXXIV): Zacharias' journey is now said to have been assisted by a cloud which travelled over his retinue to keep them cool – in other words Zacharias is now also likened, if rather clumsily, to Moses leading the Israelites through the desert.

DOMUSCULTAE

Chapters 25 and 26 of Zacharias' life are important as containing the earliest references to the foundation of agricultural units called domuscultae – four (possibly five) are mentioned, and under Hadrian I (97:54–5, 63, 69, 76–7) we meet with six more (one, c. 76, mentioned purely in passing). Archaeology adds a contribution to our knowledge, otherwise there is little contemporary information outside the LP; this gives most details for the domusculta Capracorum (97:54, 69), also the one best known archaeologically. The domuscultae provide almost the only usable evidence for studying settlement patterns in central Italy between 600 and 1000, during which time (but not necessarily in the 8th century) there was a large-scale shift in these patterns (Wickham, 1979, 87). The nature, size, number and organization of these agricultural areas are controversial.

Domuscultae were in some way novel, or lives 93 and 97 would not stress them. Chronologically it is likely to be no coincidence that they were (as far as we know) the first papal estates set up in the Campagna following the loss of the papal properties in Sicily in 732–3. The gifts of Norma and Ninfa by Constantine V (c. 20) were not enough to make good that loss, so the acquisition of new properties or the reorganization of existing ones at this time is no surprise.

Wherever the origin of the land is mentioned it is land newly acquired by the church. Thus Zacharias accepted a bequest from Theodore, c. 25. It was gifts from Leoninus (enlarged with further gifts and purchases) and from Mastalus that were organized as two domuscultae by Hadrian (97:63, 77), and the other domuscultae he founded were on what had been his own family land. But in other cases the land is of unstated origin. So we cannot exclude the possibility that some domuscultae were reorganizations of existing church land. But not all land acquired in this period was necessarily incorporated in a domusculta: Leoninus also bequeathed the massa Acutiana, and although it was 'close to' (*iuxta*) the domusculta, the language of 97:63 seems to imply it was not made part of it. Equally there is no reason to suppose that all existing papal properties were organized into domuscultae. The distinguishing factor may not be the land's origin but some peculiarity of organization, status or purpose.

The first under Zacharias (c. 25) is for the pope's privy purse, the second is vaguely for 'the church's use'. The function of Hadrian's first domusculta (Capracorum, 97:54) is to provide for the poor; where any function is stated for the others it is again vague, 'for the church's use and requirements'. These expressions do not require, but do not exclude, the possibility that domuscultae were for food-distribution at Rome; but the reference to Zacharias' privy purse would be an odd way of expressing this. A single purpose for the revenue was not the criterion for categorizing domuscultae.

Some aspect of their operation might provide an explanation. But the account of the domusculta Capracorum in the LP is the only evidence (see 97: n. 93), and on this basis Wickham (1978, 176–7) concludes that these estates 'should simply be regarded as part of the 'manorial system' of eighth-century Northern and Central Italy'. There was nothing necessarily new in the economic structure. 'That they put a lasting stamp on the economic organization of vast areas of the Campagna is unlikely'. Only in the 10th century is there evidence for the beginning of a new distinctively medieval settlement pattern (incastellamento, on which see Wickham, 1979, 84–92).

In some cases the LP draws attention to the existence (St Caecilia's, 93:25; St Hedistus', 97:63), the building (St Abbacyrus', 93:25; St Peter's, 97:69) or rebuilding (St Theodore's, 97:76; St Leucius', 97:77; also perhaps St Andrew's at the 30th mile on the Via Appia, 97:76, if it is on a domusculta) of churches on or for the domuscultae. This could suggest an increased population or the resettlement of an existing population on a domusculta. But it need not imply this: it would be extraordinary if the papacy had made no spiritual provision for the workforce. Bertolini (1952) proposed that Zacharias was bringing abandoned land at Tres Tabernae under cultivation and that domuscultae are to be seen as new foundations on land that was underoccupied or uncultivated. This is plausible, but the evidence is circumstantial and proof could only be achieved by further archaeological research. Even if correct, the explanation may not apply elsewhere, since the Campagna was not homogeneous; in any case it is nowhere stated that Tres Tabernae was in a domusculta (Ninfa and Norma are not described as one). At Capracorum, the 'homesteads' (*casales*) mentioned in the LP imply an existing population, and the text nowhere hints at resettlement or clearance (apart from the reference to the churches) (Wickham, 1978, 176). There is no impression of an abandoned countryside (Wickham, 1979, 86); the settlement-pattern at this date still seems that of late antiquity ('The Ager Veientanus', 1968, 161).

Traditionally domuscultae were seen as large coherent blocs of land, and as representing a new concept of agricultural reorganization, and the view is still tenable. It is assumed by Bertolini (1952 and 1972), by Partner (1966) 68–78, by the authors of 'The Ager Veientanus' at 161–5), and by Llewellyn (1971), 207, 243–5). But this view was challenged by P. J. Jones in 1966 (Wickham, 1978, 174–7). The domuscultae can be seen as a reorganization of the church's rural landholdings, rather than as necessarily large or coherent territories. It is doubtful whether domuscultae, even if some were large and coherent, were defined in terms of those factors. For the evidence (such as it is) see 93: n. 92; 97: nn. 94, 124, 126, 164. In fact nothing proves that domuscultae were large or that they were made up of contiguous lands: similarly, massae could vary enormously in size and their parts were not necessarily contiguous.

In the life of Zacharias the only common peculiarity of domuscultae mentioned (c. 26) is inalienability: they are St Peter's property for ever. Under Hadrian, inalienability is again remarked on. It is possible that the leasing out of much land on terms which amounted to alienation had produced a real decline in revenue (hence the insistence that domuscultae were permanently inalienable) and also a rural aristocracy with security of tenure which was becoming a rival to the church in the countryside (Noble, 246). But the impression of large-scale leasing may be misleading: it is based on the survival in summary form of 39 leases made in the time of Gregory II, and for all we know the policy did not cease then.

At this point domuscultae could become significant politically. There is no doubt that, whatever their origins and organization, they did become quasi-military: certainly by the 9th century the inhabitants were expected to act as soldiers (LP Sergius II 104:47, Leo IV 105:70, 80 with n. 106, and Duchesne, II, 137 n. 47; Whitehouse, 1973, 861–76); unlike clerics, they could be armed. But under Zacharias the Campagna was already threatened by the Lombards. Were soldier–farmers designed from the start to play a defensive role? The appearance not long after the first domuscultae of a new official, the *superista*, apparently the chief military officer at the Lateran and in charge of the *familia S. Petri* (occupying the domuscultae?), may not be coincidence (Brezzi, 1947, 25–6). From that time the Duke of Rome disappears from the sources; indeed, from Hadrian's time the Roman militia seem to have a merely ceremonial role, the traditional military organization disappears, and papally-appointed dukes have (it seems) judicial, not military, functions.

Hence Noble (248–9) hypothesizes that by adjusting and reorganizing some of their rural holdings, the popes attempted to create a military force independent of the Roman remnant of the former imperial army of Italy. He suggests that as early as

767 the rebellion of Toto of Nepi shows that the Roman duchy's regular militia had realized how the church had formed its own militia, usable against their interests; and that it may have been the *familia S. Petri* who kept Christopher in power and who carried out his reprisals in the countryside after Desiderius withdrew from Rome in 768. He notes that Hadrian founded one of his domuscultae (Capracorum) near Toto's lands (to inhibit any successor?), that one of Leo III's assailants in 799 was Maurice of Nepi, and that on the failure of the rural nobility's plot against Leo in 815, they ravaged Leo's domuscultae. Till 816 (when the nobles took over) or shortly after, it was the domuscultae that enabled the clergy to hold their own against the nobility. After that, the *familia* became a weapon in Roman factionalism until, proving useless against the Saracens, it disappeared (Whitehouse, 1973, 865). But while it existed it could have been an instrument against the interests of the lay aristocracy.

The case is persuasive. But it does not follow from their military activities in the ninth century that this was what was planned by Zacharias. Nor does it follow that the whole of the *familia S. Petri* occupied domuscultae: what other name would be given to workers on other papal estates? *Familia*, after all, means dependent populations on a *fundus* (Bosl, 1982, 33), not necessarily on a domusculta; there is, incidentally, no way of knowing whether the *familia* was made up of household or agricultural slaves, tenants or others bound to labour-service (Wickham, 1978, 176). That the domuscultae were targets of attack by lay aristocrats need mean no more than that the nobles were annoyed either at the way some (not necessarily all) domuscultae had been acquired (they might not have agreed with the LP's repeated claim that popes had paid a fair price when the land was newly acquired), or merely at the inalienability principle – ravage the land you know you will not be allowed to lease. The system of domuscultae had taken in lands which might otherwise have been granted to nobles on perpetual leases. 'The Church was moving from a bureaucratic system to ... landed lordship, on at least some of its property. The rural nobility, long accustomed to holding vast tracts of Church land, cannot have liked this diminution of the pool of available land in central Italy' (Noble, 247–8, noting this as the thesis of Hartmann, 1909).

If, then, origin, purpose, operational and resettlement factors, size and coherence are not of the essence of a domusculta, we are left with the evidence of the LP. What distinguished a domusculta was the inalienability principle; consequent on this (and possibly intended from the start) was the existence of a workforce, which would permanently remain that of the church, and could be used for military defence.

93. **1. ZACHARIAS** [3 December 741–15 March 752], of Greek origin, son of Polychronius, held the see 10 years 3 months 15 days. He[1] was gentle and gracious, adorned with all kindness, a lover of the clergy and all the Roman people, slow to anger and quick to have pity, repaying no one evil for evil, nor taking even merited vengeance, but dutiful and compassionate to everyone from the time of his ordination; he was one who returned good for evil even to those who were previously his persecutors, and when giving them preferments he at the same time enriched them with goods.

2. He found the whole province of Italy along with the duchy of Rome in great convulsion at the persecution[2] of Liutprand king of the Lombards. The king's pretext was that Transamund duke of Spoleto had taken refuge from his persecution in this city of Rome;[3] pope Gregory his predecessor of happy memory, Stephen[4] the then patrician and duke and the whole Roman army had not handed this Transamund over, and the result was a blockade by the king, who stole from the Roman duchy four cities, Amélia, Orte, Bomarzo and Blera.[5] And so the king returned to his palace[6] in August of the 8th indiction [739]. **3.** But duke Transamund, making a plan with the Romans and mustering the common army of the Roman duchy, crossed the

---

1 His earlier career is not given; he was probably born in Calabria in 679 and can be identified with the deacon Zacharias who attended the Roman council of 732 (Marcou, 1977). A contemporary fresco portrait of this pope survives in S. Maria Antiqua, whose restoration, begun by John VII, he continued.

2 The invasion of 739, cf. 92:14.

3 Cf. Paul the Deacon, *HL* 6.55, who however confuses Liutprand's expedition in 729 with that of 739 here dealt with and rightly placed by the LP; Liutprand had captured Spoleto and installed Hilderic before 16 June 739, and Transamund had fled to Rome.

4 A lead bull found at Blera has inscribed on it in Greek the prayer 'Lord, help thy duke Stephen, patrician and duke of Rome', probably referring to this man.

5 *Pauli continuatio tertia* c. 14 (*MGH SSrL,* 207), written in Italy, states that because of the refuge taken by Transamund, Liutprand took many cities and castella *de iure Romani pontificis Gregorii* – this shows how things were seen in Italy; we see below that Zacharias is determined to regain his cities, with no reference to imperial authority (Noble, 51). On Duchesne's chronology (but see n. 15) a letter of Gregory III dated 15 October 740 (*Epp. Lang.* 16, *MGH EKA* 3, 708) belongs at this point: the pope reminds all the bishops of Lombard Tuscany of their ordination oaths to St Peter to help his church in time of danger (texts of such oaths in *Liber Diurnus* 75, 76, ed. Foerster, 136–8), and exhorts them to help his envoys (the priest Anastasius and the regionary subdeacon Adeodatus) and accompany them to Liutprand and Hildeprand to demand the restoration of the four castra taken from St Peter 'last year'; if they would not do so, Gregory III would go in person, despite his ill-health. 'This action by the pope may have struck the king as a subtle but effective reminder that Rome was not without means of stirring up trouble in the *regnum*' (Noble, 48).

6 And not to assist Charles Martel in Provence?

93. ZACHARIAS

duchy of Spoleto's borders by two routes. And straightaway, in fear of the Roman army's size,[7] the people of the Marsi,[8] Forcona,[9] Valva[10] and Penne[11] gave in to Transamund. Then crossing the territory of Sabina[12] they came to the city of Rieti.[13] And straightaway the Reatini too gave in to him. Going on from there he entered Spoleto[14] in December of the .. indiction.[15] There was convulsion between Romans and Lombards because the Beneventans and Spoletans were siding with the Romans. **4.** But when Transamund duke of Spoleto did not comply[16] in carrying out what he had promised

---

7 This must refer to the contingent which seems to have entered the duchy of Spoleto along the Via Valeria, a route which will have brought them first to the Marsi.

8 The Marsi lived in the area round the Fucine Lake, 90 km east of Rome. They and the next three peoples occupied the eastern part of the duchy of Spoleto.

9 Città di Bagno, 30 km N of the Fucine Lake.

10 A small bishopric 20 km NW of the Fucine Lake.

11 Ancient Pinna, 33 km E of NE from Forcona and across the Apennines.

12 The Byzantine duchy of Rome and the duchy of Spoleto had divided the former Sabina between them, with Rieti as the westernmost city of Spoletan territory. Further Lombard infiltration meant that even the eastern parts of Sabina in the duchy of Rome (the dioceses of Cures, Forum Novum and Nomentum) had been lost by the Byzantines, and in consequence they were not now under Zacharias' control. This is the area in which were located the patrimonies Liutprand would shortly (c. 9) promise to restore to Rome; cf. n. 27, Noble, 156–7; and see further 97:32 with n. 45.

13 The second contingent apparently followed the Via Salaria through Sabina to Rieti and Spoleto.

14 The LP neglects to mention that Transamund, a papal ally, had Hilderic (installed by Liutprand to succeed Transamund at Spoleto) killed.

15 Some MSS add '8th', '7th', or 'aforesaid'; '9th' would be correct if, as seemed likely to Duchesne, the date was December 740, but no MS gives it. Noble, 45, accepts December 739 (8th indiction). The consequence of this chronology, as Noble, 48, sees and tries to justify, is that early 740 to late 741 become a historical 'blank', a peace on the status quo of late 739, with Liutprand holding the four cities; the letter cited in n. 5 would then belong in this period.

16 Transamund perhaps dared not provoke Liutprand. But the king's return, as our author knew, was likely anyway. At this point (December 739–early 740 on his chronology) Noble, 45, dates Gregory III's second letter (*CC* 2) appealing to Charles Martel: 'It is crucial to realize how difficult the pope's position was in 739–40. No military aid had come from Charles, and none was likely. The Spoletan alliance had misfired. The exarch was useless. Liutprand had attacked Rome, seized four of its cities, and then left temporarily, but his return had to have been expected at any moment'. There is some reason to believe that Charles may have interceded with the king on Gregory's behalf. The Frankish annals record that Gregory sent Charles the keys of St Peter's confessio and a link from the apostle's chains; Charles sent gifts back by Grimo abbot of Corbie and Sigebert, a monk of St Denis. These and the envoy Anthat may have mediated between Gregory and Liutprand (Noble, 46, citing Ewig, 1969, 20; but, *pace* Noble, Anthat is not mentioned in the LP). But the annalists also claim that Gregory and the Roman people proposed to depart from the empire and put themselves under Charles' protection. If

the pontiff, the patrician and the Romans, about getting back the four cities which had been lost on his account, or the other heads of his promises, and king Liutprand was preparing for a campaign against the Roman duchy, at this stage pope Gregory of happy memory was called by God and taken from this world,[17] and by God's will the aforenamed holy Zacharias was elected to the pontificate.

On him almighty God conferred such grace that he would not hesitate even to lay down his life for the Roman people's salvation.[18] So he sent an embassy to the king of the Lombards and preached what was salutary to him. **5.** Giving way to this holy man's admonishments, he promised to return the four above-named cities he had stolen from the Roman duchy. And when he began a campaign[19] and went to capture Transamund duke of Spoleto, at this holy man's urging the Roman army came out to help the king.[20] When Transamund saw he had been trapped,[21] he came out from the city of Spoleto and surrendered to the king.[22] **6.** When this king protracted his delay in fulfilling his promise to return the four cities mentioned, the pontiff Zacharias, as a true shepherd of the people God had entrusted to

---

we can accept that such a formal decision by the Romans to secede from the empire (or a realization that they had in fact done so some years earlier) is historical, we are forced to assume that unless they had chosen a foolish isolationism they intended to place themselves under the protection of another power: and that could only be the Franks. But whatever the truth, nothing came of the appeals to Charles (Noble, 47–8).

17 Charles Martel and Leo V also died in 741.

18 As Duchesne observed, the exaggeration is absurd; what had Zacharias to fear when he was abandoning Gregory III's support for Transamund against Liutprand? Even Gregory (letter cited in n. 5) had been worried only about the fatigues of the journey if he visited Liutprand. But the long account that follows in the LP is merited. It was the first time that a pope had in person undertaken a diplomatic mission outside Roman soil; Zacharias was acting as representative of the Roman people – there is no involvement of the empire at all (cf. Noble, 52).

19 This is Liutprand's second campaign; the army of Rome had now abandoned Transamund and was supporting Liutprand. Paul, *HL* 6.56, confusingly has the 'Romans' fighting for Spoleto, but he means the troops of the exarchate.

20 Zacharias saw that Gregory III's alliance with the dukes was unworkable in the long term against Liutprand and realized he had to confront the king directly if all of central Italy was not to fall into his hands; he emphasizes his reversal of Gregory's policy by helping Liutprand against Transamund. In exchange, the king was willing, initially, to hand back the four cities (Noble, 50–51).

21 *suam deceptionem*; not 'deceived', which would make it an adverse judgment on Zacharias' change of policy, out of keeping with the sympathies of this biographer.

22 Liutprand put Transamund into a monastery and installed his own nephew Agiprand as duke of Spoleto; the king then marched against Benevento, duke Godescalc was killed while trying to escape, and Liutprand installed his great-nephew Gisulf as duke (Paul, *HL* 6.56-7).

him, put his hope in God, left this city of Rome with *sacerdotes* and clergy, and made his way confidently and boldly, travelling to a place belonging to the city of Terni in the territory of Spoleto, where the king was in residence.[23]

When he reached the city of Orte[24] and the king knew of his arrival, he sent his envoy Grimuald, who met him and conducted him to the city of Narni. **7.** To meet this holy man king Liutprand sent his vassal dukes and a large army; and at the city of Narni, some 8 miles from where the king was,[25] they welcomed him (it was Friday) and conducted him from there to the basilica of St Valentine bishop and martyr in the city of Terni in the duchy of Spoleto. In front of this basilica's doors the king with the other chief men and his army welcomed the holy man, and after a prayer, and completing their welcome of each other, when he had urged him with the expressions of God and with profuse charity, he left this church in his company and went on about half a mile. And in this way they each spent that Friday in their tents.

8. But on Saturday they met again, and overflowing with God's grace he addressed him with advice pleasing to God, preaching to him that he should be still from the hostile campaign and the shedding of blood and should always pursue what makes for peace. He was swayed by his pious language and amazed at the holy man's resoluteness and advice. By the grace of the Holy Ghost he obtained everything he asked him for:[26] he gave back to the holy man the above-named four cities which he had stolen two years earlier in his blockade on account of Transamund duke of Spoleto, along with their occupants. He confirmed these arrangements by a donation, in the Saviour's oratory, built in his name inside St Peter's church. **9.** And in the title of donation to St Peter prince of the apostles, he regranted the patrimony of Sabina,

---

23 Evidently the narrator was on the journey, but his chronological notes are inadequate. Lower down the text gives the 10th indiction, 741–2; the meeting between Zacharias and Liutprand must have occurred no later than the spring of 742, since the annexation of the four cities had taken place two, not three, years before.

24 The first city in Lombard territory a traveller from Rome would reach.

25 Terni is in fact 8 Roman miles from Narni, 12 km ENE.

26 There seem to be three separate documents involved here and below at the 'Peace of Terni': a charter restoring the four towns, a charter restoring the patrimonies taken 30 years earlier, and a 20 years' truce with the duchy of Rome. Zacharias got what he wanted; it may be that Liutprand thought he had gained as well: he had got the pope to renounce the alliance with the dukes, and though he had in effect recognized the duchy of Rome as independent, this would be a small price if he now had a free hand to deal with Ravenna, and that is the direction in which he turned next (c. 12; Noble, 52, 54 and writers cited in his n. 192)

which had been stolen nearly 30 years ago,[27] those of Narni[28] too and Osimo[29] and Ancona, along with Numana[30] and the valley called Magna in the territory of Sutri.[31] The king confirmed a peace with the Roman duchy for 20 years; and as for all the captives he held from the various Roman provinces, he sent his letters both to his own Tuscia and across the Po, and gave them back[32] to the blessed pontiff along with the captives from Ravenna – the consuls Leo,[33] Sergius,[34] Victor and Agnellus.

10. At the king's request he ordained in the same basilica of St Valentine a replacement for bishop Cosinensis[35] who had passed on. When the king was present with his judges at the new bishop's consecration, God inspired them to remorse by the sweetness of the great prayer he recited; and when they saw the holy man pour out his prayers, many of those Lombards were moved to tears. That same Sunday, after the ceremonies of mass were done, the blessed pontiff invited the king to dinner to receive the apostolic blessing. Such were the graciousness and cordial hilarity while he ate, that the king himself said he never remembered when he had eaten so much.[36]

---

27 If this figure is precise, the occupation of the Sabine patrimony by the Lombards will have been in the first year of Liutprand's own reign, when Faraold II was duke of Spoleto and Constantine was pope. Duchesne noted that the Lombard occupation would have meant the confiscation of Roman church property and that now Liutprand was not retroceding sovereignty of the duchy of Spoleto, merely the revenues of property. Even given that a formal royal act of donation to St Peter was involved, this is surely right. Desiderius later ratified the return of this patrimony (*CC* 72).

28 Captured by the Lombards in the time of Gregory II (91:13 and n. 39).

29 Osimo also had become Lombard under Gregory II (91:18).

30 The dates of Lombard annexation of Ancona and Numana are not known.

31 Cf. 91:21; in 727–8 Liutprand had seized the castellum of Sutri for 140 days and had returned it stripped of its wealth – and, as we see here, of its territory.

32 Here and elsewhere *redonavit* means that the pope received it, but not necessarily that it was the pope from whom it had been taken in the first place.

33 To be distinguished from another Leo *ipatus* about 780 (Agnellus, c. 162).

34 Duchesne saw no reason to identify him with Sergius archbishop of Ravenna (on whom, 96:19, 25 and nn. 61, 68) as was done in *MGH SSrL*, 377 n. 8; the identification is accepted by Brown, 1984, 185 n. 18.

35 This is the name of a place, not a person, but the text may be corrupt. Consentia (Cosenza) is too far south, Narni and Terni are unlikely; Duchesne argues for Senensis (Siena), in Lombard Tuscany and in Liutprand's gift. Some have speculated that the new bishop was Transamund himself: Paul, *HL* 6.57, says that Liutprand made him a cleric; this could be true, but no source says that Transamund was ever a bishop, and the LP would surely have noted the point.

36 Perhaps the LP's most extraordinary example of eyewitness reporting! *Commessurum* (= *comesurum*) fulfils a remarkable function as an active past participle; this is surely the sense (it was so understood in MSS which produce variants), rather than 'he had it in mind he would never eat so much again'.

93. ZACHARIAS

11. Next day, Monday, the king bade him farewell and sent as his escort his own nephew Agiprand[37] duke of Chiusi and also Tacipert the *gastald*, Ramning the *gastald* of Tuscánia, and Grimuald; these were to be this holy man's escort to the aforenamed cities and were to hand them over with their occupants. Which is what happened – first the city of Amélia, then Orte. He reached the Castrum of Bomarzo and accepted it; it would then have been a long journey round the State's[38] territory to go to the city of Blera through the districts of the city of Sutri, so the king's envoy Grimuald took the blessed pontiff through the territory of Lombard Tuscia since it was near, that is by way of the Castrum of Viterbo, to the city of Blera.[39] This city too the *gastald* Ramning and the envoy Grimuald together handed over to the holy man. And in this way by God's favour he returned with the palm of victory to this city of Rome. He convened all the people and addressed them: in thanksgiving to almighty God they were all to set out from God's holy mother's church called *ad martyres* and make their way in common with a litany to St Peter's, prince of the apostles. And so it was done.

12. This was accomplished in the 10th indiction [741/2]. In the next indiction [742/3] the king was greatly oppressing the province of Ravenna and had made ready for a campaign against that very city and a blockade of it. On hearing of the king's campaign His Excellency Eutychius the patrician and exarch, along with John, archbishop[40] of the church of Ravenna, and the whole people of that city and of both Pentapolis and Emilia, put their request in writing and sent it to this holy man, begging him hasten to deliver them.[41] And the holy man sent Benedict, bishop[42] and *vicedominus*, and Ambrose,[43] the *primicerius notariorum*, on an embassy with gifts to request the king and

---

37 Cf. n. 22. The pope is taken on a formal tour to receive each of the four cities.

38 Noble, 52, takes this as the first unambiguous reference to papal territory as *respublica*; cf. 92: n. 52.

39 The shortest route from Bomarzo to Blera would be through Viterbo, about 30 km; whereas Bomarzo to Sutri is 28 km almost due south, and Sutri to Blera 17 km ENE. The detail proves that Lombard territory included a wedge containing Viterbo.

40 Agnellus, *Lib. Pont. eccl. Rav.* 151–3, assigns him only 8 years, but we are now in the campaigning season of 743 and John had been present as bishop of Ravenna at the Roman Council of 731. Read XIII for VIII in Agnellus?

41 A remarkable admission of imperial impotence and papal competence.

42 No doubt Benedict, bishop of Mentana, who attended the Roman Council of 745.

43 Ambrose occurs frequently in the diplomatic negotiations of Zacharias and Stephen II; he was *primicerius* from at least 742/3 (this chapter) till his death in 753 (94:23–24); after him Theodotus held the post (97: n. 3).

beg him to end his combativeness and restore the Castrum of Césena[44] to Ravenna. But he would not endure it.

And when Zacharias saw his stubborn persistence, this holy man, defended by the Trophy[45] of the Faith, left Rome to be governed by Stephen the already mentioned patrician and duke,[46] and not as a hireling but as a true shepherd he left his sheep and hastened to redeem those who were going to be lost. **13.** *On his departure, when he commended himself in prayer to St Peter prince of the apostles, with his sacerdotes and clergy and travellers, it was almighty God's will that, to prevent their being burnt by the heat, a cloud covered them by day until the place where they pitched their tents; in the evening it rested, but on the next day it was divinely raised up to protect them.* His Excellency Eutychius the exarch came to meet him at St Christopher's basilica in the place called Aquila,[47] some 50 miles from Ravenna.[48] *But the same cloud covered them and went with them to St Apollinaris' basilica in Ravenna. And then as a sign that he was to go to the city of Ticinum, there were flaming armies in the clouds, going ahead of the holy pontiff.* The men and women of Ravenna, both sexes and every age, came out from the city, giving thanks to almighty God. With copious tears they welcomed the holy pontiff, crying out and saying: 'Welcome to our shepherd who has left his own sheep and hastened to deliver us who were about to be lost!'

14. And from Ravenna he sent to king Liutprand the priest Stephen[49] and the *primicerius* Ambrose to tell him he would be arriving. These men entered

---

44 A frontier town between Ravenna and the Lombard kingdom, commanding the Via Aemilia. Liutprand may have wished merely to secure access to Spoleto through the exarchate and Pentapolis, but the pope regarded his attack as in breach of the Peace of Terni. The king then sent envoys to the emperor to ask to be allowed to keep Cesena (c. 15). Cf. Noble, 53–5.

45 The Cross, as symbol of the victory of Christ.

46 Cf. c. 2. The phraseology shows that by this date the duke of Rome was de facto subordinate to the pope. The duke of Rome is appointed by the pope, responsible to him, and rules only in his absence. The office lasted until at least 778–81; the last known incumbents were relatives of the popes or of their high officials.

47 Unknown; Duchesne suggests a location near Rimini, which he says would be about the right distance from Ravenna (but Rimini is only 48 km from Ravenna). The pope had probably followed the military road (still under imperial control) passing through Todi and Perugia, crossing the Apennines at Castrum Lucioli (above Cagli) and then rejoining the Via Flaminia; cf. BP Gregory I 66:2 and Duchesne, I, 313 n. 3.

48 Imperial protocol had required the pope to go one mile to meet the exarch; that the exarch goes 50 miles to meet the pope shows the exarch's reduced status.

49 Three priests named Stephen were at the Roman Council of 745, for the *tituli* of SS Mark, Eusebius and Chrysogonus.

the Lombards' territory at the city of Imola,[50] and discovered there was a plan to obstruct the holy man travelling thither; they let him know this in a letter written in the quiet of the night. The pontiff Zacharias learnt it and toward the dawn of Saturday, frightened by no fear of death but relying on Christ's help, he boldly left Ravenna and entered the Lombards' territory in the company of his own envoys. They went ahead of him but the king, driven by anguish,[51] would not receive them. On the 28th day of June[52] the supreme pontiff reached the Po; and there the king did send his chief men to receive him. With them he reached Ticinum where the king was in residence, and he passed right through to outside that city's walls, and at the hour of prayer, the ninth hour,[53] he went to St Peter's basilica[54] called *ad caelum aureum* to celebrate the ceremonies of mass for the eve of the prince of the apostles. And when the libation[55] was finished he entered the city and stayed there.

15. Next day, to celebrate the *natale* of the prince of the apostles, at king Liutprand's invitation he celebrated the ceremonies of mass in the same church. And there they exchanged greetings, the citizens welcoming him as well, and so they went back inside Ticinum. Next day the king through his chief men invited the holy man to proceed to his palace. He was given a very honourable welcome by the king, and addressed him with salutary admonitions, asking him no more to oppress the province of Ravenna by the

50 That Imola and Cesena, both within 40 km of Ravenna, were in Lombard hands shows how small the exarchate now was.

51 The explanation seems to be that Liutprand had regarded the Roman duchy and the exarchate as separate entities and thought he had a free hand with the latter. Finding that Zacharias regarded the Ravennates as part of his flock, he realized he could only accomplish his ultimate ambitions (whether conquering all of Italy or merely securing the duchies) at the cost of making war on the pope. And Liutprand was 'a man of sincere religious sentiments' (Noble, 55).

52 In 743; not in July, as Noble, 53, has it. 28 June was a Friday in 743, so the pope's journey of some 160 miles from Ravenna to the crossing of the Po near Pavia (he said mass there the same day) will have taken six days from the previous Saturday.

53 The normal mid-afternoon time for mass on fastdays, including those preceding a feastday; this shows that *vigiliae* means 'eve' and not vigils (nocturns).

54 The basilica of St Peter at Pavia existed before 600 (Paul, *HL* 4.31). Liutprand rebuilt it and added a monastery (id. 6.58). The present building of S. Pietro in Ciel d'oro is 12th century, its main claim to fame being the relics of St Augustine of Hippo. *Ad caelum aureum* seems to have referred to a golden mosaic ceiling.

55 For the meaning Duchesne cited a liturgical Ordo Romanus (now M. Andrieu, *Les Ordines Romani*, 1.322-3, 3.109, O.R. XV.65); after mass the pope and his ministers divested and there was a final ceremony at which they drank from three cups of wine; an even more solemn version of this occurred at the end of vespers in Easter week. In Duchesne's time it was still the custom to share a cup of unconsecrated wine after a mass in which ordinations were performed.

campaign he was starting, but instead to give back what had been taken from Ravenna's territory, and also the Castrum of Césena. The king gave way after much obstinacy and enlarged Ravenna's territory[56] as its people formerly held it, and restored two thirds of the territory of the Castrum of Césena to the side of the State;[57] but he held on to one third of this Castrum, on the pretext of an existing arrangement to restore this Castrum and its third part, which he was holding as security, to the side of the State only on 1 June[58] when his envoys were to return from the imperial city. **16.** After this the king departed, and travelling with him from place to place conducted the holy man as far as the Po; and there, bidding him farewell and setting things in good order, he gave him leave to go back, granting him as an escort his dukes and dignitaries, and also other men who were to restore the territories of Ravenna and Césena mentioned. And so it was done. And God wrought wondrously: he delivered the peoples of Ravenna and the Pentapolis from the oppression and distress[59] wherein they were held; and they were filled with grain and wine.

17. And returning to Rome with all his retinue, giving thanks to God he again[60] celebrated the *natale* of the princes of the apostles Peter and Paul with all the people; he gave himself over to prayer, asking almighty God to give mercy and comfort to the Ravennate and Roman people from that treacherous[61] persecutor, king Liutprand. God's clemency did not spurn his prayers, but took the king from this world before the appointed time.[62] And the whole

---

56 The *territorium* of Ravenna itself (as opposed to that of the exarchate) had been encroached on by the Lombards; it is a benefit to its people to get their fields and villages back, along with two thirds of the territory of Cesena.

57 Taken by Noble, 54, to mean the papal State – wrongly, if c. 12 is to be trusted ('restore the castrum of Cesena to Ravenna'); hence Noble's following observations are dubious: 'Zachary's acquisition of Cesena, moreover, is interesting because it was the first piece of soil of the old Exarchate to which any pope had secured a title. One is reminded of the papacy's acquisition of Cumae and Sutri a generation earlier'.

58 In 744. On the sending of envoys to Constantinople cf. n. 44.

59 'Oppression and distress' probably reflects the Vulgate text of Isaiah 24.12.

60 The occasion was probably the octave day of the feast, i.e. 5 July, rather than a postponement of the feast of 29 June, or the feast of Peter (not Paul) 'in Chains' on 1 August (the dedication feast of the *titulus* of Eudoxia).

61 Duchesne comments that this is hardly just; Paul (*HL* 6.58) makes Liutprand a valiant, pious, enlightened and equitable king; and under Gregory III he had respected Roman territory and had allowed the pope to gain land at the empire's expense. The LP's triumphalist view of the king's death shows that the author was contemporary: he would have been milder on Liutprand after Aistulf's expeditions against Rome.

62 Liutprand died before 22 March 744 when Hildeprand was acting as king (Noble, 55, n. 194). The LP seems to mean not that he died before *his* appointed time, but before the day appointed for the restoration of Cesena. Here, alone, the LP comes surprisingly close to

93. ZACHARIAS

persecution abated, and there was joy not only for the Romans and Ravennates but even for the Lombards themselves: since the Lombards even cast out of his kingdom Hildeprand, the ill-intentioned nephew whom Liutprand had left as king, and elected Ratchis, formerly a duke, as their king.[63] The blessed pontiff sent him a report and straightaway because of his reverence for the prince of the apostles he gave way to his prayers, and entered into a peace for the space of 20 years;[64] and the whole people of Italy was still.[65]

18. In the Lateran patriarchate[66] in front of the basilica of pope Theodore of blessed memory,[67] he newly built a triclinium and adorned it with varieties of marble, glass, metal, mosaic and painting. He adorned both St Silvester's oratory and the portico with sacred images; and he gave orders that all his wealth should be brought inside it by the hands of Ambrose the *primicerius notariorum*. He built from the ground up in front of the Lateran office a portico and a tower, where he installed bronze doors and railings, and in front of the doors he adorned it with a figure of the Saviour; making use of the stairs which went upwards to the top of that tower he constructed there a triclinium and bronze railings, and there he painted a representation of the world and decorated it with various verses. He restored the whole patriarchate almost like new – he had found the place very poverty-stricken.

19. In the church[68] of SS Peter and Paul, princes of the apostles, he provided veils of silk material to hang between the columns. In the aforesaid prince of the apostles' church he worked on the arrangement as a library of all the codices[69] he owned in his own house, which are read at matins in the

---

besmirching Zacharias by saying he prayed for the king to die.

63 Ratchis, formerly duke of Friuli, replaced Hildeprand (who ruled 7 months) about September 744. It is generally thought that Hildeprand represented the anti-Roman party among the Lombards, and that pro-Romans replaced him with Ratchis (whose wife was a Roman, cf. n. 89); but his choice by the Lombards might equally be due to his opposition to Liutprand's centralizing policies (Noble, 55–6, with nn. 196–201). Either way, the choice was good from a Roman point of view.

64 Evidently a ratification of the 20 years' truce made with Liutprand, c. 9.

65 Italian politics are not resumed until c. 23.

66 John VII had abandoned the Lateran for a residence on the Palatine (BP 88:2; Duchesne, I, 386 n. 7); the decision to return to the Lateran entailed repairs.

67 Cf. Duchesne, I, 334 n. 11. This part must have been finished before the end of October 745 when the Roman Council of that date was held in it. The work on the Lateran is therefore early in this pontificate. None of Zacharias' work survives.

68 Rather than assume an awkward expression for S. Pietro in Vincoli (the *titulus Apostolorum*), Duchesne understands *ecclesia* as plural, particularly in view of the 'lights of the apostles' below; if so, the basilicas of St Peter and St Paul.

69 A similar gift made in this very pontificate by a priest Gregory to S. Clemente is recorded on an inscription (Duchesne, III, 102).

yearly cycle. He[70] newly arranged the domusculta[71] Lauretum, adding to it the Fonteiana Estate, known also as Paunaria. He set aside 20 lb gold for the annual purchase of oil, so that the lights of the apostles would profit from the revenue, and he entailed this decree under the bond of an anathema.[72] For St Peter's he provided a gold-worked altarcloth with our Lord God and Saviour Jesus Christ's birth on it, and he decorated it with precious jewels; also 4 crimson silk veils, which he decorated with wheels and various gold-worked adornments. At his own expense he provided a crown of fine silver with dolphins, weighing 120 lb.

20. Following the usages of the church this blessed man sent an orthodox synodic letter[73] as a pledge of his faith to the church of Constantinople, and also sent another memorial to the serene prince Constantine.[74] The apostolic see's *apocrisiarii* made their way to the imperial city and discovered inside the

---

70 This sentence occurs in all the MSS, but its placing in the middle of details concerning the shrines of the apostles suggests it is an insertion.

71 For domuscultae see the introduction to this life. The location of this one (which recurs in 98:5) is not clear. The name suggested to Tomassetti the imperial villa of Lorium on the Via Aurelia but Duchesne returned to Nibby's explanation that the domusculta was located around the ancient Laurentum. The name Paunaria perhaps occurs in a diploma of Paschal II (1099-1118; *MGH Epp.* III, 106), but does not survive on the ground to clarify the location. The massa Fonteiana is presumably the same as that named in two leases granted by Gregory II (J 2197, 2206) of farms contained in it and of a fossa 20 miles from Rome; in the latter case the massa is described as in the patrimonium Appiae; so a site south of the Tiber is preferable.

72 There survives a document of Gregory II on the same subject, the full text in manuscript, and much of it on an inscription still in the narthex of St Peter's (J 2184).

73 The last time such a letter (on which cf. 91:2) was sent; it does not survive. It will have been a formal document showing the pope's orthodoxy, presumably with a fresh attack on iconoclasm. The placing of this chapter suggests Zacharias had not regarded the matter as urgent. Is it significant that the letter (which has nothing to do with that sent to the emperor, next mentioned) was sent to the church rather than the patriarch? The patriarch was still Anastasius (91:24, 92:4) whom Gregory II had not recognized (though both Gregory II and Gregory III had corresponded with him).

74 As Noble, 49 with n. 170, points out, it does not follow from this passage, in spite of the conventional wisdom, that Zacharias sent a formal notice of his election to the emperor for confirmation (which would have made him the last pope to do so); Bertolini, 1955[a], explains the passage correctly: the second document was a letter to the emperor, probably telling him to desist from iconoclasm – and (in view of the grant of Ninfa and Norma in this chapter) asking for the restoration of the Roman patrimonies taken away 10 years earlier. The pope evidently wanted a modus vivendi with Constantinople; and Constantine V (who had continued as emperor after his father Leo III's death on 18 June 741) conceded this, perhaps in view of Zacharias' help for the exarchate against the Lombards and of his own problems with the Arabs and Bulgars. It suited both sides to play down the iconoclast dispute.

93. ZACHARIAS

palace a certain intruder into the imperial power, a rebel named Artavasdus.[75] For when the emperor had gone out to battle against the Agareni people, this Artavasdus immediately bribed the people who remained in the imperial city and seized the imperial throne. Afterwards the prince Constantine gathered the multitude of the eastern[76] armies, made his way to Constantinople and manfully attacked it; he encompassed the city outside and captured it, and obtained the original summit of his realm. Immediately he plucked out the eyes of Artavasdus and his sons, and many of his rebels he made exiles from their own homes. After this he sought out the apostolic see's envoy who had happened to arrive there during the convulsion; on finding him he pardoned[77] the apostolic see. In view of the pontiff's request, he sent a written donation of two estates in public ownership called Ninfa and Norma[78] to the same holy and blessed pope and to the holy Roman church, to be occupied and owned in perpetuity.

21. In his time[79] Carloman, son of Charles king[80] of the Franks, aban-

---

75 The usurpation began in Phrygia in June 742; Constantinople was taken some time later. Zacharias sent his letter not knowing at any rate the outcome. Artavasdus was orthodox, and the pope, who in 743 dated letters by the years of Constantine V, used the years of Artavasdus in letters dated 22 June and 5 November 744 (J 2270–1). Constantinople was retaken by Constantine V on 2 November 744. Theophanes (a. 6233–5) and Nicephorus (pp. 59–62) give more details, but in no way contradict the LP. Speck, 1981, dates all these events one year earlier, and is followed in this by Noble, 49. On Artavasdus see also Ostrogorsky, 165–6. The patriarch Anastasius duly played the Vicar of Bray; Constantine forgave him though subjecting him to humiliations.

76 The troops of the theme of Anatolia, which Constantine used along with those of the Thracesian theme (Nicephorus and Theophanes, *locc. cit.*).

77 Since Constantine was merciful to the patriarch he could hardly be less so to the pope and his envoy, who in the circumstances could hardly have refused to recognize Artavasdus. So Duchesne; but does the text really mean 'gave him leave to go back to the apostolic see' (so *absolvere* in cc. 16, 22)?

78 Norma centred on the village so named on the SW slopes of the Monti Lepini and just north of the Pomptine marshes, while Ninfa was only 3 km away in the plain. The gift was large, but nothing in comparison to the confiscated Sicilian and Calabrian patrimonies.

79 On this chapter see Noble, 66–7: even if Pepin exerted some pressure on Carloman, the latter's motive for taking the habit seems to have been genuinely religious. The abdication both 'complicated and clarified' conditions in France after 747. It left the mayoral office to Pepin alone, showed how weak Childeric III was, left Carloman's young sons isolated, and exacerbated the problem of the existence of a half-brother of Pepin and Carloman named Grifo (who lived till 753). It also smoothed the path for Pepin to have himself made king: an event ignored in the LP.

80 An inaccurate use of the word king (again in 94:15, but avoided by the interpolator in 92:14); in letters to Charles, Gregory III had called him *subregulus*.

doning the glory of this present life and earthly power, came devoutly[81] with some of his loyal followers to St Peter prince of the apostles; he presented himself to this apostle of God and, undertaking to remain in the spiritual habit, he accepted the burden of clerical[82] status from the same holy pontiff. *His many other gifts presented to St Peter the apostle included a great silver arch, before the confessio, weighing 70 lb.* Some time later he set out for St Benedict's monastery in the territory of Aquino;[83] the oath of profession he took was to spend the rest of his life in it.[84]

22. At that time it occurred that many Venetian traders arrived in this city of Rome; they were prolonging the fairs and markets, and were buying up a crowd of slaves, both male and female; they were trying to export them to the pagan[85] people in Africa. When he heard this, the same holy father stopped it happening, judging it wrong for those washed by Christ's baptism to be the slaves of pagan peoples. He paid the Venetians the price they were attested to have paid to buy them, redeemed them all from the yoke of slavery and let them live the life of the free.

23. At this time[86] Ratchis king of the Lombards set out in a mighty fury to capture the city of Perugia,[87] like the rest of the towns of the Pentapolis. He surrounded it and vigorously blockaded it. On hearing this the holy pope straightaway relied on his hope in God, took some of his chief clergy and made his way at full speed to that city. At the cost of very many gifts to the king and by appealing to him exceedingly, with the Lord's assistance he secured

81 *devotus*; at least by the 12th century the word can be a noun referring to a person who has vowed himself to a saint (Niermeyer).

82 i.e. monastic status, a possible meaning of *clericatus*.

83 At Monte Cassino. This was once in the territory of Casinum, but the fact that no bishop is known for this city after the 5th century suggests that the city had lost its status, with all or part of its territory assigned to Aquino.

84 His withdrawal to Cassino is attributed by Noble, 67, to his wish to avoid visitors. Before – or perhaps despite his vow after – this, Carloman spent some time at St Silvester's monastery on Mt Soracte (*Ann. Lauriss.* 746), which Zacharias had given him (*CC* 23, cf. *CC* 42).

85 Islamic.

86 In 749.

87 Perugia was on the military road from Rome to Ravenna, and is shown by this passage to be reckoned in the Pentapolis, along with, presumably, Todi, with the duchy of Rome beginning only at Amelia. This technically imperial territory separated the Lombard kingdom from the duchies of Spoleto and Benevento. Ratchis' breach of the Peace of Terni was more likely the result of Lombard nationalists provoking him into action than of any earlier unrecorded breach by the pope (Noble, 56, with n. 204). It is clear from 96:28 and 97:24 that within 20 years Perugia was absorbed into the duchy of Rome; I suspect this was a result of Ratchis' abortive campaign in 749.

his retirement from the blockade of the city. He preached to him what was to his advantage and, with God as the cause of it, he managed to turn his soul towards the efforts of the spirit: some days later king Ratchis abandoned his kingly dignity[88] and devoutly came with his wife and children[89] to the home of St Peter prince of the apostles; by submitting to the prayer recited by the holy pope he was made a cleric and was clothed in the monastic habit with his wife and children.

24. In his time our Lord God saw fit in this city of Rome to disclose a great treasure through this bountiful pontiff. In the venerable patriarchate the holy pope discovered St George the martyr's sacred head, kept safe in a casket; in this he also found a note made out in Greek letters, indicating its identity. The holy pope, altogether satisfied, immediately convened this city of Rome's people, and caused it to be taken with hymns and spiritual chants to the venerable deaconry which is dedicated to him in this city, in the 2nd region at the Velabrum;[90] and there almighty God sees fit to work infinite miracles and benefits to the praise of his own name through this sacred martyr.

25. In his time the late Theodore, elder son of Megistus Cataxanthus, to gain the pardon of his sins, bequeathed to St Peter the estate he enjoyed from his father's legacy; it is at the 5th mile from this city of Rome on the Via Tiburtina,[91] and an oratory of St Caecilia is reckoned to be in it. The blessed pope adorned it with the large buildings he constructed and with paintings. He enlarged its territory on every side; by paying fair compensation to those who held properties in the neighbourhood[92] of this place, with no compulsion but rather as befits a father, he bought in an amicable contract all the estates alongside the place, and laid down that the place should remain to St Peter in

---

88 His abdication must have been in June 749 as Aistulf was crowned at Milan on 3 or 4 July. For the date and for explanations of the abdication see Noble, 57, with notes 206–208 (deposed by nationalists annoyed at his abandonment of the siege of Perugia; or a genuine crisis of conscience). On Aistulf's activities during Zacharias' pontificate, see the introduction to this life; they boded ill for Rome.

89 The margin of the *Monte Cassino Chronicle* c. 25 (*MGH SSrL*, 487) gives Ratchis a wife Tasia and a daughter Rottruda; he went to Monte Cassino, she (it is unclear whether wife or daughter is meant) to the monastery of Blombarolia.

90 The earliest certain reference to this church, since the date (no earlier than the 10th century, Duchesne) and authority of the addition in Leo II's life (BP 82:5) about a church of SS Sebastian and George in the Velabro are uncertain.

91 The distance suggests a location near Ponte Mammolo. A bull of Gregory VII (*PL* 148, 724) mentions a *curtis S. Caeciliae*, probably on the left when coming from Rome, shortly beyond the bridge; evidently the old domusculta.

92 Not necessarily contiguous with it (Wickham, 1978, 176, against those who argue domuscultae were large blocs of land).

perpetual ownership as a domusculta[93]; even to the present day it is called St Caecilia's domusculta. He also constructed in it an oratory of St Abbacyrus in which he also deposited many saints' relics. He marked off this domusculta for his own use, to wit that of the *ratio dominica*.[94] **26.** He established another domusculta at the 14th mile from this city of Rome, in the patrimony of Tuscia;[95] and by his decrees he entailed it to remain to the church's use, also the places granted to St Peter by Anna, the relict of the former *primicerius* Agatho.[96] By his efforts he acquired for St Peter's ownership the estates called Anzio and Formia;[97] these also he established as domuscultae. Concerning all the above domuscultae he had annexed, he composed and published apostolic decrees and gathering a sacerdotal council he laid it down under interdicts of anathema that in no way whatever should it be allowed to any of his successor pontiffs or any other person whatever, to alienate these domuscultae from the church's use in any way at all.[98]

He provided cloths on St Andrew the apostle's altar at St Peter's, most excellent.[99]

27. This blessed pope laid down that on frequent days the victuals and provisions which are even now called *eleemosyna*[100] should be taken from

93 Wickham, 1978, 175, stresses the contrast between Zacharias' policy of running papal lands himself rather than, as he and Gregory II had been doing, of granting large-scale leases to the Roman aristocracy; hence the eventual development on domuscultae of their own militia (cf. 97: n. 94) in opposition to the lay aristocracy.

94 The private account of the papal household; note how the language reflects that of the imperial administration (*ratio privata*). Noble, 225, cites this as the first hint of papal budgeting (not found elsewhere in the west before the 13th century), the revenues now being predictable; this goes further than the evidence warrants.

95 Probably on the Via Clodia: at about the 14th mile are a place called Casal di Galera and the ruins of the later Castrum Galeriae. The location seems to be the same as, or to overlap with, that of one of the domuscultae called Galeria founded (refounded?) by Hadrian I; see 97:55 and nn. 99–101.

96 Agatho was evidently a predecessor of Ambrose who held the post by 742/3 (c. 12, n. 43); is he the Agatho mentioned, with no title, in the life of pope Constantine (BP 90:10)? If the land mentioned is to be in the Tuscan domusculta, the number of domuscultae founded by Zacharias in cc. 25–26 is four, not five.

97 Anzio and Fórmia, once cities but by this date merely centres for farming. A document of 944 from Gaeta (*Tabul. Casinense* I, p. 75 line 12) mentions a *locus qui dicitur domus culta*, which makes the identification with Fórmia near Gaeta certain.

98 Compare the strong language at 97:55. The emphasis here may be to show that alienation by 'emphyteusis' (perpetual lease) is excluded.

99 *optimam*; some MSS mend the text by making it plural or the cloths singular.

100 ἐλεημοσύνη, the Greek for 'mercy' or 'pity', from which derives English 'alms', perhaps with some influence from Latin *alimonium*, 'nourishment'.

the venerable patriarchate by the cellarers and dispensed to the poor and the pilgrims who doss at St Peter's; and he decreed that this *eleemosyna* of provisions should likewise be distributed to all the destitute and the sick living in all this city of Rome's regions.

In his time it suddenly occurred that the roof of Christ's martyr St Eusebius' *titulus*[101] fell down. This holy man strove with all his might, and by his prudent exertion he repaired what had fallen and excellently restored it as it was of old. **28.** This distinguished pontiff improved the condition of many of the saints' locations, and provided excellent altarcloths for the same churches of God.

He greatly loved his clergy and gave them their annual *presbyteria*[102] in double measure and more; he welcomed them all like a father and a good shepherd, encouraged them in practical ways, and absolutely never allowed anyone to cause them trouble. In fact, in his time the people God had committed to him lived their lives in safety and joy. **29.** This blessed pope by his own prudent effort translated the four books of Dialogues produced by pope Gregory of blessed memory from Latin into Greek,[103] and enlightened many who do not know how to read Latin by the narrative they can read in them. *He performed three March ordinations, 30 priests, 5 deacons; for various places 85 bishops. He was buried at St Peter's on 15 March in the 5th indiction. The bishopric was vacant 12 days.*

---

101 One of Rome's oldest churches. The first certain mention of S. Eusebio dates from 474 (inscription on the tomb of a priest of the *titulus*), after which it was represented at the Roman Council of 499; its dedication is given on 14 August in the *Martyrologium Hieronymianum*. The earliest surviving remains do not antedate the 12th/13th century, but to the south of the transept and behind the apse are the remains of a Roman apartment house, successively modified in earlier centuries for Christian use; Zacharias' reroofing will have been of this building (Krautheimer, *Corpus* 1, 210 ff, 215–16; cf. *LNCP* 103:17 with n. 38).

102 Salaries paid by a bishop (here, and often, the pope) to the priests.

103 Cf. BP 66:1. The translation may have been initially intended for the Greek monasteries in Rome and Italy, but it had great success in the east (Photius, *Biblioth.* cod. 252). Zacharias, last of the Greek popes, was presumably fluent in the language.

94. STEPHEN II (752–757)

Seriously threatened by Aistulf king of the Lombards, Rome's links with the Byzantine empire, whose willingness and competence to offer it protection it could not trust, grew weaker. The papacy sought and received help from the Franks under Pepin; to achieve this, Stephen II became the first pope to cross the Alps. Pepin's idea of restoring to the Romans the Italian territories the Lombards had taken was to give them to St Peter, not the emperor; nor should we imagine that Stephen was unaware of this in advance.

Constantinople was certainly aware what would happen. Yet, in spite of a last-ditch effort by imperial envoys (cc. 43–45) to prevent Pepin helping Rome against the Lombards, by the end of this life the author in using the term *respublica* ('the State') is no longer thinking of Constantinople. The Greek Emperor would continue to be recognized as somehow suzerain. But it was the popes who were now 'the sovereign disposers of Italy' (Duchesne, 1908, 47): when king Aistulf died accidentally, Stephen was able to secure the Lombard throne for the candidate he himself favoured. The papacy's independence from Byzantines and Lombards was secured under the protection of a Frankish dynasty which in less than fifty years would itself be reckoned as imperial. 'The historic significance of Stephen II is that he found a way to break through all the dangers and difficulties separating Rome from Francia. ... Pepin's role in Italy was, there is no denying it, critical. Without him the Republic's history would in all probability have ceased in the middle 750s ... Thanks to Pepin that history went on for more than a millenium' (Noble, 94–97).

For this short but crucial pontificate the LP contains the longest biography, Silvester excepted, so far. Much of it is a first-rate piece of contemporary chronicling, by no means lacking human touches and excitement. The author saw no need to fall back on church restorations to fill out his text, though a few were added by a later reviser. Not that the life is perfect. The coverage of the year 755 is startlingly poor (on the traditional chronology, see n. 72); at the end there is nothing on Stephen's part in getting the dukes of Spoleto and Benevento to desert their king and submit to Pepin and the pope.

Curiously, neither the author nor the reviser mentions that Stephen turned his house into a monastery and dedicated it to St Dionysius, whether that be the third-century pope or – more likely in the political circumstances – St Denis of Paris. Another omitted foundation almost certainly belongs to this pontificate: the dedication inscription (text in Krautheimer, *Corpus* 1, 67, or Duchesne, I, 514 n. 2) of the church of Sant'Angelo in Pescheria (built on to the portico of Octavia) shows that it was dedicated (to St Paul) by Theodotus, formerly duke, now *primicerius* of the apostolic see. The date is given as '1 June of the 8th indiction in the year of the world 6263 and in the time of the lord Pope Stephen junior'. On the Byzantine era, 6263 is A.D. 755; 1 June fell on a Sunday, the normal day for church dedications, and it was the 8th indiction (see Krautheimer, *Corpus* 1, 67 and especially 75 n. 2 ff, Duchesne, III, 105). Is it coincidence that the event omitted fell in the year which (on the traditional chronology) is least adequately treated? Theodotus will have been *primicerius* after Ambrose whose death in 753 is recorded in an interpolation in c. 24. He was the uncle of Hadrian I (cf. 97:2).

Another gap in the life is Stephen's dealings with Ravenna: the most crucial stage was in (need we be surprised?) the year 755, when Stephen visited the city, and survived a plot against him (Noble, 105). Archbishop Sergius was taken to Rome and forced to remain there until pope Paul let him return. Stephen sent a priest and a duke to Ravenna to take over the exarchate on behalf of the papal State.

The writer's style is tedious, particularly in its repetitive use of epithets. Aistulf is never mentioned without being described, at the very least, as wicked; Pepin is always *christianissimus*. Both kings are given their regal titles at every mention; the pontiff and other clerics are always *sanctissimus*; anyone mentioned more than once becomes 'the aforesaid' (John the silentiary, mentioned once before, is 'the oft-mentioned'). Even so, the writer's frequent changes of subject within a sentence create problems, and doubts result on who is the antecedent of possessive and reflexive adjectives and pronouns.

The manuscripts of this life fall into three classes. The various additions, given in italics, are from the MSS BD, which continue with interpolations of the kinds seen in the preceding lives: these additions date from before the end of the 8th century (at the very latest) and are trustworthy. Of the remaining MSS, AC^{12}E^{4}G represent the 'Lombard recension', which tones down the epithets. This is not just a stylistic preference. The adapter removes especially the opprobrious descriptions relating to Aistulf, and the epithets of praise attached to the names of Stephen and Pepin. It can be presumed that he wanted to provide a text that could be read by Lombards without too much discomfort, and it is unlikely that he did this after the fall of the Lombard kingdom in 774 (Duchesne, I, CCXXV–CCXXVI). The original text is that found in C^{34}E^{1256} and Vat. Reg. 1964 (a 10th- or 11th-century MS containing, with other items, LP lives 94 to 97).

94. **1.** STEPHEN [II; 26 March 752–26 April 757], of Roman origin, son of Constantine, held the see 5 years 29 days. Orphaned in early youth by his father's death, he stayed in the venerable Lateran Chamber to learn the teaching passed on from the apostles, in the time of his predecessors the pontiffs of blessed memory. They promoted him[1] through the orders of the church one by one and ordained him to the order of the diaconate. **2.** Now when lord pope Zacharias of blessed memory died, the whole people elected themselves a priest named Stephen[2] to the order of the pontificate and placed him in the Lateran patriarchate, where he lasted two days: on the third day when he had risen from his sleep and was at his seat managing his household affairs, suddenly as he sat there he was deprived of his senses and struck dumb.[3] Next day he died. **3.** After that, God's whole people gathered within the venerable basilica of God's holy mother *ad praesepe*[4], and there they all prayed for our Lord God's mercy and that of our lady, God's mother the holy and ever-virgin Mary herself, and with a good spirit they harmoniously elected themselves the above-mentioned holy man as pontiff. Sincerely and with proclamations of praise they all brought him to the Saviour's basilica called Constantinian, and from there they followed custom by inducting him into the venerable patriarchate.

This holy pope was a lover of God's churches, who also maintained unshaken the teaching handed on in the church; quick to provide help for Christ's poor, a very resolute preacher of God's word, he visited widows and orphans with good effect, and by God's power he was a strenuous defender of his sheepfold.

4. He soon restored the four *xenodochia*[5] located of old in this city of Rome; from times past and long ago they had stayed deserted and disordered. He arranged everything they required in their various places, inside and out, and conferred many gifts on them; these he confirmed with the text of a privilege under the interdict of an anathema. He is also acknowledged

---

1 Zacharias had promoted Stephen and his brother Paul at the same time (95:1); both were present as deacons at the Roman Council of 745.

2 Three priests named Stephen were at the Council of 745 (cf. 93: n. 49). Nothing else is known about this Stephen's background. As he died before consecration, he was not reckoned as pope in the theory of the time. Only in relatively modern times (once election rather than consecration was regarded as crucial) would he be styled Stephen II: which throws out the numbering of all his homonymous successors.

3 A stroke, presumably. His death was on 25 or 26 March 752.

4 No rule tied the election to the Lateran, but other localities were now unusual.

5 Hostels for strangers. On these foundations see 98:81 with n. 169.

94. STEPHEN II

as founder of the new *xenodochium in Platana*,⁶ for a hundred of Christ's poor; he made arrangements there, decreeing the provision of their food every day. Outside the walls of this city of Rome, alongside St Peter's, he built two *xenodochia*, on which he conferred many gifts; he merged them permanently with the venerable deaconries already existing outside there – God's holy mother's deaconry and that of St Silvester⁷ – and strengthened the permanence of this by apostolic privileges. *In his time Hunald⁸ duke of Aquitania came to the home of the apostles and undertook to remain there. Afterwards with devilish cunning and cheating, and in breach of his deceitful vow, he went out⁹ to join the Lombards and urged them on in their wickedness. He got his just deserts and died by stoning.*

5. Meanwhile there took place in Rome and its subordinate cities a great persecution by Aistulf¹⁰ king of the Lombards: the king's mighty savagery was pressing, so in the third month¹¹ from his ordination to the apostleship

---

6 This is never mentioned again as such. By Leo III's time it seems to have been absorbed into St Eustace's deaconry, called in medieval documents *in Platana*; it is mentioned in the late 8th-century Itinerarium of Einsiedeln, under Leo III (98:38, 75) as a deaconry, and under Gregory IV (103:12) as a basilica (Krautheimer, *Corpus* 1, 217). A deaconry there already existed when Gregory II granted it perpetual leases on a long list of farms (J 2220). The building is described in 12th century documents as close to Agrippa's temple, and is evidently represented by the present S. Eustachio; Hülsen, 251. The name may derive from plane-trees in the gardens of Agrippa's baths.

7 But 97:66 (nn. 133–4) claims these two deaconries were only founded by Hadrian I.

8 This must be Hunald I, son of Eudes (on whom see 91:8), who in 745 was replaced by his son or brother Waifre (and not Hunald II, whose rule was ended by Charlemagne in 769). Hunald I's end is otherwise given only in the rather unreliable Metz Annals (*MGH SS* I, 328) which claim he retired to a monastery in the île de Ré. Perhaps, then, he came to Rome 7 years or more later. He was Pepin's implacable enemy, and Pepin's espousal of the pope's cause in Italy must have reawakened his hatred. The identification of Hunald, and the implications for the date and reliability of the interpolations in MSS BD, are discussed by Duchesne, I, CCXXVII–CCXXIX.

9 *exediens*, taken by Duchesne as a corruption of *exiens*; if this was during Aistulf's siege in 756, Hunald had merely to 'go out' of his monastery to be among Lombards.

10 Aistulf succeeded Ratchis in 749 and pursued a policy of taking over imperial territory in Italy. He got Ravenna and the remains of the exarchate before July 751, and also the duchy of the Pentapolis; he attacked Istria and made some kind of deal with Venice (since Gregory III had once used Venice to dislodge the Lombards from Ravenna) – events all ignored by LP under Zacharias and only vaguely alluded to in this life. There is no record of Zacharias diverting Aistulf from Ravenna as he had done Liutprand and Ratchis. The exarchate was too weak to defend itself, let alone Rome; even access to it from Roman territory was risky; and Zacharias would have had to take account of the opinions of the Roman army. Now Aistulf was in a strong position on the Adriatic coast to put pressure on the duchy of Rome even when he was at peace with it. Cf. *Pauli continuatio cassinense* c. 4 (*MGH SSrL*, 199).

11 June 752. Stephen was too weak to do other than negotiate with Aistulf. The envoys are

the holy pope immediately arranged for his own brother the holy deacon Paul, and the *primicerius* Ambrose, to take many gifts and go to the king of the Lombards, to negotiate peace and sign treaties. These individuals went to Aistulf and imparted the gifts to smooth the way for procuring this from him; they negotiated and signed a treaty with him, binding for a period of 40 years.

6. However this shameless Lombard king was contaminated by the Ancient Enemy's cunning and incurred the guilt of perjury by tearing the treaties to pieces after barely four months.[12] Many were the insults he piled on the holy pontiff and the whole Roman people, various were the threats he sent him. His intention[13] being, despite God's opposition, to take over the whole of this province, he attempted to fasten a heavy tribute on this city of Rome's inhabitants: he was eager to extract on every head every year a gold solidus each, and he indignantly claimed to subject this city of Rome and its subordinate walled towns to his own jurisdiction. **7.** The holy pope saw that the king's pernicious savagery was pressing, and he sent[14] particularly for the religious abbots of the venerable monasteries of St Vincent[15] and St Benedict,[16] and sent them in his own stead to that cruel king, and through them emphatically requested to obtain the confirmation of the peace treaties

---

both church, not civil, officials. Noble, 73, thinks the peace was not generous to Rome if Aistulf could demand tribute; but the point is surely that the demand of tribute was part of Aistulf's breach of this peace.

12 Bertolini, 1946, thinks Aistulf was buying time with a treaty he never intended to keep. Hallenbeck, 1982, 52–61, thinks Stephen broke the treaty first by appealing to the Byzantines: but cf. n. 17. Noble, 72–3, holds the view of Delogu, 1980, 170–72: Aistulf's plans, like those of Liutprand and Ratchis, were wrecked because he wrongly thought he could take Ravenna and have peace with Rome. Stephen disagreed.

13 If the tax could be imposed it would betoken submission; Aistulf would have imposed a sort of protectorate over Rome as a first step towards unifying all Italy apart from the Byzantine south under his own rule. Hallenbeck (last note) however thinks Aistulf was no real threat to Rome. Noble, 73, stresses the king's dilemma: an independent pope threatened his rule, particularly over the duchies and Ravenna; his minimum need was for a corridor to the south and for this he must hold some part of the exarchate and Pentapolis; yet, as a devout christian, he did not want war with the pope. But might there not be some basis to the LP's doubts on Aistulf's devotion?

14 About October 752; the embassy is also in *Pauli continuatio cassinense* c. 4 (*MGH SSrL*, 199); diplomacy is still the pope's only weapon.

15 Near the source of the Volturno, S. Vincenzo was founded early in the 8th century by three brothers, Paldo, Taso and Tato, Lombard nobles of Benevento (Autpert, *MGH SSrL*, 546, and Paul, *HL* 6.40); the abbot at this time was Azzo.

16 Monte Cassino; the abbot at this time was Optatus. Both abbeys were subject to Benevento and so indirectly to Aistulf.

94. STEPHEN II

and a rest for the two sections of God's people. He received them, it is true, but held them in total contempt, despised their warnings, and imperilling his own soul he dispatched them back in confusion to their own monasteries without achieving a thing, telling them not to deviate for a visit to the holy pope. When our excellent father heard this, just as he had often done before he forthwith made over and committed his own cause and that of the people entrusted to him to the almighty Lord our God, and recommended his cheerless wail of woe to God's greatness.

8. Meanwhile[17] the imperial silentiary John reached Rome bringing the holy pontiff a mandate,[18] and he brought another mandate addressed to that impious king with words of urging annexed, that he should restore to their proper dominion the places of the State that he had usurped in his devilish plot. The holy pope straightaway sent this imperial envoy, along with his brother the holy deacon Paul, to the criminal Aistulf at Ravenna. He received them and sent them away with a vacuous reply, attaching to the imperial envoy a certain individual from his own people, a wicked man imbued with devilish plots, to make their way to the imperial city. **9.** They returned to Rome, were presented to the holy pope and told him of their lack of success. Then the holy man, realizing the evil king's plan, sent his envoys with apostolic addresses to the imperial city along with the imperial envoy, asking His Imperial Clemency, as he had often written him was needed[19] in these districts of Italy, to come with all his means and deliver this city of Rome and the whole province of Italy from the teeth of the Son of Iniquity.

---

17 Noble, 72–3, talks of Stephen appealing to Constantinople several times in the early months and summer of 752, as it had not yet occurred to him to ask for Frankish help – proving that no pact had been entered into between Zacharias and Pepin in 751; and that in appealing Stephen was acting as an ally, not as a subject. But the LP does not bring Constantinople into the picture at all before this chapter.

18 Presumably this commanded the pope to try further negotiations with Aistulf and send his own envoys along with John and the imperial letter to Aistulf. As Constantinople saw it, Ravenna was still rightfully Byzantine territory – and, *pace* Noble, Constantine V (741–775) was treating Stephen as a subject. The result was Stephen's third embassy to Aistulf in one year.

19 *exercitandis*; Duchesne regards the passage as unintelligible and corrupt; but the sense seems clear. The letter (J 2308) also told the emperor to restore the images. Noble, 74, thinks that Stephen wanted Constantine V to free Rome from the Lombards on the pope's behalf, whereas the emperor had just been trying to enlist Stephen's aid to free Ravenna on the empire's behalf: 'If the emperor came to Italy, defeated Aistulf, and reestablished imperial control in Ravenna, the pope had little to lose and probably much to gain from the destruction of Aistulf. If, on the other hand, the emperor did nothing, Stephen's position was no worse, and his claims in Ravenna became potentially more effective'. The result of the papal appeal to the east becomes clear in cc. 15–17; meanwhile the LP gives no details on developments.

10. Meanwhile the atrocious king of the Lombards, no less pernicious than before, boiled over with mighty rage and, roaring[20] like a lion, kept sending pestilential threats to the Romans, claiming they would all be killed by a single sword unless they complied with his above demand and surrendered to his control. Again the holy father, gathering the whole Roman assembly, admonished them with fatherly love in such words as these: 'I pray you dearly beloved children, let us implore the Lord's clemency on our heap of sins and he will be our helper and in his most provident mercy he will deliver us from the hands of them that persecute us.' The whole people obeyed his advantageous advice and gathering singlemindedly they all shed tears and besought the almighty Lord our God. **11.** On a certain day with great humility he held a procession and litany in the usual way[21] with the holy image of our Lord God and Saviour Jesus Christ called the *acheiropoieta*,[22] and along with it he brought forth various other sacred religious objects[23]. With the rest of the *sacerdotes* the holy pope bore that holy image on his own shoulder, and both he and the entire people processed barefoot into God's holy mother's church called *ad praesepe*. Ash was placed on the heads of all the people, and they made their way with great wailing and besought the most merciful Lord our God. They attached and fixed to our Lord God's adorable cross the actual treaty which the unspeakable king of the Lombards had torn to pieces.

12. The blessed pope carefully convened all his *sacerdotes* and clergy in the Lateran patriarchate and warned them to walk in the paths of divine Scripture with all their might and devote themselves to spiritual reading, so as to prove capable in dealing with every response and every claim made by the opponents of God's church. Nor for one moment did he stop warning and comforting God's whole people to live sober and godly lives[24] and guard themselves from all iniquity. *As he was persuading all the abovenamed sacerdotes on heavenly matters, he brought them closer by granting them earthly preferments; so that they might all be found well-attired in God's*

---

20 *fremens*, but in view of c. 22 this may be for *frendens*, 'gnashing his teeth'.

21 Commenting on the occasions when the image next mentioned was used, Duchesne, II, 135 n.10 (on 105:19), suggested that 'a certain day ... in the usual way' here refers to 2 February or 25 March 753 (for the institution of the processions on the Marian feasts see BP Sergius I 86:14); however, at any rate in later use the carrying of the image was restricted to 15 August, a date which suits the present occasion neither in 752 nor in 753.

22 Literally 'not made by hands', from its supposed miraculous origin. This is the earliest certain mention of this famous icon; if it was not brought to Rome under the iconoclast emperors, it might just be the same as the *imago S. Mariae quae per se facta est* venerated at S. Maria in Trastevere, probably from the 7th century.

23 *sacra mysteria*: images, or perhaps relics.

24 Titus 2.12.

church, *he gave them the tunics, chasubles or whatever, for each order. To others he gave the amount for which they were indebted so they could be delivered from moneylenders; thus might the whole of God's church reach the highest honour.*

13. For the province's safety and that of all Christians this blessed man laid it down that all earlier negligence should be set aside and every Saturday a litany should take place: one Saturday, to God's holy mother *ad praesepe*, another, to St Peter's, another, to St Paul's. *He provided the grills in front of the altar of St Mary the ever-virgin ad praesepe, and covered it with silver, weighing 40 lb.*

14. This blessed pope restored St Laurence's basilica,[25] above St Clement's in the 3rd region; for a long time past it had stayed damaged. He restored the roofing of St Soteris' cemetery,[26] which had fallen down. *He provided an altarcloth at God's holy mother's ad martyres; he himself proceeded there with a litany, and with his own hands covered the altar with it.*

15. So, untold times and with uncountable gifts the holy man besought the pestilential king of the Lombards for the flocks God had entrusted to him and for the lost sheep – for the entire exarchate of Ravenna and for the people of the whole of this province of Italy, whom that impious king had deceived with devilish trickery and was now occupying. He was getting nowhere with him; and in particular he saw that no help would come his way from the imperial power. Now his predecessors the blessed pontiffs Gregory, Gregory and Zacharias[27] of blessed memory had sent to Charles king[28] of the Franks of excellent memory to ask for help against

25 Unmentioned elsewhere. Duchesne's identification of it with the equally unknown St Laurence ad Taurellum (97:50) was pure guesswork, and his location of it between S. Clemente and S. Pietro in vincoli (which would put it in the 3rd ecclesiastical region) was based on a false reading (Tauro for Lauro) in a 14th century catalogue of Roman churches; Hülsen, 283, 297, VZ, 3, 255 etc. However, St Laurence does appear in a surviving mosaic at S. Clemente; did the artist know of a cult of St Laurence nearby?

26 There are some surviving traces of a small basilica at this cemetery on the Via Appia, Marucchi-Josi, *Le Catacombe Romane*, 183ff.

27 This is true only of Gregory III (in 739). Gregory II's contacts were only with Eudes of Aquitania, hardly relevant; and the Continuator of Fredegar says that Gregory III's contacts were the first of the kind. Zacharias cannot have written to Charles, who died before he was pope, nor is there any other evidence that Zacharias sought Frankish intervention, unless his granting of the kingship to Pepin was part of an unknown deal (denied by Noble, 70–71; though it would mean that a friendly response to an appeal could be expected). Indirectly, Gregory II and Zacharias had probably hoped for friendship with the Frankish princes of Austrasia, with Boniface as their intermediary. Yet despite all the diplomatic activity in 752 it was only in 753 that the pope turned to the Franks.

28 Improper use of 'king', as already at 93:21 (with n. 80).

the oppressions and invasions they too had endured in this province of the Romans at the hands of the unspeakable race of the Lombards. In exactly the same way this venerable father too, God's grace inspiring him, now sent his letter[29] secretly through a pilgrim to Pepin king of the Franks, a letter written in the agony that held this province fast. He sent word incessantly to the king of the Franks: the king must dispatch his envoys here to Rome; he must have them summon him to come to him.[30] **16.** When the king of the Lombards was strongly oppressing the cities and this province of the Romans, there suddenly arrived an envoy from the king of the Franks, an abbot named Droctegang;[31] the reply the king sent through him was that he would fulfil the holy pope's every wish and request. Afterwards another envoy, a dependant of his, arrived with just the same message.[32]

17. While, as related above, the Lombards were punishing the ancient city of Rome and all the walled towns – they even took over the castellum of Céccano,[33] which belonged to the tenants of God's holy church – immediately there arrived from the imperial city John the abovenamed imperial

29 Lost; the pilgrim went incognito as the Lombards had closed the Alpine passes.

30 i.e. Stephen wants Frankish envoys to come to Rome to take him to see Pepin in person, to remind him if need be of the debt Pepin owed to the papacy.

31 The abbot of Jumièges, who arrived about spring 753.

32 Stephen sent Droctegang and a Roman cleric named John (who was to return with Pepin's reply) back to France with two letters (*CC* 4–5); one is a courteous reply to Pepin, saying that Droctegang will tell him more orally; the other letter is, unprecedentedly, addressed to all the dukes of the Franks. In this, Stephen says he expects the Franks to fight for St Peter their protector and for the needs of the church: this will bring them eternal salvation. The letters are discussed by Noble, 75–78; he points to the turmoil in France, and notes that Pepin could only help Stephen by an invasion of Italy, which would be opposed by many Frankish nobles (Einhard, *Vita Karoli* c. 6, refers, without details, to Pepin's opponents; his proximity to the royal family makes him creditworthy). They may have supported Carloman's heirs (cf. n. 68) and have resisted abandoning the policy of friendship with the Lombards, which was what helping Stephen would entail. Perhaps Pepin thought he could consolidate his hold on the kingship by becoming the pope's protector and by gaining hegemony over the Lombards; and if the Lombards overwhelmed the papacy, what would become of Pepin's right to the kingship? The reformed Frankish church would take the papal side: Pepin would have to stay on the right side of it. His problem was how to overcome opposition in France. Did Droctegang bring Stephen an oral message about this opposition? Did Pepin suggest, or Stephen and Droctegang realize, that Stephen should invoke St Peter, his most powerful weapon, in a letter to the Franks? Stephen was 'spelling out a doctrine that war against the enemies of the church was not only justified but a positive obligation for Christians' (Noble, 77).

33 Despite all the talk of persecution, threats and broken treaties, this is the first hostile act of Aistulf actually mentioned. Ciccanum, 9 km S of Frosinone, is the ancient Fabrateria Vetus, still a *municipium* in the 5th century (*CIL* X, 5651), but by this time merely a centre for farming, like Anzio and Formia, 93:26 with n. 97.

silentiary with this holy pope's envoys; he also brought with him the wicked Lombard king's envoy, whom they had fetched home, and also an imperial mandate[34] whose contents were that the holy pope should make his way to the king of the Lombards, to get back Ravenna and the other cities pertaining to it. For this purpose he at once sent his envoy to that blasphemous king to get a safe conduct for himself and those who were to travel with him.

18. Immediately after his [John's] return there also arrived the envoys of Pepin king of the Franks – bishop Chrodegang[35] and duke Autchar[36] – to bring the holy pope, just as he had sent and requested, back to their king in France: they encountered him just ready to make his way to the king of the Lombards for the gathering up again of all the Lord's lost sheep.

19. Then consulting[37] the mercy of our almighty God, the blessed pope left this city of Rome for St Peter's on the 14th day of October in the 7th indiction [753]; following him were many Romans and people from other cities, weeping and wailing – there was no way they would let him travel. So the holy man placed himself in God's power and under the protection of God's holy mother and the blessed princes of the apostles, and then in spite of being enfeebled by physical illness he resolutely set out on the gruelling journey to achieve everyone's safety, comforting the whole of the Lord's people and commending them to the good shepherd our lord St Peter, prince of the apostles. From this holy church he took with him some of the *sacerdotes* and dignitaries and other ordained clerics, also the chiefs of the militia. As he started on his journey Christ went ahead of him; and while the journey lasted the Lord granted him very calm weather.

20. So when he reached about the 40th mile[38] and the Lombards' borders, one night a great portent appeared in heaven,[39] like a ball of fire setting towards the south – from the districts of Gaul to those of the Lombards. So one of the envoys of the Franks, the duke Autchar, raced on ahead to

---

34 'This must rank as one of history's emptier commands', Noble, 78, who also comments, n. 70, that the territory next mentioned does not include the duchy of Rome – the emperor had long given up any meaningful claim to it. He remarks that, if meaningless, the command was still useful: Stephen is willing to try a face-to-face meeting with Aistulf; Zacharias' confrontations with Liutprand and Ratchis had, after all, produced results. Stephen had little to lose: if Aistulf evacuated the exarchate, Stephen would have won with no help from Byzantium or the Franks; if Aistulf was obdurate, Stephen could still play the Frankish card.

35 Of Metz. His visit is also in Paul the Deacon, *Gesta epp. Metensium* (PL 95, 709).

36 Autchar was Pepin's brother-in-law.

37 *consulens*, the word for consulting an oracle.

38 i.e. the northern edge of the duchy of Rome, around Blera and Sutri.

39 Apoc. 12.1.

Ticinum and waited for him there. **21.** When the blessed pope came near the city of Pavia, the criminal king Aistulf sent him his envoys, telling him he had better not say a single word to him in request for the city of Ravenna and the exarchate belonging to it, or about any of the other places of the State[40] that he and his predecessors as kings of the Lombards had taken over. But he sent him a reply, stating that no fear or terror would silence his requesting something of this kind.

When he reached Pavia itself and was presented to the unspeakable king, he gave him many gifts,[41] earnestly begged him and with copious tears requested him to give back the Lord's sheep that he had stolen and restore property to its owners. But there was no way he could get anything from him. As for the imperial envoy, he also made the same request and gave him the emperor's letter, but he too could achieve nothing. **22.** The envoys of the Franks leaned heavily on Aistulf to allow the holy pope to travel on to France. At this, Aistulf summoned the blessed man and asked him if it was his intention to make for France. He did not keep quiet about it but openly told him his intention – and that made him gnash[42] his teeth like a lion. On this account he secretly sent his courtiers to him a number of times in the hope they could somehow steer him away from this purpose. **23.** Next day, when holy bishop Chrodegang was present, the king of the Lombards asked the blessed pope if it was his wish to travel to France. His reply was: 'If it is your intention to let me go, it is certainly mine to travel there.'

Then he gave him leave. He took with him from this holy church of God the *sacerdotes* and clergy,[43] George bishop of Ostia,[44] Wilchar bishop of Mentana,[45] the priests[46] Leo, Philip,[47] George and Stephen,[48] archdeacon

---

40 Here meaning the Empire; Aistulf evidently knew that Stephen had been instructed by Constantine V to make a fresh demand for the return of lost territory.

41 This appears to be diplomatic protocol rather than a bribe (Noble, 79).

42 *fremere* should mean 'roar', but *dentibus* shows it is used for *frendere*; cf. c. 10.

43 The chiefs of the militia who had come with the clergy from Rome do not continue from Pavia to France. Many of the clergy mentioned are known elsewhere; the two bishops went to France several times as envoys of Stephen II and Paul.

44 He later became bishop of Amiens.

45 He perhaps later became bishop of Sens; cf. 96:17 and n. 44.

46 Two Leos, a George and three Stephens were among the priests at the Roman Council of 745; identification is thus difficult.

47 In 761 Philip signed pope Paul's donation to the monastery of SS Stephen and Silvester (J 2346) as priest of St Mark's *titulus*. Stephen's two successors used him as a diplomat and for the government of the exarchate. At least by the start of Hadrian's pontificate he had become a bishop (*CC* 36, 49, 60–61).

48 Perhaps the future Stephen III, cf. c. 50.

94. STEPHEN II

Theophylact,[49] the deacons Pardus and Gemmulus,[50] the *primicerius* Ambrose,[51] the *secundicerius* Boniface, the regionaries[52] Leo and Christopher, and others as well; and on the 15th day of November[53] in the same 7th indiction [753], he moved out of Pavia and set out on his journey for France.
24. Even after he had given him leave, the evil king of the Lombards still attempted to make him deviate from his journey. But this was perfectly clear to the holy man, so at great speed and with God going before him he came to the mountain barriers[54] of the Franks. He entered these with his companions and immediately rendered praise to almighty God. He continued his journey to the venerable monastery of Christ's martyr St Maurice[55] where it had been mutually agreed he should meet up with the king of the Franks; with the Lord's consent the blessed pope and all his companions reached there safely. While he was staying a few days in that venerable monastery – *it was there that the primicerius Ambrose caught fever and died*[56] – there arrived abbot Fulrad[57] and duke Rothard, who had been sent by Pepin the excellent king of the Franks, and they asked the holy pontiff to travel on to their king.[58] They conducted him and his companions to him with great honour.

---

49 He was to be Paul's competitor for the papacy on Stephen's death (95:1–2).

50 Gemmulus is known as a correspondent of Boniface (*S. Bonifatii et Lulli Epp.* 54, 62, 104, *MGH EKA*, I, 308, 327, 390).

51 Cf. 93:14.

52 Duchesne, I, 457 n. 25 referring to 394 n. 15, takes these to be regionary subdeacons; but all other regionaries in these lives are notaries or *defensores*.

53 Stephen had left Rome on 14 October and must have spent well over a week at Pavia. Noble, 79–80, suggests that as there was no time for correspondence between Pavia, Rome, Constantinople or France, the delay was due to Aistulf's obstinacy, and that he let Stephen go only to avoid a diplomatic incident (there were Franks on the embassy), which would have provoked the intervention from Pepin that Aistulf, who is likely to have known of Frankish opposition to Pepin, hoped to avoid.

54 *clusae*: a fortification blocking a mountain road, here the Great St Bernard Pass.

55 The abbot here at Agaune was Wilchar, former bishop of Vienne, cf. 92: n. 57.

56 Six years later his body was taken to St Peter's where it was buried beside pope Paul's oratory (95:6). Two slightly differing copies of the epitaph survive (texts in Duchesne, I, 458 and III, 103); it confirmed the place of death and gave the date as December 753, his age as about 60, and the burial date in St Peter's as September 759.

57 Abbot of St Denis, Paris.

58 Pepin was then at Diedenhofen. *Annales mettenses priores* (ed. Simson, p. 44) hint that Pepin did not know whether to expect Stephen's arrival but was filled with joy when he finally knew he was coming – for all Pepin knew, Stephen might have done a deal with Aistulf, and no pope had ever crossed the Alps; but Pepin would evidently expect to gain something himself if he answered Stephen's request to protect Rome.

25. When[59] the king heard that the blessed pontiff had arrived, he came very quickly to meet him, along with his wife, sons and dignitaries. On this account he sent his son named Charles nearly 100 miles to meet the angelic pope, with some of his chief men. He himself was at his palace at the place called Ponthion,[60] some 3 miles distant; he dismounted his horse and prostrated himself on the ground in great humility, along with his wife, sons and chief men, and welcomed the holy pope; and he made his way alongside his saddle-horse for some distance, like a groom.[61] **26.** Then the bountiful man with all his companions rendered in a loud voice glory and unceasing praise to almighty God, and with hymns and spiritual chants they all set out with the king towards the palace together, on the 6th day of January,[62] on the solemnity of our Lord God and Saviour Jesus Christ's Epiphany. There they sat together inside the oratory, and there it was that the blessed pope then besought the christian king in tears to arrange for peace treaties on behalf of St Peter and the State of the Romans.[63] And at that moment he satisfied the blessed pope with an oath that he would obey his orders and advice with all his strength, and that it would give him pleasure to restore by every means the exarchate of Ravenna and the rights and places of the State.[64]

59 Parallel accounts of all that follows are given in various Frankish sources (see Noble, 81, for references), especially the Continuation of Fredegar and the *Chronicon Moissiacense*.

60 South of Châlons-sur-Marne.

61 In the LP it is Pepin who prostrates himself and does groom-service for Stephen. *Chron. Moiss.*, usually well-informed, has the pope and his clergy in penitential garb prostrate themselves before Pepin one day after their arrival at Ponthion. This corresponds to the pope's beseeching of Pepin a few lines later in the LP, but the presentation in papal and Frankish accounts is typical of their different viewpoints on these events (Noble, 80–81).

62 In 754.

63 So too *Pauli continuatio tertia* c. 34 (*MGH SSrL*, 209–10). The Frankish sources, written later, use variant expressions: Stephen requested help for himself; help for himself and the Roman people; help for the Roman church; defence from the Lombards and the recovery of St Peter's rights; which all, from the Frankish viewpoint, amount to the same thing; and the terms used even in these sources are all of papal origin, and likely to have been learnt, without fine distinctions, by the Franks during these discussions (Noble, 81, citing Bertolini, 1968, at 514–525).

64 The 'State' must be the papal State. Details of how the 'restoration' (it is to include the exarchate!) was to be carried out are left till later, Noble, 81, citing Ewig, 1969, 22. But, whatever the exact nature of his agreement to help the pope, Pepin clearly now agreed to force the Lombards to restore their conquests. On Pepin's oath and all that has been built on it, see Noble, c. 8. A peace treaty seems odd when they had not been at war: but *pax* is a positive concept, an alliance. Either there were two separate agreements (treaty and oath), or (so Noble) a single oath of perpetual alliance; references to *amicitia* are to this alliance. It was aimed immediately against Aistulf, but was open-ended and was in fact renewed until the 820s (cf. 97:39, the oaths exchanged by Charlemagne and Hadrian; and the *Ludowicianum* of 817 which refers back to Pepin's oath to Stephen); it gave the State protection indefinitely (Noble, 276),

27. But as the season of winter was pressing, he asked the holy pope to make his way with all his companions to Paris, to spend the winter at the venerable monastery of St Denis. This he did, and he and the christian Pepin went to that venerable monastery; it was the Lord's will that some days later the holy pope anointed the christian king Pepin, with his two sons, by Christ's grace kings of the Franks.[65] **28.** As a result of the very gruelling journey and the uncertain weather the blessed pope was so gravely ill that his own companions and the Franks who were there gave up hope for him. But the inexpressible clemency of our Lord God, who does not abandon those who hope in him, willed the christian man's recovery; when they were expecting to find him dead by the morning, next day he was suddenly discovered to be well.[66]

29. King Pepin took his leave with the venerable pontiff's advice, favour and prayer, and made his way to the place called Quierzy.[67] There

---

but gave Pepin no rights to intervene within it (so Noble, though see his p. 278 n. 1). Equals pledged to support each other and not to help each other's enemies. As one of the parties was St Peter, Pepin entered into a spiritual tie. He bound his dynasty to defend the papacy; the pope bound himself to pray (seen as a powerful weapon), and more immediately he confirmed Pepin's kingship (next note).

65 Apart from shorter accounts in the various Frankish annals, there survives a description of this ceremony, the *Clausula de unctione Pippini regis*, written by a monk of St Denis about 767, and preserved at the end of a 10th-century MS of Gregory of Tours (Brussels 7666–71; edited by B. Krusch in *MGH SS Merov* 3, 465, after whom Duchesne, I, 458 n. 31; on its authenticity, no longer disputed, see Noble, 87 with n. 108). The date given in the *Clausula* is 28 July (754). If that is right, the ceremony is wrongly placed in the LP; placed later it can be seen as a reward by Stephen for Pepin's efforts and undertakings on behalf of Stephen. Pepin's wife was also anointed; all this sealed the legitimacy of the dynasty. The *Clausula* says that Stephen solemnly forbade the Franks ever to choose a king from another family – that dealt with the claims of the Merovingians, of Carloman and his sons, and of any other ambitious noble, on 'the highest moral authority the world then knew' (Noble, 87). Pepin got papal confirmation of his kingship actually in France; it was no longer founded merely on instructions from Rome some three years earlier (Noble, 88, citing Rodenberg, 1923, 13–14). In exchange Stephen gained at the very least a promise of help against the Lombards, and, if only contingently, a huge slice of Italy. The *Clausula* and *Ann. mett. pr.* say that Pepin was now styled 'patrician of the Romans'. The significance of this title is analysed by Noble, c. 9: it betokened a legal entitlement for Pepin to take on the obligation of defending the State. Pepin never used it, though the papacy addressed him by it; cf. 96: n. 39.

66 On this chapter was based a 9th-century fiction, the *Revelatio facta Stephano papae* (PL 89, 1029).

67 On the Oise, near Laon. *Contin. Fredeg.* c. 37 gives a meeting on 1 March at *Bernaco villa* (Berny). Noble, 83, accepts this as a separate earlier meeting before that at Quierzy, and this is probably right, though Duchesne argued that, since the two places are close and the LP is an eyewitness account closer in time to the event than the Frankish source, the LP's single

he gathered all the dignitaries of his royal power and imbued them with the great father's holy advice; with them he planned the achievement of what he had once by Christ's favour decided on with the blessed pope. **30.** Meanwhile[68] Carloman, brother of kindly king Pepin, who had been living a devout monastic life for some considerable time in St Benedict's monastery, was persuaded with devilish enticements by the most unspeakable Aistulf, who sent him from there to the province of France to obstruct and oppose the business of ransoming the State of God's holy Church of the Romans. When he got there he exerted himself to the full and strove mightily to subvert the affairs of God's holy church just as he had been sent to do by the unmentionable tyrant Aistulf. But God was propitious and Carloman totally failed to divert to his purpose the steadfast heart of his brother the christian Pepin king of the Franks; instead His Excellency Pepin realized the criminal Aistulf's cunning and asserted that he would fight with all his strength for the matter of God's holy church exactly as he had formerly promised the blessed pontiff. Then the holy pope and the king of the Franks consulted and agreed together: as Carloman had vowed himself to God to lead the monastic life they placed him in a monastery there in France, where some days later God called him and he departed this life.

31. The christian Pepin king of the Franks, in true loyalty to St Peter and obedience to the holy pontiff's advantageous advice, sent his envoys[69]

---

gathering, at Quierzy, is to be preferred; though he conceded that since Pepin did spend Easter (14 April 754) at Quierzy, the LP might have conflated this and an earlier meeting. At Berny, then, Pepin consulted with his nobles and agreed to go to Italy if necessary. Then, at Easter at Quierzy, now with the pope present, 'public force was given to Pepin's promise of Ponthion as a result of the agreement won at Berny. The promise of Quierzy was no more binding upon Pepin than his earlier one at Ponthion. This time, however, it had the support of the Franks. Where the promise of Quierzy differed from its predecessor was in spelling out what the Franks would do in Italy in the event they had to go there' (Noble, 83). A written document was produced at Quierzy, now known only from an excerpt in the life of Hadrian I (97:41–2). On its authenticity and the problem created by the fact that Pepin never handed over the territory defined in it, see life 97. Distinguish the donation of Quierzy from the donation of Pepin, for which see c. 46.

68 March or April 754. Carloman had been a monk since 747; Aistulf apparently forced the abbot to let him leave, and then sent him to oppose Stephen's plans and stop his brother Pepin invading Italy. Several motives may have influenced Carloman to agree to this: to support his sons, to support the anti-Pepin nobility, to prevent Pepin adopting an anti-Lombard policy (Noble, 82, gives references). Despite his understanding of Frankish affairs, he failed for unknown reasons, and was kept in a monastery till his death (which happened at Vienne). His failure may partly explain the lack of opposition to Pepin at Quierzy (c. 29).

69 *Contin. Fredeg.* and *Ann. mett. pr.* place Pepin's embassy to Aistulf immediately after the events of c. 27 (in reality the events of cc. 29–31 were more or less simultaneous), and say that Pepin sent envoys to Aistulf urging him out of reverence for SS Peter and Paul to make amends

to Aistulf the criminal king of the Lombards to negotiate for peace treaties and the restoration of the rights of ownership that the State of God's holy church possessed; again a second and third time he besought him, as the blessed pope advised, and promised him many gifts if only he would peacefully restore property to its owners. Yet the pressure of sin made Aistulf put off complying. **32.** At this the distinguished king of the Franks, seeing there was no way he could manage to soften the atrocious Aistulf's stony heart, decreed a general campaign against him. When the squadrons of the Frankish armies had gone about half way, the holy man again besought the kindly king Pepin to send one last time to the savage Aistulf king of the Lombards, in case he could somehow, late as it was, sooth his savagery and persuade him advantageously to return property to its owners without the shedding of human blood. So it occurred: again the kindly king of the Franks sent his envoys to Aistulf.[70] **33.** The blessed pope, true father and good shepherd as he was, also sent him an apostolic letter of warning and request, that the blood of Christians should not be shed; in it he emphatically adjured him by all God's mysteries and the day of judgement to come, telling him to restore the property of God's holy church of the State of the Romans[71] peacefully and without bloodshed. But his own wickedness prevented him and he chose to make no concession – far from it: he sent threats and provocations to the pontiff, His Excellency king Pepin and all the Franks.

Then trusting in almighty God's mercy Pepin king of the Franks set out on his journey,[72] sending ahead to wait for him some of his chiefs, and men from the host with them, to garrison the mountain barriers belonging to the Franks. They went there and remained at a distance, awaiting their king's

---

to the Romans, but Aistulf summarily refused. The LP has four attempts by Pepin to negotiate with Aistulf, of which the fourth (c. 32) was while Pepin was already on campaign. *Contin. Fredeg.* puts the first *before* the assembly at Berny; Duchesne thought this could be right.

70 *Ann. mett. pr.* has Pepin offer to pay Aistulf 12000 solidi if he would do justice to St Peter. This will be the gift referred to in the interpolated c. 34.

71 'God's holy church of the State of the Romans' is here used in the LP (written soon after Stephen's death) of the time while Stephen was in France; it occurs also in one of Stephen's letters, *CC* 6. 'The ecclesiastical state was, as its title implied, the Roman empire' (Miller, 1974, at 123–4). With a different nuance Noble, 95–7, sees in this 'fascinating and enigmatic title' which Stephen gave to his State a way 'to identify the Holy Church, which was not iconoclastic and heretical, with the Republic of the Romans, that is, with the *real* Romans, the Catholic ones, and not with the heretical and vain Greeks who lived not on the Tiber but on the Bosporus and who called themselves 'Romans' in Greek: *romaioi*'.

72 He went by way of Lyons, Vienne and St Jean de Maurienne. On the traditional chronology the campaign was in 754 (the battle being about August); but many now place the campaign in 755, following Hodgkin, 1899, 229–234: see Noble, 88 n. 113.

arrival. **34.** *So these kindly men, the king and the pope, reached Maurienne, and there in the church of St John, our Lord Jesus Christ's forerunner and baptist, he celebrated mass devoutly. As he had done long before, both he and all his chief men honoured the pope magnificently with many gifts, adding yet more: the gifts[73] which he had promised through his envoys to give Aistulf he now presented to God; he provided gifts for the holy man's hands to dole out; and commending himself to his prayers he followed after the above-mentioned men from the host.* **35.** So when the shameless king Aistulf heard that those Franks who had arrived to garrison their mountain barriers[74] were few in number, relying on his own ferocity he suddenly threw open the barriers and with huge forces fell on them at daybreak. But the righteous judge, our Lord God and Saviour Jesus Christ, granted victory to those very few Franks: they overcame that Lombard multitude and slaughtered them, so that Aistulf himself, when he took to flight, could only just escape from their hands and take flight without his weapons right into the city of Pavia. With some of his men he shut himself inside it for fear of the Franks, while the Franks themselves came into the mountain barriers and when the slaughter was over they took the Lombards' encampment along with much spoil. **36.** The christian Pepin king of the Franks, came with the blessed pope in his suite, and they both reached the walls of the city of Pavia.[75] The forces of the Franks laid siege to it for some days and manfully forced it to submit.

Then the blessed and angelic pope besought the kindly king Pepin that no further evil should occur and the blood of Christians should not be spilt, and with advantageous preaching he pressed for a peaceful end to matters. **37.** At this the christian Pepin king of the Franks, heard and fulfilled the advice of this blessed father and good shepherd – they entered on a peace beloved of God, and they signed in writing the treaties they agreed between Romans, Franks and Lombards.[76] The king of the Franks took Lombard hostages, and Aistulf pledged himself with all his judges under a terrible and

---

73 Cf. n. 70.

74 These *clusae* were at Vallis Seusana, *Contin. Fredeg.*, c. 37.

75 Aistulf sent envoys to the Frankish nobles to seek peace (*Contin. Fred.*), hoping no doubt to exploit Pepin's difficulties with them (Noble, 89).

76 This is the First Peace of Pavia. The Frankish annals reveal that Aistulf also had to pay an indemnity of 30000 solidi, deliver 40 hostages, and promise never to withdraw from Frankish overlordship; but he kept his life and his kingdom. Stephen and Pepin both had cause to be content with the Peace, see Noble, 89–90, but its serious flaw was its dependence on Aistulf honouring it. In fact, Aistulf failed to do so, relying on Pepin's lack of enthusiasm for campaigning in Italy, and attacked Rome.

mighty oath, and he signed the agreed treaty's written text, that he would immediately return the city of Ravenna with the various cities.[77]

After this they parted from each other, and as usual that perfidious Aistulf king of the Lombards fell into the guilt of perjury, by putting off the restoration he had sworn under oath to carry out. **38.** *The christian and God-beloved king of the Franks sent with him his own envoys, his brother Jerome*[78] *and his other chiefs with many others, to be his escort until he returned to Rome.* **39.** Now when the holy pope reached Rome, *there he encountered in the Campus Neronis sacerdotes with crosses, who were chanting and giving untold thanks to the Lord, and also a large mixed crowd of people, men and women alike, who cried out: 'Here comes our shepherd and, next to God, our salvation!'* some time afterwards, that adversary Aistulf, enemy of his own soul, was filled with a mighty rage: God was against him, not merely because he had failed to fulfil his promise[79] – **40.** *Meanwhile the blessed pope, ever reflecting on the things of God, had the nighttime offices, which*

---

77 The cities are given in *Ann. mett. pr.* as Ravenna, Narni, Ceccano and the Pentapolis. As Duchesne noted, the full list must be that given in c. 47 (without Comacchio), and one would expect all the Lombard conquests in the exarchate and Pentapolis to have been mentioned. The First Peace of Pavia seems to be the 'text of donation' (Noble, 91) that Pepin gave Stephen at this time (often mentioned in the papal letters of 755–6), rather than a separate document as Duchesne supposed; Stephen failed to get Pepin to put it into effect before returning to France. Despite the pope's insistence, Pepin accepted the oaths as made in good faith; when Aistulf broke his word, Stephen reproached Pepin for his confidence (*CC* 6–7).

78 This brother of Pepin is otherwise known only from the *Genealogia Comitum Flandriae* (*MGH SS* 9, 302) where he is said to have been son of Charles Martel by a concubine (the reference to Jerome in Einhard's *Annals* derives from the LP). Stephen's escort back to Rome was led by Fulrad; Pepin returned to France in autumn 754 on the traditional chronology, before mid 755 for Hodgkin and his followers.

79 On the traditional chronology this is a very brief account of the whole of the year 755, and even on the revised chronology it covers the last six months of 755 (the invasion of the Roman duchy and siege of Rome began only at the new year of 756, see n. 82); either way, the first period of hostilities when, despite the pope's insistence, Aistulf (now that the Franks were safely north of the Alps) refused to surrender the exarchate and the Pentapolis, and continued his depredations on Roman territory. Equally brief are the Frankish sources, which merely say that Aistulf returned to the offensive. But from this period come the two letters from Stephen to Pepin, *CC* 6–7, mentioned in n. 77. In the former, carried by Fulrad and the other Frankish envoys, Stephen cites Pepin's donation (Pavia, not Quierzy), and complains of the refusal of 'the perverse, mendacious, diabolical and perjurous Aistulf to hand over a palm's breadth of land to St Peter and God's holy church the State of the Romans'; Peter had anointed Pepin king, Peter holds the keys of heaven: Pepin should fulfil his promises. In the second letter, borne by Wilchar of Mentana, Stephen says much the same, mentioning how Peter had instructed him to undertake the difficult journey to a distant land to seek salvation from Lombard wickedness. Perhaps it was the failure of Pepin to respond that emboldened Aistulf to attack Rome itself.

had become slack[80] *for a long time, carried out in the hours of night, and in the same way he restored the daytime office as it had been of old. To the three monasteries which since ancient times perform this office at St Peter's he added a fourth,*[81] *and there he established monks who might thenceforth join together in the office, and he ordained an abbot over them. There he bestowed many gifts, both everything necessary for the monks in the monastery, and real estate outside; he established even to this day that with the other three monasteries they should chant in St Peter's, prince of the apostles.* **41.** – *but also as he started a general campaign*[82] *with the whole people of his kingdom of the Lombards and came against this city of Rome. For a period of three months he besieged it and surrounded it on every side: every day he fought strenuously against it. Everything outside the city this pestilential Aistulf devastated with fire and sword, and thoroughly wrecked and consumed it, pressing mightily on so that he could capture this city of Rome. He even dug up the sacred cemeteries of the saints and stole many of their bodies, which was greatly to his own soul's detriment.*[83] *As for the Castrum of Narni,*[84]

80 The custom had grown up, not of omitting the night office, but of anticipating it the previous afternoon or evening to ensure an unbroken night's sleep. Despite Stephen II's efforts at reform, this became normal medieval (and modern) practice.

81 The monastery of St Stephen Minor was demolished in 1776 to make way for the new sacristy of St Peter's. In the 10th century it was called S. Stephanus de Mitcino; from the 11th century it was known as *de Ungaris*, thanks to building works undertaken by Stephen I king of Hungary and a bull of 1058 assigning it to Hungarian pilgrims; in the 14th century it was called S. Stephanus de Agulia ('Needle'), from the obelisk then sited close by; Hülsen, 472, Ferrari, 328–30. On the other three monasteries, cf. 92:6 with n. 20 and 97:53 with nn. 91–92.

82 Stephen's letters to France begging for help, written on 24 February 756 during the siege, give extra details. Thus *CC* 9, addressed to Pepin, Charles and Carloman: Rome has been under siege by Aistulf and the armies of Tuscia and Benevento for 55 days since 1 January, churches outside Rome have been pillaged and burnt, monks have been maltreated and some have been killed, nuns have been violated, many Romans have been killed and others taken captive, and Narni has been occupied. *CC* 8, addressed to Pepin alone, says much the same, adding that the Lombards have even penetrated to St Peter's, and that Aistulf has said he will have mercy on the Romans if they hand the pope over; these letters both went with the envoys who returned to France with Pepin's envoy Warnehar (c. 42).

83 Stephen's letters do not mention this particular sacrilege. Duchesne commented that the Lombards' purpose in taking the bodies was probably not sacrilege or an insult to their cult, but, as with similar thefts, profit; and he compared how Einhard took the bodies of SS Marcellinus and Peter (at least Aistulf could have claimed the right of conquest). The Abbey of Nonántola near Modena claimed to possess St Silvester's body, which Aistulf had given it shortly after he founded it; but the date is based on forged documents, *MGH SSrL*, 567 ff; and in Rome at least it was believed that Silvester's body was transferred shortly afterwards (19 July 761) to the monastery of SS Stephen and Silvester (95: n. 9).

84 Cf. Stephen's letter to Pepin in n. 82. It is clear from the LP that Aistulf had restored it

94. STEPHEN II

which he had previously returned to the envoy of the Franks, he stole it from St Peter's ownership.

42. So what Aistulf had impiously done loudly resounded in the ears of the king of the Franks; and the blessed pope arranged for his envoys[85] to be sent on a journey by sea to him in France, along with a certain religious man named Warnehar who had been sent here to Rome by the king of the Franks. Everything that had happened and that the tyrant Aistulf had cruelly done he intimated in a detailed account in his apostolic reports to the christian and God-worshipping king of the Franks, and adjured him emphatically and firmly that as God would be his witness at the day of judgment he must fulfil all he had promised to St Peter. **43.** At this[86] the christian Pepin king of the Franks was roused by the ardour of his faith and again by God's power he started a general campaign, came to the districts of the Lombards and totally overthrew their mountain barriers.

Now when the christian Pepin king of the Franks was approaching these mountain barriers of the Lombards, there came to this city of Rome imperial envoys, George the chief secretary and John the silentiary, who had been sent to the king of the Franks. The blessed pope welcomed them and told them of the king of the Franks' campaign. They thought it too doubtful[87] to believe. He attached to them an envoy of the apostolic see, and gave them leave for France. They travelled by sea and reached Marseilles as quickly as they could; and when they entered it they learnt that the king of the Franks had already entered the Lombards' territory in accordance with the blessed pope's urging and the promise he had made on oath to St Peter. **44.** This realization made the imperial envoys unhappy and in their trouble they tried to afflict the apostolic see's envoy and hold him at Marseilles, to stop him making his way to the king;[88] they caused him much hurt. But St Peter

---

and then retaken it; *pace* Noble, 92, this is not a hypothesis.

85 George bishop of Ostia, and the *magnifici viri* Thomaricus and Comita, who went with Pepin's envoy abbot Warnehar (as here). Despite his clerical status Warnehar had not hesitated to don armour and defend the ramparts. Stephen tells Pepin how tricky it was to get the letters and envoys out of Rome during the siege (*CC* 9). The three letters survive; for the first two see n. 82. The third, *CC* 10, addressed like *CC* 9 to the rulers, clergy, army and entire people of France, is presented as written by St Peter himself, but the contents, corresponding with the LP's summary here, add little to the other two letters.

86 Pepin clearly could not withstand the appeal made in St Peter's own name.

87 George and John, not surprisingly, think Stephen does not want them to see Pepin.

88 Noble, 93, paraphrases this 'The papal *missus* tried to detain the imperial ones'; this is not what the LP says but is perhaps more probable. Stephen's envoy would not want George and John to put the Byzantine claim on Ravenna and the exarchate to Pepin; but George was able to escape from Marseilles into Italy and find Pepin.

prince of the apostles intervened and their cunning was reduced to nothing. So one of them, George the chief secretary, went on ahead of the apostolic see's envoy and quickly caught up with the christian king of the Franks.[89] He found him inside the Lombards' territory not far from the city of Pavia; and he much besought him and promised that many imperial gifts would be granted him, if he would grant and concede the city of Ravenna and that exarchate's other cities and walled towns, to imperial control. **45.** He was totally unable to sway the stalwart heart of the christian and kindly Pepin king of the Franks, who was loyal to God and devoted to St Peter, to grant those cities and places to imperial control. The God-worshipping gentle king stated there was absolutely no way at all that these cities could be alienated from St Peter's power and the ownership of the Roman church and the apostolic see's pontiff. He affirmed on oath that he had given himself to the struggle so often not to gain any man's favour but for the love of St Peter and the forgiveness of his sins. He stated too that there was no amount of treasure that could persuade him to steal what he had once given St Peter. This was the reply he gave that imperial envoy, and straightaway he gave him leave to return home by another way; and he, with nothing achieved, came to Rome. *At this time the holy pope provided in the church of God's mother St Mary an image*[90] *of fine gold, of God's mother seated on a throne, bearing on her knees the figure of the Saviour our Lord Jesus Christ; he adorned it with many precious stones, jacinths, emeralds, prases and pearls, and set it between the two other images of God's mother Mary, the silver ones which were there from of old in front of the altar; and these he had gilded.*

46. Now when the kindly Pepin king of the Franks was keeping the city of Pavia closely besieged, Aistulf the atrocious king of the Lombards, to gain his pardon, claimed he would by all means restore the cities listed in the agreed treaty which he had contemptuously failed to restore previously. The former agreement between the parties, produced in the past 8th indiction [754/5], was again confirmed,[91] and he restored the cities mentioned,

---

89 By 758 George was in Naples (*CC* 15). The other imperial envoy, John, stayed in France; he was still there at the start of 757 (*CC* 11).

90 *imago*: perhaps an ikon, not a three-dimensional image. Note that Constantine V had in 754 held the iconoclastic Council of Hieria (Ostrogorsky, 171–5).

91 The Second Peace of Pavia, June 756, confirming the First Peace of 754. *Contin. Fredeg.* and *Ann. mett. pr.* say that Pepin granted the wish of his nobles that Aistulf live and be king, but made him hand over hostages, give up a third of his treasury, pay an annual tribute, and swear to make restitution.

and added also the Castrum called Comácchio.[92] Concerning all the cities received, he [Pepin] issued a donation in writing[93] for their possession by St Peter, the holy Roman church and all the apostolic see's pontiffs for ever; it is kept safe even till now in our holy church's archive.

47. To receive these cities the christian king of the Franks sent his counsellor, Fulrad the venerable abbot and priest.[94] The distinguished king took his leave and straightaway went successfully[95] home to France with his armies. Fulrad the venerable abbot and priest went to the districts of Ravenna with the envoys of king Aistulf; they entered each city in turn, those both of the Pentapolis and of Emilia, and received them and at each one took away hostages; and taking the dignitaries with him along with the keys to the cities' gates, he came to Rome. As for the keys, both of the city of Ravenna and of the various cities of the exarchate of Ravenna, along with the donation concerning them that their king had issued, he placed them in St Peter's confessio; and he handed them over to this apostle of God and to his vicar the holy pope and to all his successor pontiffs for ever, for their possession and management – that is to say[96] Ravenna, Rímini, Pésaro, Conca,[97] Fano, Césena, Senigállia, Iesi,

---

92 The earliest literary mention of Comiaclum, 30 km N of Ravenna, south of the main branch of the Po, which was probably the northern boundary of the exarchate. An inscription shows that its first bishop (Vincent) was living as recently as 708.

93 This is the famous 'Donation of Pepin'. By it he gave the cities listed in c. 47, which he forced Aistulf to surrender; Narni and Ceccano had been taken by Aistulf from Rome, but the others had been taken from Byzantine control. The Byzantines had failed (cc. 43–45) to persuade Pepin of the empire's rights; in their view he gave what was not his to give. The context of the iconoclastic council of 754 is relevant: hence the stress in c. 45 on Pepin's true christianity. From this point on, papal letters to the Franks regularly ask that St Peter's rights be secured and the catholic faith be kept inviolate (Noble, 94 n. 141, citing Bertolini, 1968, at 539–41). The result was that Stephen gained various scattered pieces of land. 'If Pepin had deposed Aistulf and taken his kingdom by right of conquest, then the 'Donation of Pepin' would have to have followed the terms of the Quierzy document, but in 756, as in 755, Pepin stopped far short of wreaking maximum devastation on the Lombards' (*id.*, 93).

94 Whereas in 754 the Franks had all departed from Italy, in 756 Pepin left Fulrad behind with a small force to ensure that the terms were carried out.

95 i.e. with his army intact, as he had fought no battle (*Contin. Fred.*).

96 The list of towns will be the same as that in the treaty of 754, cf. n. 77. All the places seem to be east of a north–south line cutting the road from Ravenna to Imola. They are probably the total of Aistulf's own conquests of imperial territory, since it seems it was not Ratchis who took these places from the empire; at the death of his predecessor Liutprand the Lombard eastern frontier corresponded to such a north–south line; while Ancona, Numana and Osimo, all certainly Lombard territory under Liutprand, are not now listed in the territory Aistulf gives to the Roman church.

97 Unknown, but probably on the coast below Rímini, near Cattólica – and the river reaching the Adriatic closeby (16 km below Rimini) is indeed called the Conca.

Forlimpópoli, Forlì with the Castrum Sussubium,[98] Montefeltro,[99] Arcévia,[100] Mons Lucati,[101] Serra,[102] the Castellum of San Marino,[103] Vobio,[104] Urbino, Cagli, Lucioli,[105] Gúbbio and Comácchio, also the city of Narni[106] which the duchy of Spoleto had taken over many years previously from the side of the Romans. *At that time the blessed pope built a tower on to St Peter's;[107] he gilded it in part, and in part coated it with silver, and in it he set three bells to call the clergy and people to divine office.*

48. Meanwhile the wretched Aistulf, while out hunting somewhere, was struck by a divine blow and died.[108] Then one Desiderius duke of the Lombards,[109] who had been sent by the criminal Aistulf to the districts of Tuscia, on hearing of Aistulf's death immediately convened and mustered the entire army of Tuscia, and attempted to seize the summit of the kingdom of the Lombards. Aistulf's brother Ratchis,[110] once king and later a monk, held

98 Some walled town or fort in the territory of Forlì, usually identified with the ruins at Castro Faro, 9 km SW of Forlì and in the diocese of Forlì as known in later times.

99 Montefeletrum; strictly Montefeltro is now the name of the mountain range south of the town, which is now called San Leo; it was an episcopal city (the see was later moved 11 km SW to Pennabilli); cf. a lease by Gregory II to a priest Lupicinus of two monasteries of St Leo and St Severinus within the Castrum Montefeltro, J 2193.

100 Probable identification of Acerreagium; 24 km W of Iesi.

101 Unknown, but mentioned as in the territory of Césena in a lease granted by Gregory II of a farm in the Roman church's Ravenna patrimony (J 2192).

102 Duchesne suggested this is Serra dei Conti, 16 km W of Iesi and 10 km NE of Arcévia; but he conceded there are two other places named Serra, one 5 km W of Castel Bolognese, and one near San Marino. And there are others further afield.

103 Capital of the present Republic of San Marino.

104 Or Bobio; identified by Duchesne as Sársina, 25 km W of San Marino.

105 For Lucioli (not far from Cagli) see Gregory I and Boniface V (BP 66:2, 71:2) with Duchesne, I, 318 n. 3; probably identifiable with Cantiano.

106 As the text makes clear, Narni is not connected with the previous list; it had been captured by Faraold, Lombard duke of Spoleto, about 717–8 (cf. 91:13 with n. 39; and 93:8); which is why it alone of the cities in the duchy of Rome is mentioned in Pepin's donation here; it had 'temporarily' been restored by Aistulf (c. 41).

107 This, the earliest known bell-tower of St Peter's, was presumably of wood.

108 Aistulf died without an heir in December 756, 'while he was thinking how to avoid fulfilling his promises' (Einhard's *Annals*). In a letter to Pepin (*CC* 11), written March/April 757, Stephen reveals his joy at Aistulf's death and at later developments, particularly concerning Spoleto and Benevento, cf. n. 113.

109 Desiderius was a wealthy man from Brescia, former constable to Aistulf, and by now a duke in Tuscia; as king he reigned from 3 or 4 March 757 to June 774.

110 Despite the presentation in this chapter, it seems likely that it was Desiderius who revolted against Ratchis after the latter's return to Pavia, rather than vice versa. According to the *Catalogus regum langobardorum brixianus* (*MGH SSrL*, 503), Ratchis, after leaving Monte Cassino, 'governed the palace' at Pavia from December (756) to March (757), after which

94. STEPHEN II

him in contempt, and many other chiefs of the Lombards despised Desiderius with him; they convened and mustered many of the Transalpine[111] and other armies of the Lombards, and set out to challenge him. **49.** At this,[112] Desiderius made every effort to seek himself help from the blessed pontiff, to succeed in taking the royal dignity, promising on oath that he would fulfil the blessed pontiff's every wish; moreover he stated he would return to the State the cities that had remained,[113] and would give plentiful gifts. Then the excellent father and good shepherd adopted a plan with the venerable priest

---

Desiderius was reckoned as king. Ratchis is described as in the first year of his governorship (not kingship) in a diploma from Pisa (see Andreolli, 1966, at 322–5); but most scholars regard him as king again (Noble, 100). Stephen's preference for Desiderius will be for fear that Ratchis would behave as aggressively as he did in 749, rather than as piously as in 744; and he knew that if Desiderius was to have his help, he could drive a tough bargain: hence the promises extracted from Desiderius in c. 49 (*id.*, 100–101). Stephen was helped by the fact that (*CC* 11) on Aistulf's death Liutprand duke of Benevento and Alboin the new duke of Spoleto opted out of the Lombard kingdom and commended themselves through Stephen to Pepin (Noble, 103). Ratchis' supporters may have seen Desiderius as a creature of Aistulf, whose policies might bring Pepin back to Italy (Andreolli, 324–5). But the *Chronicle* of Benedict of St Andrea (ed. Zuchetti, p. 81) says the opposite: the Lombards chose Desiderius to avert a new invasion by Pepin. Stephen's ability to offer troops to Desiderius is a remarkable sign of papal control (and of its acceptance) in and around Rome.

111 Elsewhere in 8th-century writings, 'Alps' can refer to the Apennines.

112 The initiative seems to be that of Desiderius, not of Stephen; though to say that Stephen held aloof till Desiderius' appeal (Noble, 100) goes beyond the evidence. Stephen II (*CC*11) insisted that Pepin recognize that Desiderius had been crowned.

113 i.e. those which Aistulf had not undertaken to restore. Shortly after Desiderius' accession, when the papal envoys returned to Rome, Stephen, leaving nothing to chance, wrote to Pepin (*CC* 11): Pepin should struggle for the liberty and security of the people of the State, and should should see that the remaining cities were ceded. The cities that Desiderius had promised in Fulrad's presence to restore to St Peter are then listed: 'Faenza, Imola and Ferrara with their borders, *saltora* and all their territories, also Osimo, Ancona and Numana with their territories; and afterwards through duke Garrinod and Grimoald he undertook to return to us the city of Bologna with its territories'. Aistulf had (eventually) restored only his own conquests; the pope now wanted Liutprand's conquests as well: only 20 or 30 years earlier, imperial territory had still extended further west from Ravenna (Faenza, Imola, Ferrara, Bologna) and further south-east from the Pentapolis along the coast (Ancona, Osimo, Numana) than was the case at Aistulf's accession. The effect would be that the new Roman State would include all that had been imperial territory in the late 7th century, apart from what was north of the Po (Venice and Istria) or in the still Byzantine areas south of the Liris. As for the duchies of Spoleto and Benevento, Stephen was content with a stronger alliance rather than outright control; in this respect he was returning to the policy of Gregory III (so Duchesne). But Desiderius was not in fact willing to restore all the places Stephen wanted, see c. 51 with n. 118; early in 758 pope Paul wrote to Pepin to complain of this (*CC* 14).

and abbot Fulrad[114], counsellor of the christian Pepin king of the Franks; he sent his brother the deacon Paul and the counsellor Christopher[115] along with Fulrad to Desiderius in the districts of Tuscia. After a discussion with him, Desiderius straightaway stated in a written text and on a terrible oath that he would fulfil the whole of the promise attached above.[116] **50.** After this he [Stephen] immediately sent his envoy the venerable priest Stephen[117] with a letter of apostolic exhortation to Ratchis and the whole people of the Lombards; and the venerable abbot Fulrad made his way with a number of Franks to help Desiderius, and he arranged for many armies of the Romans, should need require, to come to his assistance. The holy pontiff's prayers in his support proved acceptable to God: the Lord almighty disposed that through his coalition with the angelic pope and without imperilling a single soul Desiderius should take the royal dignity that was his ambition. **51.** Meanwhile the holy pontiff sent his envoy and took some of those cities[118] that king Desiderius had promised to return to the blessed pope: Faenza with Castrum Tiberiacum, and Cavello, and the duchy of Ferrara whole and intact.

It was God's will that he extended the State and the whole of the Lord's people, the rational sheep entrusted to him; as a good shepherd laying down his life he delivered them all from the wiles of their foes. He finished the race – **52.** *Meanwhile in the atrium called the quadriporticus, in front of the doors of St Peter's, he renewed 8 marble sculpted columns of wondrous*

114 Fulrad's involvement in Desiderius' accession may have been more prominent than the LP admits (he may already have favoured Spoleto's revolt). The Frankish sources say it was Pepin who made Desiderius king, which is surprising since Pepin took no active role (Noble, 101–2 with n. 17).

115 Christopher played a leading role after Paul's death and under Stephen III; by late in Paul's pontificate he was not merely *consiliarius* but *primicerius*, though there is no reason to suppose he yet held the latter post as Noble (100–101) assumes. One of Paul's letters to Pepin (*CC* 36, written 764–766) eulogizes him particularly for the loyalty he had shown Stephen II and Paul himself. It is widely thought that Christopher was the key instigator of the papacy's maximum territorial ambitions.

116 *CC* 11 reminds Pepin to fulfil the 'pacts confirmed by your goodness' – apparently Stephen regarded Fulrad as plenipotentiary for Pepin, who is thus seen as full partner in the agreement. Pepin was now as much the guarantor of the new political situation in Italy as he was of the pope's earlier acquisitions (Noble, 102).

117 Probably the later Stephen III, who had been a priest since Zacharias' time and had the confidence of both Stephen II and Paul (96:1–2). The letter to Ratchis was to persuade him to return to his monastery (which he did); all in all, it seems that papal support for Desiderius wrecked Ratchis' chances of a second tenure of the kingship.

118 These were all that Desiderius would agree to return. He kept Bologna and Imola (probably also Ancona, Osimo and Numana) until the fall of the Lombard kingdom.

beauty; he linked them on top by stone blocks, and over the top he placed a bronze roof.[119] *Also, close to St Peter's and on the other side of St Andrew's, in the place called the Mausoleum*[120] *he made a basilica in honour of St Petronilla – in France he had promised the kindly king Pepin that it was there he would place St Petronilla's body; and there he put many silver canisters and many other adornments that he dedicated.* – and completed all that was needful; at God's call his life ended and he went to everlasting rest. **53.** He performed one March ordination, 2 priests, 2 deacons; for various places *15* bishops. *When he was in France he granted the pallium to holy Chrodegang and ordained him archbishop.*[121] The bishopric was vacant 35 days. He was buried in St Peter's, prince of the apostles, on 26 April in the 10th indiction [757].

119 This is the cantharus or *pigna* (fountain, BP 53:7) built by Symmachus, which did have 8 columns of porphyry, some sculpted, supporting an entablature, and a bronze cupola. Krautheimer, *Corpus* 5, 175, thinks that Stephen restored the canopy and possibly added four of the columns. The huge antique bronze pinecone enclosed inside it survives in the Vatican.

120 Stephen merely consecrated to Petronilla the mausoleum of the Theodosian dynasty, a rotunda built on to the south transept of St Peter's, immediately west of the third century rotunda which Symmachus consecrated to St Andrew, itself immediately west of the obelisk; cf. 95:3 on the cult of Petronilla by the Carolingian kings.

121 Both points are confirmed by Chrodegang's epitaph (*PL* 89, 1054). On the pallium for Gaul cf. 92: n. 56. It was a personal distinction for Chrodegang's help to the pope in France, but had further purposes. Chrodegang was a trusted associate of Pepin; with a pallium he could consecrate bishops, so Stephen was in effect putting the Frankish church in Pepin's charge (his influence over it had previously been shaky) (Noble, 273). Also, under Pepin there were various attempts to reconstruct the Frankish hierarchy. When Boniface was 'envoy' of St Peter, to restore the authority of metropolitan archbishops he asked Zacharias for the pallium for Rouen, Rheims and Sens, or at least for Rouen; Boniface himself became metropolitan at Mainz. But this attempt failed. So at a council in 755 Pepin designated some bishops as pro-metropolitans (Chrodegang was probably one of them); with authority over their colleagues they were in fact archbishops. Perhaps too, after Boniface was killed in 754, the pope wanted a new envoy of St Peter among the Frankish bishops and designated Chrodegang, who would have been the ideal choice. His biographer Paul the Deacon says he consecrated very many bishops in various cities; and in 765 at the council of Attigny he signed first, ahead of the bishops of Mainz, Sens, Rouen, Besançon, Tours and many others. Attempts to establish metropolitans continued: under Charlemagne, Wilchar of Sens was called Archbishop of the Gauls; cf. 96:17 and n. 44.

95. PAUL (757-767)

Stephen II's life is the last given in a surprising number of manuscripts. It is typical of a work like the LP, subject as it was to continuations and updating, that the later the material is the less manuscript support it has.

Paul's life is disappointing in its brevity and single-minded selectivity: despite the length and importance of the pontificate, the author deals almost entirely with church matters and his reference to politics is meagre. There occurs not a single place-name away from Rome, and as far as relations with the empire are concerned there is only the briefest allusion to Paul's dealings over iconoclasm.

We are told nothing of Paul's anxiety at Constantine V's attempt to establish relations with the Lombards and the Franks and the danger Paul foresaw should this come about, even to the existing papal state, not to mention its enlargement with the cities that Desiderius had rashly promised Stephen II as a reward for Stephen's helping him to secure the Lombard throne. These were cities the Lombards had conquered up to 40 years earlier, and the presence of many Lombard settlers in them made Desiderius reluctant to hand them over to Paul without guarantees which Paul would not give. In 757 George, a Byzantine envoy, was in France (94:43-4); and, as Paul complained in a letter to Pepin early in 758 (*CC* 14), Desiderius had not handed over the cities. In the same year Desiderius came south and subdued the Lombard duchies of Spoleto and Benevento, whose independence from the Lombard kingdom had rested on Frankish and papal protection. In so doing he damaged papal territory; Paul could only complain ineffectually at this. But the duke of Benevento (Liutprand) took refuge among the Byzantines at Otranto, thus bringing the Greeks into the picture, and, still in 758, the king visited Naples, and negotiated with the Byzantine official George, who had just returned from France. The result was a Lombard-Byzantine alliance aimed against Paul; where the Franks stood was unclear. The Greeks would hand over the ex-duke of Benevento, Desiderius would help them regain Ravenna from the pope (*CC* 15). When he met Paul in Rome, the king stated he wanted peace but refused any concessions unless Paul wrote to Pepin to secure the release of Lombard hostages Pepin was holding; if he got the hostages, he would reward Paul by handing over one of the cities, Imola. As his letters to Pepin would be read by the Lombards, Paul openly begged Pepin to release the hostages (*CC* 16) and asked him secretly not to (*CC* 17, saying that the other letter was written under force majeure).

The chronology of the next few years is obscure. Surviving letters hint at Paul's anxiety that Pepin might abandon him and his fear that Desiderius and the Byzantines would then invade the papal state to regain the former exarchate. He praises the Franks for their zeal for St Peter, reminds them of their duty to defend the church, assures Pepin he would never aid his enemies, and has to deny a rumour that he had given aid to Tassilo, the rebel duke of Bavaria and a relative by marriage of Desiderius (*CC* 36; on Tassilo, see Noble, 109 n. 58). Paul clearly feared isolation if there was a rapprochement between Franks and Lombards, given that Pepin and the Lombards had both been negotiating with the Greeks, and that it was no secret that Constantine V wanted the exarchate back from the pope. The Franks did remain loyal, though Pepin dared not intervene militarily to assist Paul, both for fear of activating the alliance between Desiderius and the Empire and because he was distracted by military problems elsewhere. At some point Desiderius put further pressure on Paul to compromise over his demand for the return of the Lombard-occupied cities by seizing from the papacy Senigállia and, in Campania, the Castrum Valentis (*CC* 21). It seems that Paul, Pepin and Desiderius all wanted peace. Finally Pepin's diplomacy secured a compromise between Paul and Desiderius; the basis was the territorial status quo as in 756 – Desiderius kept the cities he had promised Stephen II in 757; and Paul came to see that neither Pepin nor Desiderius would betray him to the Greeks. Nothing came of the Byzantine negotiations with either king, and Paul's hold on the exarchate was secure – without allies the Greeks were no real danger.

But if peace was thus achieved between Lombards, Franks and Rome, there was little hope of compromise between Rome and the Empire. Paul's reception of refugee Greek monks at Rome and his support in 763 of the other eastern patriarchs against Constantinople did not help. In 765 Constantine tried a new form of attack by approaching Pepin for support for iconoclasm, in the hope of creating a religious breach between the Franks and Rome; fortunately for Paul (who shared his predecessor's dislike of iconoclasm, c. 3 – the one aspect of all this that the biographer records), Pepin rejected these overtures: at the synod of Franks and Greeks held at Gentilly in 767 to debate iconoclasm and other doctrines the Roman view was accepted.

A further gap in the life is on relations with Ravenna; archbishop Sergius, who had been detained in Rome by Stephen II, was allowed by Paul to return home: Paul rightly judged that Sergius had no interest in the restoration of Byzantine rule and could be trusted to rule Ravenna on Paul's behalf.

It is clear from the criticism, however guarded, that the author makes of Paul that the composition of this life was not strictly contemporary. The brevity of the text and its many important omissions suggest the same; but it would be unfair to conclude from the LP alone that 'The official papal view must have been that Paul was a failure because he could neither get nor hold what had been promised to Stephen II' (Noble, 111). Paul's pontificate, as Kelly puts it, 'was a continuous struggle to defend and consolidate the young, still vulnerable papal state'. In that he did not fail. But as we shall see in the next life, his regime in Rome was to have unfortunate results.

Despite all the defects of this life, the account of building works is a valuable record, though even this as given by the original writer (whose text is represented by MSS of classes ACDEG) is not complete: in a later life (97:50) the LP records that Paul began a restoration of SS Apostoli, and something on this was added (c. 6) by the interpolator whose text is that of MSS class B. This and the other additions by the interpolator (given in italics in the translation) may have been made several decades later (cf. n. 18); one can only speculate how much more is missing. Paul's portrait appears in a fresco in the main apse of S. Maria Antiqua which (though the LP is silent) dates to this pontificate (Krautheimer, *Corpus* 2, 250).

95. PAUL

95. **1.** PAUL [29 May 757–28 June 767], of Roman origin, son of Constantine, held the see 10 years 1 month. From early youth he was handed over along with Stephen his brother and predecessor as pontiff to learn the teaching of the church in the Lateran patriarchate, in the time of lord pontiff Gregory the second junior [III]. Afterwards he was consecrated along with his brother by the blessed pope lord Zacharias to the order of the diaconate.[1] Now when his brother and predecessor as pontiff was nearing the end of his life, straightaway the people of this city of Rome were divided: some who sided with archdeacon Theophylact gathered together and took up residence in his house;[2] others agreed on this blessed deacon Paul – the majority of the judges and people sided with him rather than with archdeacon Theophylact. The holy man himself never left the Lateran patriarchate, but with the others who were faithful continued to tend his sick brother and predecessor as pontiff. **2.** But when his brother and predecessor as pontiff had departed this life and been buried with great honour in St Peter's, immediately the same gathering of people who were siding with the then deacon Paul, as they were the stronger and mightier side, elected him to the pinnacle of the pontificate. Thereafter those who had gathered with the archdeacon were scattered.[3] So by God's will this holy man was ordained to St Peter's holy apostolic see and consecrated pontiff.

He was bishop in the time of the emperors Constantine [V] and Leo [IV].[4] He was gentle and merciful, never rendering anyone evil for evil. And if to a slight extent he caused anyone affliction through his evil subordinates, he was quickly moved by piety to bring him mercy and comfort.[5] **3.** Many have borne witness how by night on his own he toured the chambers of the sick who lay

---

1 Cf. 94:1, n. 1.

2 If there was an election, the location was highly irregular. Theophylact was seen by Baumont, 1930, 8–9, as candidate of the military aristocracy; but as archdeacon he will have had clerical support against the noble Paul, though Paul too must have had such support. There is no evidence for Theophylact's supporters wanting reconciliation with Byzantium. On the meaning of the events of 757, see Noble, 193–5.

3 The faction of Theophylact caused a delay of about a month between Paul's election and consecration. In this time Paul wrote to tell Pepin of Stephen's death and his own election by the entire people (*CC* 12); he uses the forms hitherto used in writing to the exarch (*Liber Diurnus* no. 59, ed. Foerster, 113–4) and promises to stay loyal to the pact between Pepin and Stephen II. In a further letter (*CC* 13), written (evidently by Paul) in the name of the 'Senate and People of Rome' (not to be taken as proof of the survival of the Roman senate!), Pepin is thanked for his past help and asked to see that the Lombard-occupied cities be restored (Noble, 104 n. 30). Neither letter asks Pepin to ratify his election or hints that it was contested.

4 Leo the Khazar had been co-emperor with Constantine Copronymus since 751.

5 A delicate hint that Paul may have been a harsh ruler; cf. 96:18.

totally bedridden, and with his servants those of other needy people in the quiet of the night, ministering to them with plentiful supplies and bringing them help and assistance. He even visited the prisons and other places of confinement in the same dead of night; and if he found any imprisoned there, he would rescue them from the peril of death and let them go free. Many debtors, dunned and oppressed by their creditors, he redeemed from the yoke of slavery by paying off their debts; to widows and orphans and all in need he brought assistance. *To fulfil his elder brother and holy predecessor pope Stephen's advantageous arrangements, immediately that pontiff had died, this blessed pontiff gathered the sacerdotes, the whole clergy and this city of Rome's entire people, and began operations at the cemetery outside the Appian Gate some two miles from Rome where St Petronilla had once been buried. From there he removed her venerable and holy body along with the marble sarcophagus in which it lay and on which were carved letters reading 'To Aurea Petronilla, sweetest daughter'. This made it certain that the carving of the letters could be identified as engraved by St Peter's own hand out of love for his sweetest child. The holy body and the sarcophagus were laid on a new carriage and brought by his Beatitude with hymns and spiritual chants to St Peter's; he placed the holy body in the mausoleum close to St Andrew's, whose dedication in honour of this St Petronilla, Christ's martyr, had been decreed by his brother the holy pope Stephen while yet living. There he made an adequate provision of adornment in gold, silver and brocades; he restored the church itself and in St Petronilla's honour he embellished it with wondrously beautiful pictures.*[6] *In St Peter's also he made grills on each side, right and left, of the entrance to the presbyterium and coated them with fine silver weighing 50 lb.*

6 Cf. 94:52. Some later calendars record the date of Petronilla's translation as 8 October, presumably in 757, a few months after Paul's consecration. For the basilica cf. 94: n. 120. Its dedication to Petronilla had a political purpose (the Frankish royal family worshipped her), and it certainly took place before Paul received from France the shawl used at the baptism of Pepin's daughter Gisele, born in 757 (in his reply to Paul's first letter Pepin had asked Paul to be her *compater*); for in a slightly later letter (*CC* 14) Paul says he had taken the shawl into the building already dedicated to her. When the altar was restored in 1474 the sarcophagus was found (so a letter of Sixtus IV to Louis XI who was paying for it); it is described as a marble chest with sculptured dolphins on top. In 1574 the relics were transferred and the sarcophagus broken up to pave a chapel in the basilica. Copies of the inscription had been made, which confirm the LP version except that AVREAE was really AVR, i. e. Aureliae. The sarcophagus, in other words, was of an unknown Aurelia Petronilla, not of a martyr. Paul's paintings in the chapel may be those described there in 1458 as ancient ones showing the story of Constantine, which would fit the politico-religious interests of late 8th-century Rome. The decoration was renewed in 1464, but the entire chapel was torn down to make way for new St Peter's, with no proper record being made.

He strenuously defended the orthodox faith, which is why he frequently sent his envoys with apostolic letters to entreat and warn the emperors Constantine and Leo to restore and establish in their erstwhile status of veneration the sacred images of our Lord God and Saviour Jesus Christ, his holy mother, the blessed apostles, and all the saints, prophets, martyrs and confessors.[7]

4. This blessed pontiff unceasingly applied all his spiritual endeavours, his great care and his concern, to the cemeteries of the saints. He observed that very many locations in these cemeteries of the saints had been largely demolished through the neglect and carelessness of antiquity and were now nearly reduced to ruin,[8] so he forthwith removed the saints' bodies from these destroyed cemeteries. With hymns and spiritual chants he brought them inside this city of Rome, and he took care to have some of them buried with fitting honour around the *tituli*, deaconries, monasteries and other churches.

5. This holy prelate constructed from the ground up a monastery[9] in his own house in honour of St Stephen the martyr and pontiff and of St Silvester, another pontiff and a confessor of Christ. He built a chapel on to this monastery's upper walls, and with great veneration he deposited their bodies there. Within the monastery's enclosure he newly constructed from the ground up a church of wondrous beauty; he decorated it with mosaic and marble and bestowed on it all its adornment of gold, silver and other kinds; and he

---

7 Paul was worried at the iconoclast stand of Constantine V's church council at Hieria in 754. The letters referred to are lost, but one to Pepin (*CC* 36) tells how Paul had badgered the emperor on the issue; the emperor had replied claiming that letters from Rome had been written without Paul's knowledge by the *primicerius* Christopher.

8 The damage had no doubt been aggravated by the Lombard siege of Rome in 756, as Paul mentions in his privilege to St Silvester's (below).

9 The complex described is the present S. Silvestro in Capite (so called from its claim to possess the head of John the Baptist), part of whose buildings have been occupied since 1870 by the General Post Office (Krautheimer, *Corpus* 4, 149ff). A chapel of St Dionysius/Denis, part of the complex, may have been begun by Stephen II; and Mallius (*de abb.* 31) states that Stephen began and Paul finished the abbey of St Silvester *inter duos hortos*. Paul mentions his monastery and the translation of Silvester's body to it in a letter to Pepin (*CC* 42). The foundation charter from Paul to the first abbot Leontius, dated 2 June 761 and signed by 22 bishops, 18 priests and the archdeacon, is preserved in the conciliar collections (J 2346; edited by Federici, *ASR* 22, 1899, 254-264) and there are verbal similarities with the LP's account. Duchesne questioned its genuineness, but Federici (243-246) defended it and Ferrari (302-12) concurs. It describes how Paul established the monastery in the house he inherited from his parents. The translation of Silvester's body to the chapel is then dated to 19 July 761, and that of pope Stephen's body to 17 August 761. In another letter of Paul's, addressed to Leontius the monastery's abbot, and witnessed by 41 bishops and priests, Paul repeats his reasons for the foundation, tells of the transfer of relics from the catacombs, and lists the monastery's possessions and facilities. In 768 the monastery was the prison for Passibus, the opponent of Stephen III (96:12).

built there a silver canopy *weighing 720 lb. And he built there an altar at the confessio, which he clothed with fine silver weighing 300 lb;* and there with great respect and reverence he deposited the bodies of the uncounted saints he removed from the demolished cemeteries.[10] On this monastery he conferred many estates and landed properties in the city and the country,[11] and he enriched it profusely and abundantly with gold, silver, other kinds of things and all its requirements. There he established a community of monks and decreed it should be a monastery for chanting the psalms in the Greek manner,[12] and he laid it down under great excommunications that the praises to our God almighty and all the saints resting there should be carried out diligently and unceasingly.

6. Inside this city of Rome on the via Sacra close to the Temple of Rome he newly built the church in honour of SS Peter and Paul,[13] where these blessed princes of the apostles at the time they were crowned with martyrdom for Christ's name knelt down when they poured out their prayers to our Redeemer; and on this spot even now their kneeprints can be distinguished on a very hard stone as a testimony to every subsequent generation to come.[14] *Inside this city he renewed the roofing of the church of the holy Apostles near the Via Lata,*

---

10 The doors of S. Silvestro are still flanked by two inscriptions listing the male and female saints, with their feastdays as observed there; see A. Silvagni, *Monumenta epigraphica christiana*, I (Vatican, 1943), tav. xxxvii.

11 If documents of 955 and 962 are trustworthy, the monastery's property by that time was indeed extensive; it included the Milvian Bridge and all dues paid there, a monastery at Bomarzo, in Rome a dozen churches, Augustus' mausoleum, the Antonine Column, houses in the Trevi region, and lands outside the city, and in the territories of nine other towns; Ferrari 304–5, 310–11.

12 Paul made the monastery available for the numerous monks who fled from the east following Constantine V's intensified campaign against the iconodules.

13 This church is located by the LP in the same terms used for SS Cosmas and Damian's (BP Felix IV 56:2). As Paul's church cannot be either that church or S. Maria Nova and is not in the medieval catalogues, it seems it disappeared early on. De Rossi saw medieval paintings on an apse of the basilica of Maxentius where there was once an altar and thought this might represent Paul's church. Duchesne thought it more likely it was somewhere between that basilica and SS Cosmas and Damian, where Benedictus Canonicus (VZ III 219.15) places the stone. By 1375 the stone with the apostles' kneeprints was in S. Maria Nova; perhaps it had been moved there early from Paul's church. See Krautheimer, *Corpus* 1, 222 with notes 2 and 3.

14 The legend alluded to is that of Simon Magus; at least from the 5th century the story of his fall was located on the Via Sacra; Ps.-Marcellus (Lipsius, *Acta App. apocr.*, 167) says the four pieces of Simon's body joined together four stones, which remained to prove the victory of the apostles. Gregory of Tours, *Gloria martyrum* 27, says two apostolic kneeprints collected rainwater which cured sickness.

which had largely collapsed.[15]

Outside the walls of this city of Rome, inside St Peter's he newly constructed a chapel[16] in honour of God's holy mother, close to pope St Leo's oratory, alongside the entrance doors to St Petronilla's and St Andrew's, and he adorned it with mosaic and various minerals; and there he set up an effigy of God's holy mother, standing upright,[17] of gilded silver weighing *150* lb. In this chapel he also constructed his own tomb. *In front of the tower of S. Maria ad Grada, in the atrium called the Paradise, he built with wondrous work a chapel in front of the Saviour in honour of God's mother St Mary, and he decorated it magnificently.*[18]

7. When he was staying at St Paul's in the summer on account of the great heat, he was stricken with a bodily infirmity, and there his life ended; there too he was buried, and there for some three months his corpse remained interred. But afterwards all the citizens of Rome and those of other origin gathered together and took his body across the river Tiber on boats, bringing it with the honour of psalmody to St Peter's; and they buried it in the chapel which, as mentioned, he had constructed. He performed one December ordination, 12 priests, 2 deacons; for various places … bishops. The bishopric was vacant 1 year 1 month *while the trespasser Constantine was intruder into the apostolic see.*

---

15 SS Apostoli, originally the church of SS Philip and James. In view of 97:50, Paul's activity can be seen as merely the beginning of major restorations.

16 It is mentioned in the late 8th-century description of St Peter's (*Notitia ecclesiarum, CChr* 175, 310, lines 188–9); Mallius stated that it was closed off by bronze grills and women were forbidden entry. It was near the oratory of Leo and the entrance to the churches of Petronilla and Andrew.

17 *in statu*: if this means a statue, it is unique in the LP record of 8th-century Rome. Yet given the object's weight the idea is plausible (it is so taken in Vogel's index in Duchesne III, 226). If so, the Roman reply to iconoclasm is seen even more sharply.

18 The chapel, S. Maria ad Grada, was at the foot of Stephen II's tower which later took its name from the chapel (in the late 8th-century description of St Peter's, *CChr* 175, lines 311, 215, the chapel is named as *S. Maria quae Nova dicitur*); that the text calls the tower after the chapel whose foundation it is recording reveals, as does the manuscript tradition, interpolation. But it is the earliest reference to the gatehouse at the eastern portico of the atrium, and its date is confirmed by the inscription naming Paul, recorded by Grimaldi (who witnessed the building's demolition), *Descrizione* (ca. 1615, ed. Niggl, Rome, 1972), 195 fig. 8; Krautheimer, *Corpus* 5, 175.

96. STEPHEN III (768-772)

Constantine II, brother of Toto duke of Nepi, held the see from 5 July 767 till 6 August 768. His election was an attempt by members of the lay aristocracy to regain control from the clerical officials favoured by Paul; the manner of his election and ordination were irregular, though the election acts were signed by all the clergy, including the future Stephen III. But he found it difficult to gain recognition elsewhere: his announcement of his election to Pepin, and request that Pepin should maintain his undertakings to Stephen II and Paul, received no reply (cf. n. 9) from Pepin, who had recently been following a policy of non-intervention in Italy and was engaged in military affairs elsewhere; perhaps the king thought he could do nothing about the control of Rome by the Tuscan army.

There is the merest hint in the LP that the trouble originated in the harsh rule of pope Paul, and this emerges only because it was part of Constantine's defence (c. 19). The compiler's prejudices prevent Constantine being given his own biography; in c. 6 he almost seems to gloat over the fate of the bishop who consecrated him (a life of the next brief intruder Philip is hardly to be expected). We have seen (p. 76) that a number of surviving MSS end at the death of Paul's predecessor in 757; it seems that compilation of the LP was then laid aside: the eventual compiler of Paul's life was 'not strictly contemporary'. It may be that the same author wrote Stephen III's life (the expression *aegritudine praeoccupatus* occurs in both), and also part of the next, that of Hadrian I, down to the fall of the Lombard kingdom. If this is so, Paul's brief biography may have been no more than a rushed introduction by a writer whose real concern was to present his viewpoint on the events leading up to the end of that kingdom, and gain it currency by attaching it to the LP. His partisanship clearly reflects the outcome of the strife between Franks and Lombards and of that between lay and clerical parties.

Paul's regime had gained him enemies, including Toto. It was Christopher, leader of the clerical party, who had (or so he later claimed, n. 3) dissuaded Toto from murdering Paul (who was dying anyway) and had gained Toto's promise that the election of a new pope would follow tradition. Toto broke his promise by having his brother Constantine acclaimed by his own troops, installed in the Lateran and made bishop. For the first time a lay, aristocratic, military coup had been carried out by men who knew that to control Rome and the papal State they had to seize the papacy (Noble, 113).

So Christopher and his son Sergius are presented in the LP as heroes who secured

96. STEPHEN III

Constantine's removal (their refusal to serve him is stressed), but they achieved it only by calling on Lombard help. This was a surprise to king Desiderius and awkward for our author. The Lombard king was keen to grasp such a chance to control Rome, and it was with Lombard troops supplied on his instructions that Sergius staged a coup and had Toto killed and Constantine arrested.

In the LP the Lombards' role in Sergius' entry into Rome is minimized; nor are they mentioned in the account of the coup, whose success is put down to the officers of the Roman militia: at one point the Lombards are left stranded on the Janiculum, and just before Toto is killed they want to turn and flee. As a result the sequence of events in cc. 8–9 is not totally clear. Waldipert, a Lombard priest, apparently Desiderius' personal envoy (Noble, 115), tried to have a priest named Philip made pope, clearly in the Lombard interest. But Christopher saw that such a degree of Lombard involvement was unacceptable at Rome and would also thwart his own ambitions. He gambled ('in a stunning display of haughtiness', *ibid.*) by swearing never to enter Rome while Philip was in the Lateran. The gamble paid off: Christopher's supporters ejected Philip, and the 'dazzling' prospect for Desiderius of a Lombard-dominated papacy vanished. Christopher then had Stephen elected (the only certainly non-noble pope between 752 and 844 apart from Leo III), at least following traditional forms, but he clearly planned to rule in the name of a powerless pope. 'Apparently the Lateran had triumphed over the laity, and Desiderius' interests had been neatly set aside' (*id.*, 116).

In expressing disgust at the behaviour (c. 12, 14, 15) of those who mutilated Constantine, his supporters, and Waldipert, the compiler protests a little too much. Even if Stephen could not prevent this, Christopher surely could have done. Sergius (c. 16) took the news of Stephen's election to France, with the request that a council be held. The council's real purpose was to prove that unlike the regimes of Constantine and Philip, that of Stephen III was legitimate, that is, acceptable to the Franks. Significantly this synod dated its acts 'in the reign of our Lord Jesus Christ', without giving the regnal year of Constantine V. Stephen and the clerical party had to disavow the openly known fact that they had at the time recognized Constantine as pope. The Lombards had to accept the fait accompli at Rome, though as the next best thing Desiderius tried to have his own candidate installed at Ravenna: Stephen was able to stop this, but only because the Franks leaned on Desiderius (c. 26).

But with the death of Pepin (24 September 768) Frankish foreign policy began to shift. Guided by Bertrada, mother of Charles the new king, the Franks tried for an alliance with the Lombards. To cement this it was arranged that Charles marry Desiderius' daughter, and Stephen was powerless to stop what to him seemed the Franks' abandonment of their protectorate over the Roman see. He felt let down by them, and was finding Christopher's domination at Rome intolerable. Desiderius, assuming the Franks would not prevent him, seized his chance to secure control at Rome. He had found a new agent there in the person of Paul Afiarta; Afiarta was able to persuade Stephen to trust Desiderius' promises to hand over territory to the papal state. Christopher, whose power had originated when he had turned to the Lombards in 768, found his ambitions wrecked when Stephen did the same in 771. Stephen abandoned Christopher and his son to their fate at the hands of Afiarta and the Lombards, and even wrote (see n. 84) to Charles and his mother claiming that Desiderius had saved him from a conspiracy led by Christopher and Sergius. The result was that Stephen was as much under the thumb of Afiarta as he had ever been under that of Christopher. His alliance with Desiderius was proved folly when the king said he had done enough for Stephen without handing over any territory (97:5). And when in 771 Charles divorced his wife and the Franks again became Desiderius' enemies, Stephen's ineptness was clear.

All this was difficult for our compiler. In particular Stephen's own policy vacillations had to be disguised (it is *never* made clear that he sided with the Lombards), as did his reliance on Christopher and then on Afiarta. Given the Lombard involvement in Constantine's deposition, one feels that the compiler was relieved he could present Christopher and Sergius as no friends of Desiderius (c. 28), but as it was an awkward inconsistency that Stephen III abandoned them, he claims that Stephen intended to save them from their fate (c. 32). He shares Stephen's embarrassment that Stephen had gained the papacy through Christopher, but adopts an escape different from that used by Stephen himself (nn. 84–87). Almost certainly the compiler was writing with a hindsight not available to Stephen: the Lombard kingdom was to collapse two years after Stephen's death, and the Franks would be supreme. Another source (n. 78) which also favoured Christopher regarded Stephen as conniving with the Lombards and saw Stephen's death next year as condign punishment for this. Our compiler's efforts at justification end with his throwing the blame for everything onto the Lombard king (and thus onto Afiarta and the Lombard faction in Rome).

This life contains in passing the first mention of the term 'cardinal' (deacons and priests, c. 20; the 7 cardinal bishops, c. 27).

96. STEPHEN III

96. **1.** STEPHEN [III; 7 August 768–24 January 772], of Sicilian origin, son of Olibus, held the see 3 years 5 months 28 days. A man of stamina, he was learned in the divine Scriptures and imbued with the traditions of the church, in keeping to which he was resolute and steadfast. When he came as a boy from the island of Sicily to this city of Rome, lord pope Gregory III of holy memory handed him over to St Chrysogonus' monastery which he was then newly founding,[1] and there he became a cleric and a monk. Afterwards lord pope Zacharias took him from that monastery and instructed him to stay in a chamber of the Lateran patriarchate; afterwards he consecrated him priest for St Caecilia's *titulus*. **2.** But because of his modesty and chastity he kept him in his office at the Lateran. The next blessed popes, lord Stephen and Paul, also kept this holy Stephen in their service because of his pious behaviour.

But when his predecessor lord pope Paul was staying at St Paul's on account of the sternness of the summer heat, and was there incapacitated by the serious illness which brought his life to an end, this blessed Stephen was constantly at the service of his predecessor as pope day and night, and never left his bedside until he gave up the ghost.[2] **3.** But[3] when he had not yet breathed his last, straightaway a duke Toto, a longtime resident of the

---

1 Cf. 92:9; if *parvulus* in 731–45, he can have been barely 50 when he became pope.

2 Stephen himself claimed at the Council of 769 that he alone had not deserted Paul's deathbed and that consequently he could have had no part in Constantine II's election.

3 Another account of these events, prepared by the *primicerius* Christopher as a deposition to the Council of 769, survives in a 9th century Verona MS (text Mansi 12.717, and Duchesne, I, 480–1, n. 3). This confirms the LP, but adds details and naturally stresses Christopher's efforts to stop Toto intruding Constantine as pope. Christopher claims that Toto had tried to kill Paul on his deathbed, but he had prevented this and brought Toto and his accomplices to his own house where they swore to avoid a disputed election, to consider as candidates only Roman *sacerdotes* and deacons according to tradition, and to allow no peasants from the neighbouring towns into Rome. Toto and his party immediately broke the last part of this promise and mustered their peasants; at this point Paul died. All went the same day, Sunday, to the Basilica of the Apostles and swore to the people to keep to lawful procedures. Everyone went home, but Toto and Constantine used their army to install Constantine in the Lateran and have him made a cleric. Christopher wondered what to do; a notary told him with threats to attend the election, but despite his fear he preferred to die rather than do so. Next day Constantine was made deacon in an oratory of the patriarchate and so attained the papacy. Christopher could only lament and pray. The other faction killed duke Gregory who held Campania, and tried to kill Christopher. Tipped off, he and his sons fled to St Peter's. Failing to dislodge him by persuasion, Constantine came to him in person and swore at St Peter's confessio to let him and his sons stay in their homes till the following Easter, when he would let them enter a monastery. After Easter (10 April 768) they begged him to let them go to the Saviour's monastery in the districts of Spoleto; at which point the MS breaks off.

city of Nepi, with his brothers Constantine, Passibus and Paschal, gathered a sizeable army and a band of peasants from Nepi itself and the other cities of Tuscia. They came into this city of Rome by St Pancras' Gate and stayed under arms at Toto's house, where they suddenly elected Toto's brother Constantine, then a layman. Many of them were armed and wearing breastplates, and like robbers they took him to the Lateran patriarchate. They came with him up to the residence of the *vicedominus*, and immediately they forced George, the bishop[4] they had sent for, to bestow on Constantine the prayer to make him a cleric. George flatly refused to do this and fell prostrate on the ground before Constantine's feet, mightily adjuring him by all the divine mysteries to give way, abandon his intention and unholy presumption, and not be the cause of such an unheard of novelty[5] occurring in God's church. **4.** When he made this protest, many of the wicked men who had brought about this unholy election were moved to rise up against him and threaten him violently; stricken with fear he bestowed on him the prayer of clerical status. So now that he was a cleric, he intruded into this holy Lateran patriarchate. When the next day, Monday, dawned, he was consecrated by the same bishop subdeacon and deacon in St Laurence's oratory[6] inside the patriarchate, against what the holy canons lay down.[7] So he made the whole people swear him allegiance. When Sunday came, he again made his way to St Peter's with a host of armed men, and was consecrated pontiff by the same George bishop of Palestrina and two other bishops, Eustratius of Albano and Citonatus of Porto.[8] And for a period of one year and one month he held on to the apostolic see into which he had intruded.[9]

4 Of Palestrina, c. 6.

5 Constantine would start to list precedents when put on trial (c. 19). But there were in fact no precedents at Rome: Silverius, intruded in 536, was only a subdeacon (though son of pope Hormisdas), not, *pace* Duchesne, a layman; Fabian in 236 was not a Roman priest or deacon, though despite Duchesne Eusebius *HE* 6.29 does not say he was a layman – anyway this is not likely to have been known in 8th century Rome.

6 The earliest mention of the Sancta Sanctorum at the top of the Scala Santa.

7 They limited ordinations to certain days and imposed time-intervals between grades.

8 The bishops of Albano and Porto would normally have been led by the bishop of Ostia (see BP pope Mark, 35:2); but George of Ostia was in France, occupying the see of Amiens. He reappeared as one of the bishops from France who, with Italian bishops including Eustratius and Citonatus, took part in the Council of 769 (c. 17).

9 Two letters from Constantine to Pepin survive (*CC* 98–9), written to notify his ordination and gain recognition. He claims violence was used to make him accept election, and admits (apparently not considering it irregular) that people from nearby towns had taken part. The first letter got no reply; the pretext for writing again was to communicate to Pepin a letter from Theodore, the new patriarch of Jerusalem. This is omitted by our compiler, but he has to admit that Constantine

5. When Christopher the *primicerius* and counsellor witnessed this, in his faithful zeal he and his son Sergius, who was then *sacellarius*, would rather have died than see the perpetration of this unholy novelty and wicked presumption on the apostolic see. Every day they wept and lamented, pretending that they would become monks and asking to be released by Constantine: they claimed they would make for the Saviour our Lord Jesus Christ's monastery[10] and there assume the monastic habit. And he received an oath from the *primicerius* Christopher, and trusting them he gave them their release.[11] When they were journeying and reaching the Lombards' frontier, that monastery's abbot wanted them brought inside the monastery, but the *primicerius* Christopher and his son Sergius, formerly *sacellarius* and later *secundicerius*, deviated from the route, strongly adjuring Theodicius duke of Spoleto to take them across the Po to his Lombard king Desiderius; by this means they were attempting to bring about the redemption of God's holy church. And the duke of Spoleto brought them to his king. When they were brought into his presence they earnestly begged him to grant them help, that this novel error should be cut off from God's church.

While the *primicerius* Christopher and his son Sergius were staying with the king, Constantine the intruder into the apostolic see performed the ordination[12] of priests and deacons, 8 priests, 4 deacons; and in the course of that year and one month he made 8 bishops for various places. **6.** But bishop George of Palestrina who had consecrated Constantine deacon and pontiff was a few days after that consecration stricken with a serious and noxious illness and rendered immobile. He never again celebrated the ceremonies of mass: his right hand withered and shrivelled[13] – he could not even reach his mouth with it. Thus he wasted away and became weaker, and his life came to an end.[14]

---

performed ordinations: they would be an issue at the Council of 769; but he does not want to admit that Constantine and the aristocracy were accepted by nearly everyone in Rome.

10 Near Rieti in the duchy of Spoleto. Anxious to show how Christopher and the clerical party coped with the situation the compiler telescopes the time interval (the placing of c. 6 may be deliberate), during which this party was able to regroup.

11 Noble, 114–115, remarks that only in retrospect can Toto and Constantine be accused of naivety in letting them leave Rome; there was no reason to believe Pepin would intervene or that Christopher, the most bitter enemy of the Lombards in Rome, would turn to the State's oldest enemies. Christopher and Sergius were influenced by Toto's military control, Frankish inactivity, and the death of their ally duke Gregory.

12 These ordinations will have been performed at the summer Embertide (probably Saturday 4 June) 768, since Christopher had only left Rome after Easter that year.

13 *aruit et contracta est*: Vulgate, Job 7.5.

14 No bishop of Palestrina attended the Council of 769; by 770 Andrew was bishop.

7. Meanwhile, when the Lombard king let them go, Christopher and Sergius went to the city of Rieti. Sergius and the priest Waldipert[15] went ahead with men from Rieti and Forcona and other Lombards from the duchy of Spoleto; they reached this city of Rome suddenly and unexpectedly in the evening, actually at twilight, on the 29th[16] day of July in the 6th indiction [768], the eve of the martyrs SS Abdon and Sennen, and took possession of the Salarian Bridge. **8.** Next day they crossed the Milvian Bridge and came to St Peter's Gate, and they continued and came close to St Pancras' Gate.[17] Some kinsmen of Christopher and Sergius who were watching and guarding the gate saw Sergius come close to it, signalled to him and immediately opened the gate; and so Sergius and Waldipert with the Lombards entered Rome. In fear of the Roman people they climbed with a banderol[18] on to the city walls, and these Lombards never dared come down from the Janiculum, but stayed there in great anxiety. **9.** When the brothers Toto and Passibus heard of this, and did not know the crafty plan their betrayers had embarked on, they rushed to the gate with a number of men who included Demetrius the *secundicerius* and Gratiosus, then *cartularius* and later duke,[19] who were also in on the plot with the wicked betrayers.[20] As they came close to the Lombards, one of these Lombards named Racipert who was evidently an outstanding warrior came to meet duke Toto and attacked him: Toto fell on him, struck him violently and killed him. On seeing this the Lombards were attempting to turn and flee, but Demetrius the *secundicerius* and Gratiosus who were standing behind Toto struck him in the back with their lances, and so got the better of him and killed him. Passibus fled to the Lateran patriarchate to tell his brother Constantine what had happened. On hearing this, Constantine fled into the Saviour's basilica with Passibus and bishop Theodore his *vicedominus*; they went down to the baptistery, to St Venantius' church,[21] and waited there a while. Reckoning they had a better chance of

---

15 A Lombard (cf. c. 15), evidently Desiderius' envoy; the king must have agreed with Christopher that a pro-Lombard pope should be elected and sent Waldipert to secure this. The attempt failed; Waldipert did not see that while Christopher might accept Lombard help to remove Constantine, he was unwilling to lose his own influence.

16 28th in the MSS, wrongly, since the feast mentioned fell on 30th July.

17 Presumably they failed to force the Salarian, Flaminian and St Peter's gates.

18 *flammula*; a small banner or streamer used by cavalry.

19 He would succeed Toto as duke; he was related to Christopher and Sergius (c. 31).

20 The author's bias is not very consistent: he sympathizes with Christopher, but resents Rome's betrayal to the Lombards. Christopher's part in the fighting is obscure: he did not appear in Rome till c. 11.

21 Cf. BP John IV 74:2; Duchesne, I, 330 with n. 3.

safety in the *vestiarium*, they went up there, entered St Caesarius' oratory,[22] shut the doors on themselves and waited there. Some hours later the judges of this city of Rome's militia arrived, ejected them from that oratory and placed them in confinement.

10. Next Sunday the priest Waldipert without Sergius' knowledge gathered some Romans, went to St Vitus' monastery[23] and removed from it the priest Philip. They elected him and acclaimed with shouts of praise: 'St Peter has chosen Philip pope!' And following custom they took him into the Saviour's basilica. There the prayer was said by a bishop in pursuance of ancient custom, and he gave the Peace to everyone, and they brought him into the Lateran patriarchate. There too, sitting on the pontifical throne, he again gave the customary Peace; he went aloft and as pontiffs normally do he held a banquet, with some of the church's chief men and the militia's chief officers sitting with him. 11. But shortly afterwards on the same day the *primicerius* Christopher arrived and on discovering that Philip had been elected he immediately became highly angry and asserted on oath before all the Romans that he would never enter Rome until the priest Philip had been thrown out of the Lateran patriarchate. Then Gratiosus and some of the Romans came and threw Philip out of it. He came down by the staircase that leads to the bath and very reverently went back to his monastery.[24]

So next day the *primicerius* Christopher gathered all the *sacerdotes*, the chief clergy, the militia's chief officers, the whole army, the honourable citizens and the whole assembly of the Roman people from greatest to least, at the Three Fates.[25] They deliberated and with absolute and total unanimity they all agreed on holy Stephen.[26] They went to St Caecilia's *titulus* where he lived a spiritual life as a priest, and they elected him pontiff. They acclaimed him with shouts of praise and brought him to the Lateran patriarchate. It was

22 The sites of and relationship between the *vestiarium* and this oratory are unclear, though the oratory was inside the *vestiarium*, see *LNCP* 104:25; Hülsen, 234, locates them in the western part of the palace, near the Baptistery.

23 Evidently the same as the monastery of Sardas; it will have taken the dedication of the nearby but distinct St Vitus' deaconry (cf. 98:78, n. 152), as St Agatha's monastery on the Quirinal took its dedication from a nearby deaconry. The present San Vito, on the Esquiline, marks the deaconry's approximate site. Note how Sergius, in command of the troops in this coup, is made out to be in ignorance at this stage.

24 Nothing is known of his later life; in the recriminations that ensued (which cost Waldipert his eyes and his life) his genuine unwillingness must have been accepted.

25 Three statues of Sibyls (Pliny, *NH* 34.11) stood near the Rostra (where Romans of republican times had held assemblies), in the north corner of the Forum.

26 Note the hyperbole; it 'reflects a degree of consensus hoped for but not attained by the Lateran' (Noble, 116). The place of the election was irregular.

God who saw to it that everything about his election was carried out lawfully and that he assumed the summit of the pontificate.

12. While this holy Stephen was still pontiff-elect,[27] some perverted individuals, men who do not keep their eyes on God and have no fear of the dreadful judgment to come, put up to it by some plague-ridden instigators of evil who got their just deserts from the Lord, gathered together and seized Theodore, the bishop and *vicedominus*, and then – it is unholy even to mention it – they gouged out his eyes and cruelly cut off his tongue, and they gouged out Passibus' eyes as well. Such was the unholiness they showed themselves to have, that they would not even let them be taken to their homes for their own men to take care of them; they took away everything that was theirs, their servants and possessions. One of them, bishop Theodore, they had confined in the Clivus Scauri monastery[28] where tortured by hunger and thirst he breathed his last crying out for water, while Passibus they sent to St Silvester's monastery. As for Constantine who had intruded into the apostolic see, he was brought out into the open; they fixed a huge weight to his feet and made him sit on a horse in a saddle designed for a woman, and in the sight of them all he was taken to the Cella Nova monastery.[29]

---

27 'For a short time Rome was the scene of random and gratuitous violence' (cc. 12–15), until 'the Lateran had clearly regained the upper hand, but its hand was bloody and its support was far from unanimous' (Noble, 116).

28 Gregory I's foundation to St Andrew (now S. Gregorio) in his own house, Ferrari, 138–151; founded for Latin monks, by the 840s it was occupied by Greeks (John the Deacon, *Vita Greg. Magn.* 4.85), as were the next two monasteries mentioned; this change probably took place before 768. By the early 10th century the monks were again Latin. The present church is 9th–12th century. Of the original foundation the ruins of the *triclinium* and of the library of pope Agapitus survive, Krautheimer, *Corpus* 1, 320–26.

29 This is St Saba's; John the Deacon (*Vita Greg. Magn.* 1.9) talks of 'the place called Cella Nova where before now was dedicated a chapel in her name (*sc.* of Silvia, Gregory's mother, said to have lived in a hermitage here), and the famous monastery of Christ's confessor St Saba'. Ferrari, 146, notes that Greek monasteries (such as, here St Saba's, and, last note, St Andrew's) and Latin monasteries seem to have taken different sides in politics, as again at 98:11,13. It is unclear whether St Saba's was originally a Latin or Greek foundation. It is forcing John's language to say that Silvia actually founded the monastery, but if she did it was presumably Latin. One of the four Greek abbots who petitioned the Roman Council of 649 (two of the others being clearly from Rome) was John 'of the laura of St Saba in the desert near Christ our God's holy city' (Jerusalem), who had been in Rome for some years. It is widely held that he brought his monks with him from Jerusalem, established them in Rome, and dedicated the Cella Nova site to St Saba. The monastery became, or reverted to being, Latin probably in the 10th century; Krautheimer, *Corpus* 4, 51–71, Ferrari, 281–90.

13. At dawn on Saturday,[30] the day before the holy pope Stephen's ordination, some of the bishops, priests and clergy gathered in the Saviour's basilica, and Constantine was again brought into the open. The holy canons were read out, and so he was deposed. Maurianus the subdeacon came forward, removed the stole[31] from his neck, threw it at his feet, and then cut off his papal shoes.[32] And so next day, Sunday, the holy Stephen received his consecration as pontiff. The whole Roman people made their prayer of repentance and confession to God's clemency; in it they confessed that they had all sinned in the unholy ordination of Constantine the intruder into the apostolic see, in that they had not resisted it; and so Leontius the *scriniarius*[33] read out this confession in a raised voice from the ambo of St Peter's.

14. Afterwards the whole army of the city of Rome and of Tuscia and Campania mustered and went to Alatri in the districts of Campania, where there was a tribune Gracilis, an adherent of Constantine the intruder into the apostolic see, who had caused much evil to be perpetrated in Campania.[34] They put the city of Alatri under strong constraint, extracted Gracilis from it and brought him here to Rome. They put him in strict confinement and there for some days he remained imprisoned. But afterwards some wicked Campanians who had come here to Rome, encouraged by others who were even more wicked and unholy than themselves, extracted Gracilis from confinement, pretending they were taking him to a monastery; but when they reached the Colosseum,[35] there they gouged out his eyes and removed his tongue.

When a few more days had passed and the men of Tuscia and Campania had gathered here in Rome, Gratiosus and his more influential supporters, on whose warrant all the evils had been brought about, with no fear of God in them embarked on a plot. At first light he went with a squadron of soldiers

---

30 6 August 768.

31 The papal pallium; cf. the depositions of pope Silverius and patriarch Macarius of Antioch (BP 60:8, 81:13).

32 *campagi*, part of his papal insignia (Greg. Magn. *Ep.* 8.27); when pope Martin was taken to Constantinople and deposed, his shoe-straps were cut (*PL* 87.115).

33 He attended the Council of 769, when he was described also as regionary notary.

34 In 767 Campania had been loyal to Christopher, but the murder of duke Gregory (n. 3) seems to have been followed by the installation by Toto of one of his adherents, Gracilis, and to have produced divided allegiances: in this incident Campanians were fighting Campanians (cf. Noble, 116). Campania here excludes areas lost in 702 to duke Gisulf of Benevento and other areas (south of Gaeta, or perhaps of Terracina) which were still under Byzantine control in the duchy of Naples.

35 This may still refer to Nero's colossal statue or be the earliest recorded use of the word to refer to the nearby Flavian amphitheatre.

from Tuscia and Campania to the Cella Nova monastery where Constantine the intruder into the apostolic see was confined; they forced him out of the monastery, gouged out his eyes and then left him blind in the street.

15. When all this was over and done, some men rose up and said that the priest Waldipert, who was of Lombard race, had embarked on a plot with Theodicius duke of Spoleto and some of the Romans to murder the *primicerius* Christopher and other leading Romans and betray the city of Rome to the Lombard race. So a certain Christopher, the *vicedominus*, was sent with a crowd of people to arrest him. But he knew of it and fled into God's mother the ever-virgin St Mary's church called *ad martyres*. The *vicedominus* forced Waldipert out of it – he was holding the image of God's mother – and had him confined in the foul prison called Ferrata, in the large cell.[36] After a few days they brought Waldipert the priest out of that prison; they threw him to the ground close to the lane[37] to the Lateran grounds, gouged out his eyes and cut out his tongue in a cruel and unholy fashion; they despatched him to the *xenodochium* of Valerius,[38] and later his life came to an end there as a result of the gouging out of his eyes.

16. And so at the start of the high pontificate to which he had now been ordained, this holy prelate sent to their Excellencies Pepin, Charles and Carloman, kings of the Franks and patricians[39] of the Romans, in the districts of France, the same Sergius who was now *secundicerius* and *nomenclator*,[40] to request and encourage their Excellencies by means of his apostolic letter[41] to send some bishops who were skilled, learned in all the divine Scriptures and the teachings of the holy canons, and thoroughly expert, to hold a council in this city of Rome to deal with that unholy presumption of novel error and rashness which Constantine the intruder into the apostolic see had dared to

36 Apparently in the Lateran; cf. 97:10 on Sergius' imprisonment and assassination.
37 *transenda*; but Duchesne understood it as *transenna* (railing) and interpreted it to refer to the barrier marking off the Lateran grounds, especially on the north.
38 Somewhere on Monte Celio, not too far from the Lateran; cf. 98:81 and n. 169.
39 The first reference in the LP to the Frankish kings as patricians of the Romans; the title (previously conferred only by emperors) was given by Stephen II to Pepin and his descendants at St Denis in 754. From 754 it was used by popes addressing the kings; but Pepin himself never used it, and Charlemagne did so regularly only from 776. It is highly controversial whether it connoted any constitutional power. Noble (278 ff) sees it as honorific, with its possessor's power depending, in the Byzantine empire, on some other office; this would suggest that Stephen II did not intend to confer power on Pepin, merely to signify his protectorate over the State; cf. 94: n. 65.
40 Note the use of a *nomenclator* as an envoy; cf. BP Sisinnius 90:3.
41 Not extant, but mentioned in a later letter (*CC* 45); Sergius left Rome after Stephen's accession, but before Pepin's death (24 September 768) was known.

perpetrate. **17.** So Sergius went on his journey to the regions of the Franks, and found that the christian king Pepin had already departed this life. He continued his journey and reached his sons, the brothers Charles and Carloman, kings of the Franks and patricians of the Romans. He presented them with the apostolic letters and they gave him a warm reception. They showed him appropriate kindness and he gained from their Excellencies everything he had been sent to achieve – the christian kings sent from the regions of the Franks 12 bishops,[42] approved men who were very learned in the divine Scriptures and the rituals of the holy canons, namely:[43]

Wilchar, of Sens, archbishop of the province of the Gauls,[44] and the bishops of these cities: George of Amiens,[45] Wulfram of Meaux, Lullo of Mainz, Gaugenus of Tours,[46] Ado of Lyon, Hermenarius of Bourges, Daniel of Narbonne, Ermenbert of Worms,[47] Bernulf[48] of Würzburg, Erlolf of Langres, Tilpin of Rheims, and Gislebert of Noyon.

These came to Rome in April[49] of the 7th indiction [769], and the holy pope Stephen immediately gathered various bishops of Tuscia and Campania and some from this province of Italy,[50] namely:

42 The interpolated list names 13, but either the archbishop or more probably George of Amiens, whom the Council acts reckon as still bishop of Ostia, is excluded.

43 MS B⁴ alone contains the two lists of bishops. In theory the other MSS might have suppressed them; Duchesne, I, CCXXIX, preferred this view. But the lists are not quite in the form that the original compiler expected, and they must be interpolations. The compiler had intended to include them (he writes *scilicet:* and *id est:*) but did not do so. The copyists of B³C² and the lost MS B of Freher reached this point and went no further, hoping to include the lists before continuing the text, but never resuming their copying. All other MSS continue with the primitive text. B⁴'s copyist alone included what the original compiler wanted; his list is confirmed by the council acts (*MGH Conc* 2.1.75–6, 80–81), though the order of names and some details differ.

44 Probably the former bishop of Mentana (and no new bishop of that see appears in these lists), see 94:23 and n. 45. For the extraordinary title, see 94: n. 121; he gained his special status (like that of the fifth-century papal vicariate of Arles) after the death of Chrodegang of Metz, and under Hadrian I his authority even extended into Spain. In the present list the occupants of former archiepiscopal sees are not listed apart from other bishops.

45 Cf. n. 42. Pope Paul had allowed him to remain in France (*CC* 21, 37); when Constantine recalled him (*CC* 99), he did not obey. So it was a moot point of which see he was bishop: Stephen could hardly yet have decided the matter. He later went back to France, whence in 782 he came as Charlemagne's envoy to Hadrian (*CC* 73).

46 For *Toronensis* perhaps read *Rotonicensis* (of Rodez). Certainly there was no bishop of Tours so named; the list of bishops of Rodez is incomplete at this period.

47 The acts here have a garbled city name which could represent Salzburg.

48 Berohelpos, MS (Verabulpus, acts); but Bernulf is a known bishop of Würzburg.

49 The acts place the first of this council's four sessions on 12 April 769.

50 Ravenna heads the list out of honour for the city (showing also that it was at least not

the priest Valentine and the deacon John to represent lord Leo[51] archbishop of Ravenna, Joseph of Tortona,[52] Lantfred of Castrum,[53] Aurianos[54] of Tuscania, Radoin of Bagnorégio, Peter of Populonia, Filerad of Luni, the archpriest Theodore and the deacon Peter to represent Jerome bishop of Pavia-Ticinum, Peter of Caere, Maurus[55] of Bomarzo, Leo of Castellum,[56] Sergius of Ferentino, Jordanes of Segni, Ado of Orte, Ansald of Narni, Nirgotius of Anagni, Agatho of Sutri, Stephen of Centumcellae, Theodosius of Tivoli, Pinnis of Tres Tabernae, Bonifa[57] of Priverno, Leoninus of Alatri, Valeran of Trevi, Bonus of Monterano, Gregory of the territory of Silva Candida, Eustratius of the territory of Albano, Citonatus of Porto, Citonatus from Velletri, Potho of Nepi, Antoninus of Cesena, John of Faenza,[58] Stabilis of Pesaro, George of Senigallia, Maurus of Fano, Sergius of Ficuclae, Juvianus of Cagli, the priest Sabatius representing Tiberius bishop of Rimini, Florentinus of Gubbio, the priest Gregory representing Marinus bishop of Urbino.

18. When they were all gathered, the council took place[59] in the Saviour

---

openly disloyal to Rome). The rest are arranged geographically: 7 bishops (Tortona to Pavia) are from the ecclesiastical province of Milan and (at this date more significantly) from the Lombard kingdom; the low placing of Pavia itself may be because it was represented only by legates. Next come bishops from cities now in the papal state: 21 from the Roman duchy itself (Caere to Nepi), then those of the exarchate and the Pentapolis, beginning with Cesena and Faenza from the ecclesiastical province of Ravenna and concluding with 8 from the suburbicarian diocese. Noble, 118–119, discusses the significance of the list for the extent of papal rule in Italy and the current state of relations with Desiderius (who could have stopped bishops from his kingdom attending); it is clear that despite his setback in 768 he had not yet broken with Rome. Indeed Rome seems to have won some influence with the Lombard bishops after some 200 years in which contacts were tenuous. But most of the bishops are from nearer Rome, where the papal State's power then lay.

51 An error (cf. c. 25); the archbishop was still Sergius, as in the council acts.

52 Vertonensis, MS (Derzonae, acts); Tortona, seen by Noble as representing Milan.

53 The bishopric now sited at Acquapendente, 20 km WNW of Orvieto.

54 Aurinandus in the acts, perhaps rightly; bishop of Toscanella, near Imola, given the list's geographical arrangement, and not of Tuscánia 18 km W of Viterbo.

55 Maurinus in the acts.

56 Probably Città Castellana (Falerii Veteres), rather than Città di Castello in Umbria, which in the eighth century was known as Castrum (or Castellum) Felicitatis and was in the Lombard kingdom (*CC* 58) unlike the other names here from Caere on. There was a massa Castellana in Roman Tuscany (J 2207, Gregory II), and by the 9th century the name Castellum occurs, as here, for a place beween Nepi and Gallese.

57 *sic* MS; Bonisa in the acts; both forms may be corrupt for Bonifatius.

58 The acts add: (John, Antoninus?) 'were sent by Sergius archbishop of Ravenna'.

59 What survives of the acts is in Duchesne, I, nn. on 482–3, or *MGH Conc* 2.1:74 ff. The holding of the Council shows Christopher and Sergius to be safely in power: their own man was pope and Christopher's kinsman Gratiosus was duke. Their problem was that Toto's fall

our Lord Jesus Christ's basilica close to the Lateran. The blessed pope Stephen presided with all these bishops joined in session with him, and Constantine, the intruder into the apostolic see, now eyeless, was brought into the open. He was closely examined on why he as a layman had presumed to intrude into the apostolic see and perpetrate this error and wicked novelty on God's church. He professed in front of everyone that he had been pressurized by the people, elected by force and taken under compulsion into the Lateran patriarchate, owing to those burdens and grievances[60] that lord pope Paul had caused the Roman people. Falling to the ground, with his arms stretched out on the pavement, he wept that he was guilty and had sinned more times than there were sands in the sea, and implored pardon and mercy from that sacerdotal council. They had him lifted up from the ground and that day passed no sentence against him. **19.** But next day they brought him in again and questioned him on that unholy novelty. He replied that he had not acted without precedent, since Sergius archbishop of Ravenna had been made an archbishop when still a layman,[61] and Stephen bishop of Naples had also been a layman when he was unexpectedly consecrated bishop.[62] But when Constantine continued in this way, all the *sacerdotes* straightaway became angry in their zeal for church tradition; they had him buffeted on the neck and ejected him from that church.[63] **20.** Then all the registers of his acts, and the council whose written account of his supposed confirmation had been published, were brought out, and they destroyed them by fire in the centre of that church's *presbyterium*. After this the holy pope Stephen with all the *sacerdotes* and Roman people threw themselves on to the ground and cried out and wailed aloud *Kyrie eleison*, confessing that all of

---

can scarcely have encouraged harmony between the clerical and lay parties. It is likely that they aimed to create a continuity of power for the clerical party, not dependent on the person of the current pope (Noble, 117-8).

60 Cf. 95:2 and n. 5.

61 Agnellus (c. 154) adds that he was married, and on becoming archbishop he consecrated his wife a deaconess; Agnellus is muddled, but it seems that Stephen II threatened Sergius with deposition but died before this was carried out, while Paul came to an agreement with Sergius and reestablished him in his see; cf. *CC* 14.

62 The *Gesta epp. Neap.* (*MGH SSrL*, 425) tell that Stephen was consul at Naples and had ruled the duchy for 12 years, during which time his wife had died; coming to Rome he was made bishop by Stephen (III). Constantine thus proved that even after the events of 767 Stephen accepted that a layman could become bishop. Had he been allowed, Constantine might most obviously have named Ambrose of Milan. But the point at issue was that there were no precedents for the Roman see, cf. n. 5.

63 Constantine seems to have changed his tune after the first session on 12 April; this antagonized his judges, and (on 13 April according to a fragment of the acts of the session on 14 April) he was submitted to a penance (lifelong monastic confinement).

them had sinned in that they had taken communion from Constantine's hands. So as a result a penance was imposed on them all.

Next[64] the sacred canons were brought forward and clearly scrutinized, and a decision was pronounced by this sacerdotal council under interdict and anathema: no layman should ever presume to be promoted to the sacred honour of the pontificate, nor even anyone in orders, unless he had risen through the separate grades and had been made cardinal deacon or priest.[65] At the same council they also decreed the amendment of many other matters that needed canonical reproof. **21.** On the matter of the bishops, priests and deacons whom Constantine had consecrated, this council promulgated that any of the bishops who had previously been priests or deacons should revert to their former grade of office, but if they were acceptable to the people of their cities, a decree of election should again be passed in the usual manner and they should come with their clergy and people to the apostolic see and receive their blessing and consecration from the holy pope Stephen. As for the priests and deacons consecrated by Constantine, they too should revert to their former status, and later, if any of them were acceptable to the holy pontiff Stephen, he should consecrate them priests or deacons. But they laid down that those of them who were going to be consecrated should never reach a higher grade and not be promoted to the summit of the pontificate, in case this unholy error and novelty should spread in God's church. But the holy pope Stephen stated clearly before the whole sacerdotal council that he would never be induced or so far give way as to consecrate these priests or deacons. As for the laymen consecrated priests or deacons by Constantine, it was promulgated that they should adopt the monastic habit and remain for the rest of their days in their own homes or wherever they chose.

22. When such sentences had been promulgated, those bishops consecrated by Constantine immediately reverted to their former grades of office in

---

64 From here to the end of c. 21 is a summary of the Council's 3rd session (14 April), with the decree on papal elections (*MGH Conc* 2.1:86–7, Duchesne, I, 483 n. 52). The restriction of candidacy to priests and deacons (Fürst, 1967, 65–8, Noble, 196), meant that aristocrats could only hope to rule the State if they passed through the church hierarchy. Other details are that the laity and military are to be excluded from the election; only the *sacerdotes*, the church's *proceres* and the whole clergy may take part. Once the pope is elected and taken to the patriarchate, all the officers and men of the army, the honourable citizens and the whole commons of Rome must come to salute him as lord of them all, and must all sign the usual decree to this effect (only at this stage do the laity have any say). No one is to enter, or be invited or brought into, Rome from the castra of Tuscia or Campania or anywhere else. No slaves of the clergy or the militia are to be at the election, nor anyone bearing arms or clubs.

65 On the origins and meaning of the cardinalate see Kuttner, 1945, and Fürst, 1967; for the cardinal bishops, n. 74.

96. STEPHEN III

accordance with the council's sentence; then elected anew by the clergy and people, the usual decree being issued, they came to the apostolic see and were consecrated by the holy pope. As for the priests and deacons, they remained as they were till this pontiff's death, and he never consecrated them. So it was laid down in this council that everything Constantine had done in the the church's sacraments and the divine cult had to repeated, apart from sacred baptism and <the blessing of> the holy chrism.

23. After[66] all these matters were promulgated, the various testimonies of the holy Fathers were straightaway brought forward in this council concerning the sacred images of our Lord God and Saviour Jesus Christ, his glorious mother our lady the ever-virgin St Mary, the blessed apostles and all the saints, prophets, martyrs and confessors. They explored them all carefully and decreed that all Christians should venerate these holy images with great respect and honour, just as all this apostolic see's preceding pontiffs and all the venerable Fathers down to the present had observed about the respect and honour towards them, and just as all of them had handed it down, for bringing devout remorse to mind. And they disallowed and anathematized that execrable synod recently held in the districts of Greece for the removal of these sacred images.[67]

24. Once everything needing promulgation had been completed in that council, the blessed pontiff gathered all the *sacerdotes*, the clergy and the whole people, and they set out for St Peter's prince of the apostles, processing barefoot with hymns and spiritual chants. And there Leontius the *scriniarius*, mounting the ambo, read out loud to the people all that had been done in the council; and three bishops, Gregory of Silva Candida, Eustratius of Albano and Theodosius of Tivoli, mounting the same ambo in that church, announced the bond of anathema, that no one at any time should presume to transgress anything at all that had been laid down in that council.

25. When this was over it happened some time after that Sergius archbishop of Ravenna departed this life.[68] Michael, that church's *scriniarius*, who

---

66 Here begins a summary of the council's 4th and final session (15 April). A letter of pope Hadrian (J 2483 = *PL* 98.1256) says that Stephen alleged in support of the cult of images the famous portrait of Christ from Edessa, and had a letter about this miraculous image, written to pope Paul by the patriarchs of Jerusalem, Alexandria and Antioch, read out to the council. The council wrote to Constantine V (by whose year the Council had failed to date its sessions) telling him to restore the images (J 2337).

67 In 754 at Hieria.

68 Surprisingly, Agnellus has none of these details. Sergius died 25 August 769, having been archbishop since at least 752 (perhaps since as early as 742). After 751 there was no longer an exarch, so Sergius was the highest personage in Ravenna. Agnellus (c. 159) described Sergius'

discharged no sacerdotal office, immediately arose and set out for Rimini, to Maurice duke of Rimini. This wicked Maurice gathered an army on the advice of Desiderius king of the Lombards, came and entered Ravenna, and by brute force elected this Michael and took him into the church of Ravenna's *episcopium*. As for archdeacon Leo who was to have been elected[69] to the rank of archbishop, they took him away to Rimini, where Maurice had him detained, closely confined in prison. Then Michael, Maurice and the judges of Ravenna sent as quickly as they could to the blessed pontiff Stephen a promise to give him gifts in plenty if he would consecrate Michael archbishop. But the blessed prelate did not give way when promised a bribe to consecrate Michael; he stated that there was no way this could be done when Michael did not have a sacerdotal office.[70] He replied to Michael in a letter and sent his envoys with it, to entreat and recommend him to desist from his unrighteous intention. But he totally refused to accept the apostolic warnings; he gave many presents[71] to Desiderius king of the Lombards, including even the sacred equipment and ornaments of his church and various other kinds of things, and by brute force he held out for over a year[72] in the *episcopium* into which he had intruded, while he stripped it and reduced it to great poverty. **26.** But Michael's evil supporters found they could never sway the holy pontiff's mental resoluteness. Then on an occasion when envoys[73] from His Excellency Charles, king of the Franks and patrician of the Romans, were present in person, the blessed prelate sent his envoys again to warn both these envoys of the Franks and all

---

authority as like that of an exarch over a wide area extending south into Tuscia (archbishop Leo claimed the same rights as Sergius, *CC* 49). That he had been consecrated at Rome caused him problems at home, especially once Pepin was an ally of the pope and was committed to handing Ravenna over to Rome; hence Sergius' alliance with Aistulf, his detention in Rome, his return to Ravenna and his 'truce' with Rome (see pp. 51, 77); on his death the old exarchate again loosened its ties with Rome. There are remarkable parallels between events at Rome and Ravenna: the actions of the aristocrats ('judges'), their relations with the clerical élites, the roles of Maurice and Michael and those of Toto and Constantine, the appeals from both cities to Desiderius, the king's responses and his failure to get any longterm advantage; see Bertolini, 1968, 2, 549-91, Brown, 1979, Noble, 104-5, 119.

69 Perhaps this means he was in fact elected and was to have been consecrated.

70 A canonically convenient pretext (all the more so, given the decree in c. 20) to avoid accepting Desiderius' nominee to the archbishopric; both sides accept that Rome should retain its prerogative of consecrating the archbishop of Ravenna.

71 He redirected his bribes!

72 Michael held the see till the last months of 770.

73 One of them was named Hucbald, as is recorded by pope Hadrian in a letter of 788-9 to Charlemagne on procedures for electing bishops of Ravenna (*CC* 85); in this he mentions Michael's intrusion and removal. Papal authority at Ravenna was too weak to put down an intruding bishop there without help.

96. STEPHEN III

the people of Ravenna. They all immediately rose up against Michael and threw him out of the *episcopium* in disgrace. They sent him here to Rome in chains, and elected that church's archdeacon, Leo. He came to this apostolic see with the *sacerdotes* and clergy of that church of Ravenna and with that city's judges and people, and was ordained and consecrated to the office of archbishop by the holy pope Stephen.

27. This blessed prelate Stephen was one who maintained church tradition, so he renewed the ancient ritual of the church for the various grades of clergy. He laid down that every Sunday the seven cardinal bishops[74] in their weekly turns, who are on duty in the Saviour's church, should celebrate the ceremonies of mass on St Peter's altar, and recite *Glory be to God on high*.[75] He provided three silver tringles, one for St Peter's, one for St Paul's and one for St Andrew's, over the grills through which one approaches the altar, and on their cornices were placed images.

28. This blessed pontiff took great care to send send his envoys and letters[76] of

---

74 The seven suburbicarian bishops, attached to the Lateran; here mentioned for the first time as 'cardinals'. Their sees were Ostia, Porto, Silva Candida (S. Rufina), Albano, and at this date perhaps Velletri, Gabii and Palestrina (or Mentana?). By the 11th century the last three were Tusculum (Frascati, itself the continuation of the older see of Labicum), Sabina and Palestrina.

75 On the privilege of chanting this, see BP Telesphorus 9:2 and Symmachus 53:11. For early 8th-century practice in this regard see *Ordo Romanus* II.9–10 (Andrieu, 2, 116); bishops could anyway use the formula within their own dioceses.

76 Charles and Carloman quarrelled in summer 769. Some of Stephen's letters survive, *CC* 44–47. *CC* 44 is a request by Stephen for peace in France, so that the two brothers can demand St Peter's rights (next note) from Desiderius. The queen-mother Bertrada then travelled towards Rome; en route she got peace between Tassilo (Desiderius' son-in-law) and Charles, and arranged that Charles marry one of Desiderius' daughters, thus creating a triple coalition against Carloman. But at Rome and to Christopher it seemed that Frankish political problems had been resolved by a Lombard alliance just when Desiderius was plotting against Rome. *CC* 45 is Stephen's letter on the appalling rumour of this marriage-alliance with the pestilential Lombards; Stephen failed to stop the marriage, which he saw was going to leave him without an ally and give Desiderius the chance to remove Christopher and Sergius: the papal State would be destroyed. *CC* 47 was sent to Carloman; clearly in fear, Stephen offered to baptize Carloman's new son Pepin. Late in 770 Bertrada arrived in Rome; she persuaded the pope that the alliance was no threat, and that Desiderius would make restitutions to St Peter; she also offered Charles' services to settle Stephen's recent problems in Ravenna and to regain a long lost patrimony in the duchy of Benevento. Charles fulfilled both of his mother's promises: count Hucbald seized Michael from Ravenna and brought him to Rome, so that Leo could be made archbishop (cf. n. 68), and Etherius restored the Beneventan patrimony (*CC* 46). So Charles, despite his marriage, stayed loyal to the pope. The troubles in France need not worry Stephen. And Charles would keep Desiderius peaceful. All was well for Stephen – but not for Christopher. By accepting the Frankish–Lombard peace, Stephen took the chance Charles and Bertrada offered him to be his

advice to His Excellency Charles king of the Franks and his brother Carloman, also king – Christopher the *primicerius* and Sergius the *secundicerius* were involved and engaged in this – about exacting from Desiderius king of the Lombards St Peter's lawful rights[77] that with hardened heart he was refusing to give back to God's holy church. This made Desiderius boil with indignation and fury against Christopher and Sergius, and he made efforts to snuff them out and destroy them.[78] To fulfil his wicked intention and so that he could get hold of them he pretended he was coming here to Rome to pray at St Peter's, while he secretly sent presents to the chamberlain Paul, surnamed Afiarta, and his other wicked followers, to persuade them to incur the apostle's wrath.[79]

---

own man and assert his influence over Christopher. To Hallenbeck, 1974b, this proves he must not be seen as weak and easily dominated. Christopher and Sergius, losing in Rome, could only choose Carloman as their ally, whose envoy Dodo then contacted them (n. 84).

77 This may merely allude to the Beneventan patrimony (last note). But Christopher was still in power and was a 'maximalist' with regard to papal territory; he may have revived the claim to the cities Desiderius had promised in 757 (Frankish pressure had caused the claim to be dropped in Paul's time). Quite apart from his interference in Rome and Ravenna, Desiderius had also in 769 sent troops into papally-claimed Istria (whether for conquest or influence), occupying lands of the church of Grado; cf. *Epp. Lang.* 19–21, *MGH EKA* 3, 711–15: John of Grado's letter to Stephen, Stephen's letter to the Istrian bishops, and his reply to John. Stephen's promises to John and the bishops never materialized.

78 Halphen, 1950, 51–7, studied the sources for these events, showing that despite its problems the LP is the best; see Bertolini, 1968, 1, 19–61. Two other sources parallel, and generally confirm, the LP. One is *CC* 48 written shortly afterwards, for which see n. 84. The other is the 16th-century 'Aventinus' who in his Annals, year 771 (text in Duchesne, I, 484 n. 58), followed both the LP and a now lost account (generally considered authentic) by a secretary of Tassilo of Bavaria, who took a favourable view of Christopher and blamed his death on a plot of Desiderius with the pope's connivance. In this version Desiderius came to Rome as if to pray, but really to capture Christopher, who collected forces from all around Rome and forced the pope and his clergy, whom he suspected of siding with the Lombards, to swear loyalty. Next day the pope escaped from the city to Desiderius. Together they conspired against Christopher, besieged Rome, and used all means to turn as many citizens as possible against him, sowing discord among them by a threat to destroy the city unless he was handed over or at least expelled from the city. Stephen sent legates to the city gates with a message for those inside not to fight but to hand over Christopher and save themselves and the city. A riot ensued in which the gates were opened and Christopher was handed over in chains to king and pontiff, blinded, his tongue cut out, and killed. This happened during Lent in St Peter's, with everyone locked out except the pope, the king's ministers, the clergy, and the abbots of St Martin's, St Stephen's and SS John and Paul's; George, abbot of SS John and Paul, clothed in the papal vestments, came to the altar as if to say mass, threw the abbot of St Stephen's and St Martin's into chains, dragged him to St John's and stole all his equipment. An innocent man had been maltreated, the house of prayer had been turned into a den of thieves; the pope's death next year was a fitting punishment for his part in it.

79 The author blurs the facts that Stephen is now with Desiderius against Christopher and Sergius and that the king wants to discuss with him what is to be done with them.

96. STEPHEN III

And this Paul agreed to it and privately tried to achieve these men's destruction. When Christopher and Sergius found this out, and also that the shameless king Desiderius was coming to Rome, they immediately gathered a crowd of people from Tuscia, Campania and the duchy of Perugia,[80] and manfully made ready to obstruct king Desiderius with the people they had gathered. They shut this city of Rome's gates and blocked them with masonry;[81] and so they were all under arms in their own city's defence.[82]

29. Meanwhile[83] king Desiderius suddenly arrived at St Peter's with his army of Lombards. He immediately sent his envoys to the pontiff to ask him to come out to meet him; which is what happened. But when he had been brought into his presence and they were together discussing St Peter's lawful rights, the blessed pontiff went back again and entered the city. Paul and his wicked followers embarked on a plot with the Lombard king; they attempted to mislead the Roman people into rising up against Christopher and Sergius and killing them. They,[84] when told of this, gathered the people and went up under arms to the Lateran to arrest those who wanted to waylay them. When they were announced in the usual way, the whole crowd of people who had come with them rushed on with their weapons into lord pope Theodore's basilica, where the pontiff Stephen was waiting. He strongly rebuked them for their presumption in entering that holy patriarchate under arms. **30.** During their discussions, next day the pontiff went out again to St Peter's[85] to speak

---

80 Cf. 93:23, 97:24.

81 *alias ex eis fabricaverunt*; the curious expression recurs at 97:21.

82 By defending Rome they hoped to force Stephen back to an anti-Lombard stance.

83 We are now in the early months, and Lent, of the year 771 (not 770, since the pope's death in 772 was 'next year', cf. n. 78 at end).

84 *CC* 48 (to Bertrada and Charlemagne) begins its narrative here (cf. Aventinus' version in n. 78). In it Stephen follows the line taken by Afiarta and the Lombards: Christopher and Sergius are the guilty parties, the pope is saved by his 'admirable son Desiderius'. He claims that Christopher and Sergius entered a plot with Dodo (Carloman's envoy) to kill him; with an army they attacked the Lateran and smashed their way in; they found the pope in Theodore's basilica, but God delivered him from them. He gives no reasons why Christopher and Sergius should have turned from protectors into enemies, or why Carloman's envoy sided with them, or why they should attack him. It seems that in reality Christopher did not want to kill the pope but to get sureties from him and remove him from the influence of Afiarta and the Lombards to whom he had given himself when he met the king. Their main goal was, as the LP says, to seize Afiarta; in this they failed, but they did extract an oath from the pope not to hand them over. From what Hadrian I (97:5, when Desiderius had finally refused to restore anything) stated Stephen told him, it is clear that Stephen at some point before his death returned to the very different view reflected in the LP.

85 *CC* 48 implies that the pope had difficulty reaching St Peter's for refuge (from Christopher), at a time when Desiderius happened to be present to discuss the church's rights. Hence

with the king. When they had come into each other's presence, Desiderius skirted the matter of St Peter's lawful rights[86] and concentrated exclusively on tricking Christopher and Sergius. For this reason he closed all the doors of St Peter's and let none of the Romans who had come out with the holy pontiff leave the church. Then[87] the bountiful pontiff sent Andrew bishop of Palestrina and Jordanes bishop of Segni to the city gate that leads out to St Peter's, where Christopher and Sergius were waiting with a crowd of people, to exhort them either to enter a monastery if they wanted to save themselves or to be sure to come to him at once at St Peter's.[88] But they, in fear of the Lombard king's evil savagery, dared not come out to him, stating they would sooner be given into the hands of their brothers and fellow-citizens the Romans than to a foreign race. **31.** So when the people with them heard from the bishops' mouths this message sent them by the pontiff Stephen, they were immediately anxious, their hearts were broken, and they all began to desert them. Now a certain duke Gratiosus, one of Sergius' relatives, pretending to be on his way home, gathered some of the Romans and they set out together to the Gate called Portuensis. Finding it shut, they dared to lift the gate itself off its hinges, and so they went out by night to the pontiff Stephen. Christopher and Sergius saw they were being greatly tricked, and first of all on the same night at the hour the bell[89] rang Sergius went down by the wall and made his way to St Peter's. The Lombard guards arrested him on the steps of St Peter's and took him to their king. Christopher, his father, followed him, and they were brought into

---

Duchesne thought the king's presence might really have had nothing to do with the quarrel between the pope and Christopher.

86 *CC* 48 claims that Desiderius gave the pope all he wanted. In fact Stephen got nothing from Desiderius except the Beneventan patrimony (n. 77), but that the king made further promises seems likely from 97:5, where Hadrian relates how Stephen told him that Desiderius failed to fulfil them.

87 Stephen states that he sent his *sacerdotes* to Christopher and Sergius, telling them to repent and come to him at St Peter's; but with Dodo they immediately formed up their army and closed the city gates against him. But the people deserted them; many came to the pope, either over the walls or by opening one of the gates. Christopher and Sergius were forced to come to him unwillingly (in the LP, willingly, but they had little choice with no remaining supporters). The people all wanted their deaths; Stephen blocked this, and arranged to have them taken by night into Rome so they would not be seen and killed. It was none of his doing – he calls God to witness – that they were then mutilated (he does not mention Christopher's death).

88 Stephen wanted to avoid a bloodbath, but equally wanted to end the influence of Christopher and Sergius. Clearly they came to realize that, with the gradual loss of their supporters to Stephen and Desiderius, their cause was becoming hopeless.

89 In Lent the bell (that of St Peter's must be meant, cf. 94:47 and n. 107) would ring for nocturns or vigils at about midnight.

the pontiff's presence. In his desire that they survive safe, he ordered them to be made monks.

After this the blessed pontiff bade king Desiderius farewell and entered Rome, leaving Christopher and Sergius in St Peter's and intending them to be brought safe inside Rome in the quiet of the night, to prevent their enemies waylaying them. **32.** But when evening was coming on, Paul the chamberlain and his other wicked accomplices straightaway gathered a crowd of people, came to the Lombard king Desiderius, and with him embarked on an unholy plot: they removed Christopher and Sergius from St Peter's, went with many of the Lombards to the city gate, and there they gouged out their eyes.[90] And so Christopher was taken to St Agatha's monastery,[91] where after three days his life came to an end from the pain of having his eyes gouged out; while Sergius was brought to the Clivus Scauri monastery and afterwards taken to a cell in the Lateran, where he remained till the pontiff Stephen was passing away.[92]

33. All these evils resulted from the iniquitous instigations of that Desiderius king of the Lombards. The holy pontiff performed one December ordination, 5 priests, 4 deacons; for various places <*16*> bishops. He was buried at St Peter's. The bishopric was vacant 9 days.

---

90 Despite the pope's protestations of innocence (n. 87), it was clearly his present counsellors, Afiarta and his gang, who perpetrated this. Christopher and his party had not been guiltless earlier, but that had not stopped Stephen accepting the papacy from them, and even if he was not directly implicated in this attack, one may ask whether he did enough to prevent it and why he did not then break with Afiarta. Afiarta's only loyalty was to his own career: if he did not want to be pope, he wanted to be the power behind the throne: which till Stephen's death he was (Hallenbeck, 1974a).

91 Uncertain which; Ferrari, 22, opts for S. Agatha de Subura (which he identifies as that founded by Gregory II, 91:10); Cecchelli prefers S. Agatha in caput Africae.

92 *transitum*; but it emerges from the next life (97:10–11) that Sergius was taken from the prison and killed 8 days before Stephen actually died.

97. HADRIAN I (772-795)

This life is the longest in the LP so far. Duchesne (I, CCXXXIV–CCXLIII) discussed its composition and importance at length; all later work on the problems connected with it is indebted to him. The life falls into two unequal parts: the division is at the end of c. 44.

The first part is a historical narrative similar to those in lives 93, 94 and 96, and gives details of events from 772 to 774, the fullest account we possess of this crucial turning point in Italian history. Starting with Hadrian's early career and election, it covers the history of the next 2 years and 4 months down to the end of the Lombard kingdom. It is contemporary historical writing and is almost certainly by the author who compiled life 96. He deals at length with the aftermath of Stephen III's death, when Afiarta, acting in part as agent for Desiderius, hoped to maintain control. Even before his ordination Hadrian recalled those exiled by Afiarta; with no great subtlety he removed him by sending him on an embassy to Desiderius and having him arrested at Ravenna (the author exonerates Hadrian from guilt in his execution). It is clear that Desiderius hoped to restore his influence at Rome, and also to use Hadrian as an instrument for Lombard influence over the Franks: the pope was supposed to anoint Carloman's sons as kings to replace their uncle, Charles, who had been sole king of the Franks since Carloman's death in December 771. Hadrian used delaying tactics and called on the Franks to intervene. Desiderius refused a compromise; Charles invaded Italy and after a long siege he captured Pavia and removed the Lombard king. It is a great pity that the author did not continue his work beyond 774. He is not faultless (in c. 5 he forgets he is putting a speech into Hadrian's mouth and refers to Desiderius as 'the same' because the text, but not the speaker, has mentioned him earlier!); but that is a small complaint against the author of excellent material.

An estimate of the historical value of this narrative depends in part on the date of composition: if it was compiled after Hadrian's death in 795 we would expect mistakes, intentional or otherwise, to creep in. But the case for arguing that the account is nearly contemporary with the events is strong. We shall see that the second part of the life was composed in stages before the pope's death, so there is no reason why composition of the first part should have been delayed to 795; indeed, it is reasonable to suppose it was written before any of the second part, some of which was written by 780. What is more, the account has a thoroughly contemporary feel to it. Who after 795 would have bothered about these details of distant events, when the Lombard kingdom was just a fading memory? If Charles' visit to Rome in 774 was worthy of record over 20 years later, why not his two later visits? Why is there not the slightest sign of changes introduced in the light of later events? And why did the historical section stop in 774? The only possible answer is that the account was drawn up in the 770s and then allowed to stand unchanged by later compilers in a way typical of most of those who continued the LP.

But is this conclusion sustainable historically? With the account of the fall of the Lombard kingdom there is no problem.[1] It is the events connected with Charles' visit to Rome at Easter 774 that cause qualms. Two difficulties arise from the account in the LP (Duchesne, I, CCXXXVII ff). Firstly, it is asserted that the territories promised in 774 coincided with those promised by Pepin to Stephen II at Quierzy. Is it not incredible that this unfulfilled promise of huge areas, some three-quarters of Italy, was made in 754? Secondly, while no doubt some kind of promise was written down in 774 and Charles and the pope each had copies, is it credible that the version in the LP is a genuine contemporary record of such a promise, given that it does not correspond with what Charles actually did?

(1) As to the Donation of Quierzy in 754: can we believe that Pepin had promised so much to Stephen II? What the LP actually says is that in 774 Charles had that Donation read to him, that he entirely agreed with it, that he had another promise drawn up *ad instar anterioris*, in which he conceded the 'same cities and territories', and that he undertook to hand these over to the pope *per designatum confinium*, as shown contained in that donation. Clearly there is some leeway in choosing a precise interpretation of this text and in estimating its accuracy. Perhaps the writer has compared the two texts badly, perhaps he has exaggerated the coincidence of the two donations. But assuming he intends to say that they were the same, is he right? Let us consider the areas of Italy involved.

The boundary of the territory promised in 774, and therefore in 754, is described as a line from Luni to Monsélice. This defines its northern limit, cutting across the southern part of the Lombard kingdom. South and east of the line we are merely told that Venetia, Istria, the exarchate as it once was (before Liutprand's conquests) and the duchies of Spoleto and Benevento are included (as also is Corsica). Excluded is any territory on the coast or inland north and west of Luni, where Rome possessed the patrimony of the Cottian Alps (see 91:4 and n. 16); in so far as anyone in the 8th century could distinguish clearly between territorial control and property ownership, this exclusion of an area where the church had property implies that the promise was not just to return patrimonies.[2] Also excluded from the donation seem to be the

---

1 Mohr, 1955, 72–86, condemned the first part of Hadrian's life in the interests of his own theory that Hadrian changed sides from a 'Lombard' to a 'Frankish' party; Löwe, 1956, 493–8, vindicated the LP account.

2 Neither Pepin nor Charles was simply regranting Roman patrimonies lost to the Lombards since 569 (so Duchesne, I, CCXXXVIII, against Sickel, 1883, 36); though it is true that in the 7th century all the current Roman patrimonies in Italy were in imperial territory, and that after 774 no claim was ever made for patrimonies in the Lombard kingdom, if these had ever existed.

imperial enclaves in southern Italy, along with Sicily and Sardinia. Is a promise on this scale credible in 754?

With the former exarchate there is no real problem: Pepin would shortly refuse to hand it over to the emperor, on the grounds that he had regained it from the Lombards for the benefit of St Peter.

The province of Venetia–Istria was so far from the empire, once this had lost the exarchate, that it was in a vacuum. As it bordered the exarchate it was easy to treat it in the same way.[3]

For the duchies of Spoleto and Benevento the claim in the LP is at least plausible. Gregory III had already wanted to detach them from the Lombard kingdom; hence his treaties with their dukes (92:14 and n. 46), and his dangerous policy of helping them in their revolt against king Liutprand in 739. Zacharias had abandoned this policy, but after Pepin's two interventions in Italy, those duchies would again show separatist tendencies from the Lombard kingdom.

For the part of the Lombard kingdom south of the Luni–Monsélice line, the problem is greater but not insuperable. There is no trace of separatism. If Pepin promised this area to the pope, his motive must have been to increase papal territory. The Luni–Monsélice line itself may have been a convenient traditional demarcation (cf. 97: n. 63).

Duchesne argued that our knowledge from other sources of what was agreed at Quierzy between Pepin and Stephen II is too thin to entitle us to reject our author's account out of hand. He is likely to have been present in St Peter's on 6 April 774 and to have heard Pepin's donation read out; he could check its text in the archives. His testimony must be taken seriously, even as authoritative. True, there was a great difference between what had been carried out after Pepin's expeditions of 754 and 756 and what was again promised in 774, but it does not follow that what had then been done matched all that had been promised. While Pepin's envoys were calling on Aistulf to hand over the exarchate and the Pentapolis, Pepin must have thought what would happen if Aistulf refused: war, and the likelihood of complete victory, would leave the Lombard kingdom at his disposal. Why should he not have agreed to share Italy with the pope, much as Charles seems to have thought of doing in 774? True, Stephen II's letters do not mention it, but none survives dating between the donation of Quierzy and the Treaty of Pavia. In this treaty Pepin granted what he thought appropriate by that time, and Stephen had to accept it. After that, the donation of Quierzy had no real meaning, though no doubt a copy was kept in Rome. But in 774 the situation in Italy, with Desiderius under attack as Aistulf had once been, was

---

3 A letter of Stephen III to John bishop of Grado (*MGH EKA* 1, 715) suggests it was mentioned in the treaties of 754 and 756. Alone of the territories mentioned in 754 (and 774), Venetia–Istria is ignored subsequently. Despite papal interest in the area since the 720s, Hadrian makes no complaints. Istria was strategically too important for Charles to lose it to the papacy, which could probably not have controlled it anyway. As for Venice, neither the Lombards nor the Franks ever fully controlled it, and Charles, who would have regarded its strategic significance as not much less than that of Istria, was in no position to give it away.

close to returning to what it had been in 754, and its relevance as propaganda was seen; no surprise that the text was shown to Charles. Our compiler, it is true, would have found verification much easier for the donation of 774 than for that of Quierzy. But there was in fact less reason to lie about the earlier document. The value of the 774 document was that it had Charles' signature: it gained no extra weight from its conformity (or lack of it) with the donation of Quierzy. Indeed the opposite: it was risky to compare it with a donation that had remained a dead letter.

Historical probabilities, the normal veracity of the papal biographers, their editorial habits and procedures, the history of the text and the antiquity of the MSS, all impel acceptance of what the text asserts. Duchesne admitted the unsubstantiated nature of his arguments, but claimed it was enough to show that a contemporary and well-placed witness could report the facts accurately. The LP's compilers had one means of concealing what they found awkward: silence. Mendacity in the interest of a cause believed just can nowhere be traced in the LP. Even if it was not far from the Lateran that the Donation of Constantine was forged at about this time, there is no proof that the LP's compilers would have approved of this.

Duchesne's proof that the LP's account was both authentic and accurate was accepted by many writers (cited in Noble, 84 nn. 97–101), despite the remaining difficulty of explaining why the promise of Quierzy was never fulfilled and why the papacy never complained. There were sceptics. Some argued that while at Quierzy Pepin did perhaps formalize the promises he had given at Ponthion, no accurate record of the details was preserved; others, that there was a document, but the version produced in 774 was forged or at least interpolated, particularly as regards the detail of the Luni–Monsélice line (but is it credible that in 774 Charlemagne confirmed a forged copy of a document which had been signed in his own presence in 754?). Others accepted the document as given but explained it away as merely a record Lombard and papal spheres of influence (there is no evidence for such a theory). Still others suggested that Pepin merely promised to restore papal patrimonies south of the Luni–Monsélice line (but that is not what the text *says*).

It was Kehr who solved the difficulty:[4] the Quierzy document was a 'contingent treaty'. An invasion of Italy by Pepin would obviously mean the restoration of places like Céccano to the Roman duchy. But if the invasion resulted in the destruction of the Lombard kingdom, its territory would be divided along the Luni–Monsélice line, so that Pepin would get the northern heartlands of the kingdom (or Aistulf himself might keep these), while Stephen would get Tuscia and the southern duchies. The pope would have Lombard Tuscia to prevent attacks on Roman Tuscia; he would have Spoleto and Benevento, an extension of the existing policy of alliances with them, which would both weaken the Lombard kingdom and provide a buffer against the Byzantine south; as for Ravenna, Istria and Venice, these had long been areas of papal interest though hardly of control, but a papal claim on them was not inconsistent with

---

4 Kehr, 1893, 436ff. Duchesne himself, 1908, 96 n. 1, agreed with his explanation, and it has since found widespread support; cf. Noble, 85–6.

earlier policy. In other words, the treaty was a 'maximum' scheme: any lesser arrangements might have been acceptable, but it shows the papacy's maximum plan for the territory of its State. But it was hypothetical: the treaty was purely 'contingent'. In fact, the First Peace of Pavia which followed the invasion did not dissolve the Lombard kingdom, and in consequence the Quierzy document necessarily stayed unfulfilled.

(2) If so much could be promised to Stephen II in 754, there is little difficulty in accepting that the same areas were envisaged in 774. In the territories, separatist tendencies had increased and were apparent even in Lombard Tuscia (c. 33). In Spoleto and Benevento, separatism had increased during the last twenty years (for events there on Aistulf's death see 94:48ff. and n. 110). And the moment Charles entered Italy, Spoletans rushed to Rome to be incorporated in the papal state, and no doubt Beneventans would have done the same given the chance; certainly Rome would later treat Benevento and Spoleto analogously. The promise of 774, therefore, is plausible. Pavia was about to fall; the 'contingency' that had not come to pass in 754 would now occur. Hadrian will have made the maximum demands on Charles, rather than fall back on the treaties of Pavia or Desiderius' promises to Stephen II or Stephen III. It may have merely been an opening gambit; he may have been surprised that Charles agreed. Is it credible that Charles did agree? He may not have thought ahead; or he may have wished not to offend Hadrian, at whose request he had come to Italy, while the political and military future was unclear (Noble, 144).

What Charles actually did before returning to France was to take for himself the title 'Charles by the grace of God king of the Franks and Lombards', install a provisional government at Pavia, and hand over to Hadrian Bologna and Imola, two cities detached from the Lombard kingdom (though in fact, like all the cities of Emilia previously under papal control, they were now held by Leo, archbishop of Ravenna). Nothing more. He did not abandon the sovereignty he now had. Hadrian, too, claimed and exercised sovereignty.[5] But whatever his territorial claims, for now he had to be content with the return of only what Desiderius had seized.

Hadrian certainly never got the areas supposedly promised in 774. But it is important that his correspondence over the next years reveals his dissatisfaction and his pressure on Charles to concede more. The details are worth sketching, if only to provide some of the history of the expansion of papal territory that the LP fails to give.

In his first letter to Charles after his departure, Hadrian complained about Leo of Ravenna and also about the unfulfilled promises (CC 49). Early in 775 a letter from the king told Hadrian that he would arrive in October to fulfil all his promises; in

---

5 At some time between 772 and 781 Hadrian began dating documents by his own years rather than those of the emperors; for his exercise of the right to strike coins see the discussion in Noble, 290 n. 43 (Hadrian's are the first certain papal coins; earlier 'coins' back to the time of Gregory III are probably merely pilgrim tokens). In places the papal claim was accepted: at Spoleto, duke Hildeprand dated documents by the years of Hadrian's pontificate. For Hadrian acting as head of state, see 97: nn. 20, 22, 25, 35; and Noble, 132–4, 289–90.

97. HADRIAN I

reply, Hadrian expressed his confidence this would happen, so well had his envoys been received at Charles' court (*CC* 51). In another letter that year Hadrian dwelt on his high hopes (*CC* 53) though he did not refer to a visit by Charles. The matter was apparently to be dealt with by envoys; in a letter of 27 October 775 (*CC* 54) Hadrian was concerned that the envoys had not arrived. In November he sent to the government at Pavia and was told the envoys could not come to Rome immediately; this worried Hadrian, and he sent Andrew bishop of Palestrina and Pardus *hegumenus* of St Saba to Charles to encourage him to fulfil his own and his father's promises; he still had confidence in him (*CC* 55; in each of letters 53–55 the conduct of Leo is still a cause of complaint). The envoys at last set out and reached Perugia where they were met by Hadrian's envoys who were to bring them to Rome, but the Franks made their way to Spoleto claiming they had to confer with Hildeprand. Hadrian, knowing they intended to go on to Benevento, asked that they should at least do so by way of Rome; but the envoys went straight to Benevento. Hadrian wrote (*CC* 56) to remind Charles of his undertakings 18 months earlier, particularly about the possession of Spoleto which was now disputed: duke Hildeprand had accepted Charles as his sovereign by January 776. The envoys returned from Benevento to Spoleto and tried to get an agreement between Hildeprand and Hadrian. At their request the pope sent hostages to Spoleto with a safe-conduct for the duke to come to Rome. But when the papal envoys reached Spoleto they found Hildeprand plotting with the dukes of Benevento, Chiusi and Friuli (*CC* 57). By presenting this to Charles as a revolt, the pope seems to identify his own interests with those of Charles – his own enemies are the king's enemies; Spoleto was in revolt against them both: Charles, he insisted, was needed in Italy (*CC* 51–2, 58).

Charles arrived, and put down the revolt of duke Hrodgaud of Friuli. Nothing more is heard of the plot by the other dukes.[6] In the summer of 776 Charles had to leave northern Italy and return north to deal with a revolt. But it was from this time that he began to introduce Frankish personnel and government into Italy. Hadrian came to realize he was not going to get Spoleto or Benevento; he dropped the claim, but continued to request his patrimonies there.

No further papal letters to the king survive until May 778, and by that stage a change of tone on Hadrian's part can be detected. It seems that by early 778 Charles had promised two papal envoys he would spend Easter in Rome and have his recently born son Pepin baptized there. Instead he led an expedition to Spain. In May Hadrian wrote to insist on the fulfilment of the promises of 774 (*CC* 60), for the first time alluding to Constantine's donation to the Roman church by which 'it had been raised and exalted to receive power in the West':[7] Charles should be a new Constantine.

---

6 Duchesne thought they were too disconcerted by the death of Constantine V, on whose support they had relied, to continue their schemes.

7 Duchesne argued that this was no mere reference to the *Gesta Silvestri* or the LP life of Silvester, but to the famous Donation of Constantine. There now seems to be some agreement that this forgery was produced in the latter half of the 8th century in the context of the papal

But Hadrian made more plausible demands: he sent Charles charters by which emperors, patricians, etc. had given St Peter gifts in Tuscia, the duchies of Spoleto and Benevento, Corsica and the Sabine patrimony, complained that the Lombards had seized these, and demanded them back. Hadrian was using arguments based on Charles' own promises, pre-Lombard title-deeds (so confusing sovereignty and property rights) and, perhaps, on the Donation of Constantine. The use of such arguments shows that Hadrian had given up expecting the promise of 774 to be fulfilled; and a letter of May 778 (*CC* 61) shows he now realized he would have to cope on his own in Italy: he tells Charles that if the king will not aid him against Benevento, he will have to use the Roman army himself. Benevento and the Greeks of Naples were a problem (they threatened Hadrian's control of Roman Campania), and until 780 he continued to ask for Charles' help.

In 781 Charles made his son Pepin king of Italy. Charles spent Easter with Hadrian in Rome, and they began to work out a land settlement which was to be very different from what was envisaged in the promises of 754 and 774; Hadrian got much less than his maximum demands, but he got more than he had ever had before, and above all he gained freedom and independence of action. The details have to be extracted from the *Ludowicianum*, the donation of Charles's son Louis to pope Paschal I in 817, on which see the introduction to life 99. Clauses 1 to 7 (as numbered in the summary there) seem to represent Charles' grant in 781. Hadrian was granted Rome and the parts of Tuscia and Campania in the Roman duchy (clauses 1–3; Noble, 160–161). To Roman Tuscia was added (clause 7) a northward and coastal extension into the area the Lombards had held and which had never been in the Roman duchy; Hadrian had no historic right to this area, which was now detached from the Lombard kingdom for Hadrian's benefit.[8] The background in Campania was that Charles had arranged a marriage alliance between his daughter and the emperor Constantine VI; the effect of this was to neutralize duke Arichis of Benevento, who had to make peace with the Franks and Greeks. Charles could safely grant Campania to Hadrian, not just its patrimonies but its sovereignty, though within defined territorial limits (as it had existed since the penetration of the Liri valley by duke Gisulf II of Benevento in 702). The Ravenna exarchate[9]

State's liberation from the empire and that it was probably written by a Roman cleric at the Lateran; but there is no evidence (unless *CC* 60 be such) for its use at the time for political ends. It could not serve the purpose of legitimizing papal rule in the eyes of Franks, Byzantines or Romans themselves. The Franks did not need it, the Byzantines would not have believed it, and the Lateran would hardly try to fool itself. Perhaps the text was a jeu d'esprit, whose author understood the reality and believed in papal rule (see Noble, 134–7; text: *Constitutum Constantini*, ed. H. Fuhrmann, *MGH Fontes iuris germanici antiqui*, 1968; translation Mark Edwards, *Constantine and Christendom* [TTH 39, 2003], 92–115 with his comments at xl–xlvi).

8 Cf. *CC* 80. Others, with Duchesne, think that this clause represents part of Charles' grant in 787; the effectiveness of Hadrian's control of this area before 787 may well be doubted.

9 Archbishop Leo had died 14 February 777. What Rome was given was the exarchate in its restricted sense of Ravenna and its environs, not the whole areas of central and north-

and the Pentapolis[10] were also granted (clauses 4–5). From 778 to 781 the only area that Hadrian had expressed concern about was the Sabine patrimonies.[11] In 781 (clause 6) he was given the whole Sabine territory (all of what had once been Roman Sabina) except for lands within it held by Farfa[12]. This grant was at the expense of the duchy of Spoleto, and its acceptance is a recognition by Hadrian that he would not get the rest of that duchy. The *Ludowicianum* calls the area given by Charles to St Peter both a *territorium* and a *patrimonium*. Conditions in the area were such that whatever concepts then existed of property and sovereignty were liable to glide into each other, or a claim to the latter might be based on the former. Hadrian's claim was based on pre-Lombard title-deeds; what he received was sovereignty. The royal envoys, the abbots Etherius and Magenarius, fixed the boundary of Sabina with Rieti. After such a time the problems of ownership would have been huge: there was opposition from occupants of the land, which caused the abbots much trouble. Hadrian may also have gained Corsica at this time.[13]

Charles' third Roman visit, in 787, produced a further expansion of papal territory. Just as he had in 781 given Hadrian part of the duchy of Tuscia, so now in the south he gave him part of the duchy of Benevento, down to and including Capua

---

eastern Italy which had once been Byzantine (on this distinction, Noble, 181–2). Noble, 171–2, comments that from 783 Hadrian had trouble controlling the exarchate, and holds that the result was what he calls 'a double dyarchy', a sharing of rule between pope and king, with a sharing of authority between pope and archbishop.

10 Along with Bologna, Imola and the southern Pentapolitan towns of Ancona, Osimo and Numana, i. e. all the 'remaining cities' promised by Desiderius.

11 *CC* 68–72; on the Sabine patrimonies see 93:9 and n. 27; Noble, 154–7; they were already papal property, and had been confirmed as such by Desiderius.

12 Noble, 159. It is highly likely that Farfa was already involved, even though it is not mentioned in the letters from Hadrian to Charles about Sabina: there would later be boundary disputes between its abbots and the popes.

13 Corsica's history is obscure. In the 6th century it had belonged to the exarchate of Carthage. When the rest of that exarchate was lost to the Arabs it presumably came under the control of the patrician of Sicily. The Roman church had had valuable estates there and as late as 708 pope Sisinnius had consecrated bishop for it (BP 89:2), since it was in Roman suburbicarian territory. It is uncertain if it ever belonged to the Lombards; if it did, it is easier to see how Charles would be in a position to dispose of it. Hadrian's claim in *CC* 60 had been achieved by the time of Leo III who in 808 committed Corsica to Charlemagne's protection in the face of muslim attacks (Leo III, *Epp.* X, 1, *MGH EKA* 3, 88). Hahn, 1975, 78–82, concluded from the documents that the papal claim to it did go back to 754, when, as the LP says, it was named in the Quierzy donation. Its inclusion in the *Ludowicianum* of 817 is likely to reflect Charles' concession of it to Rome in 781; perhaps Charles recognized the rectors of the patrimony as governors of the island's population and it thus passed under church control (Noble, 86, 172–4). The clause of the *Ludowicianum* mentions also Sicily and Sardinia; the former was Byzantine, the latter by 754 was under Arab control. The 817 text is probably interpolated: the *Ottonianum* of 962 includes Sicily 'if God grants it', and omits Sardinia; the original 817 text may have said this of one or both islands.

(clause 9), parts of Campania which had not been granted in 781. The background was that in the presence of Greek envoys at Capua Charles had broken his marriage alliance with Byzantium. Arichis of Benevento was thus no longer hemmed in by a Frankish–Greek alliance; he might himself join forces with the Greeks and threaten Charles; and such a threat might not be restricted to Italy, as Arichis had a marriage alliance with the duke of Bavaria (both were sons-in-law of Desiderius). But Charles' own presence at Capua prompted an offer by Arichis to back down. Campania could now resume the borders it had had before 702 with the reinclusion of the cities in the Liri valley, and could be granted to Hadrian. Clause 10 is a grant of the patrimonies in Benevento, Salerno, lower and upper Calabria, Naples and any other patrimonies 'under Frankish control'; the areas named after Benevento had been taken by the emperor Leo III, and were not under Frankish control in 787 (or at the time of the *Ludowicianum* of 817); perhaps the original documents contained a 'conditional clause'. But it seems from Hadrian's letter (*CC* App. 1) that the grant even of an enlarged Campania had no effect; all Hadrian got was the bishoprics, monasteries, *curtes publicae*, and the keys of cities. He could not take over the Lombard cities of Sora, Arce, Arpino and Aquino, while Teano and Capua were by the 9th century in the duchy of Benevento. What happened was that the Greek envoys, incensed at Charles' behaviour, offered Arichis the title of patrician and induced him not to hand over anything to Hadrian (*CC* 89–80). Arichis himself died (26 August 787), but his widow, Desiderius' daughter Adelpurga, continued his policies; and the Greeks sent her brother Adalgis back to Italy with an army, and sent another army against Ravenna. Charles' response was to send Arichis' son Grimoald, whom he had been holding hostage, to rule Benevento. Grimoald defeated the Greeks, leaving both the Romans and the Franks with little to fear from the east. But fulfilment of the 787 agreement now depended on Grimoald remaining loyal. Instead, he broke away from Charles and, though he had no power to cause real trouble, the Franks never regained (and so the papacy never received) Benevento, let alone the southern Italian patrimonies.

Clause 11 concedes the tribute of the duchies of Tuscia and Spoleto; this extended the grant of part of Tuscia in 781 but, at the same time as the revenue was assigned to him, Hadrian conceded the king's authority in these duchies. This was not what Hadrian had expected in his letters from 774 to 776 or even in May 778; he now renounced sovereignty there, while at the same time Charles compensated him in terms of revenue.

As a result of 787 Hadrian gained more than he had in 774 and 781, even though the southern part of the agreement (the cities in the Liri valley) could not be implemented. At the same time he knew that Charles would not desert him; and he had peace with the Greeks. In some 70 years control of the duchy of Rome, attenuated by Lombard invasions in the 7th and very early 8th centuries, had been taken over *de facto* from the Byzantines even before the Franks were on the scene; then, thanks to Frankish help, it had escaped the Lombard threat to its existence in the 750s and the

770s, and had gained the duchy of Perugia; the Franks had helped to extend papal territory, especially through Charles' grant in 781 and 787 of territory to the south and east once lost to the Lombards, and with new territories to the north which had never been under papal control. This was a large extension of the duchy of Rome, but it fell far short of the maximum schemes as seen in the promises of 754 and 774.

Why did Charles not fulfil his promise of 774? At Easter Desiderius still held out in Pavia and Charles was not yet master of Italy; his promise need not have been insincere. If the promise at Quierzy had been 'contingent', so too was the promise made in Rome. There is no reason to suppose that he already intended to proclaim himself king of the Lombards and maintain the kingdom intact, thereby frustrating the promise. When he made that decision, he was, technically, as much in the clear as Pepin had been in not fulfilling the promise of 754. Yet a man like Charles, who did not take an oath lightly, may not have felt quite easy in conscience.

The events of 774–8 explain why he apparently went back on his word. His policy need not have been cynical. Once he took the kingdom he was less inclined, no doubt, to give away what was now his. Why destroy a political set-up that had endured 200 years? Events in Emilia, Spoleto and Benevento showed that places with separatist tendencies, which were willing to appeal to the pope against the king, had no enthusiasm to be ruled by Rome. The main purpose of his Italian wars had been to guarantee papal freedom from the Lombards. If the Roman state were given large new territories at the Lombard kingdom's expense, it would have to defend itself without calling on the Frankish king. Charles may have realized that the pope could not control territory across the Apennines. Whereas, with Charles as king of the Lombards, Rome had nothing to fear; St Peter would receive all his revenues and ought to be content. It was enough for Peter's successors to have any state, small or large, provided their independence and security were assured. Torn between his oath and his political judgment, Charles delayed: he promised he would fulfil his promise when he returned to Italy. By 781 he was much better informed about Italy and could decide where his duty lay. He realized he could not support Hadrian's maximum claims.

Hadrian's point of view changed as the years passed. At first he was puzzled. Charles, by taking his Lombard royal title, had frustrated the promise, but his arrangements before leaving for France might have been temporary. Yet he was not inactive in Italy; his envoys were there, and he was expected to return at any time; indeed he came to northern Italy in 776. As the years passed, Hadrian was more disposed to modify his claims. After 778 he stopped referring in vague terms to large claims, and mentioned specific lands instead. In *CC* 64 he even seems to regard Spoleto and Benevento as under joint sovereignty.

Why was it that after 778 and 781 Hadrian limited himself to smaller claims? Experience will have taught him that it would not be easy to achieve them, or, if achieved, to maintain them: it was little use to claim the exarchate if it were to fall into the hands of the archbishop of Ravenna. One purpose in making territorial claims (protection from a hostile king) had ceased to exist. It was wiser to limit his claims and be satisfied with the duchy of Spoleto, Campania and Lombard Tuscia, which were easier to keep under control. Northwards, the grant of the Maremma up to Populonia and the latitude of Elba, gave the pope the chance to maintain control of Corsica. Southwards, the grant of Campania with Capua and the road to it might make it possible eventually to take Gaeta and Naples from the empire, along with the Campanian patrimonies which the Roman church had vainly claimed since Stephen II's time. So he came round to the king's point of view, and the promise of 774 was quietly forgotten. As some kind of compensation the pope was given the above-named territories and also, as some kind of recognition of his rights and theoretical authority, the rents that Tuscia and the duchy of Spoleto had formerly paid to the Lombard king.

Hence, for Duchesne, the explanation why there is no reference to the donation of 774 in the letters of Hadrian and Leo III or even in the *Ludowicianum* of 817. Hence too why, although the text of the *Ludowicianum* survived long enough to come down to us (albeit with alterations of detail), we would have known nothing of the promise of 774 had it not been for the abridgment of it in the LP.

So the promise of 774 recorded in the LP need not be discarded as historically impossible. Hadrian's biographer was a contemporary, and likely to have adequate knowledge; he refers to a document of which copies existed in both the papal and royal archives, and of which an authentic copy was fixed to the confessio of St Peter for anyone to read. To suppose he would falsify it is incredible.

There may have been disappointment at Rome that the promise of 774 was not to be fulfilled. Could this explain the sharp change of policy by the compilers of the LP, who, after a remarkably brief account of the actual fall of Pavia, surprisingly fail to gloat over the fate of Desiderius, and then abandon political history entirely, thus saying nothing about the actual territorial settlement? Classen (1965, I, at p. 549) saw in this silence a disappointment at what Charles had done. Noble (141) considers that the treatment of the fall of Pavia and the silence on later events are best explained if the author was writing at the stage events had reached by about 778. There may be truth in these ideas; but there is a danger of forgetting the nature of the LP. Whatever be said of the brevity of the chapter on the fall of Pavia, the subsequent silence on political affairs need indicate no more than the interest and outlook of a different writer.

The interests displayed in the second part of the life are totally different. From c. 45 on, the contents seem to be an unsystematic mixture of donations and restorations. Except for c. 88 on the 2nd Council of Nicaea and c. 97 on the pope's death, the whole of the text is devoted to such material, which substitutes for history during the next 21 years. That Hadrian was able to devote such activity to churches, aqueducts, the city walls, the Tiber bank, domuscultae and schemes for poor relief, was only possible in the peaceful conditions that Charles' overlordship ensured (see

97. HADRIAN I

Krautheimer, 1980, 109–117). But the text shows no consciousness of this background. Theoretically the author of the first part of the life might have changed his policy. But it is certain that the life was compiled in stages and virtually certain that these stages were the work of more than one compiler.

The repetition at intervals of the same churches or other buildings (see the index under, for instance, St Paul's, St Mary Major and St Laurence) and the few dates that are given or can be inferred[14] suggest that like the preceding historical narrative, this part is arranged chronologically. The authors were satisfied to excerpt or summarize the registers of the *vestiarium* (an easy way out if they worked there), a method used also in the latter part of lives 92 and 95; and the text follows the chronological order of these sources. In places there seems an unawareness of future events;[15] compilation in sections, though not necessarily one per year, seems certain (in life 98 this method will become even more blatant). The contemporaneity of the compilers is confirmed by the absence of any criticism of the regime and by the complimentary language used of the *vestiarius* Januarius, no doubt the current compiler's superior.

Some of the sections can be delimited by internally logical sequences. Duchesne identified a section running from c. 45 to 56, a second from c. 57 to 62; he regarded the arrangement of the next part as less clear, though the placing of c. 65, dealing with the same aqueduct as in c. 62, shows we are in a fresh section; and another clearly begins at c. 83. Geertman identifies shorter sections:

(1) 45 to 51: the writer begins by listing work on the major basilicas and 11 other churches, covering restorations and donations contemporaneous with the preceding history down to August 774.

(2) 52 to 59 cover two indiction years, September 774 to August 776; the approach differs from that in the previous section; work on churches is summarized and the text then deals with work of other kinds: on the city walls, a monastery, domuscultae, and the Lateran; then 57–59 deal with St Peter's and the aqueduct supplying it.

(3) 60 to 62 treat September 777 to August 778; 60 lists St Paul's, three other named churches, the 22 *tituli* (not listed); then in 61 (after a misplaced sentence on St Peter's), 'similarly' the 16 deaconries (also not listed), then (after a misplaced sentence on the Aqueduct Iovia), 'similarly' more provision for churches; and finally in 62, work on the Aqueduct Claudia. The posited misplacings in 61 may be early interpolations such as are revealed by MSS evidence in lives 92, 93, 94, and 95; it is pure chance that no MSS of this life lack these interpolations. In bringing the text

---

14 cc. 59 and 61 record aqueducts repaired 20 years after they were damaged, presumably in 756; in c. 64 repairs to the roof of St Peter's correspond to details recorded in a letter dated 779 or 780; in c. 88 occurs the 2nd Council of Nicaea, 787; and the flood of the Tiber in cc. 94–95 is explicitly dated December 791.

15 cc. 54–55 give the number of domuscultae founded by Hadrian as four; but two more were founded later, cc. 63, 77; from the dates given above it is likely that four were founded before 776, one between 776 and 780, and one between 780 and 787. Similarly c. 61 knows of 16 deaconries, though two others were founded later, c. 81.

up to date, a compiler might well add marginal notes against earlier parts of the text, which would be incorporated in subsequent copies, not necessarily at the intended places. But interpolations cannot account for the major divisions, which must go back to the original compiler.

(4–18) Geertman identifies 15 further sections, beginning at the points where headings are provided in this translation. His scheme provides a chronologically coherent division of the mass of material contained in this part of the life. It is possible to quibble at some of the details, but the principle is sound. Each section covers a fiscal year except for 45–51 and 52–59 which each cover two years (should there not be a division at 57 as Duchesne wanted?). The few stated or inferable dates mentioned above fit into the scheme. No material is given from September 792 to the pope's death late in 795, but this comes in the next life (for the reasons, see the introduction thereto).

Continuing composition, then, seems certain and it is likely that each section was drafted not long after the events recorded. It seems clear also that there was more than one compiler: the text is a summary rather than a transcription of the source material, and the principles of selection vary. Thus the first mention of repairs to the city walls (c. 52) shows an interest not in its planning but in its expense, the viewpoint of someone in the paymaster's office; while the second mention (c. 92) suggests the viewpoint of one interested in organizing the labour force. There may well have been more than two compilers. One of them, possibly but most improbably, could have been the historian who wrote the first 44 chapters.

We turn now to the later years of Hadrian's pontificate. Even the mention of the 2nd Council of Nicaea does not inspire the compiler to explore its political consequences. Hadrian had already cooperated in Charles' schemes to reform the Frankish church by supplying him with material on liturgy and discipline. When the empress Irene summoned the Council of 787, Charles was not invited. By supporting orthodoxy, Hadrian risked a rapprochement with Byzantium which Charles, who had just broken the marriage alliance between his daughter and the empress's son Constantine VI, would find offensive. Hadrian played his hand skilfully. He sent two representatives to Nicaea, with a theological work against iconoclasm; this was applauded by the Council. He also demanded the restoration of the patrimonies confiscated over 50 years earlier by the emperor Leo III and the recognition of the Roman see's jurisdiction in Illyricum; this was ignored by the Council, as Hadrian no doubt anticipated. Consequently he could appear both as a supporter of orthodoxy and as one who had not been fully reconciled with Byzantium. The next stage was that Charles decided to oppose the decisions of a council to which he had not been invited; based on the translation of the acts into Latin (which is mentioned in the LP), he had a refutation compiled (the *libri Carolini*). Committed to defend orthodoxy, Hadrian could have found himself forced to condemn Charles; instead he stated he would excommunicate the empress and her son if the matters of the patrimonies and Illyricum were not settled in Rome's favour. Satisfied with Hadrian's loyalty, Charles held his own Council at Frankfurt in June 794 in the presence of two papal legates. This Council accepted all but one of the Nicene propositions, doing so in language borrowed from a letter of Hadrian's; the one exception, enough to satisfy Charles' honour, being a clause (in the Latin version) that images might be adored. It was then conveniently discovered that the Latin was faulty, and that the Greek original did not mention adoration. Honour was satisfied all round – except that Hadrian did not get the patrimonies or Illyricum, which he probably never expected. One wonders who planted such a diplomatic mistranslation: we are assured in the LP that it was made on Hadrian's initiative. Is this the real point in c. 97 where the compiler praises Hadrian for 'expertly' (*solertissime*) defending orthodoxy?

None of the compilers reveals the nepotistic tendencies of Hadrian's regime: he promoted his nephew Paschal to be *primicerius*. The creation of family interest was to produce problems for Leo III; but even the author of that pope's life fails to note that the leaders of the rebellion in 799 were the former pope's relatives. Despite the tensions that had existed between them, Charles grieved at the pope's death 'as if he had lost a brother or a child' (Einhard, *Vita Karoli* 19) and had masses said for Hadrian throughout his kingdom. But we learn none of this from the compiler of chapters 45–97.

97. **1. HADRIAN** [I; 9 February 772–26 December 795], of Roman origin, son of Theodore, from the region Via Lata,[1] held the see 23 years 10 months 17 days. A very distinguished man, sprung from noble ancestry[2] and born to influential Roman parents, he was elegant and most decorous in demeanour, a resolute and strenuous defender of the orthodox faith, his homeland and the flock entrusted to him, by God's power one who stoutly resisted the assailants of God's holy church and state, a merciful and bountiful comforter of the poor and all in need, and an observer of the church's tradition and the teachings of the holy Fathers.

2. On his father's death, this blessed man was left as a child with his noble mother; after his mother's death he was brought up and educated carefully by his uncle Theodotus,[3] formerly consul and duke, later *primicerius* of our holy church. From his earliest youth, while still a layman, he strongly concentrated on spiritual endeavours, modesty and chastity, eagerly staying in St Mark's church, which is near his own house. There by night and day he rendered frequent praises to our God; dressed in sackcloth he weakened his body with fasting, and he willingly and altruistically bestowed alms on the poor and needy as far as was in his power; the value of his good activity often resounded in the ears of all the Romans, which caused the fame of his nobility and purity to be broadcast far and wide. **3.** Lord pope Paul of holy memory noticed his life of pious behaviour, his spiritual activity and his exceptional character, and had him made a cleric; he appointed him a regionary notary[4] in the church and later made him a subdeacon. On lord

---

1 And near the *titulus* of St Mark (c. 2). A region where other Roman aristocrats also had property, Vielliard, 1959, 134, Krautheimer, 1980, 255, Noble, 188. Like other urban aristocrats (Castagnetti, 1979, 208–12, Noble, 197) he had rural landholdings (in Roman Tuscia, the Capracorum estate).

2 The first time the LP has stressed the nobility of a pope. Hadrian was the most aristocratic pope of the 8th century; his uncle's career (c. 2) shows that the family was part of the military aristocracy.

3 Theodotus (on whom, Halphen, 1907, 93, 136) is described as former duke, now *primicerius*, on the dedication inscription from 755 at S. Angelo in Pescheria, according to which he built this deaconry 'for the intercession of his soul and the remission of all his sins' (cf. pp. 50–1). As *primicerius* he evidently succeeded Ambrose who died in 753 (94:24), and was succeeded (between 756 when he was still *cartularius* and 764–6, *CC* 36) by Christopher who died in 771. Several portraits of him occur in St Cyrus' chapel at S. Maria Antiqua, with those of his wife and children and that of pope Zacharias (Krautheimer, *Corpus* 2, 250); in one of them Theodotus holds a model of the building, which he offers to the Virgin, and above his head he is styled 'first of the *defensores* and dispenser at God's holy mother the ever-virgin Mary's called Antiqua'. He was perhaps dispenser also at the deaconry he founded in 755.

4 Seen by Noble, 198, as a key office which Hadrian received as a result of his social rank; it also shows that Paul was recruiting nobles into the clergy.

97. HADRIAN I

pope Paul's decease, lord pope Stephen the second junior [III] was advanced to the summit of the pontificate. He too noticed the value of this blessed Hadrian's spiritual behaviour and advanced him to the order of the diaconate. From then on in various ways he was accomplished in spiritual endeavours: he bestowed enormous care not only on skilfully and lucidly evangelizing[5] the people with the message of God and the gospel, but also on putting the church's tradition into practice; and the grace of the Holy Ghost shone so brightly in his heart that he was proved efficient and capable at everything.

4. And so it happened that when lord pope Stephen departed this life, this distinguished and holy man, God's servant Hadrian, loved as he was by the Roman people's burning affection, was immediately elected to the holy summit of the pontificate.[6]

On the very day, at the very moment, of his election, he immediately brought about the return of those judges[7] of this city of Rome, both of the clergy and of the militia, who had been sent into exile when lord pope Stephen was passing away[8] by the chamberlain Paul, surnamed Afiarta, and by the other unholy officials his accomplices. He also secured the release of others who were held and imprisoned in close confinement.[9] Thus it was that all rejoiced with him when by God's favour he received consecration as pontiff.

5. So immediately after His Beatitude's consecration, Desiderius king of the Lombards sent him his envoys Theodicius duke of Spoleto, Tunno duke of Ivrea and Prandulus his *vestiarius*, with a message to persuade him that he wanted to be linked to him as by a bond of charity. This was the reply the blessed pontiff gave them: 'It is my wish to be at peace with all Christians, even with your king Desiderius; I shall endeavour to abide by the peace

---

5 This may merely mean that as deacon he chanted the gospel at mass.

6 1 February 772; that the election was apparently uncontested suggests that Afiarta's support came from Desiderius rather than from within Rome. Hadrian was candidate of the military aristocracy who were opposed to the Lombards; but since the election will have taken place under the rules drawn up in 769 (96:20), aimed against the aristocrats (Toto and his brother), some kind of consensus must have been reached between these and the Lateran bureaucracy who had promoted those rules. Noble (citing Seston, 1979) suggests there was some absorption of the aristocracy into the bureaucracy: Hadrian was a Lateran careerist despite his noble origins, which will have made him an ideal compromise candidate. This seems more plausible than the view that his election was a coup against a Lombard party in Rome (as Hallenbeck, 1968).

7 Evidently aristocratic supporters of Christopher and Sergius, removed by Afiarta and Desiderius in the hope of controlling the next papal election.

8 *transitum*, as at 96:32.

9 This was to make difficulties for Afiarta and destroy his remaining influence.

treaty[10] signed between Romans, Franks and Lombards. But how can I trust your king, given that my predecessor lord pope Stephen of holy memory recounted to me the details of his fraud and bad faith. He told me that he had lied to him in every promise[11] he made him on oath at St Peter's body concerning what he was going to do about God's holy church's lawful rights, and by his wicked artifice he went so far as to have the eyes of Christopher the *primicerius* and his son Sergius the *secundicerius* gouged out, and satisfied his will on these two church dignitaries. By this he caused us loss and damage rather than imparting any benefit on apostolic affairs. Also my predecessor, in the love he had for me his child, recounted to me that when he later sent him his envoys Anastasius the first *defensor* and Gemmulus the subdeacon to exhort him to fulfil what he had promised in person to St Peter, he sent him back the envoys with this reply: 'I have done enough for the Apostolicus Stephen by removing Christopher and Sergius who lorded it over him for there to be no need for him to ask about lawful rights. On the other hand it is certain that unless I help the Apostolicus great disaster will befall him: Carloman king of the Franks was a friend of Christopher and Sergius, and to avenge their deaths he is ready to come to Rome with his armies and take this pontiff prisoner.' That shows you the nature of your king Desiderius' bad faith and the kind of confidence and trust I can have in him.'

6. The blessed prelate Hadrian continued on this theme to king Desiderius' envoys, but they all the more insisted on oath both that their king would fulfil for this distinguished pontiff and supreme pastor all the lawful rights[12] he had not fulfilled for lord pope Stephen, and that he would remain indissolubly linked to him in a bond of charity. His Beatitude trusted their oaths and sent his own envoys, Stephen, regionary notary and *sacellarius*, and Paul, chamberlain and at the time *superista*,[13] to king Desiderius for the fulfilment of all these matters.

---

10 The treaties of Pavia in 754 and 756.

11 Cf. 96: n. 86.

12 In 757 Desiderius promised (94:49–51) the return of Ferrara, Faenza, Imola, Bologna, Ancona, Numana and Osimo, but at Stephen II's death he had returned only Ferrara and Faenza. Rather than demand the others, Paul seems to have accepted a compromise: in his last letters to Pepin he dwells on land revenues, not on territorial claims. Nothing more was done in Stephen III's time. But Hadrian now demands that at the very least the promises Desiderius made to Stephen III be fulfilled.

13 Noble, 129, notes the irony of sending Afiarta to the king to demand territorial concessions for the papacy; perhaps Hadrian just wanted an excuse to have him out of Rome. For the *superista,* here first mentioned, see glossary.

97. HADRIAN I

As[14] they left this city of Rome and went to Perugia, a message came that Desiderius had stolen the city of Faenza, the duchy of Ferrara and Comacchio, from the exarchate of Ravenna, which king Pepin of holy memory and Their Excellencies Charles and Carloman, kings of the Franks and patricians of the Romans, had granted and presented to St Peter. **7.** Not even two months had passed since this holy man obtained the summit of the pontificate, yet this atrocious Desiderius stole these cities, put the city of Ravenna under constraint on all sides, occupied the homesteads and all the estates of the Ravennates, and stole all their provisions, dependants, property and all that they had on their estates. And since neither archbishop Leo nor the people of Ravenna had any hope of survival in their great want, hunger and need, they sent their envoys, the tribunes Julian, Peter and Vitalian, here to Rome, to ask in their great woe for the holy pontiff to come with such help as he could and try to recapture those cities – they stated that unless those cities were restored there was no way they could survive.

8. Then since his envoys Stephen the *sacellarius* and Paul the *superista* were still on their way to king Desiderius, this bountiful pontiff sent the king his letters demanding that he return those cities. In his writing he strongly rebuked him: why had he abandoned the promise he had undertaken through the envoys he had sent? Why had he not restored his lawful rights to St Peter as he had promised? Above all, why had he stolen those cities that his predecessors the blessed pontiffs lord Stephen, Paul and Stephen had held? But when the holy pontiff sent this message to the shameless Desiderius to demand, warn and adjure him, he sent him back a reply that unless the bountiful prelate first came to discuss the matter with him he would never restore those cities. **9.** At that time it occurred that the wife[15] and sons of Carloman, formerly king of the Franks, took flight with Autchar to the king of the Lombards; Desiderius was exerting himself and eagerly striving that these sons of Carloman should obtain the kingdom of the Franks. This is why he was trying to trick the holy prelate into coming to him, to anoint the former king Carloman's sons as kings themselves. He intended to cause a split in the kingdom of the Franks, to divorce the blessed pontiff from the charity and attachment His Excellency Charles, king of the Franks and patrician of the Romans, had to him,[16] and to subdue the city of Rome and the whole of

---

14 With cc. 6b – 9a, cf. *Pauli continuatio tertia*, c. 48 (*MGH SSrL*, 212), *Pauli continuatio romana*, c. 6 (*MGH SSrL*, 201).

15 i. e. widow; Carloman died 4 December 771 and Gerberga had then fled with a few Franks to Desiderius in Italy (*Ann. Lauriss.*, a. 771). On Autchar see 94:18 and n. 36.

16 Sometime early in 772 even before the embassy mentioned in c. 22, Hadrian wrote to Charles (J 2396) asking for help against Desiderius, but nothing came of it.

Italy under the power of his own Lombard kingdom. But God's grace saw to it that he totally failed in this, since the blessed pontiff Hadrian remained as firm and stout-hearted as adamant.[17] Now Paul the *superista* was still with Desiderius and gave him a firm promise that the blessed pope would be brought to him: 'Even if I have to use a rope on his feet, I will bring him to your presence as best I can'. It so happened that while Paul was away on the same journey it became obvious to everyone how he had brought about the death of the *secundicerius* Sergius, blind and in his prison cell. The holy prelate was afraid this news might reach Paul's ears and cause him either to return to the king or even to deviate from his route into Lombard territory and with Desiderius perpetrate some further evil on the territory of Rome and the exarchate of Ravenna; and since he was greatly attached and loyal to him, the blessed pope therefore sent in absolute secrecy a message by the tribune Julian to Leo archbishop of Ravenna, for Leo to detain Paul in Ravenna or Rimini when he was on his way back from Desiderius. Which is what happened: on his return journey Paul was arrested at Rimini and held in confinement.

10. Then the blessed pontiff began a detailed inquest into the *secundicerius* Sergius' death. He called all the gaolers together and carefully questioned them on how Sergius had been removed from his cell. They replied: 'It was in the first hour of the night that the chamberlain Calventzulus came with the priest Lunisso and the tribune Leonatius, inhabitants of the city of Anagni,[18] and he took Sergius away; this was while lord pope Stephen was alive, eight days before he departed this life; and he handed him over to those Campanians.' This chamberlain was immediately brought into their midst and interrogated as to who had ordered him to remove Sergius from the cell and hand him over to these Campanians. He replied that his orders had been given him by the chamberlain Paul, surnamed Afiarta, by Gregory the regionary *defensor*, by the duke John, lord pope Stephen's brother, and by the chamberlain Calvulus, in the presence of the Campanians themselves.

11. The holy prelate sent his envoys into Campania to Anagni, and had Lunisso and Leonatius brought to Rome. Taken tightly bound into the apostolic presence, they admitted that their orders to remove and kill Sergius had come from the chamberlain Paul, Gregory the regionary *defensor*, John, lord pope Stephen's brother, and Calvulus, also a chamberlain and Paul's wicked

---

17 'Desiderius was no fool, and his plan was well conceived. It failed in the end because he could neither coerce nor cajole Hadrian into submitting to it' (Noble, 129).

18 Noble, 129–30, takes this to mean that all three were from Anagni, and has Sergius taken into Campania to be killed there; but the text does not say this, and cf. c. 11.

accomplice. The holy pontiff immediately sent his most trustworthy ministers with these Campanians to point out the place where they had killed and buried Sergius. They made their way as far as the Merulana, to the painted arch[19] alongside the road leading to God's holy mother *ad praesepe*. Close to this arch there, they opened one of the tombs and displayed Sergius' body lying in it, with a rope tightened round his throat and his entire body bruised and injured: there was no doubt he had been throttled and buried in the earth while half alive.

12. When all the church's chief men and the judges of the militia saw this, they and the whole people went up with one accord to the Lateran patriarchate, and prostrate before the apostolic feet they earnestly begged the bountiful pontiff to order vengeance and punishment for such an unheard of crime, in that they had presumed cruelly to murder a blind man already much tortured, for which there was no recorded precedent. They stated that if the guilt of such a disgraceful act was not atoned for, this unholy presumption and rashness would spread in this city of Rome, and perverse men would take courage from it and try to perpetrate even worse things. **13.** Then the holy prelate, acceding to the prayers of the judges and the whole Roman people, ordered the chamberlain Calvulus and the aforesaid Campanians to be handed over to the city prefect[20] for trial before the whole people

---

19 Merulana was the name of a house in region 3; Gregory I (*Ep.* 3.19, January 593) mentions an Arian church near it, which he wanted to dedicate to St Severinus (nothing more is known of this). The house gave its name (still used) to the street from the Lateran to St Mary Major. Near the Lateran the street passed under an arch of the Claudian aqueduct, which Duchesne thought might be the painted arch here.

20 Justinian gave bishops jurisdiction over the clergy and in cases between clergy and laity (Gregory I, *Ep.* 13. 50); but criminal cases, at least capital ones, had to stay out of church courts. So the murderers are handed over to the prefect. Justinian (*Pragmatic Sanction* c. 12) also laid down that provincial judges (who would include criminal ones) should be selected by local bishops and *primates*; there is good evidence (Noble cc. 6–7, Halphen, 1907, 35–6) that the pope was now appointing all Rome's officials, including judicial ones; and the prefect was certainly subordinate to papal authority (Halphen, 22–7). But nothing follows from this about papal recognition, or non-recognition, of Byzantine authority. This is the first reference to the prefect since 599 (Gregory, *Epp.* 9.116, 117; Diehl, 1888, 127; Brown, 1984, 11–12 with note 22). There is unlikely to have been any continuity in the urban prefecture (*pace* Halphen, 16–18): Hadrian himself may have recreated the office. During this time the prefect's jurisdiction, if he existed, would have have been much limited by the development of the military jurisdiction of the *dux* and other officers of the Roman army, and by the increase of church involvement in civic administration, such as the corn supply, the walls and the aqueducts. The prefect now was 'a minor lay official with an antique title because of the deeply felt consciousness of Rome's past' (Brown, 11). The title survived as that of a judge for civilian criminals till the 14th century.

of Rome, as is done with murderers. They were taken to the public prison at the Elephantum[21] and tried there before the whole people. The Campanians made the same confession in this trial as they had done before, but Calvulus' heart was hardened and he confessed the whole truth only with reluctance: it was by a cruel death that he gave up the ghost in that prison.

In order to cut off the huge and intolerable guilt of the disgraceful act, these Campanians were sent into exile at Constantinople.[22] **14.** After this the blessed pope ordered the bodies of Christopher and his son Sergius to be removed and he had them honourably buried in St Peter's. As for the record of the trial, how the chamberlain Calvulus and the Campanians had confessed their offence and guilt, the bountiful pontiff sent it to Ravenna, for Paul to have a complete and orderly digest of it. Leo archbishop of Ravenna took the record and without apostolic warrant he immediately handed Paul over to the Consularis of Ravenna;[23] he was tried before the whole people of Ravenna, and the record was read out to him; and so he showed his guilt of the great crime and confessed he had perpetrated the evil deed. That was how Paul was tried. But neither the archbishop nor any of the Ravennates informed the holy pontiff of this, though His Holiness heard it through others. **15.** Meanwhile, as the distinguished pastor and outstanding pontiff wanted

---

21 The *Elefas herbarius* in Region 8 is in the 4th-century Regionary Catalogues, in the area of the Forum Olitorium, close to the Piazza Montanara (Platner-Ashby, 199–200). The prison was not a survival from antiquity but was presumably installed in the Byzantine period in some building of that forum. It was this prison that provided the soubriquet for the church of S. Nicolà in Carcere, which marks the general site.

22 In earlier times exiles had been sent from Constantinople to Rome (e.g. Macarius, BP Agatho 81:14; and on the restoration of Justinian II in 705 the patriarch Callinicus); no doubt exiles had been sent in the opposite direction. By 772 Constantinople as a destination for exiles seems surprising, as does the request Hadrian sent to Constantinople (c. 15). Noble, 133, argues that Hadrian had no choice but to send the exiles there: he could not kill them and make them martyrs; they could not stay in Rome as that would give Desiderius an excuse to rescue them; he could scarcely send them to Desiderius; and, since at this point Charles' loyalties were still unclear, he could not send them to France; while Constantinople was powerless in Italy and could not use Hadrian's enemies against him. If this is right, it is needless to explain the references to Constantinople by saying that Rome's constitutional position had not been properly worked out. It is true that in the same year Hadrian dated at least one letter by the years of the eastern emperors Constantine V and Leo IV (*Reg. Farf.* 2 no. 99, to Probatus), but for the explanation of this see Noble, 133–4 (the same letter refers to 'our State of the Romans').

23 This official evidently acted as a criminal judge; Duchesne suggested continuity with the *consularis Flaminiae et Piceni annonarii* of the Notitia Dignitatum. Such continuity is unlikely. *Consul* and *consularis* seem identical in meaning (Bury, 1911, 26), so note the four consuls of Ravenna in 742 (93:9).

97. HADRIAN I

to save Paul's soul and prevent its eternal loss,[24] he had a request drawn up to send to the great emperors Constantine and Leo, dealing with the blind Sergius' unholy death and asking their imperial mercy for Paul: as punishment for such a great crime they should order him to be taken and held in exile and prison in the districts of Greece. His thrice-blessedness sent the same request to archbishop Leo, for him to send Paul into exile to Constantinople however he could, whether by the Venetiae or another route,[25] and send the apostolic request with him. But the archbishop, who was fervently plotting against Paul, grasped the unholy opportunity to reply to the distinguished pontiff that it was thoroughly inexpedient for Paul to be sent there, as Desiderius king of the Lombards had captured the son of Maurice duke of Venice and was holding him at court, and Maurice wanted to secure his son's release from the king by handing over Paul in exchange for him. See what an opportunity the archbishop of Ravenna cunningly grasped to snuff out Paul! And so he sent the request back to the apostolic see.[26]

16. Thereafter the holy prelate, who had sent his *sacellarius* Gregory to Desiderius the Lombard king to demand and encourage his restoration of the cities he had stolen, instructed him to warn archbishop Leo firmly, to make sure Paul was kept safe, and on his return from Ticinum to bring him with him here to Rome. When the *sacellarius* Gregory reached Ravenna, he warned the archbishop and all the Ravennate judges resolutely and firmly in the apostolic injunction's terms, in the presence of Anvald, then *cartularius* of the city of Rome, who had been sent there by the apostolic see, that Paul was to be kept safe and sound until he returned from Ticinum; he stated that he was under orders from the apostolic power to take him with him to Rome and bring him safe into the apostolic presence. After warning the archbishop in this way, he continued his journey to Ticinum. And straightaway the archbishop summoned the Consularis of Ravenna and ordered him to have Paul killed. 17. On his return from Ticinum, the *sacellarius* reached Ravenna and found that Paul was already dead. For this he greatly rebuked the archbishop

---

24 Hadrian did not want to make a martyr out of Afiarta or to give Desiderius a further pretext for troublemaking; Noble, 130.

25 Noble, 134, takes this to imply that while Rome and Ravenna were now regarded by no one as Byzantine cities, Venice and other routes were still so thought of, and in spite of the longstanding papal claim to Venice Hadrian is conceding the point. Strictly, though, Hadrian might here be making a formal claim to Venice as a route that should be under papal control, while allowing travellers to choose practical alternatives.

26 Leo's attitude may be explained by the fact that it was Lombard interference that had kept him out of his see in 769–70 (cf. 96:25–6). Leo was bound neither by scruples nor by higher policy considerations of the kind that influenced Hadrian (Noble, 130).

– why had he presumed so to deal with Paul, contrary to the apostolic injunction? So some days afterwards the archbishop, conscience-stricken, sent the tribune Julian as his envoy to the holy pope, asking him to send him apostolic letters to comfort him, as if no blame should attach to him over Paul's death, in that it was carried out to avenge an innocent man's blood. But there was no way he could sway the holy pontiff, who sent him this reply: 'You must realize what you have done to Paul – my intention, certainly, was to save his soul and I had decided on the penance he would have to undergo; that was why I sent my *sacellarius* to bring him here to Rome'.

18. Now Desiderius king of the Lombards, puffed up with pride and bluster, at the time he stole the above-mentioned[27] cities from the exarchate of Ravenna, immediately sent a number of armies and had the territories of cities occupied, namely Senigállia, Iesi, Montefeltro, Urbino, Gúbbio and other Roman cities, and perpetrated much murder, devastation and fire within their borders.[28] Thus he sent the whole army of the districts of Tuscia to Blera, and when the people of that city thinking they were at peace came out as a whole with their wives and sons and dependants to harvest their crops, the Lombards suddenly fell on them and killed all the chief men that held power in that city, and stole many men and much property as booty, laying waste everything around with fire and sword. And Desiderius gave orders for much harm and devastation to be perpetrated in the territory of Rome and other cities. He even had the castrum of Otricoli occupied. So again and again the blessed prelate sent letters of entreaty and envoys to Desiderius, begging him to repent of such evil and restore the cities he had stolen. Yet not only was he entirely unmoved to restore the occupied cities, but he had no intention at all of desisting from his evil conduct: as has been said, he did not stop cruelly inflicting much unbearable harm on the territory of the Romans.

19. Then the holy pontiff had Probatus summoned, the religious abbot of God's holy mother's venerable monastery[29] in the territory of Sabina, along with 20 of the older monks, God's servants; he sent them to Desiderius to entreat him. When they came to him – as God's servants themselves related – they fell at his feet in the presence of the Lombard judges, and

---

27 c. 6.

28 Cf. *Pauli continuatio tertia* c. 49 (*MGH SSrL*, 212). 'Roman' here means under papal, not under Byzantine, control. The action is Desiderius' reply to the pressure Hadrian had been exerting in the hope of ending the impasse in Italy, Noble, 130; and the attack on Blera (early 773) was followed by attacks into the environs of Rome.

29 At Farfa; Probatus was abbot from 770. Hadrian intended this and the later embassy to be impressive (Noble).

in the name of St Peter's vicar they tearfully implored him to repent of such evil and restore to St Peter the cities he had stolen. But they could not soften his stony heart. **20.** So, nothing achieved, these servants of God came home. Desiderius yet again sent his envoys to the blessed pontiff, Andrew the *referendarius* and Stabilis the duke, to invite him to come and discuss matters with him. The bountiful pontiff received them and gave them this reply: 'You may assure your king in my name, that before God Almighty I give you my solemn word: if he restores to me St Peter's cities, those he stole in my time, I will immediately come to him in person, at Ticinum, Ravenna, Perugia, here at Rome or anywhere else that pleases him, and I will meet him and discuss matters about the safety of God's people on each side. If he perhaps doubts this, that I might not meet him after he restores the cities, then if I do not meet him for discussions he has leave to reoccupy them. But if he does not restore the cities and fulfil our lawful rights first, let him be clear that he will never see my face. So look, I will take care to send my envoys to accompany you to your king; they can receive the cities if he will restore them. The moment my envoys receive the cities and return to me with the news, I will immediately, as I said, come to see him for discussions wherever he wishes.'

21. The Lombard envoys travelled back to their king, and to receive the cities his thrice-blessedness immediately sent king Desiderius his envoys, namely Pardus, the religious *hegumenos*[30] of the monastery of St Saba, and Anastasius, the first *defensor*. They were brought into his presence and fell at his feet, tearfully imploring him to restore the cities. On apostolic warrant they promised him on oath that if he restored them, the bountiful pontiff would immediately hurry to come to him for discussions. But they had no success in softening his iron breast and obdurate mind; gaining nothing they came home fruitlessly. Yet the pontiff did not stop sending him his envoys on this matter, both *sacerdotes* and members of each order of the monastic habit. But they could achieve nothing with him; instead he endured in his wickedness and saw to the infliction on all sides of much harm on the cities and territory of the Romans. He greatly threatened the distinguished pontiff, that he would come with all the Lombard armies to put the city of Rome under constraint. This caused the holy pontiff and his people great sorrow; and he saw to the shutting of the city gates of Rome and their blocking with masonry.[31] **22.** As he was in such difficulty and trouble, need forced him to

---

30 Abbot of a Greek monastery; on St Saba's (Cella Nova) see 96:12 and n. 29.
31 For the expression, cf. 96:28.

send his envoys by sea[32] with apostolic letters to His Excellency Charles, the God-protected king of the Franks and patrician of the Romans, to ask his Excellency to come, as his father Pepin of holy memory had done, to the aid of God's holy church and the afflicted province of the Romans and exarchate of Ravenna, and exact in full from king Desiderius St Peter's lawful rights and the stolen cities.

23. But since none of the ingenuity the wicked Desiderius attempted enabled him to persuade the holy pontiff to travel to him to anoint Carloman's sons as kings, and he failed to divorce the bountiful pontiff from the charity and attachment the christian king Charles the Great had to him, he then with obstinate courage left his palace along with his son Adalgis and the Lombard army; with him he took the wife and sons of the former king Carloman and Autchar who, as mentioned above, had taken flight to him, and tried to come here to Rome without the pontiff's knowledge. He sent his envoys, Andrew the *referendarius* and two other judges of his, to announce his arrival. When these reached Rome and were brought into the apostolic presence, he replied: 'Unless as I have already made clear he restores to St Peter the cities he stole in my time and fulfils our side's entire lawful rights first, it is quite unnecessary for him to take this trouble, as there is no possibility of his being presented to me.'

24. When Desiderius received this reply he took no notice of it at all, but continued his journey to Rome. The distinguished pastor learnt that his arrival was now at hand and gathered the whole people of Tuscia, Campania, and the duchy of Perugia[33] with some from the cities of the Pentapolis and fortified this city of Rome. All were armed and ready so that, should the king arrive, they could, with God's help and that of St Peter and supported by the holy prelate's prayers, put up a strong resistance to him.[34] His Holiness had all the adornments removed from St Peter's and St Paul's and brought all their sacred equipment and adornments into this city of Rome; he had all the doors of St Peter's closed and ordered them barred and strength-

---

32 By sea, since Desiderius had now (about April 773) started a general mobilization and was (c. 23) heading for Rome. With this appeal (J 2403), cf. the Frankish Annals for this year (e. g. *Chron. Moiss., MGH SS* 1, 295), which record that when Charles had gone to spend the winter at the villa called Theodone, Hadrian's envoy Peter came to Marseilles by sea, as the Lombards had shut the roads to Romans, and then by land to see Charles, to ask him and the Franks 'for God's service, St Peter's rights and the church's solace over' Desiderius and the Lombards.

33 At least by this date Perugia was under papal control; cf. 93:23, 96:28.

34 Hadrian wants to defend his State as best he can and not wait for any help that Charles might send in response to his appeal (c. 22).

ened inside, so if the shameless king arrived without the pontiff's leave and permission he would gain no admittance to that church unless, at the cost of his own soul, he forcibly broke down the doors. **25.** When he had made all these arrangements and had drawn up a written sentence of anathema, he immediately sent king Desiderius three bishops, Eustratius of Albano, Andrew of Palestrina and Theodosius of the city of Tivoli, to warn him of this, to inform him of the tie he was under, and to exhort and adjure him by all God's mysteries never to presume without his leave to enter or set foot in the territory of the Romans – neither himself nor any of the Lombards, and not Autchar the Frank either. On receiving from the bishops this account of the tie he was under, the Lombard king immediately and with great reverence returned home in perplexity from the city of Viterbo.[35]

26. Next the envoys of His Excellency Charles king of the Franks and patrician of the Romans, namely the holy bishop George,[36] the religious abbot and counsellor Gulfard,[37] and Albuin the king's favourite,[38] came to the apostolic see, to inquire whether the king of the Lombards had restored the stolen cities and all St Peter's lawful rights, as he claimed, falsely, when sending word to France that he had restored them all. Once they were present they found out he had restored nothing. The distinguished pontiff related to them all that had happened and gave them leave to return to France; with them he sent his envoys to His Excellency the king of the Franks with apostolic letters spelling out his advice and strongly adjuring him about what, with his father king Pepin of holy memory, he had promised to fulfil for St Peter: to achieve the redemption of God's holy church it was his duty to contend in person for the restoration to St Peter prince of the apostles of all that the treacherous Lombard king had stolen, both the cities and the other lawful rights. **27.** So the envoys of the Franks journeyed with the apostolic see's envoys, and deviated to visit Desiderius. They resolutely begged and exhorted him, as their own king had instructed them, to restore to St Peter peacefully the cities he had stolen and fulfil their lawful rights towards the

---

35 Astonishingly, Hadrian's gambit paid off: Desiderius withdrew, though he restored nothing and retained Gerberga; the result was a shortlived truce, not a final resolution of the problem. Noble, 131, agrees with Fasoli, 1968, I, 78–9, on the impact of the threat of excommunication. But perhaps Desiderius may also have doubted his ability to take Rome, and, since prominent Lombard nobles were soon to abandon him (c. 32), he may have seen the risk of his own kingdom disintegrating.

36 Probably the bishop of Amiens, formerly of Ostia, 94:23, n. 44; 96:17, nn. 42, 45.

37 Abbot of St Martin of Tours.

38 *deliciosus*; this must be Alcuin, who had already been with Charlemagne before 780 (*vita Alcuini*, c. 6).

Romans. But they completely failed to achieve any of this from him – he refused to restore anything whatever.

Receiving this reply, the envoys of the Franks returned to their own region, the apostolic see's envoys journeying with them. They carefully related all this to His Excellency the God-protected king Charles the Great and told him of Desiderius' wicked intention. **28.** And immediately the mild and truly christian Charles king of the Franks sent Desiderius his envoys, namely ... , begging him to restore peacefully the cities he had stolen and fulfil their lawful rights towards the Romans in full; additionally he promised to pay him gold and silver to the amount of 14000 gold solidi.[39] Yet neither entreaties nor gifts succeeded in bending his savage heart. Achieving nothing, the envoys of the Franks returned to their christian king.

29. Then[40] the God-protected king Charles the Great mustered the full number of the armies of his kingdom of the Franks.[41] Some of his army he sent to occupy all the mountain barriers. With many mighty Frankish warriors he came by Mont Cenis close to these barriers,[42] then waited with his armies at some distance inside the territory of the Franks. Desiderius and the whole number of the Lombard armies were waiting to put up a strong resistance at the barriers, which they carefully strengthened by building various walls. **30.** At the moment the christian king of the Franks came close to these mountain barriers, he immediately sent his envoys to Desiderius again, asking the king as before to accept the amount of solidi mentioned and restore the cities peacefully. But the shameless king chose to concede nothing whatever. When he continued so obdurate, the christian king of the Franks, desiring to get back St Peter's lawful rights peacefully, sent a message to the Lombard king that he need hand over to him no more than

---

39 Noble, 131, combines this offer with its repetition after the campaign started, c. 30.

40 On the fall of the Lombard kingdom see discussion in Schmid, 1972, 1–36. The various Frankish annals (and *Pauli continuatio romana, MGH SSrL,* 201) add details on the campaign; they have nothing on the diplomacy that follows or that mentioned lower down. They continue (cf. n. 32) that Charles consulted with the Franks and together they agreed to the papal envoy's request; a common *sinodus* with the Franks was held at Geneva; there Charles divided his army, he himself coming by way of Mont Cenis, while his uncle Bernard came with the other *fideles* by Mons Jupiter (i.e. to penetrate Lombardy from two directions); both armies reached the mountain barriers and Desiderius came against Charles; Charles and the Franks pitched camp at the barriers, and he sent his regular warriors (*scara*) over the mountains; Desiderius saw this and abandoned the barriers, so Charles and the Franks entered Italy without bloodshed; they reached Pavia and besieged Desiderius; Charles celebrated Christmas in camp there, but went to Rome for Easter.

41 Noble, 131, contrasts the scale with the modest forces Pepin twice brought to Italy.

42 This seems to refer to the division of the armies mentioned in n. 40.

three sons of Lombard judges as security for the restoration of the cities, and he would immediately return home with his armies of Franks without causing any harm or engaging in battle.

31. Even so he failed to turn his evil mind. So almighty God, seeing the evil Desiderius' iniquitous perfidy and unbearable shamelessness, when the Franks were willing[43] to return home the next day, instilled terror and mighty fear[44] into his heart, that of his son Adalgis and those of all the Lombards. That very night, abandoning their tents and all their apparatus, they all as a whole took to flight when no one was pursuing them. When the armies of the Franks saw this, they did pursue them and killed many of them. As for Desiderius, he fled with his judges at full speed and reached Pavia as fast as he could, and there he took care to entrench himself with his judges and a crowd of the Lombard people. Strengthening the city walls, he made ready to resist the armies of the Franks and defend his city with his Lombards. But Adalgis his son took Autchar the Frank and Carloman's wife and sons with him and went inside Verona, since it is the strongest of all the Lombard cities.
32. The rest of the Lombards scattered and returned to their own cities.

Before Desiderius and his Lombard armies could make for the mountain barriers, some of the individuals who held power among the people of Spoleto[45] and Rieti made their escape to St Peter, surrendered to the holy pope Hadrian, swore allegiance to the prince of the apostles and the holy pontiff, and were shaved[46] Roman-fashion. All the others from the duchy

---

43 Duchesne seemed to take *vellent* as 'wanted to', commenting that other sources give no hint of the Franks' hesitation. The translation here implies that the Franks were willing to go home if the conditions were fulfilled; this fits the other accounts and the LP account of Charles' preference for diplomacy, though the LP may have exaggerated this in order to magnify the supernatural element in the Lombard retreat.

44 No great surprise: while Charlemagne delayed diplomatically near Susa at the foot of the Mont-Cenis pass (160 km W of Pavia), his uncle was approaching down the Val d'Aosta (about the same distance, but a little W of NW from Pavia) and sending his cavalry to outflank the Lombards.

45 This Lombard duchy had long had separatist tendencies from the kingdom of Pavia (Duchesne, I, CCXXXVII) and took an early opportunity on Charles' arrival in Italy to detach itself and link up with the papal State. For Hadrian one consequence of gaining Spoleto would be to secure his control over Sabina; cf. 93:3, 9, n. 27; and, as his letters from 778–781 show, Sabina was Hadrian's main territorial concern later, when duke Hildeprand went over to Charles about December 775; in 781 Hadrian got the whole of Roman Sabina (and not just the patrimonies); Noble, 157.

46 Here and below Niermeyer assigns the meaning 'be given the tonsure'; I can see no suggestion they became clerics. Duchesne compares 92:14, where Liutprand had many noble Romans shaved Lombard-fashion. Note that the Lombards do not seem to have thought it necessary to consult Constantinople; Noble, 134.

of Spoleto were eager to surrender to the service of St Peter and the holy Roman church, but in fear of their king they dared not do so. So when all those from the various cities of the duchy of Spoleto who had taken flight from the barriers came back, they immediately came crowding as a whole to the bountiful pontiff, and falling at his feet they earnestly begged his thrice-blessedness to take them into the service of St Peter and the holy Roman church and have them shaved Roman-fashion. He welcomed them and accompanied them into St Peter's; from greatest to least they all with one accord promised God's apostle and swore with a written oath to remain with their sons and all their descendants loyal to his service, and that of his holy vicar pope Hadrian and all his successors as pontiffs. **33.** After taking the oath they were all shaved Roman-fashion, and the thrice-blessed good shepherd and father, rejoicing with them all, straightaway ratified for them the duke they had elected themselves of their own free will, namely noble Hildeprand who had previously made his escape with the others to the apostolic see.[47] So it was God's will that this distinguished pontiff by his own striving subdued the duchy of Spoleto as a whole to St Peter's ownership and power. And all the occupants of the duchy of Fermo, those of Osimo, Ancona and Castellum Felicitatis[48] too, fled from the Lombards' barriers, and came back in droves to the holy pontiff, surrendered to his thrice-blessedness, took the oath to remain loyally in the allegiance and service of St Peter, his vicar the bountiful pope Hadrian and his successors as pontiffs, and were shaved Roman-fashion.

34. But Charles the christian king of the Franks, on campaign with the whole of his armies, reached the city of Pavia and encompassed it on all sides. He sent word immediately to France and had his wife, Her Excellency queen Hildigard, and his noble sons brought to him at Pavia. When he realized that Adalgis had taken flight to Verona, he left most of his armies at Pavia while with a number of the strongest Franks he made his way to Verona. When he got there, Autchar and Carloman's wife and sons immediately surrendered freely to the kindly king Charles. His Excellency received them and returned to Pavia. Straightaway despatching squadrons of his warrior armies, he captured various Lombard cities beyond the Po and

---

47 Note that Hadrian acts as a head of state. Hildeprand is previously unknown. The date is after September 773 when Theodicius was still duke; in 774 Hildeprand dated a charter by the year of pope Hadrian and used the formula of the papal chancery to do so; but by December 775 or January 776 Hildeprand recognized Charles and dated documents accordingly; Brühl, 1971, 63–5, Gasparri, 1978, 84–5, Noble, 134, 144.

48 Fermo, Ancona and Numana were Spoletan dependencies. Castellum Felicitatis (Città di Castello) was in Lombard Tuscany and the duchy of Chiusi; cf. 96: n. 56.

reduced them to his own power.

35. When the king of the Franks had stayed at Pavia for six months[49] at the siege of the city, being very keen to visit the homes of the apostles and considering that the holy Easter festival was approaching,[50] he took with him various bishops, abbots, judges, dukes and *grafiones* with many armies,[51] and came here to Rome through the districts of Tuscia. So fast was his journey that he presented himself at the homes of the apostles on Holy Saturday itself. The blessed pope Hadrian heard he was coming and was struck with great amazement and rejoicing that the king of the Franks had come so unexpectedly; he sent all the judges to meet him at the place called Novae, some 30 miles from this city of Rome.[52] There they welcomed him with a banner.[53] 36. And when he was only a mile or so away from Rome, he sent all the *scholae*[54] of the militia, along with the *patroni* and the children who were just starting out to learn their letters, all bearing branches of palm and olive, and all chanting his praises; with shouts of acclamation and praise they welcomed the king of the Franks. His Holiness despatched venerable

49 As he reached Rome 2 April 774 (Easter was 3 April), he must have left Pavia late in March; so the beginning of the siege of Pavia was about the end of September 773.

50 Charles' motives were religious, but perhaps not exclusively. Pavia was likely to fall and cities of the Spoletan duchy were giving in to Hadrian, so Charles may have seen the need to discuss (as in c. 41) the future of Italy; Fasoli, 1968, 131, Noble, 139.

51 He may have feared opposition while crossing Tuscany; Desiderius had once been duke there; Noble, 139.

52 Protocol seems to have required a pope to go 6 miles to meet an emperor (BP Vitalian 78:2) and one mile to meet an exarch or patrician (97:36). Noble, 139, 288, thinks that Hadrian's sending of troops to a much greater distance sprang from doubts about Charles' intentions (he wanted to put on a display of force); while Hadrian's own waiting on the steps of St Peter's was a sign that he accepted no overlordship by Charles, who was not to be allowed to appear as the pope's sovereign. Novae is otherwise known only from the Peutinger Table (Ad Novas, 8 miles from Vaccanae, which in the Antonine Itinerary is 21 miles from Rome) and the Ravenna Cosmography (Civitas Nova); perhaps identifiable with ruins close to the chapel of S. Bernadino, 1 km E of Trevignano on the north shore of Lake Bracciano; it would be a staging post on the slip road connecting the Via Cassia and Via Clodia. If so, and as it would otherwise have been pointless to go round the north of the lake, it follows that Charles came by the Via Clodia but found it impracticable south of the lake.

53 Duchesne noted that the *triclinium* of Leo III gives a representation of this *bandora* in mosaic (what now survives is only an approximate copy of the original mosaic; see 98: n. 21); Noble, 235, takes the word as referring to the distinctive banners (*signa*) of the *scholae* mentioned in the next chapter. The text there seems to make the banners identical with crosses, but shortly afterwards (c. 37) it regards them as separate. If the crosses are the seven stational crosses kept in store at St Anastasia's, see LNCP Benedict III 106:28 with n. 72.

54 The companies of the Roman militia, one from each of the 12 or 14 civil regions of Rome; the *patroni* were their leaders.

crosses, that is to say standards, to meet him, just like greeting an exarch or patrician, and had him welcomed most honourably.

37. The God-appointed kindly Charles the Great, king of the Franks and patrician of the Romans, the moment he noticed those holy crosses and standards coming to meet him, dismounted his horse and so took care to come to St Peter's on foot with his judges. The bountiful pontiff rose at daybreak that Holy Saturday, and came with the whole clergy and people of Rome to St Peter's to greet the king of the Franks; with his clergy he waited for him on the steps to the apostle's hall. **38.** When His Excellency the kindly king Charles arrived, he kissed every single step leading up to St Peter's holy church, and so came to the pontiff where he was waiting in the atrium at the top of the steps, close to the church doors. He was greeted and they embraced each other; the christian king Charles held the pontiff's right hand, and in this way they entered the venerable hall of St Peter prince of the apostles. The whole clergy and all God's servants the monks chanted praise to God and His Excellency, loudly acclaiming: 'Blessed is he who comes in the name of the Lord' etc. And so the king of the Franks, all the bishops, abbots and judges, and all the Franks who had accompanied him, came with the pontiff close to St Peter's confessio. There they prostrated themselves and made their own prayers to our almighty God and the prince of the apostles; they glorified God's power, that through the prince of the apostles' prayers of intercession he had granted and ordained so great a victory.

39. Once the prayer was finished, the king of the Franks earnestly requested the bountiful pontiff's permission[55] to enter Rome to fulfil his prayers and vows at God's various churches. The holy pope and His Excellency the king of the Franks, with the judges of the Romans and Franks, went down together to St Peter's body and ratified their oaths to each other;[56] straightaway the king of the Franks and his judges and people entered Rome with the pontiff. That same Holy Saturday they entered the Saviour's basilica close to the Lateran together, where His Excellency the king with all his [followers stayed] while the thrice-blessed pontiff celebrated the sacrament of holy baptism.[57] Afterwards the kindly king returned to St Peter's.

40. Next day, as the Holy Sunday of the sacred Easter festival dawned, the holy prelate sent all the judges and the whole retinue of the militia to

---

55 This might imply an admission by Charles that he had no sovereignty at Rome, Noble, 288; or it might be no more than a courtesy.

56 To be seen as a renewal of the oaths between Stephen II and Pepin (94:26).

57 By this date the Easter vigil ceremonies, including baptism, were being anticipated on the Saturday afternoon.

97. HADRIAN I

the king at daybreak and they greeted him very honourably. He went with all the Franks who had accompanied him to God's holy mother's church *ad praesepe*,[58] and after the ceremonies of mass were celebrated for him, he went with the pontiff to the Lateran patriarchate, where they feasted together at the apostolic table. Next day, Monday, in the same way the noteworthy father and distinguished pontiff celebrated the ceremonies of mass at St Peter's as usual, and had praises[59] given to almighty God and His Excellency Charles, king of the Franks, patrician of the Romans. On Tuesday he performed mass for the king, at St Paul's as is customary.

41. But[60] on Wednesday the pontiff went out to St Peter's with his judges both of the clergy and of the militia, and he met the king for discussion. He resolutely entreated, warned and took care to encourage him with fatherly affection, to fulfil in every detail the promise[61] which the former king his father Pepin of holy memory and His Excellency Charles himself with his brother Carloman and all the judges of the Franks had made to St Peter and his vicar lord pope Stephen junior of holy memory when he travelled to France, about granting and handing over this province of Italy's various cities and territories to the possession of St Peter and all his vicars for ever. **42.** This was the promise made in France at the place called Quierzy. When he had had it read to him, he and his judges agreed with everything contained in it. Freely and with good and willing intention, His Excellency the truly

---

58 The regular *statio* for mass on Easter Sunday morning; just as St Peter's and St Paul's were regular for the Monday and Tuesday.

59 For the kind of acclamations used to Charles, see 98: n. 61.

60 As Duchesne remarked, cc. 41-44 are among the most important in the LP; he gave a full discussion, I, CCXXXVI ff. Frankish sources virtually ignore Charles' visit to Rome in 774, except for Einhard (*Vita Karoli* c. 6) who says that the king merely restored what Desiderius had 'stolen'. Italian sources say that Charles restored to Hadrian the cities and territories taken by Desiderius (*Pauli continuatio tertia*, c. 58, *MGH SSrL*, 214; Leo, *Chronicon cassinense* 1.12, *MGH SS* 7, 589; *Chronicon vulturnense*, ed. Federici, 173). In his note *ad loc.* Duchesne quotes two documents of which the first, certainly, and the second, probably, refer to Charles' visit. The first is the dedication of the Hadriano-Dionysian collection of canons, presented to Charles by Hadrian at this time, which has the acrostich: 'Pope Hadrian to his excellent son Charles, lord, great king'. The other is an inscription recorded in a 9th-century collection, evidently copied from a gold crown hung above the altar of St Peter's.

61 Stephen II's life (94:37,46,47) mentions two texts, both made after Pepin's entry into Italy: the treaty of Pavia in 754, and Pepin's donation-charter of towns that Aistulf had been forced to evacuate. But here the compiler refers to an earlier document issued at Quierzy (94: n. 67) before Stephen left France; this was a promise rather than a donation and had certainly not yet been fulfilled 'in every detail'. On the authenticity of the LP's information here see introduction to this life; it clearly did not come from life 94 which says nothing of a promise signed at Quierzy.

christian Charles king of the Franks had another promise and donation, a copy of the earlier one, written out by Etherius his religious and prudent chaplain[62] and notary. In it he granted the same cities and territories to St Peter, and undertook to hand them over to the pontiff, within the defined boundary[63] as shown contained in that donation, i. e. from Luni with the island of Corsica,[64] thence to Sori,[65] thence to Mount Bardone,[66] i. e. at Berceto, thence to Parma, thence to Reggio, and from there to Mantua and Monsélice, with the whole exarchate of Ravenna as it once existed,[67] the provinces of the Venetiae and Istria, and the whole duchy of Spoleto and Benevento.[68] **43.** Once the donation was made and the christian king of the Franks had ratified it in his own hand, he had all the bishops, abbots, dukes and *grafiones* subscribe to it; they placed it first on St Peter's altar and then in his holy confessio, and both the king of the Franks and all his judges handed

62 *capellanus*: head of the royal chapel. That Etherius (Itherius) is not called abbot, though he very soon after became abbot of St Martin of Tours, is seen by Duchesne as a sign of the LP's reliability. In the next few years he appears as one of Charles' experts on Italy (Noble, 154); with Magenarius, he works on Charles' behalf before and after the king visited Italy in 781: Hadrian wrote (*CC* 69, cf. 70, 71) that Itherius and Magenarius had conducted an inquiry into the papal patrimony in Sabina, and later (*CC* 72) he complained that evil men were stopping them handing it over. The activities of these two envoys are mentioned in the *Ludowicianum* of 817.

63 The Luni–Monsélice line may have originated in a papal-Lombard treaty of between 598 and 640 and have been part of the road-system used as a convenient line of demarcation (Caspar, 1914; Noble, 86 with n. 103, cites Rassow, 1916, 499 for the point that if the line means little to us it must have been significant to people in the mid-8th century). It would cut Lombard Tuscia away from the Lombard kingdom.

64 On the inclusion of Corsica see introduction to this life.

65 SE of Genoa. Noble, 84, has Soriano, too far north to be probable; perhaps Sorgnano, but this is too close to Luni to be mentioned. Luni and Sori/Genoa are 'in line' much as are Reggio and Parma.

66 Bardone is a now the name of a village 15 km NW of Berceto; the mountain might be Monte Barigazzo, 2 km further NW, 8 km SE of Bardi. There is also a Monte Borgogne, 7 km S of Berceto. Apart from this passage, cf. *Burdonis* in later medieval continuations of the LP (Duchesne II, 359.18, 377.5, 381.22, 418.15).

67 Including the Pentapolis.

68 On Spoleto see c. 32. As for Benevento, its acquisition would solve problems over papal control of Campania (cf. 96: n. 34), would isolate the Greeks at Naples who could no longer threaten Rome through an alliance with Benevento, and would enable Hadrian to control duke Arichis, an ambitious man installed at Benevento by Desiderius in 758, who would shortly style himself *princeps* when there was no longer a Lombard king for him to be subject to. In 778 Hadrian was concerned (*CC* 61) that Benevento had joined Gaeta, Terracina and the Greek patrician of Sicily in seizing parts of Campania; Hadrian sent in troops and regained Terracina, only to see Naples and Benevento, in alliance, recapture it.

97. HADRIAN I

it to St Peter and his holy vicar pope Hadrian, promising under a terrible oath to maintain everything included in that donation. The christian king of the Franks had Etherius write out a copy of the donation; then with his own hands he placed it inside over St Peter's body, beneath the gospels which are kissed there, as a firm security and an eternal reminder of his name and that of the kingdom of the Franks. His Excellency took away with him another copy[69] of the donation made out in this holy Roman church's office.

44. His Excellency Charles king of the Franks returned with his armies to Ticinum, to finish the war and the siege of the city of Pavia vigorously. When God's wrath raged furiously against all the Lombards inside that city and many were lost by disease and annihilation, so it was God's will that His Excellency the king of the Franks captured the city along with Desiderius king of the Lombards and all his companions, and reduced the entire Lombard kingdom into his own power.[70] He took Desiderius and his wife with him to France.[71]

45. Now[72] this blessed pontiff was a lover of God's churches and took unceasing care to carry out the adornment and restoration of them all. *[A.D. 772–4:]*

---

69 Or 'other copies'; text uncertain. Duchesne (with MSS ACE) has the inconsistent *alia ... adscriptam*; D has *aliam*; B has *adscripta*.

70 *Ann. Lauriss.*, 774: Charles captured Pavia with Desiderius, his wife and daughter and all his palace treasure; the Lombards from all the cities of Italy came there and surrendered to Charles; Adalgis slipped away and reached Constantinople by sea. *Chron. Moissiac.*, *MGH SS 1*, 295: after a ten-month siege Charles captured Pavia in June. *Monte Cassino Chronicle*, *MGH SSrL*, 487: Pavia was captured on a Tuesday in June; but since the first Tuesday was 7 June, and *MGH DK* 1, 114, no. 80 (in which Charles is already *Carolus Dei gratia rex Francorum et Langobardorum*) is dated at Pavia on 5 June, the statement is doubtful.

71 *Ann. Lauriss.*, 774: with Italy subdued and set in order, and a Frankish garrison left in Pavia, Charles, his wife and the Franks returned in triumph to France. *Ann. Sangall. maiores*, *MGH SS* 1, 75: Desiderius with his wife Ansa was exiled to Corbie, where he stayed till his death, occupied in vigils, prayers, fasting and good works. *Ann. Lobienses, MGH SS* 13, 228–9: Desiderius was placed in the custody of Adalfrid, abbot of St Amand and later bishop of Liège. Noble, 131–2, comments that Charles' solution to the Lombard problem differed from Pepin's; Pepin had settled for an unenforceable overlordship, Charles took the crown himself; but Charles did not face the problems at home that Pepin had from 751 to 756. Quite apart from Charles' sense of duty to defend Rome, Desiderius, with his scheme to get Carloman's sons anointed kings, was a real threat to Charles, and had to be removed. Charles returned to France because of a rebellion in Saxony (*Ann. regni Francorum* 773–4; *Ann. mettenses priores*, p. 62; *Poeta Saxo* 1.26, *MGH SS* 1, 230) and the risk of trouble elsewhere: further reasons to remove the risk of a continuing Lombard threat.

72 The life now abandons all political history and concentrates on gifts and repairs to churches and similar matters.

At St Peter's this angelic man[73] provided a cloth of wondrous beauty with gold and jewels, representing St Peter's release from chains by the angel.[74] In the same basilica he coated the pavement from the entrance of the railings to the confessio[75] with fine silver weighing 150 lb. **46.** Close to the great silver doors in St Peter's he provided a curtain of wondrous size, its material cross-adorned and fourfold-woven silk. For all the arches of the same basilica of the prince of the apostles he provided 65 veils of tyrian material with interwoven gold. Then in the same church His Beatitude provided the great cross-shaped light with 1365 candles,[76] hanging over the *presbyterium*, and arranged for this light to be lit four times a year, at Christmas, Easter, the feast of the Apostles and the pontiff's anniversary. In the same basilica this holy prelate provided a gold-rimmed silver chalice weighing 5 lb, which he put in the *presbyterium* to replace the one lost in lord pope Paul's time. In St Andrew the apostle's church close to St Peter's this thrice-blessed pontiff provided afresh a pure silver canopy weighing 135 lb.

47. So too in St Paul the apostle's church he coated the body of this teacher of the world with silver sheets weighing 30 lb; this holy prelate added these since the silver there previously was too damaged. Also in this same basilica, he provided the great curtain close to the main doors, its material fourfold-woven silk, like the curtain he provided in St Peter's; he also provided another great curtain, its material fourfold-woven silk, which hangs beneath the great arch close to the altar. Also for this church's various arches he provided 70 veils, their material fourfold-woven silk. Inspired by God this holy pontiff had this church's atrium paved with beautiful marble: it had previously been very desolate, and the grass that grew there was attracting oxen and horses in to graze.

48. In God's holy mother's church *ad praesepe* he provided 2 cloths over the high altar, one of fine gold and jewels representing the Assumption of God's holy mother, the other of cross-adorned silk with a purple surround. Close to the great doors in the same church he also provided a great curtain, its material fourfold-woven silk, like the one he provided for St Peter's. For

---

73 From here to middle of c. 52, distinguish restoration to individual churches from gifts of *vestes* ('cloths') or of hangings which apply to all churches. *Vestes* are cloths of precious materials, sometimes embroidered (adorned) for covering an altar. The hangings divide into the great curtains at the main door (*cortina maior*) and curtains arranged between the columns of the naves.

74 Acts 12.7.

75 The area from the grill (*rugae*) which shut the 12-column portico in front of the *presbyterium* to the entrance to the confessio.

76 *candelae*: really oil-lamps?

97. HADRIAN I

this basilica's various arches he likewise provided 42 veils, their material fourfold-woven silk. **49.** Likewise in the Saviour our Lord Jesus Christ's basilica close to the Lateran he provided a cross-adorned silk cloth and a great curtain, its material fourfold-woven silk, and for the various arches 57 silk veils, their material all fourfold-woven and cross-adorned silk. In the church of St Laurence outside the walls, the one in which his holy body is at rest, he provided a cross-adorned silk cloth, and he likewise provided another cloth in the great church.[77] He rebuilt the roof of St Laurence's great basilica, as it was then roofless and its beams were broken.

In St Valentine's basilica[78] he likewise provided a cloth of cross-adorned silk. In St Pancras' basilica he likewise provided another cloth of cross-adorned silk. As for St Mark's church, whose roof of ancient build was close to collapse, he removed the antique beams, erected other very sturdy ones, rebuilt the roof itself and the surrounding portico, and restored the church itself. The blessed pontiff rebuilt the three antique arches with the addition of 12 lb of silver. Over the high altar in the same church he provided a cloth of cross-adorned silk. For the same church's various arches he provided 27 veils, their material fourfold-woven silk, and a curtain of the same fourfold-woven silk material that hangs beneath the beam. **50.** As the roof of the basilica[79] of St Laurence *ad Taurellum* was very ancient, he replaced all the beams there and restored it; he also provided and presented a fourfold-woven silk cloth over this church's altar. As for the basilica[80]

---

77 Wrongly identified by Duchesne (I, 235, n. 12) as the church founded by Xystus III (whose foundation was S. Lorenzo in Lucina); the *basilica maior* at S. Lorenzo fuori le mura was Constantine's huge cemeterial basilica discovered in the 1950s (BP xxxiv); in c. 64 it is mentioned as dedicated to St Mary. See *LNCP* 105:26 n.42 for fuller details.

78 On the Via Flaminia, founded by pope Julius (Liberian Catalogue, BP Appendix 1, 101), rebuilt by Theodore (BP 75:5), recipient of a donation by Benedict II (BP 83:2); in the 9th century a monastery was attached to it (Ferrari, 336–40); Krautheimer, *Corpus* 4, 289–312. The original dedication date, 14 February, passed into the calendar. On the identity of Valentine, A. Amore, 1975, 13–16, concludes that he was not a martyr but was a man involved in the original foundation; the question is confused by the cult of a Valentine at Terni, also on the Via Flaminia, also on 14 February (for the basilica there, 93:7,10); one is presumably a duplicate of the other.

79 Cf. 94: n. 25.

80 The earliest reference to this church (it recurs in Benedict III 106:25). It was destroyed around 1500; to judge from Bufalini's plan it was behind and a little north of the present S. Trinità dei Monti, while Lanciani ('L'Itinerario di Einsiedeln', *Mon. d. Lincei* I, 456) located it just east of S. Trinità in the Villa Malta (Bobrinsky), and believed that the tower which joins this house was in fact the bell-tower of S. Felix's. The church must have originated as the house chapel of the *domus Pinciana*, home of the Anicii; the dedication saint was Felix of Nola; Hülsen, 252.

of St Felix *in Pincis*, which was in ruins and roofless, he built a roof and freshly renewed the church itself and provided and presented a fourfold-woven silk cloth over this church's altar. He also renewed the roof of the basilica of St Laurence *in Damaso*, and there too he presented a cross-adorned silk cloth over its altar, and he provided another cloth for behind the altar, where St Damasus' body is at rest.[81] At the Apostles' basilica on the Via Lata, he renewed the surrounding portico, which had previously been begun but not completed by his predecessor lord pope Paul; by God's favour this blessed pontiff repaired all of it and also restored the great roof. This blessed pontiff realized that this church's apse was close to collapse and had this apse strengthened with iron buttresses[82] and so renewed it. In the same church he provided a cross-adorned silk cloth over the high altar. He also renewed SS Peter and Marcellinus' cemetery[83] on the Via Labicana close to St Helena's basilica; he rebuilt its roof, both of St Tiburtius' and of SS Peter and Marcellinus'; and he rebuilt the steps down to their sacred bodies as there was then no access down to these holy bodies. **51.** In St Hadrian's[84] basilica he provided silver candlesticks weighing 12 lb, and 2 silver *laudimae*[85] weighing 8 lbs, which he placed over the *presbyterium* railings where the silver arch is. He also provided two cross-adorned silk cloths, one over St Hadrian's altar, one over St

---

81 Damasus had been buried in his basilica on the Via Ardeatina, BP 39:6, confirmed by the 7th-century Itineraries *CChr* 175 pp. 294, 308, 316, 327; but the compiler of the Lorsch I sylloge of inscriptions in the 8th or 9th century believed that the body rested in the *titulus*, a view apparently here shared by the LP unless the compiler has confusingly shifted his attention to the basilica outside the walls, cf. Krautheimer, *Corpus* 2, 146–7..

82 *cancalis*: presumably a form of *cancellus* ('railing'), required by the context in a structural rather than an ornamental sense.

83 See BP Silvester 34:26–7 with xxxiv–xxxv; the saints' bodies had been left in their tomb when Paul moved others into Rome, and were stolen on Einhard's behalf in 827.

84 Cf. BP Honorius 72:6, and in this life cc. 73 and 81 where it is restored and made into a deaconry; it recurs in Gregory IV 103:15, 17; Hülsen, 260–61. It was Lanciani (1883) who showed from various documents that St Hadrian's was the Curia Senatus, last rebuilt by Diocletian, and that Honorius adapted it as a church by adding an apse (the outside walls were otherwise untouched) and inserting 2 rows of columns to provide a nave and 2 aisles (the columns ceased to be visible in the remodelling of 1654, when the paving was raised and the bronze doors were removed for use at St John Lateran); it was restored to its original state between 1931 and 1937. North of St Hadrian's, the church of St Martina was installed similarly in the Secretarium Senatus; the two buildings were joined by a covered portico and a sort of court whose plan was surveyed by Antonio da Sangallo (Lanciani, pl. I), but the Via Bonella was cut between the buildings in the 17th century.

85 Perhaps lighting-fixtures of some kind?

97. HADRIAN I

Martina's altar.[86] In the same church he provided 15 veils, their material fourfold-woven silk. Then he rebuilt the roof of St Prisca's *titulus*[87] which was then on the point of collapse and was in ruins; there too he provided a cross-adorned silk cloth. At SS Cosmas and Damian's church at the Three Fates[88] he provided a cross-adorned silk cloth; a curtain in front of the apse, its material fourfold-woven silk; and 20 veils of the same fourfold-woven silk and 20 of linen.

[A.D. 774–6:]

52. Now[89] for the various *tituli* and other churches and all the deaconries and monasteries, as many as are inside the wall of this city of Rome, this holy pontiff fired by God's inspiration provided and presented cloths of silk materials, that is cross-adorned silk and tyrian. And as a good shepherd he restored and decorated for the praise of God all God's churches both outside and inside this city of Rome's walls.

Furthermore[90] he renewed the walls and towers of this city of Rome that had been demolished and destroyed to their foundations, and restored everything around as required; to which he devoted much money, both on pay for those who built the wall and on their sustenance, also on limestone and various requirements, and spent up to 100 lb gold.

---

86 Cf. n. 84; here St Martina's is regarded as an altar, as part of St Hadrian's; in c. 96 it is regarded as a separate basilica.

87 Its priests signed at the Council of 499; the tombstone of a possibly 5th-century priest of this *titulus*, Adeodatus, survives in the cloister of St Paul's. In 1776 close to the present church was discovered an ancient christian oratory with badly damaged paintings then identified as of the apostles. De Rossi argued that the legend identifying Prisca with the wife of Aquila, the two being mentioned in the New Testament, was well founded, and he linked in the name of the Cemetery of Priscilla; in 98:73 (but not 98:10, 83) the *titulus* is called that of Aquila and Prisca, which shows the legend is at least that old; Hülsen, 424; Krautheimer, *Corpus* 3, 260–276.

88 This description of the basilica of SS Cosmas and Damian results from the inaccurate extension of a term applying to the area around the rostra, the arch of Septimius Severus and the Curia (St Hadrian's), to a site along the Clivus Viae Sacrae (which was the direct prolongation of the road along the NE side of the Forum, and began precisely where the name Tria Fata, on which cf. 96: n. 25, strictly belonged).

89 The compiler here telescopes his source documents.

90 The Einsiedeln Itinerary provides as an appendix (*CChr* 175, 341–3) a full count of the towers, battlements, posterns, latrines and windows in the stretch of wall between each of the 16 gates and at the Hadrianium (Castel S. Angelo); in all it reckons 383 towers, 7020 *propugnacula* (battlements), 5 posterns, 116 latrines, 2066 large windows (but the actual figures add to 387, 7080, 5, 120, and 2047; and 2143 or 2144 small windows are not included in the total); de Rossi (*Piante di Roma*, 70) suggested that the survey was compiled on this occasion. Further similar restorations occur in c. 92, with details of the labour force then used.

53. Fired by God's inspiration this blessed prelate established a community of monks in St Stephen's monastery *cata Barbara patricia*[91] at St Peter's, where he appointed a suitable person as abbot; and he laid down that they should perform unremitting praises at St Peter's, just like the other three monasteries, and that the two monasteries alongside that church should chant praises to our God, since that monastery had been largely inactive, neglected and uncared for, and no office for worshipping God was being maintained there.[92]

54. This blessed prelate created and newly established 4 domuscultae.[93] One was called Capracorum,[94] in the territory of Veii about 15 miles from

---

91 Mentioned also at 98:77, 90 as *cata Galla patricia* (so too in a bull of Stephen II in 757, Mansi 12, 552, cf. Ferrari, 319 n.3) and at 98:47 as St Stephen Major (so too in Paschal I 100:2, 27). Its church survives as S. Stefano degli Abessini behind St Peter's (Duchesne, 1914, 315 = *Scripta minora*, 261; Hülsen, 477–8; cf. bibliography to 1957 in Duchesne III; Krautheimer, *Corpus* 4, 178–198). Galla was no doubt the matron Galla, daughter of Symmachus consul and patrician, mentioned by Gregory I (*Dialogues* 4.13); widowed after a year of marriage, she became a nun close to St Peter's and survived many years at a convent there; monks must have taken over later, not necessarily on exactly the same site. For Barbara (whose name is firmly attached to a monastery close to St Andrew's on the Esquiline) see 91:3 with n. 14; Ferrari, 319–27; the association of her name with St Stephen Major may be a slip. Ferrari, 330, reports the view of Cancellieri that Galla was responsible for St Andrew's at St Mary Major's and Barbara for St Stephen Minor (not Major), and that the names of Gregory's two friends were muddled and used interchangeably; but St Stephen Minor was founded long after Gregory's time (94:40) and the bulk of the early evidence would associate Barbara with St Andrew's and Galla with St Stephen Major.

92 Since it was only 20 years since Stephen II (94:40) had made precisely the arrangements Hadrian was now making, it can be seen how quickly rules of this kind were neglected; but the particular trouble here may have been caused by discord among the monasteries at St Peter's shortly before Hadrian's accession (see 96: n. 78).

93 In fact 6, not 4; cf. Duchesne, I, CCXXXXIV b, and introduction to this life. On the domuscultae in general see introduction to life 93.

94 On this domusculta see also c. 69 with n. 138; its proximity to the lands of Toto of Nepi might be an attempt by Hadrian to provide military force against any new Toto (Noble, 248–9). It was centred on S. Cornelia, 15 km N of Rome, midway between Veii and Formello (6 km N of Veii, 17 km S of Nepi), a site rediscovered in 1958 and excavated by Charles Daniels in 1962–64. Its identification with the domusculta was made by J. B. Ward Perkins (*Antiquity* 37, 36–45); the arguments are summarized by Whitehouse, 1980, 128; see also 'The Ager Veientanus', 1968, 161–5; Wickham, 1978, at 172–8. Partner, 1966, 68, reckons that Capracorum was some 8 or 9 by 24 km, running from Prima Porta to Calcata; the authors of 'The Ager Veientanus', 163, reckon a continuous strip of territory midway between the Via Cassia and the Via Flaminia, about 25 km north to south, with a total area between 100 and 200 square km; Duchesne had described it as a huge estate, starting at the 15th mile, on the east of the Via Cassia, and as becoming the replacement for Veii as the next population centre north of Rome. But all this is very doubtful. Hadrian's central bloc need have been only a few square km;

97. HADRIAN I

Rome. Of this, he originally held as a legacy in succession to his parents the Capracorum farm itself with many other farms contiguous to it, which had been his for some time; there he purchased many other farms, homesteads and estates, paying fair compensation[95] to various persons in return, and added them to this domusculta. He laid down by an apostolic privilege[96] under very binding anathemas that this domusculta Capracorum, with the estates, farms, homesteads, vineyards, olive-groves, watermills and everything pertaining to it, should remain for the use of our brethren Christ's poor for ever; the wheat and barley grown every year on the lands of the domusculta should be carefully brought to our holy church's granary and stored separately; the wine and the various legumes grown every year on the estates and lands of this domusculta should also be diligently brought to our holy church's cellar and stored apart. As for the pigs tended at pannage

---

though he accumulated much land, nothing shows it was a single *latifundium*. It presumably included (apart from the church of S. Cornelia) the castrum Capracorum (referred to in Vatican charters), identified with the castello at Monte Gelato beside the river Treia above Mazzano near the modern Mola di M. Gelato, in Faliscan territory. But despite Partner, 1966, 74-5, it presumably excluded the estates given by Eustathius and others to the deaconry of S. Maria in Cosmedin (Bertolini, 1947, 143-4) since a deaconry was not controlled directly by the pope (*ibid.*, 127-30); these included the fundi of Trea (cf. the river Treia), Scrofanum (Wickham, 1978, 168), Agelli (*id.*, 169) and Antiquum (the castello of Calcata in Faliscan territory was later described as *in fundum qui vocatur Antico*). The territory of the domusculta could be that detailed at the foundation of the 11th-century monastery at S. Cornelia. Its occupants took part under Leo IV in the building of the walls of the Leonine City, as is recorded in a surviving inscription placed in 1634 above the present Porta Angelica; a cast now exists in that part of the Passetto restored by Prandi (*PBSR* 1979, p. 33); A. Prandi gives the best text (1951 at 152 note 1); cf. Gibson and Ward Perkins (1979, at 32-3). After 1026-35 the domusculta was dismembered and gave birth to the towns and villages of Formello, Campagnano, Mazzano, Calcata and Faleria (the medieval Stabla or Stabia), and a number of deserted sites of which Castel Porciano, Roncigliano and Maggiorana can certainly be identified. The omissions of Isola Farnese (on the ruins of the acropolis of Veii) and Sacrofano may be no coincidence if the territory of the domusculta was not a single bloc, *pace* the authors of 'The Ager Veientanus', *loc. cit.*

95 This phrase, repeated in c. 63, looks like special pleading in view of the trouble Leo III was to have with aristocrats who claimed the church had taken over their lands forcibly. But it is not a sign of late composition: in 93:25 the same insistence on fairness occurs. No doubt all through there were others whose view was different. For the attack on the domuscultae at Leo's death, Astronomus, *Vita Hludowici* c. 25 (*MGH SS* 2, 620). For the tensions leading to this and the development of a militia on domuscultae separate from the forces of the aristocracy, cf. 93: n. 93.

96 It looks as if the compiler was following the text of a formal document at this point (J 2486). This passage provides the only description of the working of a domusculta. Daily supplies to Rome suggest that the domusculta did not have its own storage arrangements: the cellar (*paracellarium*) is clearly at the Lateran.

every year on the homesteads of this domusculta, a hundred head of them should be slaughtered and stored in the same cellar. His thrice-beatitude decreed and promulgated under mighty ties and interdicts that every day a hundred of our brethren Christ's poor, and even more if available, should be gathered at the Lateran patriarchate and be stood in the portico[97] close to the stairs going up into the patriarchate, where the painting of the poor is; and 50 loaves, each loaf weighing 2 lb, and 2 *decimatae*[98] of wine, each *decimata* weighing 60 lb, and also cauldrons full of broth should be disbursed every day to these poor by the hands of a trusty cellarer, each of them receiving a portion of bread, a drink of wine, that is 1 beaker containing 2 cupfuls, and a ladle of broth. So his bountiful thrice-beatitude, with the sacerdotal college, laid down and promulgated that the revenues of the produce and the various properties of this domusculta should be disbursed or expended on no other needs, but all the profit should be for, and should be disbursed for ever on, the assistance and daily sustenance of these our brethren Christ's poor.

55. The other three domuscultae are: Galeria,[99] on the Via Aurelia at St Rufina[100] about 10 miles from Rome, with farms and homesteads, vineyards, olive-groves, watermills and everything pertaining to it. The other two are: the other Galeria,[101] on the Via Portuensis about 12 miles from

---

97 This portico was at ground level on the north front of the palace, between St Laurence's oratory and the great staircase. Rohault de Fleury (1877, 378) found some traces of it, with the debris of frescoes which might have belonged to Hadrian's decoration.

98 A liquid measure.

99 Note that this and the next domusculta have the same name, though P. Partner (1966, p. 68 n. 6, following Tomassetti, *La Campagna Romana*, III, 36–47) thought the two were really one, stretching from the Tiber northwards, 15 km beyond the Via Aurelia, right up to the ruined village of Galeria beside the Via Claudia. The name Galeria survives as that of a stream which runs southwards through this area, presumably within a mile or so of both domuscultae, and joins the Tiber some km east of Porto. One of Rome's ancient rural tribes was called Galeria; its territory may have been approximately that of Hadrian's two domuscultae. The use of the name for the domuscultae may be accounted for by either the stream or the tribe.

100 S. Rufina (Boccea, ancient Buxum) is on the Via Cornelia: if this is not a simple error, either both roads were known as Aurelia at this date, or perhaps the 10th mile of the Via Aurelia was one of the boundaries of a domain whose administrative and religious centre was at S. Rufina – but the shrine of SS Rufina and Secunda (with the bishopric of Silva Candida) was not called Galeria. A little to the north at Casal di Galera was the later Castrum Galeriae (where in 1059 the antipope Benedict IX was besieged by the troops of Nicholas II and Hildebrand), the probable location of the domusculta founded by Zacharias (93:26 with n. 95). Hadrian's domusculta may be a refoundation of the earlier one, or it may have absorbed it. On the domusculta Galeria and its extent on the banks of the Galeria and the Arrona between the Via Clodia and the Via Aurelia see Silvestrelli, 1917, 279.

101 The name of the second domusculta Galeria is kept by Ponte Galeria, a station on the

Rome, with farms and homesteads, vineyards, watermills and St Laurence's monastery[102] on the island of Porto Romano, with vineyards pertaining to it and the lettuce farm[103] called Asprula. The other domusculta is called Calvisianum,[104] with farms and homesteads, vineyards, olive-groves, watermills and everything pertaining to it, on the Via Ardeatina about 15 miles from Rome. His thrice-beatitude laid down[105] by an apostolic privilege under strongly binding anathemas that these three domuscultae – Galeria, Calvisianum and the other Galeria – should remain for ever for our holy Roman church's use and its requirements.

56. But as well as all the spiritual endeavours that this thrice-blessed and bountiful pontiff had both for fulfilling the growth, requirements and benefits of the holy Roman church, and for the restoration of God's churches and the improvement of divine worship, it is clear that he also had great concern and solicitude, affection and love for the patriarchate's holy and venerable house. So with great fervour and love for the honour of St Peter prince of the apostles and this holy patriarchate's decoration, he newly constructed and built there[106] a tower adorned with wondrous beauty, adjoining the portico which goes down to the bath; and there he had a gallery, a veranda[107] that is, built very beautifully, with bronze railings. He also rebuilt the portico itself, which had been destroyed by age, as was much needed; and he adorned that tower and all his new constructions with painting and marble.

---

railway to Fiumicino. On 1 August 1018 Benedict VIII (J 4024; *PL* 139, 1617) included it in his endowment of the bishopric of Porto.

102 St Laurence at Porto is a church mentioned in Benedict VIII's charter (last n.), by when the monastery was the bishop's residence; an account in 1256 relates how the bodies of the martyrs of Porto (Eutropius, Zosima and Bonosa) were translated from this church to Clairvaux; this suggests that the church was that built for these martyrs about 400 by bishop Donatus (Amore, 1975, 243–4). The 'island' (Isola Sacra) seems identical with that called Assis or Arsis in the LP (BP Silvester 34:28; Leo IV 105:76).

103 *lecticaria*: the word is unknown, and Duchesne offers no suggestion; as the context requires an agricultural meaning I assume a derivation from *lactuca*. The name Asprula is equally unknown.

104 On this domusculta see Lanciani, *Röm. Quartalschr.* 29, 1915, 49. It was located at Solforata, at the 15th mile of the Via Ardeatina, between that road and the Via Laurentina to the east; the name occurs in a bull of Honorius III.

105 No doubt in a similar document to that given above in more detail for the domusculta Capracorum.

106 These buildings occur in no later document, and are not mentioned by Rohault de Fleury, 1877; they must have been in the eastern part of the palace, slightly in front of the apse which has the copy of Leo III's mosaic.

107 *deambulatorium* is qualified by *solarium* to show that the building was in the open rather than in a church.

57. So[108] this thrice-blessed and truly noteworthy father, good shepherd and distinguished prelate, burning with great love and affection for his mentor St Peter prince of the apostles, when he had provided and presented all the decoration for this apostolic hall, splendid cloths with gold and jewels as well as various silk materials and other gold and silver ornaments in the same apostolic hall, he also renewed all its great steps going up to the atrium and also those from the two porticoes on each side which go up into the church; and he renewed the whole pavement of the church itself where the marble was broken, employing other beautiful and better marble. As for the porticoes on each side of this church, in which the beams were broken and the roof was close to falling, he put new beams in place and rebuilt and restored the roof itself. **58.** His thrice-blessedness also provided six images coated with silver sheets, three of which he placed on the railings at the entrance to the *presbyterium*,[109] where he also provided a cornice of coated silver and placed these three images on this cornice: in the middle, the image with the Saviour's face painted on it, and on each side of it images with painted representations of angels, one of St Michael, the other of St Gabriel. On the second railings, those in the middle of the *presbyterium*, he provided another cornice of coated silver and placed on it the other three images: in the middle one representing God's holy mother's face, and on the two sides one with St Andrew the apostle's face painted on it and on the other with St John the evangelist's. Both sets, all six images, as said above, were made very beautifully of silver sheets, which he gilded; on these images he put 100 lb silver.

59. The Sabbatina aqueduct[110] had now been badly broken for a period

108 Duchesne (I, CCXXXV) places here the beginning of the third part of this life.

109 The *presbyterium* here is the area in front of the confessio, bounded at the east by the 6 outer columns, which already had an iconostasis provided by Gregory III (92:5), with Christ and the apostles on one side, Mary and other virgins on the other. Still unadorned were the 2 grills between the central columns of the 2 colonnades, one in the outer colonnade, the other in the inner colonnade. The triple image now provided for the inner colonnade had the Virgin as its centre, with those saints to right and left who had special sanctuaries to the right and left in the basilica.

110 An obscure interpolation of uncertain value in pope Honorius' life (BP 72:5) claims that 'he established a mill on the wall at the place of Trajan (near the outlet of the Aqua Trajana or Acqua Paola) close to the city wall and (repaired?) the channel which brings water into (from?) Lacus Sabbatinus (Lake Bracciano), and under it a channel which brings the water of (to?) the Tiber (the discharge channel which joined it to the Tiber)'. Like all the aqueducts, the Aqua Trajana/Sabbatina had been cut by Vitiges in 537 (Procopius, *BG* 1.15); its particular value had been that its water turned the mills on the Janiculum. It must have been restored at some time before Aistulf cut it again in 756, and although Gregory I (*Ep.* 12.24) had been concerned

of twenty years;[111] through it used to run the water for the waterpipe[112] to the atrium of St Peter the apostle's church, also for the bath close to the same church where our brethren Christ's poor, who come at the Easter festival every year to receive alms, used to wash, also for the various mills which used to grind on the Janiculum; the water from this aqueduct was running neither into St Peter's atrium nor into the city. When this aqueduct, as said above, was wrecked, since 100 of its arches, built up to a great height, had been demolished and destroyed from their foundations, there seemed to be no hope of rebuilding and restoring these arches and the aqueduct; the blessed and holy prelate gathered a crowd of people and personally came to build and restore this aqueduct, and he put great care and concern into this aqueduct's building, in that he renewed it and restored it afresh from its foundations. As for that waterpipe which ran from this aqueduct to St Peter's atrium, since through great neglect and unconcern most of the waterpipe's lead had by now been removed by stealth, while the lead that remained was damaged, straightaway this distinguished pastor added a great amount of lead and built the waterpipe afresh, and, with God as the author, he caused the water to run abundantly, as it had of old, to St Peter's atrium, to the bath, and also into the city – that is to the Janiculum where the mills used to grind.

[A.D. 776–7:]

60. At St Paul's basilica this blessed pontiff provided three images of silver sheets, which are placed on the railings at the entrance to the *presbyterium*,[113] one with the Saviour our Lord Jesus Christ's face painted on it, and the images on each side of it have painted representations of angels, weighing 24 lb. In the Apostles' basilica on the Via Lata he provided veils, 20 of silk material and 20 of linen. In St Laurence the martyr and

---

about the state of the aqueducts, the LP's interpolator may be right to attribute the restoration to Honorius.

111 The 20 year interval occurs below also for the Aqua Jovia; the reckoning will be from Aistulf's siege in 756.

112 *centenarium*; also at Nicholas I 107:16. Originally *fistula centenaria* (Vitruvius 8.208) denoted a pipe 100 inches in circumference (0.60 m in diameter). In the LP it clearly means a large lead pipe (the word *forma*, here always meaning an aqueduct, also once had a more restricted meaning); but Duchesne thought that since the LP is dealing with buildings and foundations, it should here mean the structure into which the pipe debouched (in, rather than to, St Peter's atrium). But, just below, the *centenarium decurrebat* from the aqueduct *in atrio*, which surely means we are dealing with a connecting pipe, not a structure; here and there *atrio* is (so to speak) accusative, not, as Duchesne apparently took it, ablative.

113 The scheme was like that just carried out at St Peter's, but at St Paul's there was only one row of columns in front of the altar, so only 3, not 6, images were needed.

deacon's church outside this city of Rome's walls he provided veils, 20 of silk material and 20 of linen.[114] In God's holy mother's church *ad martyres* he also provided veils, 20 of silk material and 20 of linen. This holy pontiff provided for the various *tituli* veils of cross-adorned silk and tyrian, 20 for each *titulus*, and 20 of linen; which totals 440 silk veils.[115] **61.** This[116] distinguished pontiff provided an image of silver sheets, gilded, with a representation of the Saviour our Lord Jesus Christ, weighing 50 lb, which is placed over the entrance to St Peter's basilica where the silver doors are. For the various deaconries he also provided veils of cross-adorned silk and tyrian, 6 for each deaconry; which totals 96 veils.[117] Again[118] this holy prelate had the Jovia[119] aqueduct restored from its foundations; for a period of twenty years it had lain badly broken. In St Pancras the martyr and deacon's[120] basilica outside the walls of Rome he also provided veils, 38 of cross-adorned silk and tyrian, 38 of linen. In St Stephen the first martyr's basilica on the Caelian

---

114 Krautheimer, *Corpus*, 2, 138, takes this (in view of 97:64) to refer to the east basilica (that of Pelagius), but suspects that the text should mention two sets of 30 rather than of 20 veils (there are 15 intercolumniations at each of two levels). If the text is faulty one might as well read two sets of 15; but note that the donations of veils in this chapter seem to be part of a programme of honouring basilicas and *tituli* equally with sets of 20.

115 There were therefore 22 *tituli* at this date. It would be stretching plausibility to say that there were other *tituli* which did not receive these gifts: the number of deaconries inferable from a similar phrase below is certainly correct. There were still 22 under Leo III; that more than 22 names occur is due to the use of varying names for the same *titulus*. In the 5th century there had been 25 (Duchesne, I, 165 n. 5). Since the 5th century that of Fasciola (SS Nereus and Achilleus) had been made a deaconry; the two other 'lost' *tituli* are no doubt SS Peter and Marcellinus and SS Silvester and Martin, the latter of which was now a deaconry (cf. 98: n. 100). By the later middle ages the number was up to 28. Cf. Kirsch, 1918, 6–17; Vielliard, 1959; and bibliography in Duchesne III (under Edifices sacrés).

116 Geertman places this sentence at the start of c. 60. Duchesne already reckoned it was an interpolation like those often found in lives 94 and 95; it clearly interrupts the account of gifts of silk and linen veils.

117 There were therefore 16 deaconries, which is correct at this stage in Hadrian's pontificate. Hadrian would later raise the number to 18 (c. 81), and this would remain the number in the middle ages.

118 Geertman places this sentence at the end of c. 59.

119 The *forma Iobia*, no doubt named after Diocletian ('Iovius') who may have restored it, was a branch of the Aqua Marcia which crossed the Via Appia at the so-called Arch of Drusus near the Porta S. Sebastiano and brought water to the Baths of Caracalla; it is mentioned also in the Einsiedeln Itinerary (*CChr* 175, 333 line 43: *ibi [sc. porta Appia] forma Iopia, quae venit de Marsia et currit usque ad ripam;* 340, lines 228ff: *De porta Appia usque scola Graeca. In Via Appia. Forma Iobia. Coclea fracta. Arcus Recordationis. Thermae Antoninianae* ... .

120 Legend did not make Pancras a deacon; the word (*levita*) may have been a marginal note intended to apply to Stephen, then wrongly inserted in the text.

97. HADRIAN I

Hill he provided veils, 20 of cross-adorned silk and tyrian, 20 of linen. Also in St Apollinaris' basilica[121] he presented veils, 10 of eightfold-woven silk, 10 of linen. Also in St Valentine the martyr's basilica outside this city of Rome's walls he provided veils, 22 of cross-adorned and eightfold-woven silk, 22 of linen.

62. The Claudian aqueduct,[122] which used to provide the water for washing at the Lateran bath and used to run to the baptistery of the Saviour our Lord Jesus Christ's church and to many churches on holy Easter day, had been demolished for a period of years, and only a small amount of water from this aqueduct was running into the city. And so when he realized this the distinguished and angelic prelate gathered a crowd of people from the districts of Campania and he personally came to take his turn in building and restoring this aqueduct. He put great care and concern into this aqueduct's building, in that he renewed and restored it afresh from its foundations. He straightaway caused the water from this aqueduct to run abundantly, as it had of old, into the bath and into the city.

[A.D. 777-8:]

63. In his time died Leoninus, consul and duke and later a monk. To gain[123] the pardon of his sins [he bequeathed] three twelfths of the estate Aratiana, which he enjoyed from his parents' legacy; it is at the 16th mile from Rome on the Via Ardeatina and St Hedistus' church is reckoned to be in it.[124] The blessed pope adorned it with the large buildings he constructed; he enlarged these three twelfths of this estate Aratiana with a further six twelfths [bequeathed] by the count Peter, by Agnes, the former *scriniarius* Agatho's

---

121 Duchesne thought the church (mentioned in Einsiedeln Itinerary) near the Piazza Navona was intended; had it been the one by St Peter's, one would have expected it to be mentioned in connexion with other donations there. But see 98:72 with n. 127.

122 There are substantial remains of this on Monte Celio and near the Lateran; in the Einsiedeln Itinerary it is referred to both under this name and as *forma Lateranensis*.

123 The language of this c. is lifted from 93:25; the necessary adaptations have produced some obscurity and even the lack of a principal verb!

124 The massa Aratiana may not have been a coherent bloc of land (Wickham, 1978, 176), any more than the domusculta need have been. The domusculta S. Edisti was alongside the domusculta Calvisianum (c. 55). The problem is that the martyr Hedistus (Aristus, Orestes; 12th October in the Hieronymian Martyrology) was apparently buried on the Via Portuensis (interpolation in the *Notitia ecclesiarum*, CChr 175, 309). Savio, *Röm. Quartalsch.*, 31, 1915, 29-53, 121-40, 250-59, dealt with the saint's legend and suggested, implausibly, an early translation of relics away from the Via Ardeatina site, which he located at Castel Romano; Lanciani (*Röm. Quartalsch.*, 29, 1915, 50) indicated the area of the Monte di Leva; but these are guesses. Where this church of St Hedistus was, and whether it was the site of the saint's original cult, remain unknown.

widow, and by Theodota, the former *praefectorius*[125] Dominic's widow. He also brought the boundaries together on every side: by paying fair compensation, with no compulsion but rather as befits a father, he bought in an amicable contract all the estates alongside the place, and laid down that the place should remain to St Peter in perpetual ownership as a domusculta; and even to the present day it is called St Hedistus' domusculta. The same Leoninus also granted to St Peter the estate Acutiana, close to that domusculta.[126]

64. Again in the great basilica named that of God's holy mother,[127] which was close to St Laurence the martyr and deacon's basilica where his holy body is at rest, outside this city of Rome's walls, the thrice-blessed prelate presented veils, 65 of cross-adorned and fourfold-woven silk, 65 of linen. As for the roof of St Clement's *titulus* in the 3rd region,[128] which was now about to collapse and in ruins, he restored it afresh. Also at St Silvester the confessor and pontiff's basilica *in Orfea*, which was already in ruins and its roof had been removed, he built the roof and freshly renewed the church itself. [A.D. 778–9:]

Also in the famous, world-renowned and venerable basilica of St Peter prince of the apostles, as the beams there dated from ancient times, this distinguished pontiff took notice and sent Januarius[129] his *vestiarius*, whom he knew to be a suitable person, with a crowd of people, and replaced 14 beams there; and he freshly restored that basilica's whole roof and porticoes.[130] **65.** The same bountiful prelate, filled with God's inspiration and

125 An agent of the Roman prefect rather than an ex-prefect; cf. the *praefectiani* in LP Hormisdas (BP 54:3).

126 But evidently not part of the domusculta; further evidence (cf. 93: n. 92) that domuscultae were not necessarily large blocs of land.

127 Cf. c. 49 and n. 77, with *LNCP* 105:26 n. 42.

128 Apart from a casual reference at 94:14 this is the earliest mention of S. Clemente in the LP, surprisingly so for one of Rome's oldest churches, Hülsen, *Chiese*, 238.

129 The compliments to Januarius here and just below showed Duchesne that the present compilation was made while he was in office; he will have been a successor of Miccio the regional notary who held the post in 772 (J 2395) and a predecessor of the priest Sergius and of Leo (the future Leo III).

130 It was for this restoration at St Peter's (cf. c. 74) that Hadrian wrote to Charlemagne (*CC* 65), asking that the beams Charlemagne was supplying in response to Hadrian's request be delivered on site by 1 August (779 or 780); for the repair of the *camaradum* (panelling, ceiling) which is glossed in Greek as *hypochartosis* (apparently meaning a covering of walls or ceilings, especially with plaster), Hadrian wanted a *magister* to see what timber was required; Charlemagne should then send the *magister* to the territory of Spoleto to fetch the right timber, as there was none in Roman territory; so archbishop Wilchar need not now tire himself in coming while the wood was drying out, as it could not be used while still green. See further 98:108 and n. 191.

97. HADRIAN I

moved by pity, realizing like a kind and dutiful pastor that the aqueduct Virgo[131] had been for a period of years thrown down and fully ruinous, and that only a little water came into Rome, restored it afresh and there gushed forth a great abundance of water which satisfied almost the whole city. Then he freshly restored the roof of St Januarius' basilica outside the Gate of St Laurence the martyr and deacon. Also at the cemetery of the martyrs SS Abdon and Sennen outside the Portuensis Gate he provided and presented a cloth of cross-adorned silk.

[A.D. 779–80:]

66. Now this angelic man, fired by God's inspiration, established three deaconries outside the Gate of St Peter prince of the apostles: one of our lady God's mother the glorious ever-virgin St Mary at the Hadrianium;[132] another of our same holy and undefiled lady outside the Gate of St Peter the apostle at the head of the portico;[133] and the other deaconry, that of St Silvester, close to St Gregory's hostel.[134] These deaconries the bountiful man had found hidden away, producing no works of mercy, and he freshly restored them; and to them, for the cure of his own soul, he presented many gifts movable and immovable, and established that on Thursday every week they should make their way with psalms from the deaconry to the bath and an orderly disbursal of alms should take place for the comfort of the poor.

67. This same bountiful prelate also observed that in the basilica of St Paul the apostle and chosen instrument the beams there were ancient and in part likely to fall, and just as above at St Peter's he assigned Januarius

131 Mentioned in the Einsiedeln Itinerary (*CChr* 175, 335 line 106; 336 line 128), in the latter case as 'broken', suggesting for the Itinerary a date before Hadrian's restoration of it.

132 The Mausoleum of Hadrian (Castel S. Angelo) kept its old name in the 8th century; cf. *Sylloge Einsiedlense* (*CChr* 175, 343 line 52). The church concerned was first called S. Maria Transpadina, later Transpontina; it was demolished in 1564 and replaced in 1566 by a new church on a different site, further from the Castel and Ponte S. Angelo, in the Borgo Nuovo, a road built by Alexander VI; Hülsen, 370–71. On the Vatican deaconries see Duchesne, 1914, 331–38 = *Scripta Minora*, 277–84.

133 Located at the other end of the portico which went to the basilica from St Peter's Gate close to Castel S. Angelo, i. e. at the St Peter's end ('head') of the portico; the *caput portici* is mentioned in a diploma of Leo IV (10 August 854; Marini, *Papiri diplomatici*, p. 14 n. 13) as the location of the garden of St Mary in Oratorio. The deaconry itself seems to have existed already under Stephen II (94:4) who attached a *xenodochium* to it; it is mentioned in 98:70 as 'outside St Peter's gate'; there is no trace of it after the 9th century; Hülsen, 324.

134 *hospitale*; both deaconry and hostel were in front of the great staircase of St Peter's on the present site of the obelisk. The deaconry is said to have been demolished by Pius IV in 1565 to enlarge St Peter's Square (Hülsen, 468). Vignoli (II, 83) cited Grimaldi that the church was called S. Maria de Virgariis (Hülsen, 374) or S. Gregorius Armenorum (Hülsen, 256), but these were probably different structures in the same area, as was S. Gregorius de Cortina.

his trusty *vestiarius* and a crowd of people, the thrice-blessed pastor often personally taking part, and he freshly restored all of it: in it he replaced 35 great beams, and round that church he freshly restored all the porticoes.

68. This thrice-blessed and apostolic man in a loving investigation found that the onetime pope Honorius' monastery[135] had through some kind of negligence become very desolate, so moved by divine inspiration he freshly rebuilt and enriched it, and appointed an abbot with other monks to live there according to a rule. He laid down that they should celebrate the office – matins, prime, terce, sext, none and vespers – in the Saviour's basilica also called Constantinian close to the Lateran patriarchate, in two choirs: one, the monks of St Pancras' monastery located there,[136] who formerly used to chant on their own antiphonally;[137] the other, the monks of the just-mentioned monastery of SS Andrew and Bartholomew called that of pope Honorius. In this way they should diligently chant their psalms of pious praise, re-echoing with chants in hymn-singing and God-pleasing choirs, and render glorious melody to the Lord in this venerable pontiff's name, composing his memorial in song for ever.

69. On the domusculta called Capracorum, which this holy prelate presented from his own ownership to his mentor St Peter prince of the apostles for the sustenance of the poor, he founded and built from the ground up a church,[138]

---

135 See 98: n. 135.

136 See 98: n. 133.

137 The author seems to be saying that hitherto one choir had been divided into two parts to chant alternate verses of psalms, in what would be described now as antiphonal singing; whereas henceforth the opposite choirstalls would be occupied by two separately based choirs for the same kind of singing, or perhaps more probably two choirs would perform their duties on different days. Another monastery (SS Sergius and Bacchus) would be added by Paschal I (100:22).

138 The original church was a small three-aisled basilica with a western apse and a baptistery separate from the church ('The Ager Veientanus', 1968, 164), with a *loculus* for relics beneath the site of the high altar; probably before it was rebuilt in the 11th century it acquired a campanile at the N.E. corner. By the time of this church's refoundation in 1041 as part of the monastery of SS Cornelius and Peter (founded between 1026 and 1035), the church was dedicated to the saints whose relics are mentioned in the text below, Cornelius, Lucius, Felix and Innocentius. This, and the fact that a casale named S. Cornelia (sic) has kept the name of one of this church's patrons, are among the reasons for identifying the site excavated (n. 93) as the administrative centre of this domusculta. The monastery was in use in 1238 (Wickham, 1978, 177). On its abandonment (before 1647) Cornelius' head was moved to St Laurence's church at Formello, Tomassetti, *ASR* 5, 140, 149. Cornelius and Lucius had originally been buried in the cemetery of Callistus, Felix and Innocent in two different cemeteries on the Via Portuensis; but it is not clear whether they had already been removed from their original sites before Hadrian's time.

beautifully adorning it and dedicating it to the name of his patron, God's same apostle, and depositing in it relics of the Saviour our Lord God Jesus Christ, his mother the ever-virgin Mary, the 12 apostles and other revered martyrs. He made his way to this sacred church with all his clergy and the Roman Senate, all of them in glory, joy and triumph, and he distributed the large customary alms to the poor; he translated and deposited in it the bodies of holy martyr-pontiffs, the body of St Cornelius martyr and pontiff, that of his successor St Lucius martyr and pontiff, the body of St Felix martyr and pontiff,[139] also the body of St Innocentius confessor and pontiff; in his love for the holy apostolic see in which they too had presided, this bountiful man who delighted in the sacred gave them honour which befitted his patrons in the Lord.

70. He also freshly restored the roof of St Susanna the martyr's *titulus ad Duas domus*, close to St Cyriac's, which was then on the point of falling and in ruins. He also freshly restored St Cyriac the martyr's *titulus*[140] and St Laurence's church *ad Formonsum*.[141]

[A.D. 780–81:]

He also freshly renewed the Saviour's basilica also called Constantinian, close to the Lateran patriarchate, which was in ruins, along with its square colonnades and atria, and the baptistery, just as he had the churches of the princes of the saints, Peter and Paul; in it he replaced 15 great beams. **71.**

---

139 That Felix is called pontiff shows that he was already being identified with the antipope Felix II (Duchesne, I, CXXV), and the same view is taken by the Sacramentary of Hadrian in its entry for his feast on 29 July.

140 Cyriac was said to be a deacon and martyr in Diocletian's time (*passio Marcelli, AASS Jan.* II, 371, 373, cf. Duchesne, I, XCIX), in a tradition which provided a foundation legend for the *titulus* (which existed by the time of the Council of 499 and was probably much older). The building was demolished under Sixtus IV. It was located on the Via XX Settembre at the level of the NW corner of the Ministry of Finance, near the ancient baths; see Kirsch, 1918, 75–7; Hülsen, 245; A. Rava, 1928, 160–8; Krautheimer, *Corpus* I, 115–7. On Cyriac in the martyrology, Kirsch, 1924, 51–3.

141 Otherwise S. Lorenzo in Panisperna, on the Viminal; it recurs in 98:37, 40, 73; mentioned in the Einsiedeln Itinerary as *in Formonso* and as the place where Laurence was supposed to have been grilled alive (*CChr* 175, 335–8, lines 94–5 (*ubi ille assatus est*), 144/5 (*ubi assatus est*), 171); but the catalogues from 1192 on (Cencius, Hülsen, 16, VZ III.267; Paris, Hülsen, 21, VZ III.277; Turin, Hülsen, 32, VZ III.302), Mallius in his list of Roman monasteries (VZ III.439), the *Mirabilia* (VZ III.187), and the *Descriptio Lateranensis ecclesiae* (VZ III.362) know the place as Panisperna, 'breadbasket', perhaps the name of an ancient *vicus*; there are variant readings of the word, but this is more plausible that Armellini's explanation (Armellini-Cecchelli, 250), which takes it as a corruption of Perpennia, on an ancient inscription in a nearby chapel. The older name, variously spelt, should probably be Formosus, presumably the name of the founder; Hülsen, 292–3.

Also this bountiful prelate, finding St Laurence's monastery *in Pallacinis*[142] to be desolate, freshly restored it and in every way enriched it, amalgamating it with another monastery located close by, that of St Stephen *Vagauda*;[143] he appointed monks and established that they should discharge the office in the *titulus* of St Mark pontiff and confessor, that is that they should chant the psalms of matins, prime, terce, sext, none and vespers for the repose of his own soul. In this basilica of St Mark he provided another 6 silver arches, weighing in all 55 lb, and also for the catholic procession[144] he restored 7 service chalices of fine gold weighing 9½ lb.

[A.D. 781–2:]

72. This farsighted man realized many people's safety was at risk since the road was narrow and jammed on the riverbank in the portico leading to St Peter the apostle's, and there was a crush when they crossed to St Peter's prince of the apostles; so he laid a foundation of more than 12000 blocks of tufa on the river channel's edge, and repaired the portico on a wondrous scale from the ground to its rooftop: he freshly restored this portico right to the steps of St Peter's. The deaconry of God's mother the ever-virgin St Mary *in Cosmedin*,[145] formerly only a small building, was in ruins, as a huge

142 This monastery (which recurs in 98:76, 103:41, 106:23 – where it is near both St Mark's and St Silvester's – and 107:15) must have been at the *porticus Pallacinae*; cf. Platner-Ashby, 381–2; on the ruins of the Circus Flaminius under the present Palazzo Petroni (Hülsen, 292; Ferrari, 192–5).

143 *Vagauda* (or *Bagauda*) seems to be unexplained; Hülsen, 486, noted that a priest named Bacauda signed the acts of the Roman synod of 531; and the name is that of the bishop who took Gregory the Great's synodical letter to John of Constantinople in 590 (Greg. *Ep.* 1.4, cf. 9, 10 etc.). Duchesne and Kehr (*Italia Pontificia* I, 101) thought that this monastery's church survives as S. Stefano del Cacco (so named from the image of a dog's head found on the site it occupies, a site which was once inside, or very close to, the southern end of the sacred precinct of the Isaeum). But Hülsen, 486, objected that this is too far from the area of the Pallacinae. Ferrari, 313–14, placed it near St Mark's, merely because of the location of the monastery with which it was to be united.

144 Apparently the *Litania Maior* procession, which took place on 25 April (in Rome not yet, it seems, St Mark's day) and set out from this church; cf. 98: n. 25.

145 The oldest literary mention of this deaconry, which was located partly on the podium of a classical temple and partly on a late 4th-century portico ('Loggia') alongside the Forum Boarium. Apparently in the 6th century the Loggia was adapted as a deaconry building (in fact though perhaps not yet in name: the concept of deaconries at Rome is 7th-century); while Hadrian's activity consisted in extending this eastwards using the temple podium as a foundation. The present S. Maria in Cosmedin is the result of a thorough remodelling under Callistus II (1119–24). In the porch is an inscribed donation charter from the late 7th century, naming one Eustathius, *dux, diaconiae dispensator*, and a damaged inscription recording a gift by the notary Gregory in Hadrian's time (Giovenale, 1927, 62). The tufa building behind it, which Hadrian decided to demolish, was identified by Hülsen, 148, as the temple of Hercules built

97. HADRIAN I

monument of Tiburtine tufa was tilting over it; for the period of a year he gathered a great crowd of people there, set fire to a huge pile of wood and demolished it. This distinguished bishop collected the rubble, cleared the site, and building it from its foundations he broadened the space in the said basilica on this side and that; in it he constructed three apses, and his fresh repairs made it capacious and truly *Cosmedin*.[146] **73.** As for St Laurence the martyr's *titulus in Lucina*,[147] St Martin's church close to St Silvester's *titulus*, and St Agapitus the martyr's basilica outside the walls close to St Laurence's: these churches were in decay for a long time and were reduced to a heap of ruins. The distinguished bishop, burning with love of the Holy Ghost, renewed them entirely together with their porticoes, to a fresh state of great beauty. He also freshly renewed the building of St Xystus' *titulus*[148] and of St Hadrian's basilica.[149] As for St Pancras the martyr's basilica, which was destroyed and brought to ruins by its great age, this bountiful prelate totally restored all of it and brought it to a fresh state of great beauty, along with St Victor's monastery[150] located there.

[A.D. 782–3:]

74. God's holy mother's basilica *ad praesepe* was wholly in decay for a long time; this distinguished prelate restored it on this side and that, and he

---

by Pompey near the Circus Maximus. The deaconry was in the centre of the Greek district at Rome, whose people were organized into a corporation called the Schola Graecorum or Graeca, a name found in the Einsiedeln Itinerary (24; 228; *CChr* 175, 332; 340); the expression Ripa Graeca is found in a diploma of Otto III. See Giovenale, 1927; Hülsen, 327–8; Krautheimer, *Corpus* 2, 277–307.

146 A play on words – Greek κόσμος, pure, neat, tidy, elegant. The name *Cosmedin* (Cosmidion, found also for churches at Ravenna and Naples) may derive from this, or from the district in Constantinople which contained the famous church of St Cosmas (cf. how Blachernae is found at Rome and Ravenna, and Lateran is found at Aachen). Krautheimer (*Corpus* 2, 305) thinks that the LP implies that another, false, Cosmedin had fomerly existed elsewhere, and Hadrian erected a true one in Rome, perhaps for iconodule refugees from the false one – the Cosmidion of Constantinople? – but concedes it is unlikely this can apply to all of the occurrences of the name in Rome, Ravenna and Naples.

147 See Krautheimer, *Corpus*, 2, 184.

148 Here first mentioned as such in the LP; its priests had attended the councils of 595 and 721 and it recurs in 98:45, 73. But it may be the church called Crescentiana founded by Anastasius I (BP 41:2) and represented at the council of 499. Now S. Sisto Vecchio; Hülsen, 470–1; Krautheimer, *Corpus* 4, 163–77.

149 Cf. c. 51 with n. 83, and c. 81.

150 The earliest reference to the actual name of the monastery which provided the services at St Pancras' (cf. 98:77), organized in 594 by Gregory I (*Ep.* 4.18, appointing Maurus as the first abbot); by 1018 it was called the monastery of SS Victor and Pancras, and the latter name eventually prevailed; Ferrari, 341–4.

put 20 great beams in place for that church's roofing. He[151] also renewed and restored St Eusebius' basilica on all sides. The apse-vault[152] of St Peter's was entirely wrecked and destroyed; he renewed it by engraving it in various colours on the ancient model.[153] He freshly restored the portico leading to St Paul's, from the Gate and the church of St Euplus[154] as far as St Paul's basilica itself. He freshly constructed the portico leading to St Laurence's outside the walls, from the Gate as far as the basilica itself. **75**. This bountiful Oracle freshly restored this side and that[155] this same basilica of St Laurence the martyr where his holy body is at rest and which adjoins the great basilica this prelate had previously constructed. Also he renewed on all sides St Stephen's church[156] close to them, where the body of St Leo bishop and martyr is at rest, along with St Cyriaca's cemetery and the climb up to it. He also restored on every side the Jerusalem basilica at the Sessorian, and its ancient beams which had decayed, replacing them marvellously. Also at the Apostles' *titulus*, Eudoxia's *ad vincula*, he freshly renewed its whole church. **76**. He renewed with great care SS Rufina and Secunda's basilica at the *episcopium* of Silva Candida,[157] which

151 Geertman places this sentence at the end of c. 73.

152 *camera*: the meaning here is discussed by Geertman, 192–3, 'wooden ceiling', and not 'wall revetment'; cf. c. 64 with n. 127, and *CC* 65, concerning this same repair of the *cameradum*. Duchesne (I, 240 n. 6; cf. 193 n. 64) assumed that the repair was to the apse mosaic, already restored in 640 by Severinus (BP 73:5), and which may have dated from the time of Leo I.

153 *exemplum*: picture, image, drawing; the replacement followed the original design.

154 A church mentioned already in the LP as an oratory built by pope Theodore (BP 75:5); de Rossi noted a 4th or 5th century sarcophagus found at the site. The church is mentioned again in 1145 (Monaci, *ASR* 27, 1904, 384, n. 13); and shortly afterwards gave its name to a hospital, listed in the Turin Catalogue, but there is no later reference to the church's existence. Close to the hospital was (till 1849) a church called S. Salvator de Porta, which Duchesne (following Martinelli) was probably wrong to regard as identical with that of St Euplus (Hülsen, 250, 450).

155 Cf. Krautheimer, *Corpus*, 2, 138.

156 Mentioned in the LP as dedicated by pope Simplicius (BP 49:1) close to the basilica of St Laurence; fragments of the epitaph of a bishop Leo (not a pope, nor despite the LP and the Itineraries a martyr) were found near the ruins of an ancient triapsidal oratory, not far from the SE corner of the present S. Lorenzo, close to the steps leading up to the modern cemetery which covers the Coemeterium Cyriacae; and de Rossi identified the oratory with that of St Stephen. As many of the inscriptions were of 4th century date, Simplicius may merely have dedicated a pre-existing building to St Stephen; cf. Duchesne, I, 250 n. 3; also c. 85 and n. 182.

157 Llewellyn, 1971, 244, remarks that Hadrian was restoring derelict churches at a time when peace had been restored in the campagna; the cathedral of Silva Candida was restored to serve the newly-settled population on one of the domuscultae of Galeria; but it cannot be inferred that there was new settlement. This bishopric was united to that of Porto by Callistus II, but there is still a small rural church on the site of St Rufina's (Tomassetti, *ASR* 3, 306); cf. n. 100.

had decayed from great age, along with the baptistery. As for St Andrew the apostle's basilica[158] on the Via Appia *in silice*, beyond St Thomas the apostle's, not far from the 30th mile, which had reached desolation and ruin, he freshly restored it along with the baptistery and decorated it on a grand scale. Also he freshly renewed the whole of SS Cosmas and Damian's basilica at the Three Fates, whose beams had also decayed and failed through great age. St John[159] the Baptist's church[160] at the Latin Gate had reached ruin, and he freshly renewed it entirely. He freshly restored the Apostles' church[161] at the third mile outside the Appian Gate, in the district *Catacumbae*, where the bodies of St Sebastian and others are at rest, which had reached ruin. He freshly restored Pudens' *titulus*, which is St Pudentiana's church, which had reached ruin. He renewed from the ground up St Theodore's basilica in Sabellum, close to the domusculta Sulpiciana,[162] and St Peter's basilica at the estate Marulis,[163] which had been destroyed for a long time.

77. Then in his time died Mastalus[164] the *primicerius*; for his soul's sake

158 Cf. 98:30. The two churches here named may have been somewhere near Cisterna; for St. Andrew's, Kehr, *Italia Pontificia* II 106–7.

159 Geertman places this and the next two sentences before the last sentence of c. 75.

160 A lapsus calami for St John the Evangelist, as is clear from the collect in the Gregorian Sacramentary's mass on 6 May for the *natale S. Iohannis ante portam Latinam*. Tertullian (*de praescr.* 36) already located at Rome the legend of St John the Apostle being boiled in oil before his exile to an island, and Ado's Martyrology (H. Quentin, *Les martyrologes historiques*, 1908, 632) specified the church at the Latin Gate as marking the site. The present church was consecrated by Celestine III in 1191 as a surviving inscription records (Forcella, *Iscrizioni delle chiese di Roma* (1867), XI, p. 161 n. 297). Work undertaken in 1914 revealed the painted decorations of that pope's era and also some traces of Hadrian's building. On the basilica see Krautheimer, 1936, 485–95; *Corpus* 1, 304–319; Hülsen, 297.

161 The basilica of S. Sebastiano; on it and the *Memoria Apostolorum* see bibliography in Duchesne, III (Cimitières – Via Appia). The dedication to Sebastian occurs first in the Itineraries. Xystus III (BP 46:7) had founded a monastery *in Catacumbas*, restored by Nicholas I (107:53); Hülsen, 460; Krautheimer, *Corpus* 4, 99–147.

162 Castel Savelli, slightly below and to the west of Lake Albano, records the site of this church and of the domusculta Sulpiciana. The only ruins there are of a post 9th-century castle (Tomassetti, *ASR* 2, 147). Castel Savelli is close to St Euphemia's and the Lacus Turni (BP Silvester 34:30, with Duchesne, I, 200 n. 104; Donus 80:1, with Duchesne, I, 348 n. 3).

163 The estate name is unexplained; it was located at the 12th mile of the Via Latina, and first occurs in a charter of Sergius I (printed in Duchesne, I, 380, line 33); it and St Peter's rural church occur under Gregory II (J 2204), and the church (as *in Maruli*) is mentioned in Leo IV 105:62; two charters of the monastery of St Silvester at Rome in 955 and 962 (J 3669, 3692) show it was by then abandoned. No traces seem to have been found in the presumed area, the Valle Marciana south of Grottaferrata.

164 A bull of Leo IV (J 2653) deals with a *campus Mastali* on the Via Aurelia (Tomassetti, *ASR* 3, 327). The point of the complicated passage that follows seems to be that Mastalus gave

he bequeathed to the power of this bountiful pontiff what was to be disbursed to Christ's poor out of his own legacy. In consequence Mastalus' heirs with one accord gave and sold to this great prelate their respective shares, farms and homesteads along with St Leucius' church,[165] on the via Flaminia at about the 5th mile from Rome, for 200 gold mancuse[166] solidi; this was what Mastalus' heirs gave Christ, also for the sake of his soul. As for the share which the *secundicerius* Gregory was acknowledged to have in these homesteads of St Leucius, Gregory himself granted it to this bountiful prelate in exchange for the office[167] of *secundicerius*. Since he found that St Leucius' church was in ruins and besieged by thorns and brambles, he freshly restored it and built there a domusculta on a wondrous scale and granted it for ever to St Peter his mentor; he enlarged its boundaries partly by a legacy from the late Paschal, partly by exchange with the heirs of the late Lucia and John the *primicerius*, partly with various other places.

[A.D. 783-4:]

78. In St Petronilla's basilica at St Peter's he provided 6 silver arches weighing 50 lb. He totally renewed[168] St Praxedes' *titulus* which was partly ruinous. He freshly restored[169] St Eugenia's basilica both inside and out; he

---

part of his property to the church for the poor and that Hadrian managed to induce Mastalus' other heirs to give or sell their inheritances so that Mastalus' property remained intact; the property was then extended as a result of deals with the heirs of Paschal, Lucia and John, and the domusculta was established with St Leucius' church as its centre. See Llewellyn, 1971, 244. But note how the domusculta is clearly made up of fragments, not necessarily as a single bloc (Wickham, 1978, 176).

165 Gregory I (*Ep.* 11.57 to Peter, bishop of Otranto and administrator of the see of Brindisi) mentions the monastery of St Leucius at the 5th mile, Ferrari, 198; the monastery is otherwise unrecorded. Leucius was a martyr of Brindisi. In the 18th century Galletti stated that the apse and bell-tower were still visible; but the location (south of Prima Porta) is now marked by no ruins other than the Tor di Quinto, perhaps of 11th century date; Tomassetti, *La Campagna Romana*, III 239-42.

166 *mancusus*: Dozy derives this from Arabic preterite participle *manqûsh*, 'engraved', 'struck'; Grierson, 1954, derives it from Latin *mancus*, 'deficient', thus a light-weight gold solidus. The latter explanation is preferable if the origin of the coin is italo-byzantine rather than arab.

167 *honor*: preferment. The LP implies there was a custom of paying on admission at least to lay dignities at the papal court; cf. the ancient *summae honorariae*.

168 Despite this, Paschal I had to rebuild the church totally, and on a different site, LNCP 100:8 with nn. 18-22.

169 This sentence deals with each of the 3 sanctuaries between the Porta Latina and St Stephen's: 1) the basilica of St Tertulli(a)nus; 2) the basilica of St Eugenia (cemetery of Apronianus; see also c. 82 and note) with the tombs of Claudia, Stephen, 18 or 28 clerics, Nemesius, Olympius, Sempronius, Theodotus or Theodorus, Superius, Obloteris and Tiburticanus; 3) the basilica with the bodies of Gordian and Epimachus, with the cubiculum of Quartus and

97. HADRIAN I   161

also freshly renewed SS Gordian and Epimachus' basilica and the cemetery of the same church of Simplicius and Servilian and of Quartus and Quintus the martyrs and of St Sophia along with St Tertullinus' cemetery outside the Latin Gate. He freshly restored[170] the church of SS Tiburtius, Valerian and Maximus and St Zeno's basilica along with the cemetery of SS Urban the pontiff, Felicissimus and Agapitus, and of Januarius and Cyrinus the martyrs, all adjoining in one place outside the Appian Gate; they had decayed for a long time. **79.** He freshly and totally renewed on every side God's mother the ever-virgin St Mary's *titulus*, called Callistus' in Trastevere. He also freshly restored St Marcellus' *titulus* on the Via Lata. He renewed on a wondrous scale the basilica[171] of the cemetery of the martyrs SS Hermes, Protus and Hyacinth, and Basilla. He restored[172] on a wondrous scale St Felicitas' cemetery on the Via Salaria along with the churches of St Silanus the martyr and St Boniface the confessor and pontiff, all adjoining on one piece of ground. He renewed St Saturninus' basilica[173] on the same Via Salaria, along with SS Chrysanthus and Daria's cemetery; and he renewed St Hilaria's cemetery. **80.** He freshly restored the cemetery of the Jordani, that is the one of the martyrs SS Alexander,

---

Quintus, and the crypts with the tombs of Sulpicius (Simplicius in the LP), Servilianus, Sophia and Trophimus; see the conspectus of the Itineraries in *CChr* 176, 625–6. None of these sites has been securely identified.

170 The sanctuaries of the cemetery of Praetextatus on the Via Appia: two churches above ground, that of Tiburtius, Valerian and Maximus, and that of Zeno, linked by a large crypt containing four tombs, those of Urban, Felicissimus and Agapitus, Januarius, and Quirinus. There are still recognizable traces of the two churches, one circular with 5 apses, the other rectangular with 3 square niches.

171 On the Via Salaria Vetus; cf. BP Pelagius II 65:2 for its (re-)construction. On topographical grounds Duchesne preferred *basilicam* (adopted here) in MS E to *basilicas* in BCD, yet printed the latter. Most of St Hermes' entirely underground basilica survives; 'wondrous size' is just: it is the largest of the underground cemeterial churches at Rome; Krautheimer, *Corpus* 1, 196–209; Josi, *RAC* 17, 1940, 195–208.

172 The LP now follows the Via Salaria Nova outwards from Rome. Nineteenth-century excavation revealed the church of St Silanus, described as *deorsum* in the Itineraries, which put St Felicitas' *sursum*. The latter was built by Boniface I (BP 44:6) in the cemetery of St Felicitas 'close to her body', which seems to mean that his church did not then contain her tomb, and the language of the LP implies that Felicitas and Silanus were in a single *sepulchrum*. The Itineraries imply separate tombs, that of Felicitas being now inside the church. Boniface's building is presumably what the LP here refers to as St Boniface's church, and has not been found, see Duchesne, I, 229 n. 13. In the LP pope Boniface I's tomb is described, as is the oratory, as 'close to St Felicitas' body'; the itineraries put his tomb *in altero loco* within St Felicitas' above-ground church; no doubt it was in its own tomb, separate from the altar which by the date of the Itineraries enshrined St Felicitas.

173 Already restored by Felix IV (BP 56:2); again by Gregory IV (103:5); a modern chapel in the Villa Potenziani-Massimi marks the site; Hülsen, 458–9.

Vitalis and Martial and of the seven holy virgins. On the same Via Salaria he renewed the cemetery of St Silvester the confessor and pontiff and of many other saints, which was in ruins. He freshly restored St Felix's church outside the Portuensis Gate; also he restored the basilica of SS Abdon and Sennen and of St Candida,[174] along with other cemeteries of saints together there.

[A.D. 784–5:]

81. This distinguished prelate established as deaconries[175] those basilicas he freshly restored, St Hadrian the martyr's and SS Cosmas and Damian's; in them he provided many goods for his own everlasting memory, and granted them fields, vineyards, olive-groves, slaves male and female, various possessions and movables, so that their revenue should provide for regular refreshment for Christ's poor at the deaconry bath-house.[176] In that deaconry of St Hadrian he presented 12 canisters, 1 ama, 1 scyphus, 1 paten, 1 sacred chalice, 1 offertory amula, in silver, weighing in all 67 lb.

Also in his great and expert concern and industry he freshly built from the ground up an aqueduct from the Sabbatina aqueduct,[177] and brought flowing water to his mentor St Peter the apostle's, both for the basilica's baptistery, which was being filled from waggons, and for this basilica's atria and the bath, for the needs of pilgrims and those who serve there.

82. He freshly restored St Secundinus' basilica[178] at Palestrina, where his body is at rest, which was in ruins. The first martyr St Stephen's basilica on

---

174 On the Via Portuensis. The *Notitia Ecclesiarum* regards Candida's church as different from that of Abdon and Sennen, but the LP MSS have *basilicam*.

175 This raised to 18 the number of deaconries; cf. c. 61 and n. 117 and glossary.

176 *lusma*; Duchesne suggested that Greek λοῦσμα (from λούω) is to be explained from c. 68, where the distributions take place at the *balneum*: the cleanliness of the poor could be seen to at the same time as their other needs. In Greek, however, the word seems to have a metaphorical meaning only, 'washing', and to refer to baptism (see passages cited by Lambe). But could the derivation be from λύω, 'release', 'deliver'? One would expect **lysma* or **lisma*; but if so, translate: 'so that their revenue should provide for regular delivery from the deaconry for the refreshment of Christ's poor'.

177 For the repair of the Aqua Sabbatina (that of Trajan), see c. 59. Duchesne regarded the present c. as a duplication (analogous to the two different mentions in this life of repairs to the city walls) and to be explained as a reflection of work which lasted a number of years, possibly with interruptions; particularly as the reference in c. 59 is not a 'primitive' part of the text (I, CCXXXV). But this c. does not say that Hadrian repaired the same aqueduct, merely that he provided a *formale* from that aqueduct to St Peter's; at the most this may mean the completion of (or a replacement for) the *centenarium* recorded in c. 59.

178 The Hieronymian Martyrology records St Secundinus on 1 August at the 30th mile of the Via Praenestina. The church is mentioned in 1021 in the *Registrum Sublacense* no. 173, and, though undiscovered, it must have been below Genazzano.

97. HADRIAN I

the Caelian Hill had decayed for a long time, and he freshly and marvellously renewed both the pile of the basilica and the porticoes inside and outside by bringing huge beams to it. At St Eugenia's basilica which his bountifulness had a while ago renewed, bestowing expert care on it, he freshly built there from its foundations a monastery[179] for girls and decreed that they should chant praises to God there continually, prime, terce, sext, none, vespers and matins; and he presented many gifts to it, fields, vineyards, houses, slaves male and female, various possessions and other things movable and immovable. At the *titulus* of Pammachius, SS John and Paul's, which had decayed with the passing of the years, he renewed all the roofing for that *titulus*.

[A.D. 785–6:]

83. In his great love this distinguished *sacerdos* elegantly adorned the whole of St Peter's confessio inside with fine gold in sheets with various representations, using in all 300 lb weight; and on the upper door of the same sacred confessio 13 lb fine gold; also on the lower threshold of the apostle's confessio 25 lb; for the face of the altar above this bountiful confessio, and on the right and left sides close to the stairs that adjoin the confessio, he added 136 lb silver on it, and carefully renewed it and magnificently gilded its representations with 18 lb fine gold. He also renewed 10 chandeliers in the same church of God's apostle, adding 100 lb silver on them. In front of the silver gates he provided 9 silver canisters weighing in all 45 lb; also on the tower 12 canisters weighing 36 lb. For the various crowns in the same church of St Peter he provided dolphins from 100 lb silver. **84.** In St Paul's church he likewise allotted 80 lb silver for the dolphins; also in the Saviour's church called Constantinian, he provided silver dolphins, 80 lb. He provided for the various oratories in St Peter's 12 silver canisters weighing in all 40 lb; and in the *presbyterium* on the men's and women's sides, railings[180] of fine silver, weighing in all 130 lb; also other railings at the head of the *presbyterium* in front of the confessio, of silver weighing in all 104 lb. In God's holy mother's church in Trastevere he provided 5 silver canisters weighing in all 15 lb. In God's holy mother's basilica *ad praesepe*, on the altar[181] of the Manger itself he provided sheets of fine gold with painted representations, weighing in all

---

179 Cf. c. 78; Ferrari, 132–3; no trace of church or convent seems to survive.

180 The grills of the three gates which gave entry into the portico (*presbyterium*) in front of the apse and confessio (like the three doors of a Greek iconostasis); in the LP the three are distinguished as on the men's side (left), the women's side (right) and 'at the head' (centre).

181 The earliest mention of an actual altar over or near St Mary Major's famous relic; the altar must have been inside a small oratory as at present, though not on precisely the same site, see *LNCP* 100:37 with n. 102.

105 lb; within the confessio above mentioned, 2 silver panels weighing in all 15 lb. **85.** He freshly restored St Agnes the martyr's church and St Emerentiana's basilica, also St Nicomedes' church outside the Nomentan Gate, and St Hippolytus the martyr's cemetery close to St Laurence's, which had decayed for a long time. He also restored the church of Christ's martyr St Stephen close to that cemetery of St Hippolytus.[182] In[183] St Paul the apostle's confessio, inside over his sacred body, he provided an image representing[184] the gospels, of fine gold weighing 20 lb.

[A.D. 786–7:]

86. This prelate, distinguished in all that is good, freshly dedicated and established SS Hadrian and Laurence's monastery;[185] it was decaying into ruin and had for long been occupied by men of the world like cave-dwellers. This outstanding bishop freshly restored it, and built it in the name of those saints Hadrian and Laurence; to it he gave many goods, gold and silver, fields, dependants and various properties, also movable goods. He decreed that by chanting day and night they should perform the accustomed praises to God in God's mother the ever-virgin St Mary's basilica *ad praesepe*, in[186] the other monasteries there established. **87.** In the confessio of St Laurence the martyr outside the walls this farsighted bishop provided an image representing the gospels and including a representation of St Laurence, of fine gold weighing 15 lb. In front of the vestibule[187] of the altar in the Saviour's

---

182 Evidently not the church of St Stephen close to S. Lorenzo fuori le mura (c. 75 with n. 151), though it cannot have been far away. De Rossi believed it was identical with the cemeterial basilica of St Hippolytus, still so described in the Itineraries (which do not mention St Stephen), but the LP clearly regards them as different.

183 This sentence is placed by Geertman after the first sentence of c. 87.

184 *in modum*: the same expression in cc. 87 and 95 (twice). Is the LP thinking of icons of the four symbols of the evangelists (based on the four living creatures of Ezekiel 1.5ff, man, lion, ox, eagle), or a picture showing copies of the four gospels? But note that Liutprand of Cremona (*Leg.* 13, ed. Becker, 183 line 23) uses *modus* to mean 'wording', 'tenor'; could the LP mean aniconic images containing phrases of the gospels?

185 Evidently Hadrian was restoring an older institution dedicated to St Laurence; it recurs as St Hadrian's monastery close to the *praesepe* in 98:77. The Turin Catalogue has a church of St Adrianellus close to St Mary Major, between St Andrew and St Vitus, which seems to be the church of the monastery here mentioned, and the name recurs in a document of 1364; the diminutive Adrianellus reflects the size of the chapel. The monastery was located near the southern corner of St Mary Major and was demolished in the 15th century, cf. 91: n. 14; 98:77 n. 143; Duchesne, 1907, 484 = *Scripta Minora*, 334; Hülsen, 261; Ferrari, 179–81.

186 Does the author mean 'along with'?

187 Explained by Duchesne as an iconostasis-portico like that in front of the confessio at St Peter's.

97. HADRIAN I

church called Constantinian he provided 3 gold bowls weighing 10 lb. For the various crowns in God's holy mother's basilica *ad praesepe* he provided silver dolphins weighing 24 lb. As for the silver image of the Saviour, God's holy mother, the apostles SS Peter, Paul and Andrew, which had formerly been there in St Peter's at his body,[188] this noteworthy bishop made it of fine gold of wondrous size, weighing 200 lb.

[Second Council of Nicaea, 787:]

88. This tasteful prelate and strenuous preacher of the true faith sent his envoys, the venerable Peter archpriest of the holy Roman church and Peter the religious abbot of the venerable monastery of St Saba called Cella Nova, to the emperor Constantine and his mother Irene, to encourage them and faithfully preach to them through his apostolic letters,[189] to set up the sacred images, as they are orthodoxly venerated in the holy catholic and apostolic Roman church by the warrant of the Scriptures and the traditions of the approved Fathers from olden times to the present. These emperors revered and welcomed this apostolic letter, and had a council of some 350 bishops gathered at Nicaea. Their belief was in clear accord with the teaching of this apostolic letter, as was the resolution they promulgated. They defined a universal synodic decree, a wonderful affirmation on the setting up of the venerable images. The same envoys brought with them this synod's decrees in Greek along with the emperors' mandates[190] with their actual signatures. The noteworthy bishop bade them be translated into Latin[191] and deposited in the sacred library, and so created a worthy everlasting memorial to his own orthodox faith.

[A.D. 787-8:]

89. This noteworthy pope wonderfully adorned the altar of St Paul's, along with the doors of his confessio, with sacred representations delineated on pure gold, weighing 130 lb. As the roofing of the *titulus* of SS Quattuor Coronati was close to collapse, he erected many beams there and freshly restored everything. Also in St Peter's he provided a paten and chalice for everyday services, of fine gold weighing in all 24 lb.

---

188 *ecclesia beati Petri ad corpus*: probably a way of describing St Peter's basilica (rather than the actual shrine).

189 The letters given to the envoys were dated 26 October 785 (J 2448-9); there were two letters, one to Constantine and Irene, the other to the patriarch Tarasius. The Council held eight sessions, from 25 September to 22 October 787.

190 The imperial letter is lost, but that of the patriarch Tarasius survives.

191 This was the Latin translation that offended the Frankish clergy and caused Charlemagne to oppose the 7th Ecumenical Council with the famous *Libri Carolini*. The translation does not survive (except for fragments in the *Libri Carolini* and in Hadrian's reply, J 2483), as it was replaced by that made under John VIII by Anastasius Bibliothecarius.

[A.D. 788–9:]

Also in God's holy mother's church *ad praesepe* this holy man provided a paten and sacred chalice of refined gold weighing in all 20 lb. Also at Eudoxia's *titulus* – St Peter *ad vincula* – he provided 12 canisters weighing in all 36 lb, and for the various crowns 35 dolphins weighing 8 lb. Also he freshly repaired St Sabina's church in the territory of Ferentinellum.[192]

[A.D. 789–90:]

90. In St Paul's this bountiful prelate provided a paten of refined gold, with a sacred chalice, weighing in all 20 lb. Also in St Laurence's church outside the wall he provided of fine gold a paten with a sacred chalice, weighing in all 16 lb. Also at SS Sergius and Bacchus' deaconry,[193] this deaconry's alms-distributor, out of fear of a temple sited above it, overturned it over this church and obliterated the basilica to its foundations and was totally unable to restore it; moved with pity and with love for those martyrs,[194] this farsighted bishop restored and enlarged it to a state of great beauty. **91.** The basilica of the monastery of Christ's martyr St Anastasius,[195] along with the *vestiarium, hegumenarchium*[196] and other buildings, caught fire in the quiet of the night thanks to the monks' lack of care, and was ablaze from its foundations to its rooftop. Hearing this, the merciful prelate ran in haste very early in the morning and found it still burning. Only the chest of the martyr's relics was saved, lying in

---

192 Is this Ferentillo, 13 km ENE of Terni? Duchesne does not consider this, while remarking on the existence of a cult to St Sabina in the Terni neighbourhood. But the Subiaco register (no. 173) has a territory of Ferentinellum *maius* or *minus* in the valley below Subiaco, though never referring to a church of the right name.

193 This was on the site of the imperial Rostra, between the arch of Septimius Severus and the Temple of Saturn, below the Temple of Concord (whose destruction is recorded here). The deaconry recurs in 98:38, 75, and 103:12; the building was abandoned in 1562; see Lanciani, *Storia degli scavi* II, 6; Hülsen, 461–2.

194 By the 16th century the martyrs whose relics were claimed to be there were not Sergius and Bacchus but Felicissimus, Agapitus and Vincent; on the deaconry's abandonment these were moved to S. Maria della Consolazione; Hülsen, 461.

195 Located *ad Aquas Salvias*, near Tre Fontane on the Via Ostiense; it recurs in 98:38, 76 (and perhaps 98:80 with an oratory of St Mary) and in later lives (103:28, 105:15, 106:24, 107:36). The first certain mention of it is at the Roman Council of 649, as the monastery *de Cilicia ad Aquas Salvias*, its dedication not stated. De Rossi (*Roma sott.* I, 114, 182–3) accepted a 10th-century tradition that the monastery was founded by Narses (d. 572) and believed it was originally dedicated to St Paul; the relic (his head) of St Anastasius, who was martyred in Persia in 627, will have arrived before the middle of the 7th century (the date of the *De locis sanctis*, *CChr* 175, 316, 31, VZ II.109, which mentions it there). The monastery still survives, named SS Vincenzo ed Anastasio (Vincent shares Anastasius' feastday on 22 January); Hülsen, 173; Ferrari, 33–48.

196 Residence for the *hegumenos*, abbot.

97. HADRIAN I

the middle of the site. The rest of the sacred objects and furniture in the church and the *vestiarium* had been melted by the fire. In great sorrow he and his servants strove to put out the fire, then he immediately put all his efforts into freshly renewing what was saved from the smouldering ruins and restoring the church, *vestiarium*, *hegumenarchium* and other buildings to a better state than before. He conferred on it more and better sacred objects, furniture and adornment than those burnt there.

[A.D. 790–91:]

92. This God-protected prelate observed that this city of Rome's walls[197] had been in ruins for a long time and that in places many of the towers were overthrown to the ground. With his expert care he gathered all the cities of Tuscia and Campania, along with the people of Rome and its suburbs and all the church patrimonies, and apportioned it stretch by stretch[198] to them all, and with apostolic outlay and stewardry he restored, renewed and adorned it round the whole city.

93. At the high altar of St Peter's he provided various representations of fine gold weighing 592 lb, and inside the confessio an image representing the gospels, of refined gold weighing 20 lb, along with a railing in front of the confessio, of fine gold weighing 56 lb; total for the altar, inside the sacred confessio this side and that, the image representing the gospels, the upper and lower doorposts, the railing and on the body, 1328 lb refined gold.

[A.D. 791–2:]

94. In this noteworthy pontiff's 20th year, in December of the 15th indiction [791], the river Tiber left its channel, swelled and spread itself over the plains. In great spate it entered the Gate called Flaminia, overthrowing that Gate to its foundations, and reached the arch called Three Sickles.[199] Meanwhile in some places it even overlapped the walls and it extended itself through the streets beyond St Mark's basilica after turning a right angle[200] by

---

197 Cf. c. 52 and n. 90.

198 *per pedicas*: *pedica* ('foot') was a unit used in measuring building works.

199 The arch of Marcus Aurelius over the Via Flaminia (Platner-Ashby, 35), where the Via della Vite meets the present Corso, not far from S. Lorenzo in Lucina. The arch was demolished in 1662, but most of its sculptures are preserved on the Capitol. The name Three Sickles (*Tres Falciclae*) presumably referred to some detail on the monument; in the *Mirabilia* it was called the Arch of Octavian.

200 *regammans*. The Tiber reached the end of the Via Lata and met the Capitol which forced it to turn by the portico of St Mark's; cf. 91:6. The Pallacinae district was near the NE end of the Circus Flaminius, and the vicus Pallacinae may even correspond with the present Via di S. Marco, Platner-Ashby, 381–2: possible fragments of the portico were found in the Via degli Astalli.

the Pallacinae portico as far as the Bridge of Antoninus;[201] it overthrew the wall itself to escape and rejoin its own channel; so that on the Via Lata the riverwater rose up to twice a man's height. The waters dispersed themselves from St Peter's Gate to the Milvian Bridge, and the force of the river took it as far as near the Remissa. **95.** It overturned houses and desolated fields, uprooting trees and crops and sweeping them away. At that time the greater part of the Romans were not even able to sow; which meant that great trouble was in store. Hearing this, since the river was coursing through the city for three days as if in its own channel, the distinguished prelate bewailed greatly and, prostrate on the ground, continued in prayer; through his prayers God showed his mercy and next day the spate ceased. But for many days yet the water held Rome in its grip. The distinguished bishop was moved by God's inspiration to use dinghies[202] and supply food for those living on the Via Lata, so they would not die of hunger, as the enormous flooding totally prevented them leaving their homes. Afterwards, when the water dried up, he comforted everyone in that region of the Via Lata with gifts.

96. This sacred prelate carefully brought great bronze decorated doors[203] of wondrous size from Perugia and elegantly set them up in St Peter's at the tower. At St Mark his mentor's *titulus* he provided a paten and sacred chalice of fine gold, weighing in all 11 lb, also 4 silver chalices weighing in all 12 lb. As for SS Cosmas and Damian's basilica, he presented a paten and chalice of refined gold, weighing in all 11 lb. On St Hadrian's deaconry equally he conferred a paten and chalice of pure gold, weighing in all 11 lb. In St Hadrian the martyr's deaconry he provided 2 silver arches weighing in all 20 lb, and in St Martina's basilica 3 silver arches weighing in all 30 lb. In the ever-virgin St Mary's church *ad martyres* he renewed the canopy of silver, which had been worn away by age, added 60 lb silver to it and set it up again in its former place; and in the same venerable church he provided a silver arch weighing 12 lb.

[Hadrian's death and burial:]

97. This blessed and distinguished pontiff completed all things needful and fresh, both as to alms for the poor and as to the adornment of holy churches, finishing the race and expertly maintaining the orthodox faith. At God's call his life came to an end and he went to everlasting rest. He performed two

---

201 Now the Ponte Sisto.

202 *sandala*: small boats, manoeuvred by a scull (a short, light, spoon-bladed oar).

203 Evidently from some ancient building in Perugia, now to be the doors of the atrium of St Peter's.

97. HADRIAN I

March ordinations, 24 priests, 7 deacons;[204] for various places 185 bishops. He was buried[205] at St Peter's on 26 December in the 4th indiction [795].

204 From these figures it follows that virtually the entire electoral college in 795 were appointees of the aristocratic Hadrian; yet they elected a non-noble as pope, and the nobles revolted against him in 799. Hadrian cannot have shown undue favour to the nobles in making appointments (Noble, 197).

205 His tomb was in the chapel half way along the west wall of the south transept. Duchesne (I, 523) prints the text of his epitaph with its respectful and affectionate verses, said to have been composed by Alcuin; the original magnificent marble slab survives in the porch of St Peter's, 'a masterpiece of Carolingian art'; see Ramackers, 1964; Wallach, 1951.

98. LEO III (795–816)

The longest of all the lives in the LP, that of Leo III includes a lengthy section on the Roman revolt of 799, Leo's flight and return, and the coronation of Charlemagne in 800 – the most detailed account we possess of that crucial event. Liturgical developments are represented by an account of the introduction of the Gallican Rogation Days at Rome. But, like the preceding life, this life is almost entirely made up of extracts from registers recording expenditure on churches, which virtually take the place of history. Even the earthquake of 801 seems to be mentioned only to justify the repairs required to St Paul's basilica. However dry the great bulk of donation lists may appear, they provide a remarkable insight into the non-political activities of the papacy in Carolingian times. The record of the enormous expenditure on the programme (already begun by Hadrian I) of building, repairing and decorating christian Rome throughout the pontificate reflects well on Leo's efficient management of the church patrimonies; but one may doubt how conscious the compiler was of this. The compiler's principles of extraction of the material from his source documents allow him to give iconographical details of the 'cloths' (fabrics and tapestries) so frequently provided – the triumph of orthodoxy at the 2nd Council of Nicaea in 787 was clearly cause for celebration at Rome.

But this substitution for history does not inspire us with confidence in the compiler's capabilities as a historian. There is nothing on Leo's second journey to France (he spent Christmas 804 with Charlemagne at Aachen), the negotiations on the *Filioque* (809–10), the conspiracy of the Roman aristocracy (815) or the bloody means by which it was suppressed. It is of course no surprise that the author plays down Charlemagne's position to exalt that of Leo. No mention here of how Leo not merely announced his election to the Frankish king, but even sent him the keys to the confessio of St Peter and the banner of Rome (thereby recognizing some kind of overlordship possessed by 'the patrician of the Romans'), and asked for an envoy to come to receive oaths of fidelity from the Romans; nor of the king's reply on how it was Leo's duty to pray for the army and the kingdom while the king defended and promoted the faith. No word on how it was the king's initiative that led Leo to support various religious reforms in Charles' realm. Nor are we told that, when Leo had fled to Paderborn in 799 and his Roman enemies arrived with their accusations of adultery and perjury against him, many of the Franks thought these charges well founded. Leo's return to Rome was followed by an investigation into the charges by Frankish agents; but our author does not make it clear that their referring of the matter to the king reflected a suspicion that the pope was guilty. When the king arrived in Rome, the imperial-style ceremonial with which he was greeted is played down. Charles' coronation as emperor is presented as if it were a surprise thought up by Leo to honour a mere secular ruler (much the same view is taken by Einhard), yet it is difficult to believe the whole ceremony was not prearranged. Nor does the compiler care to mention that Leo himself knelt in obeisance to Charlemagne (the only time a pope did this to a western emperor), though we could hardly expect him to mention that Leo dated his coinage in terms of Charlemagne's regnal years. And there is nothing on the repeated complaints Leo had to make to Charles against involvement by the latter's agents in the affairs of the papal State. The compiler lost an opportunity to exalt Leo against Charles: Leo's one show of resistance, his objection to the singing of the Creed with the addition of the *Filioque*, is missed. Nor does he seem aware of the independence Leo was able to assert after Charles' death on 28 January 814: in 815 Leo condemned on charges of treason, and then executed, many who had conspired against him, and was able to satisfy the court at Aachen of the propriety of an action which Charlemagne would never have tolerated.

There is an extreme paucity of MSS for this life. There exist copies of the various later-medieval recensions, which have many alterations to the text and invariably shorten it by excising most of the material on donations and repairs to churches. These MSS provide, in Duchesne's view, no help in any of the difficult passages. Otherwise there are only six MSS of the original text, and of these the two most recent are of little value. Duchesne saw no point in printing their readings, but he gives the readings of the other four, DVCE[1], virtually in full. His preference goes to D, the MS from Tours written before mid 871.

THE CHRONOLOGY OF THE LIFE OF LEO III

As Duchesne (II, p. III) observed, the compiler has preserved the chronological arrangement of the registers he was copying, and, though he did not give annual headings, the opening formulas and renewed activity in churches previously mentioned would enable the headings to be inserted with fair confidence: the year divisions are much clearer than in life 97. Duchesne's hint was taken up by C. Hülsen (1921/23, 107–119) and Hülsen's scheme has been refined by H. Geertman (*More Veterum*), who showed that the chronology follows indiction years running from September to August (one such is specified in c. 31), and that the last three years of Hadrian's pontificate are in fact covered in this life. The reason for this may be that the new pope had spent the last years of Hadrian's pontificate in charge of the *vestiarium*, precisely where these records were kept, and could no doubt claim responsibility for organizing the donations; but for another possible reason see p. xvii, note on MS B[2]. The main chronological anchors are the earthquake (c. 31) dated 30 April 801, and the need for c. 106 on Ravenna to be after January 814 (cf. n. 191). In the translation that follows, year-headings are inserted following Geertman's chronology.

THE CATALOGUE OF DONATIONS IN 807

The special list of Leo's gifts in 807 to all the ecclesiastical institutions in Rome and to some at least of those outside the walls provides the fullest list of Roman churches to survive before the compilation by Cencius Camerarius (the future pope Honorius III) in 1192; it is fully discussed by Geertman (*op. cit.*, 82–129). The list is placed in the LP between the records of the indiction years 806/7 and 807/8, and its nature suggests an origin different from the regular lists that make up so much of this life. As transmitted in the LP the 807 list contains two accidental repetitions at the beginning of c. 81; in their earlier and correct place these are numbers 29 and 62 in a total of 117 items (without these repetitions; or down to the last item before the repetitions, 113 items). One may hazard the suggestion that the source document for the donations in 807 was a *libellus* of four pages with 28 to 33 items per page.

The order in the list is a curious compromise between the importance of the church's status (basilicas, *tituli*, deaconries, monasteries, and *xenodochia*) and the importance of the saint to whom the building was dedicated. Generally institutions dedicated to the Virgin are anticipated near the top of the list, followed by those dedicated to other New Testament personages, then those dedicated to martyrs. Similar much shorter lists show traces of the same arrangement: it is seen in some of the catalogues in the LP itself, in the seventh-century list appended to the *De locis sanctis martyrum* (*CChr* 175, 321–2; like the present list it puts St Mary ad martyres, difficult to fit into any category by its status, immediately after St Mary Antiqua), and in at least one much fuller 13th-century list. Total consistency in applying these principles is scarcely to be expected. At least as good a guide to the relative importance of each institution is the value of the gift it was given.

The list begins with the major basilicas, but the number of anticipated items leaves this fact rather opaque. At the point (c. 73) where the *tituli* not yet mentioned are listed, St Clement's, as dedicated to a martyr, is given priority, but the list then pursues a roughly geographical order starting at the Aventine and working anticlockwise round to Trastevere; however, St Xystus' is separated from Pammachius' *titulus* by three churches dedicated to St Laurence (one of them, in Formonsis, not even a *titulus*), presumably on the 'historical' grounds that Laurence was Xystus II's archdeacon. The total number of *tituli* given is 22. The deaconries begin at c. 75; including those anticipated there are 23 listed, 19 inside the Aurelianic walls, and 4 outside, connected with St Peter's. Of the last group, 3 had been established by Hadrian I (97:66), and to them had since been added that of St Martin, no doubt attached to the monastery so named. The other 19 no doubt include the 16 that existed in 776–7 (97:61), and in 784–5 Hadrian had added 2 more (St Hadrian the martyr's and SS Cosmas and Damian); the 19th may have resulted from the transfer of SS Silvester and Martin from titular to deaconry status (though see n. 100). The eventual standard number of deaconries to which the cardinal deacons would be attached would be 18, but in our period the deacons of the Roman church remained 7 in number and were not attached to particular deaconries (cf. Duchesne, I, CCXXXIV).

A further peculiarity of the 807 list is that although at the very end (c. 81) the *xenodochia* are listed without that dedicated to the Virgin, already anticipated early in the list, curiously the anticipations are not made in the list of monasteries which intervenes in cc. 76–80. Duchesne's analysis of the 49 monasteries listed was: first the major ones, then those attached closely to basilicas, then the less important monasteries and oratories, then monasteries for women. But Geertman saw that the arrangement was: 7 Greek monasteries, 16 Latin monasteries serving basilicas, 12 other Latin monasteries and 10 convents, 3 Latin convents serving basilicas, finally 1 Greek convent; headings are inserted in the translation accordingly. On the Roman monasteries see the study by Ferrari (1957).

OMISSIONS FROM THE CATALOGUE OF 807

The following intramural churches mentioned elsewhere in this part of the LP do not appear in the list:

Various oratories at the Lateran: of St Peter; of the Saviour; of St Laurence; of the Archangel; of St Caesarius; these will have had no separate status. The oratories of the Cross (BP Hilarus 48:2) and of St Venantius (98:32 as an altar, not a chapel, unlike the chapels of the 2 Johns which follow there and do occur in the list) may be only apparent omissions; see nn. 135–6.

St Abbacyrus' altar at Archangel's deaconry (clearly no separate status);

St Agatha's monastery/church, and St Agatha's monastery, are doubtless one or other of the dedications to Agatha which do occur in the list;

St Andrew's oratory cata Barbara at St Mary Major's is either St Andrew's Massa Juliana or St Andrew's close to the Praesepe;

St Martin iuxta titulum S. Silvestri; 98:75 shows that SS Silvester and Martin was now reckoned as a single deaconry;

St Martina in Tribus Fatis (*basilica, ecclesia*); in 97:51 it is merely an altar, closely connected with St Hadrian's basilica, and therefore with no separate status;

St Stephen in Vagauda; 97:71 states that Hadrian united it with St Laurence in Pallacinis, hence its non-appearance;

the *xenodochium* in Platana (but cf. St Eustace's deaconry);

St Andrew's oratory near St Mary Antiqua;

St Barbara's oratory in the Subura (99:4, unique reference);

St Basilides in Merulana (98:94, unique reference);

St Felix in Pincis (97:50; 106:25);

St Laurence above St Clement's;

St Laurence ad Taurellum (97:50, unique reference, unless it is the same as the last);

SS Marcellinus and Peter iuxta Lateranis;

St John iuxta Portam Latinam;

SS Peter and Paul's church on Via Sacra;

The last nine items may be only apparent omissions if they were in 807 closely connected with monasteries which do occur in this list; or they may have been privately owned chapels; or they may have been derelict. It may then be true that the list includes all intramural churches which had a separate 'legal' existence in 807.

The number of extramural churches active at this time but omitted is a greater problem. None more than 3 miles from Rome is included. A checklist of those omitted within that radius is subjoined:

At St Peter's: oratory of the Cross; altar/oratory of the Virgin in Mediana; pope Paul I's oratory of the Virgin; oratory of St Leo; altar of St Gregory; tower (with a chapel) of St Mary ad Grada; altar of St Martin; oratory of Saviour. Like the oratories at the Lateran these 8 will have had no separate legal existence. Perhaps the same applies to the hostel of St Gregory and the hospice and church of St Peter at the Naumachia.

Via Aurelia: SS Processus and Martinian (mil. 2) and St Callistus' basilica (cemetery of Calepodius, mil. 3).

Via Portuensis: St Candida's basilica and SS Abdon and Sennen (both these are the cemetery of Pontianus or *ad ursum pileatum*, mil. 2); St Felix's church (cemetery *ad insalatos*, mil. 3).

Via Ostiensis: St Euplus; St Mennas (cf. Paschal I 100:26,27); and SS Felix and Adauctus (cemetery of Commodilla).

Via Ardeatina: St Petronilla's cemetery (SS Nereus and Achilleus, cemetery of Domitilla).

Via Appia: St Mark's basilica (cemetery of Balbina); St Soteris' cemetery; St Xystus' (and St Cornelius'; cemetery of Callistus); SS Tiburtius, Valerian and Maximus, SS Urban, Felicissimus, Agapitus, Januarius and Cyrinus' cemetery, and St Zeno's basilica (all referring to cemetery of Praetextatus); SS Apostles' = St Sebastian's (monastery, Nicholas I 107:53, saying he founded it; the monastery *in Catacumbas* was originally founded by Xystus III but perhaps it did not exist at this date; Ferrari, 163–5).

Via Latina: SS Gordian and Epimachus' basilica, mil. 1; SS Simplicius, Servilian, Quartus, Quintus and Sophia's cemetery (part of the same cemetery); St Tertullinus' cemetery; St Stephen's, mil. 3.

Via Labicana: SS Peter and Marcellinus; St Helena's basilica; St Tiburtius' (all three are the cemetery *ad duas lauros*).

Via Tiburtina: St Januarius' outside St Laurence's Gate; St Agapitus' by St Laurence's (church built by Felix III); St Laurence Major = St Mary's by St Laurence *ad corpus* (probably no separate status from St Laurence's); St Cyriaca's by the basilicas of St Laurence *ad corpus* and Major (cemetery *in agro Verano*); St Stephen's church by St Laurence's basilica; St Stephen's church by St Hippolytus' cemetery; St Hippolytus' by St Laurence's (cemetery of Hippolytus); St Genesius' church (and altar of Saviour; same cemetery).

Via Nomentana: St Nicomedes' (cemetery of Nicomedes) and St Emerentiana's (cemetery *Maius*).

Via Salaria vetus: St Hermes' basilica (its foundation: Pelagius II c. 2; cemetery of Basilla).

Via Salaria nova: St Boniface's church and St Felicitas' cemetery (both parts of cemetery of Maximus); St Chrysanthus and Daria's cemetery and St Saturninus' basilica (both parts of cemetery of Thraso); St Hilaria's cemetery; SS Alexander, Vitalis, Martial and VII cemetery (cemetery of the Iordani); St Silvester's cemetery (cemetery of Priscilla, mil. 3).

98. 1. LEO [III; 27 December 795–12 June 816], of Roman origin,[1] son of Atzuppius, held the see 20 years 5 months 16 days. From early youth[2] he was brought up and educated in the *vestiarium* of the patriarchate and was spiritually trained in all the church teaching; being accomplished both in psalm-chanting and God's holy Scriptures he was made subdeacon and was advanced to the office of the priesthood.[3] He was chaste, eloquent and of resolute mind. When he encountered a distinguished monk and servant of God, he did not cease to spend time with him talking deeply of the things of God and in prayer; and he was a most cheerful giver of alms. What is more, he was a frequent visitor of the sick, and while preaching to them in accord with scripture he saved them with his almsgiving. Many listened to his preaching and whatever they gave him on Christ's behalf he quietly disbursed to the poor day and night, continually and beneficially presenting God with a harvest of souls. While he was thus distinguishing himself during his time at the *vestiarium* and the *vestiarium* itself was under[4] his expert care, he gained everyone's full love and affection. 2. That was why by God's inspiration all the *sacerdotes*, the dignitaries and the whole clergy, also the leaders and all the people of Rome[5] elected him with one heart and mind by God's bidding, on the feast of St Stephen the first martyr; and next day, the feast of St John the apostle and evangelist, to the praise and glory of almighty God, he was ordained to the pontiff's apostolic see.

He was a defender of the church establishment and a stenuous adversary of its assailants; he was very mild, and greatly loved those who favoured the church. Slow to anger and quick to have pity, repaying no one evil for evil, nor taking even merited vengeance, but dutiful and compassionate, from the time of his ordination he shone in seeing justice done to all. For his clergy he greatly increased the stipend for priestly functions.[6]

1 This claim puts Leo in line with all other popes from 752 to 844 except Stephen III; but Leo seems to have been Apulian, of Greek or even Arabic ancestry (Noble, 187–8, citing Beck, 1969). With the same exceptions all popes in that period were nobles.

2 The eulogy here and in c. 2 is closely based on 91:1 and 93:1.

3 Presumably by Hadrian, whose appointments therefore were not limited to his fellow nobles; cf. 97: n. 204. Leo's *titulus* was St Susanna's (c. 9).

4 The sharp variation on the meaning of *degere* (= *regeretur* the second time, as also in c. 11, *degeret* for *regeret*), suggested by Duchesne, is surely right: a cardinal priest cannot have had a superior in his own department. Leo thus gained bureaucratic, as well as pastoral, experience before his election.

5 It is difficult to see in what way all these were involved in the actual election, given the terms of the decree of 769 (96:20).

6 *roga ... in presbiterio*: the latter word (cf. 93:28 and n. 102) should signify the wages paid by the pope to the priests. But by this date the cardinal priests were not paid a regular

98. LEO III

[A.D. 792–3:][7]

3. In front of the vestibule of the altar in the basilica of his mentor St Peter prince of the apostles he provided a gold thurible weighing 17 lb; in the apostle's confessio, a grill[8] of fine gold with various jewels, weighing 49 lb; also 3 great silver crowns weighing 307 lb; and a white all-silk curtain with roses, with a gold-studded cross in the middle and an interwoven gold fringe. He freshly and totally restored the whole of the roofing of St Peter's from end to end – that is, the main vault, the other vault above the altar,[9] with the square colonnades, the water fountains[10] in front of the silver doors and the tower[11] with its chambers. Moreover the image of the Saviour, with the screens[12] of wondrous beauty painted to adorn this church, he placed on the canopy under the great arch. **4.** He provided and set up images also in St Paul's basilica and in that of the Saviour. He freshly restored with loving effort the roofing of St Anastasia's *titulus* which had decayed for a long time through lack of care and was about to collapse. He also carefully renewed St Sabina's *titulus*; in it this distinguished prelate provided 5 silver crowns weighing 14 lb; 2 six-light canisters weighing 3½ lb; 9 chased bowls weighing 11 lb.

[A.D. 793–4:]

In God's holy mother's basilica called *ad praesepe* he provided a canopy of fine silver weighing 590 lb, also silver railings at the entrance to the *presbyterium*, weighing 80 lb, and a great white silk curtain with a fringe and cross of interwoven gold. On the holy high altar, a gold-studded cloth representing the Lord's birth, St Simeon, and in the middle the *Chaeretismos*; also the apse-vault of this church, and in the colonnade;[13] and 4 silver crowns

---

salary (they received the revenues of their own churches); so the increase seems to have been in gratuities paid on important feastdays.

7 There follow the donations omitted in the previous life, beginning with the indiction year 792–3 and covering the last three years or so of Hadrian I's life; the lists then continue into Leo's own pontificate with no break; see introduction to this life.

8 Duchesne suggested that the grill was a lattice at the upper part of the confessio with the crowns (lights) suspended in front of it; the curtain closed off the bay itself.

9 i. e. the transept, whose roof in old St Peter's was significantly lower than that over the nave. *Navis* here has its older meaning of 'vault', rather than the later meaning of the area (nave) beneath it.

10 The alternative reading (MSS CEV: *et ad fontes*) makes this refer to the baptismal fonts (north end of the transept), but the context shows the fountains in the centre of the atrium within the colonnade are meant.

11 Stephen II's bell-tower (94:47).

12 Duchesne explains these *regiae* as a triptych.

13 The Chaeretismos is the Annunciation (Luke 1.26–38); from Greek χαῖρε ('Hail!').

weighing in all 145 lb 9 oz. **5.** Also in the basilica of Christ's martyr St Laurence outside the walls, he provided 3 silver images, of the Saviour, St Peter and St Laurence, weighing in all 54½ lb; and on the holy altar a tyrian gold-studded cloth representing the Lord's passion and resurrection. He also renewed the roofing of SS Felix and Adauctus the martyrs', close to St Paul's; the basilica of St Mennas;[14] the *titulus* of Christ's martyr St Vitalis; the cemetery of SS Xystus and Cornelius on the Via Appia; the cemetery of St Zoticus on the Via Labicana;[15] and the church of God's mother the ever-virgin our lady St Mary on the [estate] Fonteiana;[16] these had decayed for a long time and collapsed.

[A.D. 794–5:]

6. At the confessio in the basilica of the world's teacher St Paul the apostle he provided a grill of refined gold with precious jewels, as at St Peter's, weighing 156 lb; and above that holy altar a gold image of the Saviour and the 12 apostles, weighing 75 lb; and he rebuilt the apse-vault of this basilica like that of St Peter's; moreover, 3 silver crowns, weighing in total 220 lb; 15 great all-silk veils with roundels and with a fringe and a cross both of purple and of interwoven gold; 43 various great veils coated with fourfold-woven silk, which hang in the arches; 20 small veils with roundels, adorned with fourfold-woven silk, which hang in the smaller arches; 10 small veils of cross-adorned silk which hang in the arches, and 10 more, 3 of them with a gold-studded fringe; 4 matching Alexandrian veils; a crimson veil with wheels on it, with a fringe of wheels with birds on it, and in the middle a cross with chevrons and 4 matching wheels of tyrian. In St Andrew's basilica at St Peter's, silver railings weighing 80 lb. In the Saviour's basilica called Constantinian, an apse-vault of wondrous size.

What Leo did for the apse-vault and the colonnade is not clear (one MS, C, omits *in* before colonnade, *quadriportica*); perhaps further draperies are meant. There is no other evidence whatever that S. Maria Maggiore had an exterior atrium or colonnade.

14 The basilica (also in Paschal I 100:26–27) of this Egyptian martyr (whom the MSS here regard as female) was some distance out of the Porta Ostiensis towards St Paul's (Einsiedeln Itinerary, *CChr* 175, 332 line 30), and dated at least from Gregory I's time (he delivered one of his 40 homilies there); Hülsen, 387. It was probably the chapel of the Alexandrian corporation (σωμάτιον) mentioned in a copy of a lost inscription set up in 589 (De Rossi, *Inscr. Christ.* 2, 455). From the same area came another lost inscription recorded in the Einsiedeln collection (*ed. cit.*, 333 lines 54–63; CIG 5900) to L. Julius Vestinus, (pagan) highpriest of Alexandria and Egypt, administrator of the Museum (at Alexandria) and of the Greek and Latin libraries at Rome, teacher and secretary of the emperor Hadrian; which suggests that the Egyptian connexion with this area was not specifically christian.

15 At the 10th mile.

16 Cf. 93:19.

98. LEO III

[A.D. 795–6:]

7. On the high altar of St Peter prince of the apostles' this bountiful prelate provided a gold-studded cloth adorned with precious jewels and representing both the Saviour granting St Peter the power of binding and loosing, and the passion of Peter and Paul princes of the apostles, of wondrous size, and resplendent on the feast of the apostles. On the altar in Eudoxia's *titulus*, a tyrian cloth with great griffins and two gold-studded wheels with a cross and a purple and gold-studded fringe.

[A.D. 796–7:]

8. In St Peter the apostle's basilica this distinguished prelate provided a silver light in front of the *presbyterium* with 30 silver bowls and an eight-sided canister in the middle, weighing 63 lb; and in the silver chandeliers both round the altar and in the *presbyterium* he placed silver candles, weighing in all 212 lb. On St Petronilla's altar he placed a silk cross-adorned cloth with a purple and gold-studded fringe. In the Saviour's basilica, the Constantinian, he provided a cloth representing the crucifixion and resurrection of our Lord Jesus Christ, with a gold-studded fringe;[17] and in St Clement's basilica a silk cross-adorned cloth with a gold-studded fringe. In the silver arch of St Paul the apostle's church he provided white veils for use at Eastertide and very beautiful veils of cross-adorned silk for use on the feast day of God's apostle.

[A.D. 797–8:]

9. At the *titulus* of St Susanna for which this distinguished pontiff had been ordained priest, as it was of small construction and the walls had decayed for a long time, in his great love he increased the building's size: by freshly digging deep down he laid a firm foundation, and providing an even surface he built on these foundations a wonderfully lofty church, with an apse filled with mosaic,[18] wonderful galleries[19] and a decorated apse-vault, and he adorned the *presbyterium* and the pavement with beautiful marble. In the construction he used marble columns on right and left and for the porticoes. On to this basilica he established a baptistery, where he presented gifts: 3 gold-rimmed bowls weighing 3½ lb; 2 gold crosses with jewels, weighing 1 lb, with silver staves weighing 4 lb 7 oz; a silver lantern weighing 5 lb;

17 Perhaps *periclisis* here is plural, 'fringes'.

18 There survives a drawing of this mosaic, destroyed in 1595, showing Leo III and Charlemagne both wearing the square *nimbus*. The inscription beneath referred to the dark and narrow building's decayed state, Leo III's rebuilding it from the ground with elegant adornment, and his burial there of the martyr St Felicitas.

19 *caticuminia*: galleries or tribunes for catechumens, of whom there can have been few in 8th century Rome; the word survived in Greek for galleries above floor level.

3 silver images weighing in all 35 lb. He built the altar's *confessio* of fine silver weighing 103 lb 2 oz; 8 silver columns with 2 chevrons and 2 arches, with 5 crosses and 15 bowls, weighing in all 150 lb; 1 sectioned[20] cross weighing 14 lb, with 1 16-light canister weighing 12½ lb; 1 great silver crown with 32 dolphins, weighing 22 lb; 1 silver canister weighing 18 lb; another silver canister weighing 18 lb; 1 silver-gilt colander ladle weighing 4 lb 3 oz; Saxon silver bowls with gilt griffins on them, weighing 2 lb; 2 silver crowns with 18 dolphins, weighing 18 lb. **10.** In the same church this distinguished bishop provided a gold-studded cloth with a gold-studded fringe; another purple cloth, in the middle of which is a gold-studded cross, 4 gold-studded panels adorned with jewels and 4 gold-studded chevrons on the cloth itself, with a gold-studded fringe. In the Lateran patriarchate he built in his own name a *triclinium*[21] greater than all other such, adorned on a wondrous scale: he laid firm foundations for it and decorated it all round with marble sheets; he laid the floor with pictorial marble and decorated it with various porphyry and white columns, and with carvings, bases and lily-shaped ornamentation on the doorposts. He adorned the apse-vault and the apse with mosaic and on the 2 other apses he painted all around various representations on the marble construction. In St Prisca's basilica[22] this bishop provided a gold-rimmed and gilt chalice, and 3 crowns, of which

20 *diacopton*; some connexion with the Greek verb διακόπτειν seems inevitable. Whether the LP means made of 2, 3 or 4 sections, or somehow split so as to support the next item, is unclear.

21 The ruins of this hall in the eastern part of the Lateran palace survived into the 18th century; the LP claims it was larger than earlier such halls in the Lateran (only one has been mentioned, 93:18); Leo III was to construct an even larger one later (c. 39). The mosaic was much 'restored' in 1625, but following its final destruction a copy, still surviving, was placed alongside the nearby Sancta Sanctorum; see Lauer, 1911, 105–119, Schramm, 1928, 4–16, Ladner, 1941, I, 114–5, figs. 94–5, 100–101, Noble, 323. Since the original dated before the coronation of 800, it is a valuable record of church relations with the Franks shortly before that point, and clearly reflects Leo's ideal of cooperation between himself and the secular authority. According to a description (made before 1625) the central subject, beneath Leo's monogram, was Christ giving the 11 apostles their mission to preach, with an inscription of the last two verses of Matthew's gospel; outside the apse-vault itself was a semi-circular border inscribed 'Glory be to God on high and peace on earth to men of good will'. To the onlooker's right was Peter giving the pallium to Leo (kneeling on Peter's right) and a standard to Charlemagne (kneeling on Peter's left), and beneath: 'St Peter, give life to pope Leo and victory to king Charles.' To the onlooker's left was a parallel scene of Christ seated, giving the keys to Silvester and a banner to Constantine, both kneeling. The banner signifies military command; the pallium, priestly rule by those who may not themselves fight but can order others to do so against God's enemies.

22 Cf. 97:51 with n. 87.

one has 10 dolphins and the other two 9 each, and 8 bowls, weighing in all 28 lb; an all-silk white cloth adorned all round with byzantine purple and on the front a gold-studded cross.

[April 799–early 801:]

11. So[23] this venerable and holy prelate was conducting the affairs of the holy catholic and apostolic Roman church in the manner of the church, was maintaining the ritual of the orthodox faith, and was on all sides elegantly constructing and adorning the various churches and the interior of the patriarchate with large buildings. But the day came when he was to process as usual in what everyone calls the Major Litany, in which the people meet and join him as a matter of religious duty, so that following the annual custom he would celebrate the litany and the ceremonies of mass with the *sacerdotes*, and pour forth prayer to the almighty Lord for the well-being of the christian people. According to ancient tradition the litany had been announced in advance by a notary of the holy Roman church at the church of Christ's martyr St George on his feastday, and all the men and women devoutly crowded to the church of Christ's martyr St Laurence *in Lucina*[24] to join in at the gathering announced to take place there.[25] When the venerable pontiff had come out[26] from the patriarchate, the wicked and unspeakable *primicerius* Paschal,[27]

---

23 The coup attempted against Leo has similarities with Toto's activity in 767–8; see Mohr, 1960, and Zimmermann, 1968, 25–36, Noble, 199–202. The attempt on Leo III's life (on 25 April 799) is given also in the *Ann. Lauriss. mai.* a. 799, and in the *Annals* of Einhard; Duchesne thought the latter based on the LP, yet there are extra details.

24 Called St Laurence in Craticula by Einhard, from the gridiron preserved there.

25 The Litania Maior on 25 April was regularly announced two days earlier on St George's day while this was being celebrated at St George *in Velabro*. Like the pagan Robigalia held on the same day (Ovid, *Fasti* 4.905–42), the Litany was aimed at securing divine favour on the crops. Even the processional route was similar: it left Rome along the Via Flaminia, crossed the Milvian Bridge, and then, in pagan times, continued to the temple of Robigo at the 5th mile on the Via Clodia, but in christian times, turned sharply left to St Peter's. The festival had been christianized by April 598 at the latest: the formula for the prior announcement used that year survives (Greg. *Ep. app.* 3) – and even uses the expression 'what everyone calls the Major Litany'. The so-called Gregorian Sacramentary gives the starting point as St Laurence in Lucina, with stops for prayers at St Valentine's, at the Milvian Bridge, at a now unlocatable cross, in the atrium of St Peter's, and finally in St Peter's for mass.

26 On horseback (Einhard).

27 A letter from Hadrian I to Charlemagne in 778 (*CC* 61) preserves the significant information that Paschal was that pope's nephew; he was already important enough to take part in embassies to the Franks, and had become *primicerius* by 20 April 793 (J 2498). Einhard (*Annals* 801) calls him *nomenclator*. Theophanes (a. 6289) says that the chief conspirators were Hadrian's relatives. It seems that Leo's personality, or his actions since his unanimous election, had led to hostility among the Roman nobles.

who was not wearing a chasuble,[28] came to meet him and hypocritically begged his pardon with the words: 'I am ill and have had to come without a chasuble'. The holy prelate granted him pardon. And Campulus,[29] who was equally involved in their treachery and was travelling in the pontifical retinue, was in conversation with him, using sweet words he did not have in his heart. Meanwhile some malign, wicked, perverse and false Christians, or rather heathen sons of Satan, full of wicked scheming, devilishly came together on the route, in front of the monastery of SS Stephen and Silvester which the former lord pope Paul had founded, and secretly waited there under arms.[30] They suddenly leapt out of their place of ambush so as to slay him impiously, as has been said. Showing him no respect they rushed at him, while in accordance with their iniquitous plot Paschal stood at his head and Campulus at his feet. **12.** When this happened, all the people round him, who were unarmed and ready for divine service, were scared of the weapons and turned to flee. The ambushers and evil-doers, just like Jews, with no respect for God or man or for his office, seized him like animals and threw him to the ground. Without mercy they cut his clothes off him and attempted cruelly to pluck out his eyes and totally blind him. They cut off his tongue and left him, or so they thought, blind and dumb in the middle of the street; among them were the malign Paschal and Campulus.

But afterwards, like really impious heathens, they dragged him to the confessio in that monastery's church and in front of the venerable altar itself, again for the second time they cruelly gouged his eyes and his tongue yet further. They beat him with clubs and mangled him with various injuries, and left him half-dead and drenched in blood in front of the altar. Afterwards they kept him under guard in the monastery.[31] **13.** As they were afraid he might be stealthily rescued from there by Christians, they adopted a malign

28 At this date clergy of all ranks wore chasubles (*planetae*) on ceremonial occasions, over a long tunic. The LP implies not that Paschal was half-dressed but that high dignitaries of the papal administration, such as Paschal, were clerics who on non-ceremonial or non-official occasions had begun to dress like lay aristocrats.

29 Campulus, already a notary in 781 (*CC* 67) when he assisted Hadrian in judging a case concerning S. Vincenzo al Volturno, was by now *sacellarius* (c. 13; Einhard).

30 Einhard puts the scene close to St Laurence's church, the pope's initial stopping point, but this is very close to St Silvester's. The conspirators will have mingled with the crowd who were to join in the procession; Duchesne perhaps rightly inferred that many of the crowd supported them. It was only the pope's immediate entourage who fled (next c.), and the conspirators do not seem to have feared the crowd.

31 Other (pro-Leo) sources report a formal ceremony at St Silvester's to depose Leo: Leo III, *Ep.* X, 6 (*MGH EKA* 3, 63), Alcuin, *Epp.* 179 (*MGH EKA* 2, 297).

plan, as the deposition of the *hegumenus* of St Erasmus' monastery[32] records: the malign Paschal, then *primicerius*, Campulus the *sacellarius* and Maurus of Nepi[33] made him come to them secretly at night and sent him with many of their wicked accomplices in evil to that monastery of St Silvester, and in this way they removed him from there by night and took him to St Erasmus' monastery where they locked him up in strict and close confinement.[34]

But almighty God who, with his foreknowledge of their malice, had so long borne it patiently, wonderfully wrecked their iniquitous efforts. God acted and St Peter the apostle's prayers interceded, and it happened when the pope had been left by his butchers in prison at St Erasmus' monastery that he recovered his sight and his tongue was restored him so he could speak:[35] such was God's will, such the intercession of St Peter, keybearer of the kingdom of heaven. **14.** When almighty God in his customary mercy displayed this great miracle through his servant, it was his divine will that faithful christian men – Albinus the chamberlain with others of the God-fearing faithful – secretly rescued him from that cloister and brought him to St Peter's, where the apostle's holy body is at rest.[36] All who heard and saw God's wonders, how he had snatched an innocent and righteous pontiff from the hands of his enemies, gave glory to God and said: 'Blessed be the Lord, the God of Israel, who alone works great wonders and has not forsaken those who hope in him but fulfils his mercy in him, that God's glory and wonders may be made manifest in him; as he promised those who hope in

---

32 Located in front of S. Stefano Rotondo adjoining the aqueduct, this monastery was where pope Adeodatus (672–6) was brought up (BP 79:4); that pope enlarged it and perhaps gave it full status as a monastery. Much later legend connected its origin with Placidus the disciple of St Benedict and a member of the Valerii: the *xenodochium* of the Valerii was somewhere on Monte Celio nearby (Ferrari, 119–131).

33 Despite Duchesne's doubts, Maurus was clearly not the bishop of Nepi but a military aristocrat, a neighbour both of Toto and of Hadrian I (Noble, 200).

34 The LP is no doubt right to give a second, less public, attempt at mutilating Leo inside St Silvester's, followed by his imprisonment there; the other sources seem to know of only one place where Leo was imprisoned, and Einhard gives it as St Erasmus'. Both monasteries were Greek; for politics and monasteries cf. 96:23.

35 The LP's style is that of a panegyric. There is no evidence that Leo himself ever claimed a miracle; 9th-century writers were divided on the matter; by 1673 the miracle was held to be certain enough to justify Leo's inclusion in the Roman Martyrology.

36 Leo's rescuers took him outside Rome to safety at St Peter's. *Ann. Lauriss. mai.* has Charles' envoy abbot Wirundus of Stavelot, and Winichis duke of Spoleto, already there; Einhard implies the same but says Winichis had only come on hearing of the murder attempt. The length of Leo's imprisonment is unknown: Einhard says that the rescue was by night, not on the first night. Winichis cannot have heard the news, gathered an army and reached Rome before early May.

him, in the words of the psalmist: 'The Lord is my light and my salvation; whom shall I fear? The Lord is the stronghold of my life; of whom shall I be afraid?'; and again: 'Thy word is a lantern to my feet, Lord, and a light to my path.'"[37] In very truth the Lord rescued him from darkness and gave him back to light, restored his tongue and speech, strengthened all his limbs, and in all his works wondrously guided and comforted him. As great as was the joy for Christians and the faithful, so great was the sorrow and sadness of the afflicted, who knew not what to do; reckoning the danger they were in, they wondered whether to kill each other. **15.** Finding nothing else to do, they laid waste and destroyed the house of Albinus who was loyal to St Peter and the pontiff. The pontiff had gone to the hall of St Peter the apostle, and straightaway Winichis, the glorious duke of Spoleto, came with his army to meet him. When he saw that the supreme pontiff was able to see and speak, he received him reverently and took him to Spoleto, glorifying and praising God who had manifested such wonders in him.

On hearing this, the faithful from the various cities of the Romans came to him; and along with some from those cities, bishops, priests and Roman clerics, and leading men from the cities, he set out to visit His Excellency lord Charles, king of the Franks and Lombards and patrician of the Romans.[38] **16.** The christian, orthodox, distinguished and merciful king, immediately he heard of it, sent to meet him Hildebald the archbishop and chaplain[39] and Ascheric the count; and afterwards again sent to meet him his own son His Excellency king Pepin and other counts, and he brought him to meet the great king himself where he was.[40] He welcomed him reverently and honourably with hymns and spiritual chants as the vicar of St Peter the apostle. They greeted and embraced each other in tears. The pontiff began the *Glory be to God on high*, all the clergy took it up, a prayer was said over the whole people, and then the kindly lord king Charles the Great gave thanks for seeing the pontiff to God, who had worked so great a marvel for his servant at the intercession of Peter and Paul the princes of the apostles,

---

37 Vulgate, Psalms 26 (27), 1 and 118 (119), 105.

38 As patrician, Charles was the pope's protector; Leo's journey was at Charles' request (Einhard).

39 Archbishop of Cologne, he had succeeded Angilram (died 791) bishop of Metz as the king's chief chaplain (Council of Frankfurt, 794, c. 55); in 811 he would witness Charlemagne's will, and in 814 administer the last rites.

40 At Paderborn, where Charlemagne (with his whole army) had come to await either the return of his son Charles (*Ann. Lauriss. mai.*) or the pope himself (Einhard). The Pepin mentioned here was Charlemagne's son by Hildegard, was king of Italy and died in 810, not Pepin the Hunchback who died in 811, Charlemagne's son by a concubine.

98. LEO III

and had brought those iniquitous men to nought.

17. The serene king kept him at his court in great honour for some time.[41] Meanwhile when these iniquitous sons of the devil heard this, and after they had horribly and wickedly burnt the properties and goods of St Peter the apostle, they attempted despite God's opposition to lay false charges[42] against the holy pontiff and send them after him to the king, charges they could never have proven, as it was they who were causing these unspeakable things through their own plotting and wickedness, in their desire to humiliate the holy church. **18.** While the pontiff was staying in great and fitting honour with the merciful great king, from every side there arrived archbishops, bishops and other *sacerdotes*; on the advice of the pious great king and all the Frankish notables, with God going ahead, they despatched him to return to Rome honourably to his apostolic see, with great honour as was fitting.[43] And city by city, where he was welcomed as if he were the apostle himself, they brought him back to Rome. **19.** In great joy the Romans welcomed their pastor. On the eve[44] of St Andrew the apostle all of them as a whole – the leading members of the clergy[45] and all the clergy, the chief men, the senate,[46] the whole militia and the entire Roman people, the nuns and deaconesses,[47] the noble matrons[48] and all the women, and all the *scholae* of foreigners – Franks, Frisians, Saxons and Lombards[49] – all united together

---

41 For some days (Einhard). Charles clearly did not recognize Leo's deposition.

42 Alcuin, *Ep.* 184 (*MGH EKA* 2, 309) says he destroyed a report that Arn (who accompanied Leo back to Rome) sent him on his investigations into Leo in 799; perjury, simony and adultery seem to have been the charges. Noble, 292, has Charles sending investigators to Rome fruitlessly before Leo returned to Rome, but surely Arn at least cannot have made the journey twice.

43 Along with the king's envoys (Einhard). Alcuin, Charles' adviser, argued in a letter (*Ep.* 179, *MGH EKA* 2, 297) to Arn that no earthly power could judge the pope; so Charles' decision to have Leo escorted back to Rome merely left in abeyance the question whether Charles had any judicial power over the pope, or in Rome at all.

44 29 November 799.

45 Cardinal priests and deacons; and the clerics who headed the chancery and other departments, *primicerius, secundicerius, arcarius, sacellarius* etc.

46 Occurring after the aristocracy and before the militia, this expression seems to mean the army commanders; it does not mean the Roman imperial senate.

47 The wives of deacons, but no doubt including the wives of other clergy.

48 The wives of lay aristocrats.

49 These four corporations of foreigners settled in Rome were gaining importance at this time, and could play a military role (e. g. during the Saracen invasion of 846). The Saxon *schola* may be the earliest; its foundation is attributed to Ine king of Wessex (Matthew Paris) or to Offa of Mercia (William of Malmesbury); Duchesne thought it could even date to the late 7th century when close relations between Saxon kings and the papacy began, and when Cedwalla

and with standards and banners they welcomed him at the Milvian Bridge with spiritual chants. They brought him to St Peter's where he celebrated the ceremonies of mass, and they all faithfully shared together in the body and blood of our Lord Jesus Christ.

20. Next day, following ancient custom, they celebrated St Andrew's feastday, and he came into Rome amid great joy and gladness and entered the Lateran patriarchate. Some days later, the loyal envoys who had come with him in the pontifical retinue – the reverend archbishops Hildebald and Arn,[50] the reverend holy bishops Cunipert, Bernard, Atto and Jesse, bishop-elect Erflaic,[51] and the glorious counts Helmgoth, Rottecar and Germar – were in session in lord pope Leo's *triclinium*[52] and for a week and more they questioned those wicked evil-doers, Paschal, Campulus and their followers, on what evil they alleged against their pontiff, but these had nothing to say against him.[53] Then the great king's envoys arrested them and despatched them to France.[54]

21. A short time afterwards the great king himself[55] reached St Peter's

---

of Wessex began the series of royal pilgrimages to Rome. The other three *scholae* are presumably of 8th century date. Each had its own quarter in the area between St Peter's and Castel S. Angelo, areas identifiable from the churches which served each group and are named in a bull of Leo IV, 10 August 854 (Hülsen, 384). The *schola Francorum* had as its chapel the church of the Saviour *in ossibus* or *in macello*, whose ruins are in the Campo Santo Teutonico (Duchesne confused it with a different church); Hülsen, 455. The Frisians had the church of St Michael, first mentioned in 854 (Hülsen, 388), now SS Michele e Magno in Borgo. The Anglo-Saxons had a chapel then dedicated to St Mary, now S. Spirito in Sassia, newly built about 850 (Leo IV 105:86; Hülsen, 363). The Lombards had the church of St Justin, destroyed in or after the 15th century, located in the Cortile di S. Damaso near the modern chapel of S. Martino dei Svizzeri (Hülsen, 279).

50 Archbishops of Cologne (cf. c. 16) and Salzburg respectively.

51 Atto and Jesse were bishops of Freising and Amiens, Bernard probably of Worms; the sees of Cunipert and Erflaic are unknown.

52 The building whose construction is recorded in c. 10.

53 A rather biassed presentation of what in all but name was a trial of Leo himself!

54 If so, they were later brought back to Rome for trial, c. 26.

55 Charles decided to go to Rome, but only did so in the autumn of 800, hardly 'a short time later'; the delay was perhaps caused by his uncertainty how to proceed in the case of Leo, who had appealed to him as protector, and when Charles himself had no clear right to hold any trial in Rome, let alone that of a pope. Contrast the details of Leo's return to Rome with the absence of detail on Charles' arrival! The Frankish Royal Annals tell how Leo met Charles at Mentana, 12 miles out of Rome, where they dined together. Next day, 24 November 800, there was a solemn reception on the steps of St Peter's. Discussion of the charges against Leo, the main purpose of Charles' visit to Rome, began seven days later not at a secular court but at a Roman synod, over which Charles presided: for the first time a Carolingian took a part in judicial proceedings at Rome. He began by explaining that the council's purpose was to examine the

basilica and was greeted with great honour. In that church he gathered the archbishops, bishops, abbots and all the nobility of the Franks and the senate of the Romans. The great king and the blessed pontiff sat down together and had the archbishops, bishops and abbots take their seats, while the other *sacerdotes* and leading men of the Franks and Romans were in attendance, to clear up the charges alleged against the bountiful pontiff. All the archbishops, bishops and abbots listened and with one accord said: 'We dare not pass judgment on the apostolic see which is the head of all God's churches; it is all of us who are judged by it and its vicar; just as the custom was of old, it is judged by no one.[56] But as the supreme pontiff has decreed it, we will obey according to the canons'. The venerable prelate said: 'I follow the precedents set by my predecessors as pontiffs, and am ready to clear myself of these false charges whose evil flames engulf me.'

22. Another day,[57] all the archbishops, bishops, abbots and all the Franks who were in the great king's service, and all the Romans, [came] together, again in St Peter's. In that church and in their presence the venerable pontiff embraced Christ's four holy gospels, and in their sight he went up into the ambo, and stated aloud on oath:[58] 'I have no knowledge of these false allegations which those Romans who wickedly persecuted me bring against me, and I know that I have not committed such crimes.' This done, all the archbishops, bishops and abbots and the whole clergy performed a litany and gave praise to God, to his mother our lady the ever-virgin Mary, St Peter prince of the apostles and all God's saints.

23. Afterwards when the birthday of our Lord Jesus Christ arrived, they all gathered again in St Peter's. Then with his own hands the venerable bountiful pontiff crowned him with a precious crown;[59] and all the faithful Romans seeing how much he defended and how greatly he loved the holy Roman church and its vicar, at God's bidding and that of St Peter, keybearer

---

charges; the council replied it did not wish to sit in judgment on the pope. As no one would prosecute, Leo declared himself ready to swear his innocence.

56 Charles was to accept this principle, already advocated by Alcuin (n. 43).

57 *alia die* might have meant 'next day', but this plenary session of the council did not take place until 23 December 800.

58 The quotation is a fragment of the actual oath Leo took, Wallach, 1977, 301–3; the effect of swearing the oath was that Leo threw the onus probandi onto his opponents.

59 The inauguration of the western emperors had been an entirely secular affair. In the east Leo I had been the first to be crowned, in 457, by the patriarch of Constantinople (Theod. Lect. 2.65). Justin, already crowned by the patriarch (Hormisdas, *Ep.* 67, Thiel, 863) was re-crowned by pope John I at Constantinople in 526 (BP 55:4), but there is no evidence for pope Vigilius crowning Justinian I or pope Constantine crowning Justinian II when they were in the city.

of the kingdom of heaven, cried aloud with one accord: 'To Charles, pious Augustus crowned by God, great and pacific Emperor, life and victory!'[60] Three times this was said in front of St Peter's sacred confessio, with the invocation of many saints;[61] and by them all he was established as Emperor of the Romans. **24.** Straightaway the holy bishop and pontiff anointed Charles, his excellent son, as king, on that same birthday of our Lord Jesus Christ.[62]

After the celebration of mass, when the dismissal was given, the serene lord Emperor presented a silver table with its legs, weighing .. lb. In the confessio of God's apostle he, his excellent sons the kings, and his daughters, presented various vessels of fine gold for the service of this table, weighing .. lb; a gold crown with large jewels, which hangs over the altar, weighing 55 lb;[63] a large gold paten with various jewels, with the inscription 'CHARLES', weighing 30 lb; a large chalice with jewels and two handles, weighing 58 lb; a gold-rimmed chalice with a drinking-tube, weighing 37 lb. He presented another large gold-rimmed chalice, weighing 36 lb, on St Peter's sacred altar; and in St Paul's basilica, a smaller[64] silver table, with its legs, weighing .. lb, with various silver vessels of wondrous size, needed for

60 The Frankish Annals comment that this was followed by *adoratio* of Charles, in the manner of ancient emperors, and that the titles Augustus and Imperator now replaced that of patrician.

61 The *laudes*, as the Annals (last note) actually call them. The chant is the well-known *Christus vincit, Christus regnat, Christus imperat*, whose text obviously varied much, depending on who was the object of the praise and which saints were regarded as appropriate. Duchesne (II, 37 n. 33) printed a version dating 795–800 (Leo is pope, Charles is still king), also given in H. Kantorowicz, *Laudes regiae* (Berkeley and Los Angeles, 1946), 15–16; it was perhaps used when Leo and Charles were together at Paderborn in 799 or at Rome in 800, though before this coronation. One slightly earlier version is known, *PL* 138, 885ff, cf. Kantorowicz, 21.

62 Papal anointing of Frankish kings goes back to the start of the Carolingian dynasty: Pepin, Charles and Carloman were anointed at St Denis by Stephen II. In 781 Hadrian anointed Charlemagne's sons Pepin (cf. n. 40) and Louis (the Pious), but Charles, though the eldest son, was not yet anointed. There is no evidence for the Merovingian kings being anointed by anyone, let alone by the pope; nor will there have been any earlier occasion for a pope to anoint any other king. The anointing of Anglo-Saxon kings may not have begun till after the mid 8th century. The idea (in so far as it was not simply based on scriptural references to the anointing of kings) may have come from Spain, where at least from the 7th century the archbishop of Toledo anointed the Visigothic kings. Duchesne notes that the countries which practised royal anointing were also those where priests were anointed at ordination (an imitation of Old Testament anointing of priests), a rite not used in Rome till the 10th century and never adopted in the east. Theophanes alone has the coronation of Charles preceded by an all-over anointing, probably by confusion with the anointing, here, of Charles' similarly-named son.

63 This crown survived at least till the 11th century (De Rossi, *Inscr. Chr.* 2, p. 198).

64 If this is the meaning of *subminor*, a contrast with the table already presented by Charles to St Peter's is perhaps intended.

use on this table. **25.** In the Saviour our Lord's basilica called Constantinian, he presented a cross with jacinths, which the bountiful pontiff assigned for the litany procession as the pious Emperor suggested;[65] an altar with silver columns and canopy; and a gospel-book with a cover[66] of fine gold, adorned with jewels, weighing .. lb. In the basilica of God's holy mother *ad praesepe* he presented a large silver necklace, weighing .. lb.

26. Afterwards, when those wicked evil-doers Paschal, Campulus and their followers, had been brought into the pious lord Emperor's presence, with the noble Franks and Romans in attendance, and they were all satisfied about their evil plotting and activity, Campulus turned on Paschal and rebuked him: 'It was a bad moment when I first saw your face, as it was you who put me in this danger.' The others did the same, each damning the other and proving their guilt. When the pious Emperor realized how cruel and wicked they were, he sent them into exile in the districts of France.[67]

[A.D. 798–9 and 799–800:]

27. This holy pontiff built a great *triclinium*[68] close to St Peter's, at the

65 Duchesne refers to a description of the Litania Maior (for which see now M. Andrieu, *Les ordines Romani du haut moyen-âge* 2, 135–170, *Ordo* IV). At the head came the poor from the *xenodochium* with a wooden painted cross, then seven *staurofori* carried the crosses of each of the seven ecclesiastical regions, on each of which were fixed three lighted candles; then came the clergy, and finally the pope who was accompanied by the deacons and preceded by two crosses carried by subdeacons. Charles' cross will have been for use as one of these last two.

66 *battici*: the word may be based on *battitum*, a possible past participle of *battuo*, the idea being that of gold beaten into a sheet to form the book's cover.

67 Unless the LP (c. 20) was anticipating this occasion, the malefactors had already been sent to France, and it seems plausible that this had been done because the Frankish envoys feared disturbances in the city before the king reached a decision on the matter. If so, they had been brought back for the trial, which was certainly held at Rome in their presence shortly after Christmas 800 (so Einhard). Charles condemned them to death under Roman law for *maiestas* (but against Charles or Leo?); on Leo's intervention the sentence was commuted to one of exile. So Charles, now emperor, acts as a judge at Rome, perhaps impossible for him earlier. He spent the rest of the winter settling the public, private, and church affairs of the Romans, Rome and Italy, and sent an expedition under his son Pepin against Benevento; after Easter (25 April 801) he left Rome for Spoleto. While still in Rome, on 4 March 801 he gave judgment in a dispute between Siena and Arezzo (neither in papal territory, *MGH DK* 1, 196, p. 264); in this diploma he avoided the title emperor. On 29 May 801 at Bologna (*ibid.*, 197, p. 265), in a diploma for Nonántola, he described himself as 'emperor, crowned by God, governing the Roman empire' (but not actually 'Roman emperor'); see Noble, 294–6. The LP now abandons political history.

68 The building was used for solemn audiences: in 855, Leo IV 105:111; in 901 under Benedict IV, a charter of Louis III (*Fonti per la storia d'Italia* 37, p. 29) refers to an audience held 'in the palace founded close to St Peter's, in the large apse (*laubia maiore*) of that palace'. The apse and traces of the two side apses survived to be described in the 15th century by

Needle;[69] it was decorated with wondrous beauty, with an apse adorned with mosaic and two other apses to right and left, resplendent with depiction on marble; he had the pavement laid with marble designs and had other spacious and elegant buildings constructed at the stairs up to the *triclinium* and behind it. Also in St Peter's he provided a gold-studded cloth decorated with precious jewels, representing the Lord's resurrection; white silk veils for the silver arches;[70] and for the same arches very beautiful cross-adorned silk veils for use on the feastday of God's apostle, after his return.[71] **28.** In his great love he had the *presbyterium* of his same mentor elegantly set up afresh, all of it with beautiful shaped marble; over the high altar he provided 4 all-silk crimson veils to cover all four sides, with gold-studded daffodils[72] and roses; and on the same altar, another tyrian cloth representing the Lord crucified. In the church of St Paul the world's teacher, 4 all-silk crimson veils for all four sides, a white gold-studded altar-cloth representing the holy resurrection, another gold-studded cloth representing the Lord's birth and the holy Innocents, and another tyrian cloth representing the blind man being given his sight and the resurrection. **29.** The same holy prelate provided for St Mary's basilica *ad praesepe* a white gold-studded cloth representing the holy resurrection, and another cloth with gold-studded disks representing the annunciation and SS Joachim and Anne. The prelate provided in St Laurence's church outside the walls, a white cloth, with roses and gold-studded, and over his sacred body another white cross-adorned gold-studded silk cloth with pearls. In the *titulus* of Callistus, a gold-studded cloth of byzantine purple representing the Lord's birth and St Simeon. In St Pancras' church, a tyrian cloth representing the Lord's ascension. In St Mary *ad martyres*, a tyrian cloth, as above. In St Sabina's *titulus*, as above. In St Boniface's deaconry,[73] as above. In St Mary's deaconry called *Cosmedin*,

---

Vegio (De Rossi, *Inscr. Chr.* 2, p. 351). Gregory IV (103:35) added some living quarters 'at the Needle' for the pope and his retinue to rest in when visiting St Peter's for matins and mass.

69 *aculia*; the Vatican obelisk (in its former position south of the church). Hence the *triclinium* came to be known as the Domus Aguliae (12th century *Ordo* of Benedict); Duchesne, 1914, 338-349 = *Scripta Minora*, 284-295.

70 The arches of the balustrade surrounding the *presbyterium* (Duchesne).

71 To Rome, 29 November 799.

72 Given the roses next mentioned, *astellis* may represent *hastulis*, 'little spears', also 'asphodels' (daffodils); but possibly 'little stars', cf. c. 93 (gold-studded *stellae*).

73 On the Aventine, near the ancient shrine of Jupiter Dolichenus. A basilica with St Boniface's body existed by the 7th century; the saint was not a Roman martyr (the only Roman St Boniface was the pope, died 422), and there is no reliable account of his history. The body may have been brought to Rome by monks fleeing from the Islamic occupation of Syria in the 7th century. St Boniface's monastery is referred to in a 12th-century interpolation in the LP's

as above. In SS Cosmas and Damian's basilica, a cloth of byzantine purple with a gold-studded fringe and pearls. In St Valentine's church, a gold-studded cloth, and another very beautiful cloth with interwoven gold. In St Nereus and Achilleus' deaconry,[74] a cross-adorned silk cloth. In God's holy mother's deaconry called *Domnica*,[75] a cross-adorned silk cloth. **30**. In St Saba's venerable monastery this bountiful pontiff provided a silver cluster[76] with its canister, weighing 12 lb, and a cloth of cross-adorned silk with gold studs and pearls. In St Erasmus' monastery, a cloth of cross-adorned silk with crosses and chevrons, along with its tassels,[77] with a gold-studded fringe. In the monastery of Clivus Scauri, a cloth of cross-adorned silk with a gold-studded fringe. In Pammachius' *titulus*, 2 cloths, one of cross-adorned silk with a gold-studded fringe, the other cloth of *ymizinum*.[78] At St Andrew the apostle's church *in silice* at the 30th mile on the Via Appia, this holy prelate freshly renewed the roofing, along with the baptistery and the portico. He appointed a priest for that church, and there presented gifts, silver, cloths and books.

[A.D. 800–801:]

31. In the 9th indiction the menace of our sins brought about a sudden earthquake on 30 April.[79] The earthquake shook St Paul's church and all

---

life of Xystus III as containing the body of St Alexius, whose cult is unrecorded before the 10th century (were his relics translated here then?), about the time when Benedict VII in 977 gave the monastery to Greek monks. They named the location Blachernae after the district in Constantinople; as SS Alessio e Bonifacio the monastery still survives. See Duchesne, 1890, 225–250 = *Scripta Minora*, 115–140; Hülsen, 171–2; Krautheimer, *Corpus* 1, no. 6.

74 Cf. c. 111 and n. 202.

75 The earliest mention (though the Einsiedeln Itinerary may be slightly earlier) of this surviving church. It was already ruinous by 818–9 when Paschal I (100:11) rebuilt it, so it is likely to be considerably older, but no traces earlier than Paschal's time have been found; Hülsen, 331–2; Krautheimer, *Corpus* 2, 308–321.

76 *butro* (also Leo IV 105:13, 60, both at St Peter's): cf. Probus, *botruus non butro* (a cluster). Some kind of lighting-fixture seems meant, perhaps one with a group of sockets for candles; cf. *policandilum*, c. 58.

77 *paratrapetae*: NGML cites the word from this passage only and guesses a derivation from παρά and τάπης (carpet, rug). Could it mean 'tassels'?

78 Given the occurrence in the LP of adjectives from places (Tyre, Alexandria, Byzantium, Naples), is this 'Emesene'? But cf. *imizilo* (Paschal I, 100:35,36); this, and *mizinum* in Nicholas I, 107:16, suggest a kind of material rather than a colour is meant.

79 The day and the effects on St Paul's (much of its roof with the beams fell down) are confirmed by Einhard, who gives the time as the second hour of the night and says the whole of Italy was badly shaken; Charles was at Spoleto by now. Structural damage to St Paul's may have been mainly to the roof (*navis* here meaning 'vault' as in c. 3) of the transept, above the altar where most of the silverware would be located.

the roofing collapsed. Seeing this, the great and distinguished pontiff was greatly afflicted and began to bewail the damage and destruction to the silver and other valuables therein. But by the Lord's will and by the prince of the holy apostles' protection, the pontiff put all his efforts into the task of restoring it as it was of old; with indefatigable industry he improved it and decorated it with marble of greater value; he faced the *presbyterium* and the whole church with marble, and renewed its porticoes.[80] He also freshly restored all the roofing in the vault above the altar; and there he presented three gold images, of the Saviour our Lord Jesus Christ, and of SS Peter and Paul the princes of the apostles;[81] over the doorway at the entrance he put another silver-gilt image of the Saviour, weighing 60 lb, and he freshly restored all the silver there that was damaged. He also decorated this church's wondrously beautiful windows with the mineral gypsum.[82] **32.** In the Saviour's basilica called Constantinian, this prelate and pontiff provided 2 cloths over the altar, one of them gold-studded and bejewelled, representing the Saviour entering the holy city, the other, gold-studded and with very precious jewels, representing the Lord's resurrection; and round the altar 4 red and 4 white silk veils, gold-studded; and 3 with edging, in front of the images; and 27 other white silk veils. On the altar of St Venantius, a cloth with interwoven gold, and 2 veils. In the oratories of both of the saints John, 2 gold-studded cloths of cross-adorned silk, and 2 veils. **33.** Over the altar of St Peter's this pontiff provided a cloth with a vine of fine gold with very precious jewels and pearls, representing in the centre the Saviour's face and those of God's holy mother and the 12 apostles, on which he used 25 lb gold; another gold-studded cloth representing the Major Litany; and another cloth with 3 gold-studded panels and representing the Lord's passion, with the inscription: 'This body which shall be given up for you' etc.[83] **34.** Also a great curtain with interwoven gold; and in the silver arch, 93 veils for use at Eastertide, with cross-adorned silk fringes, 5 of them gold-studded; and in the great arches 48 white veils. Also 18 gold-rimmed bowls of fine

80 Duchesne, II, 39 n. 45 speculated that Leo had to repair the 5th-century mosaic of the triumphal arch, whose style leaves much to be desired if it is really of late imperial times. He also noted an inscription at St Paul's (J 2535) containing a curse by a pope Leo (III ?) on anyone trying to purloin the furnishings of this church.

81 These three images became 'landmarks' in the basilica; a marble inscription of Gregory VII at St Paul's listing altars where mass had to be said each day ordains 'third mass, at the image of the Saviour also of the apostles'.

82 i. e. he provided the windows with stucco gratings (Krautheimer, *Corpus* 5, 100).

83 The wording, based on 1 Cor. 11.24, is strictly that as sung in the communion antiphon on the 5th Sunday of Lent, i. e. Passion Sunday.

gold, with jewels, to hang on the pergola in front of the altar, weighing 65½ lb; and a panel in front of the confessio, of fine gold weighing 28 lb. He put 2 silver-gilt images over the great main doors, weighing 90 lb, and provided 2 silver chandeliers in the *presbyterium*, weighing 50 lb. He decorated this church's windows with the mineral gypsum, and decorated other windows with glass of various colours. **35.** In the basilica of St Paul the world's teacher he provided a gold-studded cloth, representing in the centre the Saviour and on right and left SS Peter and Paul preaching to the nations, with a gold-studded fringe and most precious jewels. Over St Andrew's altar he provided a gold-studded cloth with pearls, and he adorned the *presbyterium* with designs in marble. On St Petronilla's altar, a white all-silk cloth with gold-studded panels and a cross; and there he decorated the *presbyterium* with designs in marble; he provided 6 silver columns with 2 cornices of fine silver, weighing in all 80 lb; and over the body of St Gregory, confessor and pontiff, a white all-silk cloth with gold-studded panels and a cross. **36.** In God's holy mother's basilica *ad praesepe*, an Alexandrian curtain with a cross-adorned silk fringe; another white one with a purple fringe to hang over the altar; in front of the Manger, white veils with purple fringes; and 12 inside the great main doors and in front of the *secretarium*. Inside the Manger, a crimson gold-studded cloth. In St Laurence the martyr's basilica outside the walls, a tyrian curtain with a cross-adorned silk fringe. In St Pancras the martyr's basilica, a canopy of fine silver, weighing 367 lb. In the *titulus* of St Callistus, in honour of God's mother the ever-virgin Mary, a silver canopy weighing 504½ lb. **37.** In Eudoxia's *titulus*, a white cloth with a gold-studded fringe. In St Caecilia's *titulus*, a cloth of cross-adorned silk. In St Eusebius' *titulus*, a cloth with interwoven gold. In St Vitalis' *titulus*, a cloth of cross-adorned silk with a gold-studded cross. In St Pudentiana's *titulus*, a cloth, as above. In St Anastasia's *titulus*, a cloth with interwoven gold. In St Praxedes' *titulus*, a cloth of cross-adorned silk with a purple fringe. In St Laurence's basilica *in Formonsum*, a fourfold-woven cloth. **38.** In St Anastasius' monastery, a gold-studded cloth depicting that martyr's passion, and a silver light with an eight-sided canister weighing 25 lb. In St Silvester's monastery, 2 cloths, one byzantine and gold-studded for the larger basilica, the other with interwoven gold for the oratory. In St Lucy's monastery in Renatus',[84] a gold-studded cloth with interwoven gold. In the

---

84 One of Rome's oldest monasteries, existing already in Gregory I's time; Probus, a diplomat, is mentioned by Gregory (*Dial.* 4,12) as its abbot; on 5 October 600 (Greg. *Ep. app.* 9) he is called abbot of the monastery of SS Andrew and Lucy. Monothelitism brought exiled Greek monks to this monastery; their abbot Thalassius appeared at the Lateran Council of 649

Holy Angel's on Faganum,[85] a cloth with interwoven gold. In St Lucy's deaconry *in Septem Vias*,[86] a cloth with interwoven gold. In SS Sergius and Bacchus' deaconry,[87] a cloth of cross-adorned silk. In St Lucy's deaconry *in Orfea*, a cloth of cross-adorned silk. In St Eustace's deaconry, a cloth of interwoven gold.

[A.D. 801–2:]

39. In the basilica of St Peter his mentor this God-protected venerable and bountiful pontiff provided in the centre of the basilica a crucifix[88] of fine silver weighing 72lb. In the Lateran patriarchate he built a decorated *triclinium* of wondrous size with a mosaic apse and 10 other apses on right and left, painted with various representations of the apostles preaching to the nations, adjoining the Constantinian basilica.[89] He arranged dining

---

as abbot of the monastery of the Armenissae established at Rome which is called Renatus' (Mansi 10, 903); in signing a petition he styled his monastery that of God's mother and St Andrew. His monks were probably Armenian refugees from the Arabs or from the Monothelites, just as there were Cilicians at St Anastasius' at this time. At the Council of 681 a monk from here named George represented the monks of Italy (Duchesne I, 355 n. 8). The LP mentions the monastery several times (e. g. 103:29); it is recorded in 936–9, 952 and 980 (*Reg. Sublac.* nos. 45, 121–2, 109). Duchesne located it near the bend in the Tiber just below Ripetta, where there are two churches 100 metres apart, one of them formerly S. Andrea dei marmorari (now S. Ivo dei Brittoni; Hülsen, 188), the other called, at least by 1002, S. Lucia iuxta posterulam quatuor portarum (now S. Lucia della Tinta; Hülsen, 303). Comparison of the documents of 980 and 1002 led Duchesne to believe that between these years the monastery ceased to exist but its double dedication survived: the inscription of 1002 provides the earliest evidence for the church of St Lucy; that of St Andrew is first recorded in a bull of 1194. But Ferrari, 276–80, objected that Duchesne's ingenuity was guesswork, and suggested a location on the Esquiline, near the Trofeo di Mario, somewhere between S. Maria Maggiore and the Porta Maggiore; Armellini-Cecchelli, 1000–1001, 1034, Hülsen, 304–5.

85 A church (104:23) on the top of what is now Monte S. Angelo, 7 km south of Tivoli. The derivation of Faganum is unclear; Duchesne suggested *fagus* ('beech').

86 The district south of the Palatine is so called in the Einsiedeln Itinerary (*CChr* 175, 333 line 49: 'Thence to the Seven Roads; there, St Lucy and the Septizonium'); it is arguable whether that reference to the church is much older than this part of the LP. The church recurs in c. 75 and in Gregory IV 103:29. The seven roads are (or were) those coming from different directions to the area near the Arch of Constantine.

87 Unclear which of the two deaconries so named is meant; cf. c. 75 with n. 132.

88 Apparently a crucifix, not merely a cross, erected on a transverse beam in the centre of the main nave; the Roman *Ordines* talk of a *locus crucifixi* in the Lateran at which the procession to vespers at Easter paused before continuing to the altar.

89 This *triclinium* was to the west of the patriarchate's main buildings and may have been joined to the north of the basilica; the area is now occupied by the 16th-century Lateran palace inside which its foundations have been traced. Councils were held in it under Nicholas I (107:30, 62), and banquets in the 12th century (*Ordines* of Benedict and Cencius); no doubt also receptions and legal proceedings. It may have been modelled on the hall with 19 dining-

couches there, and in the centre a porphyry shell pouring water; and he laid the pavement with various marble. **40.** In St Cyriac's *titulus* he provided a cross-adorned silk cloth with a purple fringe, a gold-studded surround and in the centre a cross of pearls. In St Xystus' cemetery of the Via Appia, a cross-adorned silk cloth with a gold-studded cross in the centre. In the *titulus* of Callistus on the altar behind the apse, a cross-adorned silk cloth with a gold-studded cross in the centre, and also there 6 cross-adorned silk veils. In the *titulus* of SS Quattuor Coronati, a cross-adorned silk cloth with a gold-studded cross in the centre. In St Marcellus' *titulus*, a cross-adorned silk cloth. In St Sabina the martyr's church, a cloth with interwoven gold with a purple fringe and a gold-studded cross in the centre. In St Laurence's basilica *in Formonso*, a cloth with interwoven gold. **41.** The church of St Paul the apostle called Conventus, in the territory of Orvieto in the district bounded by Sovana, Chiusi, Tuscania and Castrum,[90] had decayed through its great age; cattle were finding refuge in it and the relics had been stolen from it. This holy pontiff ordered it to be cleaned up and he freshly restored all its roofing with the porticoes; on its altar he placed a cross-adorned silk cloth, and he ordered relics to be deposited. **42.** The basilica of St Peter the apostle at Albano[91] was about to collapse through its great age; he freshly restored all its roofing and porticoes. In St Hippolytus the martyr's basilica in the city of Porto[92] this bountiful pontiff provided 2 cross-adorned silk cloths, one over his body, the other on the high altar. In St Sabina the martyr's *titulus*, a cross-adorned silk veil for all four sides, with a purple fringe. In God's holy mother's oratory in the *xenodochium* Firmis,[93] a very beautiful cross-adorned silk cloth.

---

couches at Constantinople, also used for banquets (Lauer, 1911, 101ff). The 11 apses may have had designs based on the stories of the 11 apostles, as a 'follow-up' to the design of Christ giving them their mission in the *triclinium* inside the palace (c. 10). The main apse had a prayer in mosaic lettering for God, who protected Peter and Paul from drowning and shipwreck, to protect this house and all living in it who enjoy the good things the apostle provides.

90 From Orvieto, Sovana is 38 km S of W, Chiusi 36 km NNW, Tuscánia 36 km SSW, and Castrum (Acquapendente) 20 km N of W. But this rural church is unlocated.

91 Almost certainly the basilica founded by pope Hormisdas on the property Mefontis (BP xliii, 54:1); mentioned again in c. 107 and in a charter of 985 (*Reg. Sublac.* no. 138), it still survives.

92 Opposite the buildings of the bishopric of Porto on Isola Sacra is a modern church of St Hippolytus and the remains of the earlier church. The saint is identified by the *Martyrologium Hieronymianum* (23 August) with a martyr Nonnus at Porto; Prudentius (*Peristephanon* 11) already confused him with the Hippolytus buried on the Via Tiburtina, and further confusions followed; cf. Duchesne, I, 145 n. 2; Amore, 'Note su Ippolito martire', *RAC* 30, 1954, 63–97.

93 See n. 169.

[A.D. 802–3:]

43. This God-protected and distinguished pontiff decreed that litanies be celebrated on the three days before the Lord's ascension:[94] on Monday the pontiff, all the clergy and the whole people, were to come out of God's holy mother's church *ad praesepe* with hymns and spiritual chants, and make their way to the Saviour's church called Constantinian; on Tuesday, to come out from St Sabina the martyr's church and make their way to St Paul's; on Wednesday, to come out from the Jerusalem church and make their way to St Laurence the martyr's church outside the walls. **44.** In St Agapitus the martyr's basilica[95] at the city of Palestrina this holy prelate provided a cross-adorned silk cloth with a fringe with interwoven gold and in the centre a gold-studded cross. In St Clement's church at Velletri[96] this distinguished prelate provided a cross-adorned silk cloth. In St Chrysogonus' *titulus*, a cross-adorned silk cloth with a purple fringe. In St Laurence's *titulus in Lucina*, a cross-adorned silk cloth with a purple fringe. In St Mark's *titulus*, a cross-adorned silk cloth with a purple fringe. **45.** In St Laurence's *titulus in Damaso*, a cross-adorned silk cloth with a fringe. In St Xystus' *titulus*, a cross-adorned silk cloth with a purple fringe. In St Hadrian's deaconry, in St Martina's church and in the deaconry *Antiqua*, cross-adorned silk cloths with a fringe. In the Holy Archangel's deaconry, 3 cloths, one of cross-adorned silk with a purple fringe, the other two of tyrian with a fringe with interwoven gold, representing elephants. In St Theodore's deaconry,[97] a cross-

---

94 Hitherto the only litany on a fixed day in the Roman liturgical books was that on 25 April (see n. 25). Rome now adopted the 'Rogation Days', first introduced at Vienne around 470, extended throughout Gaul by the First Council of Orleans in 511. Other litanies could always be held on an ad hoc basis for particular crises.

95 Its ruins were discovered in 1863–4 on the Campo di Quadrelle below Palestrina. Marucchi, *Guida archeologica dell'antica Preneste*, 140ff, gave an in-depth study and a restoration of two inscriptions concerning the basilica, one perhaps of the 4th century (*CIL* 14, 3415), the other of the 9th, perhaps mentioning the bishop Constantine who attended the Roman Council of 826 and commemorating the church's consecration after the repairs mentioned here: it attributes the original foundation to Constantine (most of the texts are in Duchesne II, 40–41 n. 59).

96 The present cathedral.

97 Like those of nearby churches (St George, St Anastasia, St Mary in Cosmedin), St Theodore's dedication reflects its origin in the Byzantine period. Little in the present building antedates the 15th century except a brick arch and the apse with a much restored mosaic of perhaps late 6th-century date (Krautheimer, *Corpus* 4, 279–88; Hülsen, 489). It was in a church of Theodora that pope Boniface I was elected in 418 before his consecration as bishop in the *titulus* Marcelli; Duchesne noted the mention in the *Passio Abundii* of a house of Theodora in the vicus Canarius, a vicus located by the *Mirabilia* (c. 10) at St George in Velabro. This suggests that Theodora's church could be St Theodore's deaconry. But the *Mirabilia* are unreli-

adorned silk cloth with a purple fringe. In St George's deaconry, a cloth with interwoven gold, with various representations including elephants, with a purple fringe. In the Holy Archangel's basilica at the 7th mile,[98] a cross-adorned silk cloth with a purple fringe. In St Agapitus' monastery *ad Vincula*,[99] a cross-adorned silk cloth. In SS Silvester and Martin's deaconry[100] this merciful prelate provided 2 cross-adorned silk cloths, one with a fringe with interwoven gold, the other of purple. In St Vitus' deaconry,[101] a cross-adorned silk cloth with a fringe with interwoven gold. In the deaconry *in Aquiro*, a cross-adorned silk cloth with a purple fringe. In the deaconry on the Via Lata,[102] 2 tyrian cloths with a purple fringe. In St Agatha's deaconry, a cross-adorned silk cloth with a purple fringe. **46.** In St Agnes the martyr's

---

able; and St Theodore's is on the site of a classical building (cf. A. Bartoli, 'Gli horrea Agrippiana e la Diaconia di S. Teodoro', *Monumenti dei Lincei* 27, 1922, 339 ff) which can hardly have given way to a church as early as 418. No *titulus* of Theodora occurs in the subscriptions to the Council of 499, but it could have changed its name by then.

98 This is the church to St Michael whose dedication on 29 September gained a permanent place in the calendar (*Martyrologium Hieronymianum* 29 September: 'At Rome, 6th (*sic*) mile on the via Salaria, dedication of the angel Michael's basilica'; *Leonine Sacramentary*: '*Natale* of the Angel's basilica on the Salaria'); it must have dated back at least to the 5th century. It was on the hill (near ancient Fidenae) called Mons S. Angeli till the 14th century, later Castel Giubileo.

99 The monastery, also in c. 78 and probably in 99:3, evidently provided services at the *titulus* Eudoxiae, S. Pietro in Vincoli; by 1014 there was a monastery of St Mary *ante venerabilem titulum Eudoxiae*, in 1015 is recorded an abbot of St Mary ad vincula, and the abbey of St Mary *in monasterio ad S. Petrum in vincula* is in Mallius' list of Roman monasteries; it was opposite S. Pietro in Vincoli in the present square (Fedele, *ASR* 29, 1906, 183), and is not to be confused with the nearby S. Maria della Purificazione; cf. n. 164. Duchesne concluded that the dedication to St Agapitus gave way to St Mary, and Hülsen, 165, concurred; Ferrari, 14-18.

100 At 97:73 St Silvester's was still called a *titulus*, though that may have been traditional rather than accurate even then, since 1) no priest from it had appeared at the Councils of 721 or 745 or in the list of witnesses to pope Paul's charter for St Stephen's monastery, and since 2) the number of *tituli* was already 22 in 777 (97:60 with n. 115), presumably the same 22 as listed later in Leo's life (i.e. the former 25, without SS Nereus and Achilleus, SS Silvester and Martin and SS Marcellinus and Peter, the first two of these now being deaconries). St Silvester's was again titular by Paschal's time (Sergius II 104:3: Paschal made the future Sergius II priest of it).

101 Cf. n. 152.

102 The earliest express mention of S. Maria in Via Lata, but it was probably one of the 16 deaconries existing in 777 (97:61 with n. 117; Duchesne, I, CCXXXIV). The structure was a third-century building with first-century elements, converted to christian use at least by the early 7th century, in view of the murals on at least three of the six chambers underlying the present church, which was constructed 1491-1506. The building had nothing to do with the Saepta Julia as sometimes stated but originated as a *horrea*; Krautheimer, *Corpus* 3, 72-81; Hülsen, 376.

church, where her body is at rest, this merciful prelate provided a cloth with interwoven gold, with a purple fringe. In St Apollinaris' church,[103] a cross-adorned silk cloth with a purple fringe. In St Eugenia's church, in which her body is at rest, a cross-adorned silk cloth with a violet[104] fringe. **47.** In St Stephen's church on the Caelian Hill, 2 cross-adorned silk cloths, one on the high altar, the other over the bodies of the martyrs SS Primus and Felician. In St Euphemia's basilica,[105] a cross-adorned silk cloth. In the holy Archangel's basilica on the Vicus Patricius, a cross-adorned silk cloth. Over St Sebastian the martyr's tomb on the Via Appia at Catacumbae, 2 large cloths, one of cross-adorned silk, the other with interwoven gold; and inside there, over the graves of the apostles Peter and Paul, 2 purple cloths of cross-adorned silk with interwoven gold. In St Laurence the martyr's basilica within the city of Tivoli[106] this holy prelate provided a cross-adorned silk cloth. In St Stephen's oratory called Major, by St Peter's, a cross-adorned silk cloth. In St Hyacinth's basilica in Sabina,[107] where his body is at rest, a very beautiful cross-adorned silk cloth. **48.** Over the altar of St Peter his patron this God-protected and distinguished pontiff provided a gold-studded cloth of wondrous size, representing the Lord's birth and adorned with very precious jewels and pearls; in the same church, 65 veils of cross-adorned silk and with interwoven gold, to hang between the great columns on right and left; and 3 other large all-silk white veils to hang at the entrance in front of the main doors; in it His Beatitude also provided a crucifix of fine silver

103 See n. 127.

104 *leoconblatea*: apparently λευxο-*blattea*, 'white-purple', therefore 'violet'.

105 St Euphemia's is mentioned also under Sergius I (BP 86:13; Duchesne, I, 380 n. 39) and as in the Vicus Patricius by the Einsiedeln Itinerary. It was connected (as here) with the Holy Archangel's basilica; the two churches will be those of the monastery of SS Euphemia and the Archangel, which was in the Vicus Patricius, very close to S. Pudenziana (c. 79). It was destroyed in the late 16th century to make way for the Via di S. Maria Maggiore (Hülsen, 249–50; Ferrari, 134–5). A copy of part of its apse mosaic shows the saint with arms uplifted in prayer and crowned by God's hand, with a menacing serpent on each side (Duchesne).

106 The cathedral of Tivoli.

107 The *Martyrologium Hieronymianum* has Hyacinth's feast *in Sabinis* 30 miles from Rome on 9 September; for '30', read perhaps '25'. A place *ad S. Iacintum* is mentioned in charters of Lupus duke of Spoleto in 746–7; a *casa beati martyris Iacinthi* in a charter of 747. 'Where the body is at rest' may reflect current popular tradition rather than a real local martyr; there may have been relics (part of the body, or cloths which had touched the body) of another Hyacinth, perhaps the one culted with Protus on 11 September on the Via Salaria Vetere, or less probably the Hyacinth culted on 4 August on the Via Labicana. Compare Valentine, on the Via Flaminia and on 14 February both at Rome and Terni (97: n. 78), and on this very Via Salaria the instruction by Gregory I (*Ep.* 9.49) for the deposition of relics of Hermas, Hyacinth and Maximus in St Mary's basilica at Rieti (Delehaye, *Comm. Mart. Hieron.*, 497–8).

weighing 52 lb, adorned on a wondrous scale, which stands close to the high altar. There too, 6 bowls with crosses of fine silver weighing 12½ lb, which hang in front of the great arch on right and left; and in it the distinguished pontiff provided 96 cross-adorned silk veils which hang in the silver arches round the altar and the *presbyterium*, 2 of them with gold-studded crosses and disks in the centre, and 8 others with a gold-studded fringe. In the same church, an arch with its columns in the middle of the *presbyterium*, of fine silver weighing in all 251½ lb. **49.** There too this bountiful pontiff provided a cross of fine gold, chased and decorated in relief, hanging on the pergola in front of the altar, with 12 candles, weighing 14½ lb. In the basilica of St Paul the world's teacher this venerable pontiff provided 11 great gold-rimmed chalices of fine silver, out of the apostle's own gifts, which hang in the great arches, and 40 others which hang between the great columns on right and left, weighing in all 267 lb. In St Paul's basilica this bountiful prelate, filled by God's inspiration, provided a canopy with its columns over the altar, decorated and of wondrous size and beauty, of fine silver weighing 415 lb; and a cross of fine gold, chased and carved in relief, hanging on the pergola in front of the altar, weighing 13 lb; and a red veil which hangs in front of the altar, with a gold-studded cross in the centre and a gold-studded fringe. **50.** Also, in God's holy mother's basilica *ad praesepe*, 5 bowls of fine gold, weighing in all 8½ lb; a cross of fine gold weighing 10 lb; and a great crown of fine silver weighing 36 lb. Also in it 42 white all-silk veils, 11 of them with roses, to hang between the great columns on right and left;[108] round the altar there, 4 more white all-silk veils with roses, one of them gold-studded and with pearls, to hang in the arches of the canopy; and another great white veil which hangs at the entrance in front of the main doors. He freshly repaired all the roofing of St Aurea's church at Ostia. This bountiful pontiff entirely and freshly restored St Marcellus' church at the 14th mile,[109] which had been burnt out by fire.

[A.D. 803–4:]

51. In the Saviour's basilica called Constantinian, this distinguished pontiff provided white all-silk veils to cover all four sides round the altar, one of them having in the centre a panel with a gold-studded cross and around it gold-studded edging. In the same basilica he renewed the high altar, beautifully decorated on a wondrous scale, of fine silver weighing 69

---

108 42 is the number of intercolumniations at S. Maria Maggiore.

109 This is the church (presumably on the via Aurelia) of the *plebs S. Marcelli*, mentioned in a diploma of John XIX to the bishop of Silva Candida (J 4076) and in two other documents (Tomassetti, *ASR* 4, 249).

lb. In God's holy mother's basilica *ad praesepe* he provided a gold-studded cloth adorned with pearls, representing the Lord's birth; also 2 silver arches in the *presbyterium* with 4 columns, and 5 other arches, weighing in all 133½ lb. **52.** In God's holy mother's basilica *ad praesepe* this distinguished prelate provided a red crimson cloth with a gold-studded panel in the centre representing our Lord Jesus Christ and St Simeon, when he was presented in the temple, and around it gold-studded edging; and another gold-studded cloth representing the passing over of God's mother St Mary, beautifully decorated on a wondrous scale, adorned with precious jewels and pearls, with a gold-studded fringe and around it gold-studded edging. In our lady's deaconry called *Domnica*, a red crimson cloth with a gold-studded panel in the centre representing[110] God's mother, adorned with pearls and with a gold-studded fringe. In her deaconry called *Antiqua* he provided over the high altar a canopy of fine silver weighing 212 lb. **53.** In the basilica of St Peter his mentor, this venerable and distinguished pontiff provided a bowl of fine gold, decorated in relief, adorned with precious jewels, weighing 7½ lb, which hangs in front of the apostle's image at the entrance of the vestibule. He coated with deep yellow gold, weighing in all 453 lb 6 oz, the face of the prince of the apostle's sacred altar from bottom to top, with the pedestals below and above, also the Saviour standing inside the confessio with his apostles SS Peter and Paul on right and left, both with crowns of precious jewels, and also the pavement of the confessio. Over this sacred altar he provided a gold-studded cloth representing the Lord's ascension and Pentecost, with a gold-studded fringe. **54.** There too, an image of the prince of the apostles on the men's side, of fine gold, with very precious jewels, beautifully decorated on a wondrous scale, weighing 19 lb 3 oz. There too this blessed pontiff provided cast railings at the entrance of the *presbyterium*, at the head on right and left, and at the entrance of the vestibule, of fine silver weighing in all 1573 lb. Also 8 pairs of fluted columns, both at the entrance to the body on right and left and at the head of the *presbyterium* on right and left, and on the men's and women's sides, weighing in all 190 lb. Also 8 silver arches, weighing in all 143 lb. **55.** In St Andrew's basilica at the same place, this blessed pontiff provided a diadem of fine gold, adorned with precious jewels, weighing 2 lb 5 oz. Over St Petronilla's altar at the same place, a gold diadem with very precious jewels, weighing 2 lb 3 oz. Also at the same place over God's holy mother's altar called *Mediana*, a cloth with interwoven gold, with a gold-studded fringe, representing the

---

110 *cum storia*: probably not 'with scenes from the life of'; LP Nicholas I 107:17 has 40 veils with a *storia* which is *leonum figuras*; Niermeyer, *historia* 3, 'picture, design'.

Lord's annunciation. **56.** In the basilica of St Paul the world's teacher this blessed pontiff provided 47 canisters of pure silver, weighing in all 247 lb. In St Agatha the martyr's monastery[111] over the Subura, a red crimson cloth with a gold-studded panel in the centre, with a gold-studded fringe. In St Pancras' monastery[112] behind the Saviour's basilica called Constantinian, a cloth with interwoven gold.

[A.D. 804–5:]

57. For his patron St Peter, gold gospels adorned all round with jewels, prases and jacints, and pearls of wondrous size, weighing 17 lb 4 oz; a special gold chalice, adorned with various precious stones, weighing 28 lb; also a gold paten weighing 28 lb 9 oz. Also in this apostle's basilica, 4 Cherubim of fine silver-gilt, weighing 93 lb, which stand over the capitals of the silver columns under the canopy. This distinguished prelate provided in the same place a gold image of the Saviour, weighing 79 lb, which stands on the beam over the entrance of the vestibule. **58.** In the basilica of St Paul the world's teacher he provided 2 angels of fine silver-gilt, weighing 100½ lb, which stand close to the Saviour's image at the entrance of the vestibule.[113] Also[114] a multi-chandelier of porphyry, to hang on the pergola in front of the confessio, on small gold chains weighing 1 lb. Above the 5 main doors at the entrance of this basilica, 5 silver images weighing in all 229 lb. In the same place, 2 pairs of handbasins gilded with purified gold,[115] weighing in all 14 lb. **59.** In the same place this farsighted bishop provided great hammered candlesticks, carved in relief, of fine silver, weighing in all 36 lb 8 oz, and 2 great cast lanterns, with two wicks, carved in relief, weighing in all 57 lb. His Beatitude decreed that they should burn on weekday nights in front of the apostle's altar. Inspired by God's grace he coated the great beam under the principal arch with fine silver, weighing 1452 lb overall. **60.** In the same place this distinguished pontiff provided on the high altar a gold-studded

---

111 Ferrari, 19–22, identifies this with the monastery founded by Gregory II (91:10).

112 Cf. n. 134.

113 i. e. adjoining the entrance to the chancel.

114 It is unclear whether the *policandilum* and the next items belong to St Paul's; by the end of c. 60 the reference to St Petronilla shows we are at St Peter's.

115 *antipento*: the word recurs in c. 64. MLW derives it from Greek πέσσειν and defines it *aurum obryzum*, 'of purified gold'. Although the objects concerned seem to be of silver (certainly so in c. 64), this may be right if it refers to the gold used for gilding (or in c. 64 for the gold rim), and is preferable to an explanation based on *antependium* (a hanging attachment?). MLW usefully cites John of Naples, *Gesta epp. Neap.* 42 (*MGH SSrL* 425, 36): *Ad sanctae enim ecclesiae ornamentum fecit crucem auream, mirabili fabrefactam opere, quod spanoclastum et antipenton vocitatur.* On 'spanoclist' see next note (all 'spanoclist' items in this life are in fact of gold).

cloth beautifullly decorated on a wondrous scale, representing our Lord Jesus Christ, his holy mother and the 12 apostles, with a gold-studded fringe, adorned all over with pearls and decorated with gold-studded purple on both sides; the noteworthy prelate decreed it be placed there on the Apostles' feastday. In the same place, a great cross of deep yellow *spanoclist*[116] gold adorned with precious jewels, and over it there he placed 3 others of pure gold, weighing 42 lb 2 oz; and 4 pairs of candlesticks, coated with silver-gilt, weighing in all 77 lb. In the same place over St Petronilla's altar this venerable and distinguished pontiff provided a canopy of fine silver weighing 348 lb, with porphyry columns, decorated on a wondrous scale; and a silver image standing under the arch of this canopy, weighing 10½ lb.

[A.D. 805–6:]

61. Over the high altar in the basilica of St Paul the world's teacher this God-protected and distinguished pontiff [provided] a gold-studded cloth representing the Lord's resurrection, adorned with pearls, with a gold-studded fringe also adorned with pearls; and 2 images of the apostles, silver-gilt, weighing in all 86 lb. 62. Over the high altar in God's holy mother's basilica *ad praesepe* this merciful prelate provided a gold-studded cloth, representing the Lord's resurrection, beautifully decorated on a wondrous scale, with a gold-studded fringe, adorned all over with pearls. In the holy mother of God's *titulus* called Callistus', a crown of fine gold to hang over the high altar, adorned with precious jewels, weighing 1 lb. In God's mother's deaconry called *Domnica*, a crown of fine gold to hang over the high altar, adorned with precious jewels, weighing 2 lb. 63. In God's mother's basilica *ad praesepe* at the entrance to the Manger this blessed prelate, filled by God's inspiration, provided main doors coated with fine silver weighing in all 128 lb; over those doors a small veil with interwoven gold, with gold-studded edging round it; and over the great main doors at the basilica's entrance 3 other large tyrian veils with a fringe with interwoven gold. 64. In St Peter's basilica this noteworthy prelate provided 18 great chalices of fine silver with purified gold rims,[117] which rest on the silver beams, weighing in all 182½ lb. In the same place, great cast candlesticks of fine silver, which stand in

---

116 Holder-Egger (*MGH SSrL*, 425 n. 4) accepted Du Cange's derivation of this from ἐπανωκλειστός; Stephanus has *in summo clausus* (as with an imperial or royal crown); if this means 'that which can be closed on top' it is difficult to see the relevance; and the initial *s* is troublesome. More probably the word refers to a technique of refining gold (σπανός in the sense of 'rare'? or could it be a skill used in Spain, where gold-mining was well-known?). John of Naples' spelling (last note) suggests a derivative of κλάειν, 'break in pieces', which is implausible.

117 See c. 58.

front of the confessio, weighing in all 198 lb. In the same place he coated the beam over the gold images at the entrance to the vestibule with fine silver weighing 126½ lb. <In[118] the same place he provided 2 cast lanterns with 2 wicks, of fine silver weighing in all 27 lb; and he decreed that they should stand on either side close to the lectern on Sundays and on saints' solemnities to shine with bright light for the reading of the holy lessons.> **65.** In the same place over the high altar at St Andrew's he provided a canopy of fine silver which weighs overall 305 lb. This God-inspired distinguished pontiff, realizing that the baptistery in the same place was now close to collapse from its great age and that the place for people coming to baptism was too constricted, improved its condition by building the baptistery from its foundations as a rotunda of adequate size, set the font in the wider central space, decorated it all round with porphyry columns, placed a column in the middle of the font, and on the column a lamb of fine silver, pouring water, weighing 18 lb 10 oz. He also built the high altar beneath the apse, and to beautify this holy altar he coated its face, confessio and grills with fine silver weighing in all 48 lb; over it he placed a cross-adorned silk cloth; in the same place he provided a cornice coated with fine silver and on the cornice he placed a silver arch and chevrons[119] weighing in all 80 lb; there too he placed 3 images weighing in all 37 lb 10 oz. The baptistery itself he decorated all round with various paintings. **66.** The oratory of the holy Cross in the same place was about to collapse through its great age; this distinguished pastor erected it from its foundations with fresh construction, along with the apse, and brought it to completion; he decorated this apse with mosaics, various pictures and marble, adorning it with wondrous brightness. There he presented: a canopy over the altar with its columns, and he coated the face of this altar with fine silver weighing in all 121 lb 2 oz; a *spanoclist* crown of fine gold with a cross in the centre, to hang over this altar, weighing 1 lb 11 oz; also 4 other silver columns, and over these columns a cornice coated with fine silver weighing in all 64 lb 3 oz; 3 silver arches weighing 43 lb 8 oz; 3 silver-gilt images weighing in all 30 lb; 12 chased silver canisters weighing in all 78 lb; 21 chased silver bowls with gold rims, and 1 cross, weighing in all 50 lb; 1 altarcloth with interwoven gold, another gold-studded purple one, and another white gold-studded cloth with roses; a small gold-studded veil with crucifix and adorned with pearls;[120] 7 cross-adorned silk veils; 4

---

118 The bracketed sentence recurs, more appropriately, in c. 67; the compiler's eye strayed and he anticipated an entry in the register he was copying.

119 *gammadiae*: decorations, like *gammulae* elsewhere? Or pointed arches?

120 Perhaps a crucifix stretched from pearls is meant.

veils with interwoven gold; 6 small tyrian veils which hang on the cornice in front of the images; 12 white silk veils, adorned all round with interwoven gold; 1 great white veil with roses, adorned on top with fourfold weave, and another red veil with a gazelle,[121] which hang in front of the great main doors; 3 small cross-adorned silk veils which hang on the cornice in front of the images; and 11 other various silk veils. In the same place at the baptistery he provided 3 tyrian veils which hang on the cornice in front of the images, and 21 other silk veils.

[A.D. 806–7:]

67. For St Peter his mentor he provided a special *spanoclist* gold chalice adorned with various precious stones, weighing 30 lb; a *spanoclist* gold paten also adorned with various precious stones, weighing 25 lb; over the canopy of the high altar of St Peter's, 4 great chandeliers of fine silver, with silver-gilt candles in the centre, weighing in all 140 lb. In the same place this distinguished pontiff provided an apostolic thurible[122] of fine gold weighing 2 lb 5 oz; over the high altar a gold-studded cloth adorned with various pictures, which he decreed to be placed there on the four Ember Saturdays during the year.[123] In the same place he provided 3 great crowns of fine silver weighing in all 154½ lb; in the same place, a decorated lectern of wondrous size and beauty, of fine silver weighing 114 lb; candlesticks of fine silver, to stand close to this lectern, weighing in all 49 lb; and over these candlesticks 2 cast lanterns with 2 wicks, of fine silver weighing 27 lb; and he decreed that they should stand on either side close to the lectern

---

121 *bubalus*: unless this is an unknown technical term, a gazelle or similar animal was depicted on the veil; 'stag' is possible, which has a christian significance (Ps. 42; cf. the water-pouring stags placed above fonts, BP 42:5 etc.), but one would expect *cervus*.

122 The excavators of the confessio of St Peter's (*Esplorazioni*, p. 200; E. Kirschbaum, 1959, 75 and plate 16b) found in the side of the narrow rectangular vertical shaft, lined with green porphyry and connecting the Niche of the Pallia with the tomb beneath, a sturdy nail used as a peg to support the gold 'apostolic' thurible which hung down into the space below.

123 *quattuor temporibus per annum in duodecim lectiones*. The *Quattuor tempora* are the Ember Days, a time of fasting to mark the changing seasons, so called as occurring four times each year, and held on the Wednesday, Friday and Saturday after the 3rd Sunday of Advent, the 1st of Lent, Whitsun (or sometimes about 3 weeks later) and in the 3rd week of September. The Saturday in each Embertide was called *sabbatum in XII lectiones*, a name referring to the series of lessons at mass that day, once celebrated in the evening as a vigil for the Sunday. As in the Roman Missal until 1969, the epistle and gospel were preceded by five Old Testament lessons; the number 12 is explained on the grounds that each lesson was read in both Greek and Latin. This is unsatisfactory: the arithmetic requires that 2 of the lessons were read only once. There was probably a stage, before the oldest surviving lectionary (7th century), when there were actually 12 different lessons (as in the Easter Vigil until 1956).

on Sundays and on saints' solemnities to shine with bright light for the reading of the holy lessons; 14 chandeliers in the *presbyterium* of fine silver weighing in all 332 lb 3 oz; 9 columns and 4 arches, of silver weighing in all 174 lb; in the same place, 64 gold-rimmed silver chalices, which hang between the great columns on the basilica's right and left, together weighing 461 lb. **68.** In the same place at St Andrew's this farsighted bishop coated the high altar with fine silver-gilt, adorned with wondrous beauty, weighing overall 135 lb; 12 chandeliers of fine silver weighing in all 52 lb; 12 silver canisters weighing in all 78 lb. In the same place he coated St Petronilla's altar with fine silver-gilt and adorned it with various pictures, weighing overall 178 lb 8 oz. He coated St Gregory the confessor and pontiff's altar[124] with silver-gilt weighing overall 127 lb. In the same place in the body of St Peter's basilica, a great all-silk Alexandrian curtain, with an accessory of interwoven gold in the centre and adorned all round with interwoven gold. This distinguished prelate provided an apostolic thurible of pure gold for the procession to the *stationes*, weighing 2 lb 8 oz. In St Paul's basilica this holy pontiff provided 2 apostolic thuribles of fine gold, one of which weighing 2 lb he placed inside over the apostle's body, the other weighing 2 lb 5 oz. **69.** This bountiful prelate coated the face of God's holy mother's altar *ad praesepe* with fine silver-gilt weighing 86 lb. In the same place he provided 2 crowns of fine silver, weighing in all 54½ lb; 1 great all-silk Alexandrian curtain adorned all round with interwoven gold.

[Donation list of 807:][125]

This distinguished prelate, by the bounty of almighty God and the apostle St Peter, the kingdom of heaven's keybearer, to gain pardon of his sins, presented crowns or canisters of fine silver for all the saints' holy churches of this bountiful Rome. He provided in:

[major basilicas and other institutions dedicated to major saints:]

the Saviour our Lord's church called Constantinian, fine silver crown, 23 lb

God's holy mother's basilica *ad praesepe*, pure silver crown, 13 lb

her church in Callistus' *titulus*, silver crown, 13 lb 3 oz

---

124 Evidently Gregory I by now had an altar at his tomb, before Gregory IV (103:6) in 828–9 moved his body to a new oratory inside the basilica. The tomb at this time was presumably still in its original place *ante secretarium* (BP 66:5), which Duchesne (III, 122 new n. 3) understood as meaning in the portico outside the basilica. The appendix to the *Notitia ecclesiarum urbis Romae* (CChr 175, 311 lines 214–5) puts it between 2 oratories (*antiqua* and *nova*) dedicated to the Virgin at St Peter's (Gregory's death-bed was also preserved near St Petronilla's, lines 208–10).

125 On the arrangement of this list see the introduction to this life.

70. her deaconry called Antiqua, silver crown, 13 lb
her church called *ad martyres*, silver crown, 12 lb 3 oz
her deaconry called Cosmedin, silver crown, 12 lb
her deaconry called Domnica, silver crown, 9 lb
her deaconry on the Via Lata, silver crown, 9 lb
her deaconry in Aquiro, silver crown, 8 lb
her deaconry outside St Peter's Gate, silver crown, 5 lb 8 oz
her deaconry at the Hadrianium, silver crown, 5½ lb
her oratory in the *xenodochium* Firmis,[126] silver canister, 2 lb 7 oz
71. St Peter the apostle's church, fine silver canister, 22 lb
St Paul the apostle's church, fine silver canister, 22 lb 8 oz
St Andrew the apostle's church at St Peter's, pure silver crown, 18 lb
St Andrew the apostle's church close to the *praesepe*, silver crown, 7 lb
St Peter the apostle's *titulus* called Eudoxia's, silver crown, 9 lb
St John the Baptist's church close to the Lateran patriarchate, silver crown, 5 lb
St John the apostle and evangelist's church also located there, silver crown, 5 lb
St Stephen the first martyr's church on the Caelian Hill, silver crown, 7 lb 10 oz
the Apostles' basilica on the Via Lata, silver crown, 13 lb
72. St Petronilla's mausoleum at St Peter's, silver crown, 20 lb
the Jerusalem church at the Sessorian, silver crown, 5 lb
St Laurence the martyr's church outside the wall, silver crown, 13 lb
St Apollinaris the martyr's church,[127] crown, 5 lb 4 oz
St Pancras the martyr's basilica outside the wall, silver crown, 8 lb

---

126 On this and the other *xenodochia* see c. 81 and n. 169.

127 Taken by Duchesne and Hülsen, 200, to be the surviving church alongside Piazza Navona (Domitian's stadium), mentioned in the Einsiedeln Itinerary in conjunction with S. Agnese in Agone, rather than the small chapel of S. Apollinaris ad Palmata connected to the atrium-façade of St Peter's, founded by pope Honorius (BP 72:3) and destroyed about 1610. But Geertman (*More Veterum*, 170–183) reaches the opposite conclusion: the Piazza Navona church may not have existed in 807, and could even be a later foundation by Leo III himself (given the entry in Einsiedeln it cannot be later), whose dedication for political reasons stressed the connexion with Ravenna; note that this life does include, uniquely, a papal gift to St Apollinaris' at Ravenna. But if so, why is the new foundation not mentioned in this life? And note that both here and already in 97:61 (with n. 121) the basilica is listed in surprising company if it was merely a small chapel. In c. 46 the church of St Apollinaris is listed immediately after S. Agnes ad corpus on the Via Nomentana, which may suggest that the mention of St Agnes brought to the compiler's mind (or that of his source) the Piazza Navona church of St Agnes, and he therefore listed the nearby St Apollinaris at that point.

98. LEO III

St Valentine the martyr's church outside the wall, where his sacred body is at rest, silver crown, 6 lb
[the remaining tituli:]
   73. St Clement the martyr and pontiff's *titulus*, silver crown, 15 lb
   St Sabina the martyr's *titulus*, silver crown, 8 lb
   SS Aquila and Prisca's *titulus*,[128] silver crown, 6 lb
   St Balbina's *titulus*,[129] silver crown, 5½ lb
   St Xystus the martyr and pontiff's church, pure silver crowns, 5 lb 2oz
   St Laurence the martyr's *titulus* called in Lucina, silver crown, 4 lb 10 oz
   his *titulus* called in Damaso, silver crown, 5½ lb
   his church in Formonsis, silver canister, 2 lb 7 oz
   Pammachius' *titulus*, silver crown, 10½ lb
   Aemiliana's *titulus*,[130] silver crown, 4½ lb
   74. St Eusebius' *titulus*, silver crown, 6 lb
   St Praxedes's church, silver crown, 5 lb
   Pudens' *titulus*, silver crown, 9 lb
   St Vitalis the martyr's *titulus*, silver crown, 9 lb 3 oz
   St Susanna's *titulus*, silver crown, 17 lb
   St Cyriac's *titulus*, silver crown, 5½ lb
   St Marcellus the martyr and pontiff's *titulus*, silver crown, 8 lb
   St Mark the martyr and pontiff's *titulus* called on the Via Lata, silver crown, 10 lb
   St Anastasia's *titulus*, silver crown, 7 lb 8 oz

128 Even in this same list (c. 80) this *titulus* is referred to simply as that of Prisca, which was correct and still normal; for the addition of Aquila see 97:51 with n. 87.

129 Not hitherto mentioned in the LP, but this *titulus* occurs in the signatures at the Council of 595 and on the tombstone of a priest, perhaps of 6th-century date, which was found at the cemetery (not the *titulus*) of Balbina, where the LP records the construction of a basilica by pope Mark in 336. The two institutions with the same dedication may have been closely linked long before the foundress was reckoned to be a martyr of Hadrian's reign and assigned a feastday on 31 March (*Acts* of pope Alexander). The *titulus* may be the *titulus Tigridae* listed at the Council of 499; the building itself may have been constructed as a church, but was more probably the hall of a private house (of a design similar to that of the basilica of Junius Bassus) converted for church use at some subsequent date; see Krautheimer, *Corpus* 1, 84–93.

130 The *titulus Aemilianae* is named at the Council of 499 and in the LP here, 103:22, and 106:15, the last entry suggesting it was not far from the Lateran. It is now generally accepted (Duchesne, II, 43, n. 77; Kirsch, 1918, 9–10, Geertman, *More Veterum*, 205 n. 1 to p. 1) that it was identical with SS Quattuor Coronati named at the Councils of 595 and 745, and in the LP (in 15 chapters of the life of Leo IV, 105). No document presents the two names as those of different churches. The rough geographical order of the present list seems to require Aemiliana's *titulus*, if it is not SS Quattuor Coronati, to be either an unidentified and not surviving *titulus* or the *titulus* of SS Marcellinus and Peter (on which see 92: n. 44).

St Caecilia's *titulus*, silver crown, 10 lb 1 oz
St Chrysogonus the martyr's *titulus*, silver crown, 5 lb
[the remaining deaconries:]
75. SS Nereus and Achilleus' deaconry,[131] silver crown, 6 lb 5 oz
St Lucy's deaconry in Septem Vias, silver crown, 6 lb 7 oz
St Boniface's deaconry, silver crown, 7 lb
St George's deaconry, silver crown, 5½ lb
St Theodore's deaconry, silver crown, 6 lb 8 oz
SS Sergius and Bacchus' deaconry,[132] silver crown, 6 lb
SS Cosmas and Damian's deaconry, pure silver crown, 5 lb 8 oz
St Hadrian the martyr's deaconry, silver crown, 6½ lb
the holy Archangel's deaconry, silver crown, 6 lb
St Eustace's deaconry, silver crown, 6 lb 5 oz
St Lucy's deaconry in Orfea, silver crown, 6 lb 2 oz
St Vitus' deaconry,[133] silver crown, 6 lb
St Agatha's deaconry, silver crown, 5 lb
SS Silvester and Martin's deaconry close to Orfea, silver crown, 6 lb 2 oz
St Silvester's deaconry close to St Peter's, silver crown, 4½ lb
St Martin's deaconry also located there, silver crown, 5 lb 4 oz
[Greek monasteries:]
76. This God-protected and distinguished pontiff provided in:
St Saba's monastery, pure silver crown, 8 lb 10 oz
St Anastasius the martyr's monastery, silver crown, 8 lb 4½ oz
St Andrew's monastery in Clivus Scauri, pure silver crown, 5 lb
St Agatha the martyr's monastery over the Subura, silver crown, 5 lb
St Erasmus' monastery on the Caelian Hill, silver crown, 4 lb 2 oz
St Silvester's monastery, silver crown, 6 lb 3 oz
St Laurence the martyr's monastery called Pallacinis, silver canister, 2 lb 7 oz
[Latin monasteries serving basilicas:]

---

131 On this deaconry see c. 111 with n. 202; Hülsen, 388–9.

132 Duchesne takes this as the deaconry of SS Sergius and Bacchus at St Peter's (92:13 and n. 40), but this is never mentioned later and may by now have been turned into a residence for the imperial envoy. The present one is more probably the homonymous deaconry below the Capitol rebuilt by Hadrian I (97:90 with n. 193).

133 Cf. n. 152.

St Pancras' monastery[134] close to the Saviour's basilica, silver crown, 5½ lb

SS Andrew and Bartholomew's monastery called Honorius',[135] silver canister, 3 lb

St Stephen the first martyr's monastery[136] close to the Lateran, silver canister, 2 lb

his monastery at St Peter's,[137] silver canister, 3½ lb

77. SS John and Paul's monastery[138] close to St Peter's, silver canister, 3 lb

St Martin's monastery[139] also located there, silver canister, 4 lb 2oz

134 This monastery and the next two served the Lateran; the three are named in order of foundation; St Pancras' existed before Gregory I's time (*Dial.*, 2, prolog., referring to one of its abbots, a disciple of St Benedict, implies that it was not new and that it was the only Lateran monastery) and was roughly on the site (or slightly to the west) of the present cloister south of the transept; Hülsen, 409–10, Ferrari, 253. It is often held that it was here that the monks of Monte Cassino fled from the Lombards in 577, but the story is late, intended to link the refoundation of Monte Cassino by Petronax in 717 with the original Benedictine community; Ferrari, 242–3.

135 Mentioned as *Monasterium Honorii* in the Einsiedeln Itinerary (*CChr* 175, 338–9, lines 177–8, 207); otherwise SS Andrew and Bartholomew. No doubt it was founded by pope Honorius, as is recorded in an interpolation in that pope's life (BP 72:6). The double dedication implies that there were two oratories in it. The present chapel of S. Andrea in the Ospidale di S. Giovanni (near the Lateran Baptistery) has been thought to represent one of these, Hülsen, 195. But St Andrew's chapel had its part in the ceremonies of vespers at the Lateran in Easterweek, and is once called 'S. Andream ad crucem', which suggests its proximity to or identity with the oratory of the Cross (founded by pope Hilarus) that adjoined the Lateran Baptistery; if these were identical, the surprising omission of the oratory of the Cross in the present list (which has the less important oratories of the two Saints John) would be explained.

136 The only reference to this monastery, on which Ferrari, 315–18. Some LP MSS make St Stephen's chapel at the Lateran a foundation of pope Hilarus (BP 48:12; Duchesne, I, 247 n. 11). This was either adjacent to or identical with the surviving oratory of St Venantius (founded by John IV, BP 74:2); if the latter, the absence of St Venantius' from the present list is explained (cf. the connexion of Holy Cross chapel with the monastery of pope Honorius, last note). Whether St Stephen's monastery originated in the time of John IV or even that of Hilarus remains unknown.

137 St Stephen Minor, the first, but newest, of the four monasteries at St Peter's (Duchesne, 1914, 314 = *Scripta Minora*, 260; Ferrari, 328–330). On them see 92:6 with n. 20 (inscription naming the 3 then existing: SS John and Paul, St Stephen, St Martin), 94:40 with n. 81 (St Stephen Minor, added to the older 3); 97:53 with n. 91 (St Stephen Major cata Barbara patricia, the one here called cata Galla patricia).

138 Founded by Leo I (BP 47:7); also called the Monasterium Maius, Ferrari, 166–72.

139 Located behind the apse of St Peter's, this monastery is first recorded in 680 when its abbot John, archcantor of St Peter's, was sent to England; then in the synodal acts of 732 (92:6, n. 20), Ferrari, 230–40.

St Stephen's monastery there, called cata Galla patricia, silver canister, 2½ lb

St Caesarius' monastery[140] at St Paul's, silver canister, 3 lb

St Stephen's monastery there,[141] canister, 2½ lb

SS Cosmas and Damian's monastery[142] close to the *praesepe*, silver canister, 2 lb 2 oz

St Andrew's monastery called Juliana Estate, silver canister, 2½ lb

St Hadrian's monastery[143] close to the *praesepe*, silver canister, 2 lb 2 oz

St Cassian's monastery[144] close to St Laurence outside the wall, silver canister, 2 lb

St Stephen's monastery[145] also located there, silver canister, 2½ lb

St Victor's monastery at St Pancras', silver canister, 2 lb 7 oz

140 On the site of the monastery now at S. Paolo, south of the basilica, next note.

141 Located inside the atrium (*intro atrio*) of S. Paolo (*Liber Diurnus* V87=C72 =A67, ed. Foerster, 167, 247, 382), where around 635–645 already stood an oratory on whose altar was the stone with which the first martyr was said to have been killed (*De locis sanctis martyrum* 5, *CChr* 175, 316 lines 27–29). Ferrari, 261, thinks 'inside' means that the monastery flanked the atrium and was entered from it. Gregory I in 604 (*Ep.* 14. 14) has the earliest mention of St Stephen's monastery: it was then for women, and had a garden between St Paul's portico and the Tiber. The formula in the *Liber Diurnus* reveals that by its date some pope had united this deserted monastery with another, presumably St Caesarius'. Gregory II (91:3) repaired monasteries (plural, but no names) at St Paul's; Duchesne suggested this was at the time of their unification, and it seems agreed that the document incorporated in the *LD* refers to this occasion; but the formula in the *LD* may be earlier than this, and perhaps Gregory II was in fact separating them. At any rate in the present list they are separate. Charters dated 961 and 967 (*Reg. Subl.* nos. 127, 139) show there was a single abbot, Roizo, of the monastery of SS Stephen and Caesarius called *quattuor angulos* at St Paul's. The 'four corners' were the junction of two ancient streets (the present Via delle sette chiese and Via Annunziatella) with the Via Ostiense: in effect the site of the present St Paul's monastery. Hadrian I and Leo III had dealings with Charlemagne about St Stephen's (*MGH Epp.* 4, nos. 92, 146–7, 150, 156); Ferrari, 254–71. From the 10th century on, the monastic complex was known simply as St Paul's.

142 This and the next two monasteries served St Mary Major; on them see 91: n. 14.

143 Otherwise SS Hadrian and Laurence's, cf. 97:86.

144 This monastery and the next served St Laurence's (Ferrari, 182–9). St Cassian's origins are unknown; the dedication saint is presumably the martyr of Forum Cornelii (Imola), whose feast happened to fall the same day (13 August) as that of St Hippolytus, whom legend closely connected with St Laurence (on Hippolytus' identity see n. 92). At any rate in the 7th century, St Cassian's was for women (*Miraculum s. Anastasii martyris*, *An. Boll.* 11, 1892, 234), but its place in the present list suggests that by 807 it was for men. Leo IV (105:30) united it with the next.

145 No doubt connected with the 'basilica' of that name founded by pope Simplicius (BP 49:1, cf. Duchesne I, 250 n. 3) and mentioned in 97:75; Ferrari, 182–9; at 184 he identifies it with the monastery founded at St Laurence's by Hilarus (BP 48:12), suggesting that the dedication to St Stephen was only acquired later.

St Chrysogonus's monastery, silver canister, 2 lb
[other Latin monasteries:]
   this bountiful prelate provided in:
   St Mary's monastery called Ambrose's,[146] silver canister, 2½ lb
   St Mary's monastery called Julia's,[147] silver canister, 2½ lb
   St Andrew's monastery close to the Apostles' basilica,[148] silver canister, 2 lb
   78. St Stephen's oratory in Dulcitius',[149] silver canister, 2 lb 5 oz
   SS Sergius and Bacchus' oratory in Callinicum,[150] silver canister, 2 lb
   St Agapitus' monastery close to Eudoxia's *titulus*, silver canister, 2½ lb
   St Agnes' oratory in the monastery called Dua Furna,[151] silver canister,

146 The Turin Catalogue has a monastery S. Maria de Maxima between S. Angelo in Foro Piscium, S. Stefano de Massima and S. Maria in Campitello, in the district of the modern S. Ambrogio della Massima, a church which may well be identical with S. Maria de Maxima; it was suggested long ago by Grimaldi and Martinelli that it is also identical with St Mary's called Ambrose's (Ambrose will have been the founder; there need be no original connexion with the Saint of Milan). The area would be that of the *porticus maximae* (CIL 6, 1184; Platner-Ashby, 423–4), which would explain part of the later name. But all this ingenuity may be unsound (Hülsen, 344, Ferrari, 199–200).

147 Certainly by about 1320 (Turin Catalogue) this was for women. From the 16th century the church of this monastery was known as S. Anna in Julia, later as S. Anna dei Funari; it was pulled down in 1887; Hülsen, 340, Ferrari, 201–2.

148 Later known as S. Andreas *de Biberatica;* by the 14th century it was for women. The site is the eastern part of the present Palazzo Colonna; Hülsen, 181, Ferrari, 49–50. It had a chapel of St Thomas (Stephen V 112:14, the only other reference to this monastery before 1192).

149 Unknown; Ferrari, 118.

150 Dedications to these saints occur in Leo III's time for deaconries at the Forum and the Vatican (cf. c. 75 with n. 132), and for two monasteries, this one (which recurs under Benedict III 106:26; Hülsen, 463) and one in c. 79 (which seems to be the women's monastery 'behind the Lateran patriarchate's aqueduct', Paschal I 100:22; Hülsen, 462). The latter is evidently that of S. Sergii de Forma or de Formis in the medieval catalogues; these also mention the (surviving) church of St Sergius de Subura, which may be the monastery in Callinicum here listed; so Hülsen, 463. Ferrari, 49–50, identifies it with the present Madonna del Pascolo (Armellini-Cecchelli, 259).

151 St Agnes' monastery called Dua Forna is mentioned in a lease granted by Gregory II (J 2215, Ferrari, 3 n. 1), and with a longer name in a document of 998–9 (Fedele, *ASR* 27, 1904, 43 n. 2, Ferrari, 4 n. 7), 'the monastery of Christ's martyrs SS Laurence and Hadrian and Christ's virgins SS Praxedes and Agnes *ad Duas Furnas*'; while a document of 1091 (Fedele, *ibid.* 63 n. 10, Ferrari, 4 n. 8) refers to the *titulus* of SS Praxedes and Agnes called Duas Furnas near St Mary Major; and the LP, 103:29 and 105:15, has a monastery of St Praxedes which seems the same as that of St Agnes. All this suggests that the monastery was located near St Praxedes' *titulus*, and it happens that when Paschal I continued Leo III's work on St Praxedes he 'provided in the same monastery an oratory of St Agnes' (100:9, 11); while an inscription at S. Prassede

2 lb 8 oz
>   St Vitus' oratory in the monastery called de Sardas,[152] silver canister, 3 lb
>   St Bibiana's monastery,[153] silver canister, 2 lb 9 oz
>   **79.** St Lucy's oratory in the monastery of Renatus', silver canister, 2 lb
>   St Mary's oratory in Michael's monastery,[154] silver canister, 2 lb 2 oz
>   St Sergius' monastery,[155] silver canister, 3 lb
>   *[other Latin convents:]*
>   this bountiful prelate provided in:
>   St Agatha the martyr's monastery[156] in Caput Africae, silver canister, 3 lb

records that on 20 July 817 Paschal put the bodies of SS Alexander, Eventius and Theodulus in the oratory of St Agnes located above in the monastery (Duchesne, II, 64; Hülsen, 168–9). As for SS Hadrian and Laurence, a monastery dedicated to them occurs at 97:86, and as St Hadrian's in the 807 list. Was it afterwards united with St Agnes' Dua Furna? Cf. 97: n. 185.

152 The LP has a monastery of St Vitus, a deaconry of St Vitus, and a monastery *de Sardas* with a chapel of St Vitus. Presumably these were not three different institutions. The medieval catalogues have two dedications to St Vitus, in Macello and in Campo; Hülsen, 499–500. The former is the deaconry (cc. 45, 75) still surviving, or rather rebuilt by Sixtus IV close to the ruins of the ancient deaconry; the latter's place in the Turin Catalogue suggests it was nearby, and a catalogue drawn up under Pius V has at this place 'due chiese di S. Vito vicine l'un all' altra'. LP 96:10 (and n.23) and the 10th century Subiaco charters mention a monastery of St Vitus, without precise location. There was a house with a church of St Vitus *regione VII in transenda* (*Reg. Sublac.* p. 29 n. 12, 10 May 998). Ferrari, 345–52, discusses the problems: around 800, either there was a deaconry of St Vitus and also a monastery of St Vitus which evolved out of the monastery de Sardas; or there was a monastery de Sardas and also a monastery of St Vitus which was connected with the deaconry. He concludes that the deaconry and monastery were distinct, and that the sources on an oratory and a monastery are referring to a single monastery. Was there a colony of Sardinians in this part of Rome? Compare the Corsicans at St Caesarius' monastery, n. 159.

153 This monastery, here first mentioned, had evidently grown up round the 5th-century basilica of St Bibiana (BP Simplicius 49:1), to which Leo II had added a chapel for other saints (BP 82:5) whose names are found attached to that of Bibiana in some medieval references to the convent (by 981 it was for women); Ferrari, 68–73.

154 Otherwise known only from a bull of 1116, by which 'St Mary's church in Michaele' was united with the basilica of the IV Coronati; Hülsen, 348, Ferrari, 241.

155 Ferrari, 294–6, agrees with Duchesne that this is the one mentioned under Paschal I (100:22) as SS Sergius and Bacchus located behind the aqueduct of the Lateran patriarchate (cf. n. 150); Paschal removed the nuns and replaced them with monks who were to sing the office at the Lateran, as the monks of St Pancras, SS Andrew and Bartholomew (so 97:68) and (probably) St Stephen by the Lateran already did.

156 Unknown elsewhere, unless it is the later church of St Stephen de Capite Africae in the medieval catalogues (Hülsen, 475–6), located on the ancient vicus Capitis Africae (the Via della Navicella) on the northern side of the Caelian Hill. The area was the site of the ancient *paedagogium Caesaris* in which young slaves were trained for service in the imperial house; the 'Head of Africa' may have been a statue on that building; at any rate the district Caput Africae was on

98. LEO III

SS Euphemia and Archangel's monastery close to Pudens' *titulus*, silver canister, 5½ lb

St Isidore's monastery,[157] silver canister, 2 lb

St Agatha the martyr's oratory in Tempulus' monastery,[158] silver canister, 2 lb

St Caesarius' oratory in the monastery de Corsas,[159] silver canister, 2 lb 3 oz

80. St Symmetrius' monastery,[160] silver canister, 2 lb

St Mary's oratory in the monastery of Aqua Salvia,[161] silver canister, 2 lb

---

the Caelian between S Stefano Rotondo and SS Quatro Coronati; Hülsen, 165; Platner-Ashby, 98–9, Ferrari, 26. Alternatively, it may be Gregory II's monastery of St Agatha, not otherwise in the present list (unless, as Ferrari holds, it is St Agatha de Subura).

157 Unknown (not the present church of S. Isidoro), but its approximate location may be inferred from the Einsiedeln Itinerary (*CChr* 175, 336 lines 139–140) which has a church of St Isidore between the Porta Tiburtina and St Eusebius'. A charter of 965 (*Reg. Sublac.* no. 130) has a 'vineyard of St Isidore' in the territory of Albano, which might have belonged to this Roman monastery; Hülsen, 278, Ferrari, 174–5.

158 Apparently the women's monastery of St Mary *Tempuli* or *in Tempuli* in a charter of 977 and two of 1035 (*Reg. Sublac.* nn. 120, 98, 99), St Mary *in Tempulo* in a bull of 1135, the monastery *Tempuli* in the list of 1192, and other documents of that period; then (with the name corrupted) the church of S. Maria *in Tempore* in a bull of 1221 (transferring the nuns from it to S. Sisto Vecchio), the Paris catalogue and that of Turin (in which it is *destructa, non habet servitorem*). The Turin Catalogue implies a location between S. Sisto and S. Lucia *in VII soliis*, and the identification with a building alongside the Passeggiata Archeologica is now accepted. See Hülsen, 167; Ferrari, 225–7; A. Zucchi, 'Il monasterium Tempuli', *RAC* 14, 1937, 353–360; Krautheimer, *Corpus* 3, 61–64. Legend made Tempulus, the founder, an exile from Constantinople, with his brothers Servulus and Cervulus, who in the time of Sergius I installed in this monastery an icon of the Virgin (painted by St Luke); such was the icon's fame that the dedication of the church to St Agatha gave way to St Mary.

159 The monastery *de Corsas* or *Corsarum* was near S. Sisto Vecchio (Leo IV 105:25; cf. next note); Ferrari, 96–9. A. Zucchi (*Roma Domenicana, note storiche*, Florence, 1938, I, 297–8) located it across the Via Appia from S. Sisto, at the junction with the Via Latina. But there is no evidence other than that it is in the right neighbourhood for Duchesne's view that its oratory became the surviving church of S. Cesario at this spot (Hülsen, 230–231, 233–4). The Corsicans might be refugees from Saracen attacks who settled in Rome, cf. the Sardinians in c. 78 n. 152.

160 Mentioned in a letter of Gregory I in 599 (*Ep.* 9. 191). Its precise location is unknown. But it is listed here after the monastery *de Corsas*; when Leo IV (105:58, cf. 105:25) restored the latter, he dedicated it to SS Symmetrius and Caesarius, so it is likely he was uniting two neighbouring monasteries (Duchesne; Hülsen, 487–8).

161 The earliest mention of the chapel in the monastery of Tre Fontane. The *Miraculum s. Anastasii martyris* (*An. Boll.* 11, 1892, 233ff), written 708–15, refers to a *mansio* of St Mary where Paul was beheaded and the relics of St Anastasius were kept. Ferrari, 41 (following Marucchi, *Le catacombe romane*, 132ff), thinks the chapel may have been an adaptation of the

St Donatus' monastery close to St Prisca's *titulus*,[162] silver canister, 2 lb 5 oz

St John's monastery in Appentinum,[163] silver canister, 2 lb

St Mary's oratory in the monastery de Lutara,[164] silver canister, 2½ lb

[Latin convents serving basilicas:]

the Jerusalem monastery at St Peter's,[165] silver canister, 2½ lb

St Agnes' monastery outside the Nomentan Gate,[166] silver canister, 5 lb

St Eugenia's monastery outside the Latin Gate, silver canister, 5½ lb

[Greek convent:]

St Gregory's oratory in the Campus Martius,[167] silver canister, 3 lb

81. this bountiful pontiff provided in:[168]

<St Sabina's *titulus*, fine silver crown, 8 lb

SS Silvester and Martin's deaconry close to Orfea, silver crown, 6 lb 2 oz>

[the remaining xenodochia chapels etc.:]

St Lucy's oratory in the *xenodochium* called Aniciorum,[169] silver canister,

---

tomb of St Zeno and his companions. The chapel was rebuilt in the 16th century and is now known (after an episode in the life of St Bernard) as S. Maria in Scala Caeli.

162 The otherwise unrecorded monastery presumably served the *titulus* (Hülsen, 248, Ferrari, 274–5). By 1030 there was a monastery called St Prisca's (Ferrari, 275 n. 4); probably an original dedication to St Donatus had given way to that of the *titulus*.

163 This name was taken by Grimaldi to refer to the Aventine, and the monastery was identified by him with that of S. Maria in Aventino, which flourished in the 11th century; but the identification is unproven (Hülsen, 270, Ferrari, 173).

164 Unknown, Ferrari, 116; its identification by Grimaldi and others with S. Maria in monasterio (Hülsen, 341, 347–8) is incompatible with the identification of the latter with St Agapitus ad Vincula (c. 45 with n. 99).

165 Listed apart from the other monasteries at St Peter's, presumably as one for women; it recurs only at Leo IV 105:109. It was located on uncertain evidence by Cancellieri on the northern side of St Peter's, where St Vincent's church, which he regarded as its continuation, was sited; see Duchesne, 1914, 314 n. 2 = *Scripta Minora*, 260 n. 2. Ferrari, 156–8, notes the existence of a chapel of the Cross at the end of the north transept of St Peter's: a relic of the Cross could have supplied the name Jerusalem to a convent nearby.

166 The first mention of the convent annexed to S. Agnese; Ferrari, 27–32.

167 In 937 the *Reg. Sublac.* (no. 121) mentions the convent of SS Mary and Gregory as in the Campus Martius. Called in later catalogues S. Maria in Campo Martio, it claimed to have the body of Gregory of Nazianzus, brought there in the time of pope Zacharias, who founded the convent for refugee iconodule nuns (Hülsen, 320–321; Ferrari, 207–9).

168 The two items following are accidental repetitions of two earlier entries, see introduction to this life.

169 The list ends with the chapels attached to the three *xenodochia* not already mentioned (the one in Firmis, with a chapel to the Virgin, is near the top of the list), and a hospital. For a fifth *xenodochium* no longer ranked as such see 94:4 and n. 6. Belisarius founded the first

2 lb 8 oz

St Abbacyrus' oratory in the *xenodochium* called a Valeris, silver canister, 2½ lb

SS Cosmas and Damian's oratory in the *xenodochium* called Tucium, silver canister, 2 lb 1 oz

St Peregrinus' oratory in the Lord's hostel at the Naumachia,[170] silver canister, 5 lb 1 oz.

[A.D. 807–8:]

82. In the Saviour our Lord Jesus Christ's basilica called Constantinian this bountiful pontiff provided on the high altar 2 gold-studded cloths, one representing the Lord's resurrection, the other the Lord's life-giving adorable Cross; 7 fine silver chandeliers weighing in all 27 lb 7 oz; there too he covered the railings in front of the entrance to the altar in fine silver weighing 48 lb 8 oz; a crown of fine silver weighing 12½ lb. There too at the baptistery, 10 all-silk white veils adorned all round with interwoven gold and fourfold-woven silk. He entirely and freshly restored all the roofing of this church with the porticoes and the baptistery. He decorated and sealed the apse windows with glass of various colours, and repaired the basilica's other windows with mineral gypsum. In the body of the basilica he provided 2 curtains, one large white one with interwoven gold, the other smaller and white with roses. **83.** In God's holy mother's basilica called *ad praesepe* this prelate provided 2 pure silver chandeliers, weighing in all 23 lb; 2 columns weighing 21 lb 5 oz; a cross and bowl of fine silver weighing 5 lb. In God's mother's deaconry called *Antiqua*, 4 all-silk crimson

---

recorded *xenodochium* (BP Vigilius 61:2, 'hostel for strangers') in the Via Lata, whose chapel is the present S. Maria di Trevi or in Trivio (medieval S. Maria *in Xenodochio*, Hülsen, 365), and which should be the *xenodochium in Firmis* whose oratory was dedicated to the Virgin. Gregory I refers to three: Aniciorum (*Ep.* 12.29), Valerii (*Ep.* 9.28) – both in the present list – and Viae Novae (*Ep.* 1.44). The last of these might be the Tucium of the present list (its oratory's dedication to SS Cosmas and Damian is recorded only here), but its location is unknown (there were 2 Viae Novae, one from the Palatine to the Velabrum, the other leading into the Baths of Caracalla). That of Valerius (mentioned also in 96:15, but its oratory's dedication to S. Abbacyrus is given only here) will have been on the Caelian, near S. Stefano Rotondo and St Erasmus' monastery: in the 4th century the residence of the Valerii was in this area. That of the Anicii may be identifiable with one of the later known churches dedicated to St Lucy; eliminating the 2 deaconries in Orfea and in VII soliis, and S. Lucia della Tinta which belonged to the monastery of Renatus, we are left with, as the most likely of the remaining possibilities, S. Lucia delle Botteghe Oscure on the northern side of the Circus Flaminius, in view of *CIL* 6, 1676, found in the Via delle Botteghe Oscure and recording building works of the Anicii; Hülsen, pp. 301, 306.

170 See c. 90 and n. 178.

veils to cover all four sides, adorned all round with fourfold-woven silk. There too[171] in St Andrew's oratory, 2 all-silk veils adorned as above. In God's mother's *titulus* called Callistus', an all-silk white cloth with roses, with a gold-studded panel in the centre representing our Lord Jesus Christ's presentation and St Simeon, with a tyrian fringe; 4 red crimson veils to cover all four sides, with crosses and chevrons, and a fringe all round of tyrian; 1 large tyrian veil which hangs in front of the images, with a purple fringe; 3 small red crimson veils with cross-adorned silk in the centre, which hang in front of the silver images, with a purple fringe; 1 large all-silk curtain in the body of the basilica. Also 3 silver-gilt images, one of them with jewels; 1 silver arch with its chevrons; 1 pair of candlesticks; 2 thuribles weighing in all 95 lb 7 oz. **84.** In St Peter's this farsighted bishop provided a gold chalice adorned with precious stones, for the procession to the *stationes*, weighing 13½ lb. In the same apostle's basilica, a gold-studded veil which hangs over the entrance of the vestibule, also another great gold-studded veil which hangs on the silver beam in front of the Saviour's image, over the entrance of the vestibule; a great crown of fine silver weighing 53 lb 8 oz; a silver light to hang beneath that crown, weighing 23 lb; 4 silver crowns weighing 57 lb; 8 canisters weighing in all 40 lb. There too in his love for and as a safeguard for the orthodox faith he provided 2 silver shields, each inscribed with the Creed, one in Greek, the other in Latin, placed right and left over the entrance[172] to the body, weighing in all 94 lb 6 oz. There too in the body of the church he provided 1 great all-silk curtain with interwoven gold,

171 If this oratory was in or near S. Maria Antiqua it is unknown. But is the reference really to the penultimate item, and the oratory that of St Andrew cata Barbara patricia near St Mary Major?

172 The door into the confessio. Leo III's inscribing of the Creed is mentioned by Photius, *Ep.* I, 24 (cf. *Mystag.*, 88). The text inscribed will have been the Nicene–Constantinopolitan Creed, used at baptisms in Rome since the 6th or 7th century in place of the older ('Apostles'') Creed; the 7th-century Gelasian Sacramentary provides the text in both languages (without *Filioque*, and with other Latin variants from the familiar text) as part of the ceremony of its *traditio* to the catechumens in Lent. Throughout the east this Creed was now used at the Eucharist, also in Spain since the 2nd Council of Toledo (589), and in Gaul from Charlemagne's time. Leo's action cannot but be connected with the dispute in 809 on the inclusion of *Filioque*. When Frankish monks on the Mount of Olives at Jerusalem used the word as they did at Charlemagne's court, native monks complained. Leo sent a copy of the traditional text to Jerusalem and later told Charlemagne's envoys of his regret that the text had been tampered with. He suggested that, as it would be difficult to stop the faithful singing this form, the use of the Creed should be gradually dropped. Clearly the Franks continued to use it, and with *Filioque*; it was finally included in the mass at Rome in the 11th century. But Leo III's inscription, no doubt of the older text, at the most sacred place in Rome, is an assertion of his own orthodoxy and shows his concern about those who added to the text.

98. LEO III

adorned all round with interwoven gold; 1 other great all-silk roseate veil which hangs on the great beam over the gold images, adorned all round with interwoven gold. There too in the baptistery, 9 white silk veils, adorned all round with interwoven gold. There too he coated St Leo the confessor and pontiff's altar with fine silver-gilt weighing 109 lb, and coated St Gregory the confessor and pontiff's altar with fine silver-gilt weighing overall 127 lb. **85.** This God-protected and distinguished pontiff coated the altar of St Paul's with fine silver and gilded it, weighing 155 lb; he coated his confessio and the face of the altar with fine gold weighing in all 121 lb 9 oz; over the entrance to the body he provided a shield of fine silver, on which he ordered the Creed of the orthodox faith inscribed,[173] weighing 32 lb; there too, 3 great crowns of fine silver weighing 93 lb. In St Sabina the martyr's basilica he provided in the body of the basilica a very beautiful great all-silk fourfold-woven curtain with interwoven gold.

[A.D. 808–9:]

86. Over the high altar in St Peter his mentor's basilica this venerable and distinguished pontiff provided a canopy with its columns of fine silver-gilt, with various representations, beautifully and marvellously decorated on a wondrous scale, weighing overall 2704 lb 3 oz; the canopy he took away from there he placed over the high altar in God's holy mother's basilica called *ad praesepe*. He provided a cross of pure silver and placed it in there, weighing 12 lb 3 oz; there too, 4 red crimson veils to cover all four sides, one of them gold-studded. In St Petronilla's mausoleum at St Peter's he provided white veils, 3 large, 8 small, adorned all round with fourfold-woven silk, and 1 great white curtain, adorned all round with interwoven gold. **87.** In front of the confessio of this prince of the apostles, this distinguished pontiff provided angels of fine silver-gilt on right and left, weighing in all 146 lb, and 2 other angels of fine silver-gilt which stand on the great beam over the entrance to the vestibule on right and left close to the Saviour's gold image, weighing in all 64 lb; there too, 4 other smaller angels of fine silver-gilt on right and left, weighing in all 68 lb; there too, 6 colonnettes of fine silver-gilt at the entrance to the vestibule, painted with various representations, weighing in all 147 lb; a great cross of fine silver-gilt, which stands close to the high altar, weighing 22 lb; there too, a great arch of fine silver-gilt, over the entrance to the vestibule, weighing 131½ lb; there too inside the confessio of St Leo confessor and pontiff, a gospel-book of fine silver-gilt, weighing 6 lb 3 oz. **88.** In the basilica of St Paul the world's teacher this same pontiff provided an image of the Saviour of fine silver-gilt over the

---

173 On a single shield, in contrast to St Peter's, so presumably in Latin only.

entrance to the vestibule, weighing 49½ lb. There too, 1 column of fine silver weighing 17 lb.

[A.D. 809–10:]

In the holy Archangel's deaconry this God-protected and distinguished pontiff provided a paten and chalice of fine silver, weighing 10 lb. Protected by God's inspiration, he provided in the Saviour's basilica called Constantinian a canopy with its 4 columns of fine silver, painted with various representations, and, with its railings and colonnettes beautifully decorated on a wondrous scale, weighing altogether 1227 lb. He freshly restored all the roofing of God's mother our lady the ever-virgin St Mary's basilica called *ad praesepe*. **89.** The chambers[174] close to the prince of the apostles St Peter's church had decayed through great age and were now on the point of collapse; this noteworthy prelate improved them by rebuilding them very firmly from the foundations. There too he provided a bath, placed on the higher level close to the great column,[175] a round construction marvellously decorated. He freshly restored this basilica's entrance steps, both those below the portico and those at the actual entrance.[176] Close to these steps, on the righthand side[177] of the atrium he built from the foundations up a house beautifully decorated on a wondrous scale, and in it placed dining couches. Close to this house he built from the foundations up a wondrously decorated bath for the benefit of Christ's poor and pilgrims. **90.** By God's inspiration this distinguished bishop newly constructed from the foundations up a hospice to St Peter at the place called Naumachia,[178]

---

174 *cubicula*; the *accubita* of 92:13 (with n. 42); but the latter word is used for 'dining couches' near the end of this chapter.

175 The obelisk (in its ancient position).

176 The LP distinguishes the flight up to the portico east of the atrium from the steps at the west end of the atrium leading into the basilica.

177 The north side, where the Vatican Palace is now. Leo is providing extra accommodation for poor pilgrims apart from the repaired chambers just mentioned and the hospice in the next chapter. On these houses for the poor, see Duchesne, 1914, 348 = *Scripta Minora*, 294.

178 The 4th-century Regionary Catalogues have 5 (but read 2) Naumachiae in Rome; one was on the Janiculum near the Porta Portuensis, but the relevant one (mentioned also by Procopius, *BG* 2.1) was in the area still known in the middle ages as Naumachia between the Vatican Palace and Castel S. Angelo; for this see Duchesne, 1902, 9 = *Scripta Minora*, 187. The *Mirabilia* and Mallius state that it contained the legendary *Sepulchrum Romuli quod vocatur meta*, a funerary pyramid destroyed by Alexander VI, close to the present church S. Maria Transpontina. The oratory of St Peregrinus existed in time to receive a gift in 807 (c. 81); construction-technique supports a Carolingian date and the apse-painting of Christ blessing is probably 9th-century work (Krautheimer, *Corpus* 3, 177 citing De Waal, though Cecchelli (Armellini-Cecchelli, 972) regards it as 10th-century). We are here told that (in 809–10) Leo built the hospice with a church to St Peter, and endowed the hospice; Paschal I (100:18) gave the hospice of St Peregrinus at St Peter's in the naumachia, which (S. Peregrinus' or St Peter's?)

decorated the various buildings of the houses there, and constructed anew a church in honour of St Peter prince of the apostles. To this church he transferred bodies of Christ's holy martyrs and buried them there, and constructed everything necessary for the hospice. For the sustenance of Christ's poor, of strangers and pilgrims coming from distant regions, he presented there urban and rural estates, to raise up God's holy church and to save the Roman people. Christ's martyr St Stephen's monastery called *cata Galla patricia* had by now decayed from its great age and part of it had fallen down; this farsighted pontiff undertook the task of improving it from its foundations, along with the oratory, by laying a firm foundation. He rebuilt anew the steps[179] which are the entry into St Peter's from St Andrew's, which had been worn away by age. St Martin the confessor and pontiff's monastery, located in that place, was flawed through great age; he restored almost all of it from the foundations. **91.** He freshly restored the roofing of St Andrew's basilica called *cata Barbara patricia* which for a long time had been worn away by age; newly rebuilt the roofing of St Lucy the martyr's *in Orfea*; restored and improved the roofing of St Balbina the martyr's which was on the point of collapse; marvellously restored the roofing of the martyrs SS Cosmas and Damian's basilica on the Via Sacra; restored and improved the roofing of St Martina the martyr's basilica at the Three Fates; and freshly restored the roofing of St Laurence the martyr's *titulus* called that of Damasus. By his wise effort this holy and distinguished pontiff marvellously rebuilt anew the roofing of St Valentine the martyr's basilica on the Via Flaminia, which was now about to collapse through its great age; as for the square colonnade of the Apostles' basilica on the Via Lata, he freshly restored all its roofing inside and out; and freshly restored the roofing of St Agatha the martyr's basilica over the Subura, which had now decayed from great age.

[*A.D. 810–11:*]

92. In the Lateran patriarchate this holy prelate built from its foundations

---

Leo had built, and its endowments, to the monastery of SS Agatha and Caecilia. Did Leo in 809–10 add a chapel of St Peter to an existing (pre-807) one of St Peregrinus? Did Leo found both? Or (most likely) is St Peter's in the present passage a slip for St Peregrinus', while in Paschal I 100:18 'which' refers to St Peregrinus' and 'at St Peter's' refers to its location near the Vatican basilica? Thanks to its oratory's dedication, the hospice itself could easily be called St Peregrinus'. The saint himself was a third-century martyr at Auxerre; it was his name which made him a suitable dedicatee of a church for pilgrims (*peregrini*). S. Pellegrino's church survives on the east side of the Via del Pellegrino in Vatican City; it is now the chapel of the Vatican Gendarmerie. Its dedication feast was 26 May. For the older remains see Hülsen, 416, Armellini-Cecchelli, 970 ff, 1490; Krautheimer, *Corpus* 3, 175–8.

179 For these steps, BP Symmachus 53:7 (end).

an oratory in honour of the holy Archangel;[180] he constructed it stoutly in *opus Signinum*[181] and adorned it all over with mosaics, various pictures and very beautiful marble minerals in various colours; and there he presented all the sacred gold and silver equipment and various veils. The *macrona*[182] of this Lateran patriarchate, which stretches from the grounds to beyond the apostles' images, was about to collapse from great age; he freshly restored it from its foundations along with its roofing and veranda[183] from bottom to top, and improved it by laying it with solid marble; he built anew the apse-vault of this *macrona* and marvellously decorated it with various representations in painting. **93.** Round St Peter his mentor's altar, this God-protected, venerable and distinguished pontiff provided a red crimson all-silk veil to cover all four sides, with gold-studded panels and disks painted with various representations, with gold-studded stars and in the centre gold-studded crosses adorned with pearls, beautifully decorated on a wondrous scale, and put in place on feast days for adornment. There too, another white all-silk Easter veil with roses, to cover all four sides, with gold-studded panels and disks, and gold-studded crosses adorned with pearls, with a gold-studded fringe. There too, 4 other small veils for each column of the canopy, with gold-studded tigers, and adorned all round with purple. He also placed 4 other small veils like these on the canopy columns in the basilica of St Paul the world's teacher. **94.** This venerable pontiff freshly improved and restored the roofing of St Agapitus the martyr's basilica at Palestrina, and the roofing of the other basilica[184] close to that one, which were now about to collapse through great age. He freshly repaired the roofing of St Stephen the first martyr's basilica on the Via Latina[185]

180 This chapel recurs in Paschal I 100:29; the only other evidence is part of its façade-inscription found among ruins during Sixtus V's construction of the present Lateran Palace, stating that Leo III had it built in honour of the Archangels (*sic*); Hülsen, 202.

181 A kind of plaster made from potsherds and lime, and used for walls and pavements; named after Segni in Latium.

182 *macron(e)a*: 'prolongation', 'extension'. Duchesne, I, 378, n. 26, explains it as the north portico of the outer (western) palace. The 'grounds' (*campus*) were about where the Lateran obelisk now is; the images were at the palace's northern façade.

183 For this veranda (*solarium*) see Leo IV 105:11 (by which time it was ruinous).

184 Citing De Rossi, Duchesne inferred from 'other basilica' that St Agapitus' was a double basilica like St Laurence's (a misunderstanding of the history of S. Lorenzo) and St Symphorosa's. More plausibly the compiler has forgotten the name of the other basilica at Palestrina (St Secundinus'), restored in 784/5 (97:82). Note how Leo restored the two separate basilicas at Albano (c. 107).

185 For its foundation see BP Leo I 47:1. The excavators in 1858 thought some of the sculpted marbles found could be of Leo III's time; they found an inscription recording how Lupo, a shepherd, presented a bell to the church in 844-7. Except for LP, Leo IV (847-55)

at the 3rd mile, which had now been worn out by age for a period of many years and was close to collapse. He freshly restored the roofing of St Basilides the martyr's in Merulana.[186]

[A.D. 811–12:]

95. In the Saviour our Lord Jesus Christ's basilica called Constantinian this God-protected and venerable pontiff provided from his own money 5 of the basilica's crowns with their dolphins, 35 canisters, 8 bowls, weighing in all 276 lb. In God's mother our lady the ever-virgin St Mary's basilica called *ad praesepe*, a curtain with interwoven gold and adorned all round with purple, marvellously decorated, which hangs over the perch above the throne; 40 various veils with interwoven gold, of cross-adorned and fourfold-woven silk adorned all round with purple. There too in front of the entrance to the Manger, a net-shaped light of fine silver, with 5 canisters, weighing in all 37½ lb. **96.** Bathed in the Holy Ghost's enlightenment, this holy prelate provided for St Peter his mentor a special gold *spanoclist* square chalice, adorned with various precious stones, weighing 32 lb, and a gold *spanoclist* paten beautifully decorated on a wondrous scale, weighing 26 lb 6 oz. In the same basilica, a net-shaped light with canisters and crosses of fine silver, which hangs beneath the principal arch, and another great net-shaped light with 20 canisters to hang beneath the great silver beam, to adorn God's holy church, weighing in all 2104 lb 7 oz. **97.** In the basilica of St Paul the world's teacher he provided a crucifix of fine silver, beautifully decorated on a wondrous scale, weighing 52 lb. There too, a white all-silk veil with roses, to cover all four sides, of which one has in the middle a gold-studded cross and gold-studded chevrons; and 9 white all-silk veils adorned all round with tyrian. There too, 8 gold-rimmed chased bowls of fine silver, which hang on the bronze light in the middle of the basilica, weighing in all 14 lb. This prelate adorned the entrance to the body there[187] with white marble of wondrous beauty, and he placed the bronze main doors there. On the marble columns which stand round the teacher of

---

105:43, that is the last record of the church till its rediscovery by Lorenzo Fortunati in 1857; Krautheimer, *Corpus* 4, 241–253.

186 Evidently on the Via Merulana, but totally unknown, even to the 807 list; Hülsen, 208. Equally unknown are any traces of the saint's tomb-shrine. Basilides was a Roman martyr culted on 12 June at the 12th mile on the Via Aurelia (*Itin. Malm.* only), the site of ancient Lorium, between Bottacia and Castel di Guido.

187 At the crypt-entrance under the altar, Leo erected a portal, known from the copy of an inscription once placed above the entrance: 'Leo III, bishop by the grace of God, adorned this entrance with wondrous beauty for God's holy people'. The *presbyterium*, east of the altar, was bounded by the colonnade mentioned below. Leo was probably repairing Gregory I's arrangements of the crypt and *presbyterium*; cf. Kirschbaum, 1959, 191.

the world's altar, where there had formerly been wooden beams which had now decayed through great age, this sacred bishop had lilies[188] placed on these columns, and over these lilies he placed slabs of solid marble and decorated the work with various pictures of wondrous size and beauty. There too he provided 5 great Alexandrian veils, marvellously decorated, which hang over the great doors at the basilica's entrance.

[A.D. 812–13:]

98. In God's mother our lady the ever-virgin St Mary's basilica *ad praesepe* this holy and distinguished pontiff provided a white all-silk veil with roses, to cover all four sides, marvellously decorated. There too, within the Manger, a white all-silk cloth with roses, adorned all round with gold studs and with a cross in the centre and gold-studded disks; 4 white all-silk veils with roses, adorned all round with tyrian. In God's mother's deaconry called *Domnica*, a white all-silk cloth with roses, with a panel of tyrian in the centre representing the crucifixion, and gold-studded wheels, adorned all round with fourfold-woven silk. There too, a curtain with interwoven gold, adorned all round with purple. **99.** In God's mother's deaconry called *Cosmedin*, a white all-silk cloth with a gold-studded panel, representing the Lord's resurrection, and gold-studded edging all round. At St Mary *ad martyres*, a white all-silk cloth with roses, with a panel of tyrian, representing the crucifixion, and a gold-studded wheel, adorned all round with tyrian. In God's mother's deaconry outside St Peter's Gate, a cloth of tyrian, marvellously decorated. **100.** In St Peter his mentor's basilica this venerable and distinguished pontiff provided 22 chased canisters of fine silver, both in the square colonnade and in the body of the basilica, weighing in all 125 lb; 48 gold-rimmed bowls with Christ's sign[189] which hang both in the square colonnade and on the bronze light in the body of the basilica, weighing in all 101½ lb; 4 silver lights which stand on the silver beams, weighing 93 lb; 2 silver arches weighing in all 41 lb 9 oz; 30 great purple veils, adorned all round with fourfold-woven silk, which hang on the silver beams right and left of the *presbyterium* and round the throne; 47 small veils with interwoven gold, adorned all round with byzantine purple and coated with neapolitan purple. In the body of the basilica, a great Alexandrian curtain beautifully decorated on a wondrous scale, adorned all round with tyrian; 25 small white all-silk veils with roses, adorned all round with purple, one of

---

188 New lily-shaped capitals were provided for the colonnade enclosing the *presbyterium*; and the slabs (*platomae*) on them replaced wooden architraves; Krautheimer, *Corpus* 5, 100.

189 *signochristas*; Niermeyer, citing this passage and 103:26, defines as 'adorned with crosses'; this may be right (*stauracis* has the same meaning but is used for silk only). But the mark could have been the chi-rho symbol (the *chrismon*).

them adorned with cross-adorned silk. **101.** There too over St Andrew's altar, a white all-silk cloth with roses, with a gold-studded panel representing the Lord's resurrection, and all round a gold-studded edging. Over St Petronilla's altar, a white all-silk cloth with roses, with a gold-studded panel representing the Lord's resurrection, and all round it a gold-studded edging. There too in God's holy mother's oratory *in mediana*, a white all-silk cloth with roses, with a gold-studded cross in the middle and adorned all round with tyrian. There too in God's mother's oratory called that of lord pope Paul, a white all-silk cloth adorned all round with ermine; 1 white all-silk veil adorned all round with ermine. There too in St Martin's monastery, a white all-silk cloth with roses, with a gold-studded cross in the centre and a tyrian fringe. **102.** Over the high altar in the Apostles' basilica on the Via Lata, a white all-silk cloth with roses, with a panel in the centre of cross-adorned silk representing the Lord's resurrection, and all round a gold-studded cloth, and gold-studded disks with a tyrian fringe; a small red veil to cover all four sides,[190] adorned all round with interwoven gold, one gold-studded; 2 small red Alexandrian veils, adorned all round with cross-adorned silk. There too in the body of the basilica, a marvellously decorated great curtain with interwoven gold, adorned all round with tyrian and with crosses of tyrian in the centre. **103.** Over the high altar in St Sabina the martyr's *titulus* this noteworthy prelate provided a white all-silk cloth with roses, with a cross-adorned silk panel in the centre representing the Lord's resurrection, and all round gold-studded edging. Over the high altar in St Susanna the martyr's *titulus*, a white all-silk cloth with roses, with a gold-studded panel in the centre representing the Lord's resurrection, and all round gold-studded edging. **104.** In St Stephen the first martyr's basilica on the Caelian Hill, a white all-silk cloth with roses, with a cross-adorned silk panel in the centre, representing the Lord's resurrection, and a gold-studded cross. Over the high altar in St George the martyr's deaconry, a white all-silk cloth with roses, with a cross-adorned silk panel in the centre, representing the crucifixion, adorned with tyrian and with gold-studded roses.

[A.D. 813–14:]

105. In his great love for our lady, this God-protected, venerable and distinguished pontiff provided in God's holy mother's basilica called *ad praesepe* a light of fine silver with its lantern and candle-holder weighing in all 40½ lb. His Beatitude decreed that on Sundays and saints' solemnities it should stand close to the lectern to shine with bright light for the reading of the holy

---

190 *tetravela*, neuter plural, is a single veil for all four sides of an altar; in this case one side of the veil was gold-studded. But it is possible that a number has dropped out of the text and the plural is real: '.. small red veils, one of them gold-studded'.

lessons. In St Peter's also he provided a light of fine silver-gilt, decorated with wondrous beauty, with its lantern and candle-holder, weighing in all 90½ lb. There too beneath the Saviour our Lord Jesus Christ's image at the crucifix in St Peter's he provided a wonderfully designed shell of fine silver, and placed it there out of love for our Lord Jesus Christ to brighten the lighting; it weighs .. lb. **106.** As for St Apollinaris the martyr and pontiff's basilica, founded close to the city of Ravenna,[191] its beams had much decayed through great age with the passing of the years from ancient times and were at that time almost on the point of collapse; this venerable father, inspired by God, sent there and through his expert and farsighted care he freshly and solidly restored and improved all that church's roofing with its square colonnades. Over this sacred basilica's altar he provided, in honour of Almighty God, and of St Peter from whose gifts and presents it came, a white silk cloth with roses, with a gold-studded cross in the centre, with disks and wheels of silk representing the annunciation, birth, passion and resurrection of our Lord Jesus Christ, his ascension into heaven and Pentecost, adorned all round like the cloth itself with gold studs; there too, a fine silver canister with its chains, weighing 15 lb. **107.** By some negligence or carelessness, through the devil's contriving, the *episcopium* of Albano along with the church founded in St Pancras' name caught fire after matins and was burnt down, from the foundations to the rooftop.[192] By God's inspiration and the Holy Ghost's enlightenment this merciful and expert pontiff laid a firm foundation and freshly and entirely restored this church to a wondrous design, along with its roofing, and with God's help improved it. As a true lover of God and devotee of God's holy churches, he provided over this church's high altar 2 cloths, one of them with large wheels with griffins, adorned all round with interwoven gold, the other cloth with interwoven gold; and 4 crimson silk veils to cover all four sides of its altar, adorned with best tyrian all round.

191 Agnellus (c. 168, life of bishop Martin of Ravenna, *MGH SSrL.* 387) also provides an account of Leo's works on Sant' Apollinare, which he places immediately after the death of Charlemagne on 30 (sic) January 814: 'Then Leo, bishop of the Roman church and city, sent his chamberlain Crisafus and other bricklayers, restored the roofs of St Apollinaris and all of the beams and ceiling-panels with fir (or deal?), and all that martyr's roofing; along with his own expenditure, all the suburban cities contributed; all the Ravennate citizens took turns in the corvée with all the roof-frames, tiles, fir-trees and other necessities, with ropes, machines(?), etc. The bricklayers set the beams on the walls and all was completed; the pontiff (Martin?) ordered the fixing only of the *hypochartosis*' (cf. 97: n. 130 for this word); but contrast the translation of the last words offered by D. Mauskopf Deliyannis, 2004, 297. I have profited much from discussing issues raised by this passage with Jonathan Bardill; see Bardill, 2005, nn. 75–77.

192 Almost certainly this is Constantine's foundation at Albano (BP Silvester 34:30 with xxxv–xxxvi); the original dedication was to St John the Baptist.

There too at St Peter's church,[193] an adorned cloth representing our Lord Jesus Christ when he reached out his hand and caught[194] St Peter out of the waves of the sea. **108.** In St Cyriac's basilica[195] this blessed and distinguished pontiff provided a white all-silk cloth, with a fringe round it with interwoven gold and in the centre a representation of the resurrection; and round the altar a white veil to cover all four sides, with fringes of tyrian. In St Vitalis' *titulus*, a white all-silk cloth with an interwoven gold fringe and in the centre a representation of the resurrection. In the holy Archangel's deaconry[196] he placed a white all-silk cloth with a tyrian fringe and in the centre a representation of the ascension; there too over St Abbacyrus' altar he presented a similar cloth. **109.** In St Agatha the martyr's deaconry this holy pontiff provided a white all-silk cloth with a tyrian fringe round it and in the centre a representation of the resurrection. In Pammachius' *titulus* over the altar of SS John and Paul, a white all-silk cloth, adorned around with interwoven gold, representing the crucifixion, ascension and Pentecost. In St Clement the martyr and pontiff's church, a white gold-studded cloth representing the Lord's resurrection and ascension, also Pentecost. In St Cyriac's church[197] on the Via Ostiensis, 5 veils of fourfold-woven silk representing the Saviour calling the disciples from the ship;[198] and over that martyr's holy altar he placed a cloth with interwoven gold.

[A.D. 814–15:]

110. In God's mother our lady the ever-virgin St Mary's basilica called *ad praesepe* this God-protected and distinguished pontiff provided 12 silver crowns with their dolphins, weighing 102 lb 9½ oz; there too, 7 silver chandeliers with their dolphins, weighing 85½ lb. In front of the *presbyterium* in St Peter his mentor's basilica this blessed prelate provided a twisted[199] light of fine silver with crowns and crosses, weighing in all 136 lb 6 oz. There too down below where the prince of the apostles' holy body is at rest he renewed

---

193 Cf. c. 42 and n. 91.

194 Matthew 14.31.

195 Probably the *titulus* of S. Cyriacus in Thermis (97:70 with n. 140; Hülsen, 245–6), since the basilica on the Via Ostiensis is mentioned just below.

196 For this see LNCP Gregory IV 103:12 with n. 23.

197 St Cyriac's martyr-basilica at the 7th mile, rebuilt by pope Honorius (BP 72:4 and Duchesne, I, 326 n. 12).

198 Perhaps the scene in Mt 14.28–9 is intended, where however it is only Peter who is called to walk from the ship over the waves; or Jn 21.4–6, where Christ speaks from the shore to Peter and six other disciples, and they meet him on the shore though they are not strictly called to do so; or Mt 13.2–3 = Mk 4.1 = Lk 5.3, where Christ on a boat addresses the people on the shore.

199 No doubt intended to match the 12 twisted (spiral) columns; cf. 92:5 and n. 17.

the gold image representing the face of the Saviour our Lord Jesus Christ, of God's mother our lady St Mary, of the apostles SS Peter, Paul and Andrew, and of St Petronilla the martyr, where he added 21 lb 3 oz refined gold. There too in front of St Andrew's he coated Christ's confessor St Martin's altar[200] with fine silver-gilt, out of what abbot Fridigisus[201] had formerly sent, weighing overall 17½ lb. In the basilica of St Paul the teacher of the gentiles he provided 5 chandeliers of fine silver with their dolphins, weighing 67 lb 4 oz.

[A.D. 815–16:]

   111. This God-inspired, venerable and distinguished pontiff observed that SS Nereus and Achilleus' church[202] was now giving way through great age and being filled with flood water. On a higher site close to that church, he freshly constructed from its foundations a church beautifully decorated on a wondrous scale, in which he presented gifts: a silver canopy weighing 225 lb; 6 silver canisters weighing in all 15 lb; a chalice and paten of fine silver-gilt, weighing 12 lb 10 oz; over the altar a crown of fine gold adorned with various precious stones, weighing 2 lb 6 oz; 2 cloths, one of them white all-silk, representing the Lord's birth, resurrection, ascension and Pentecost, adorned all round with gold studs, the other of tyrian. 112. In God's holy mother's basilica *ad praesepe* he provided a crown of fine gold *spanoclist* adorned all round with various precious stones, weighing 4 lb 7 oz. In St Peter his patron's basilica, a crown of fine gold adorned with various precious stones, weighing 7 lb. He provided 24 communion chalices of fine silver, for each region, for the acolytes to carry in procession to the *stationes*, weighing in all .. lb. In SS Nereus and Achilleus' deaconry he provided .. various all-silk veils. He freshly restored the roofing of St Agapitus the martyr's, close to St Laurence's basilica outside the wall, which had decayed through great age.

200 In the corridor connecting St Andrew's and St Petronilla's. The 8th-century *Notitia ecclesiarum urbis Romae* (c. 37, *CChr* 175, 310) confirms this; after the 12th century the altar was dedicated to St John Chrysostom.

201 Or Fridugisus, abbot of St Martin at Tours and of Sithieu, who with three other abbots witnessed Charlemagne's will (Einhard, *Vita Karoli*, 33); the gift has nothing to do with Charlemagne's legacies to Rome but is the abbot's show of piety to his own monastery's patron. Duchesne takes *quondam* with the abbot's name and thinks the LP is in error since Fridugisus lived at least till 833; perhaps so, but the linking of *quondam* with *transmisso* seems preferable.

202 Despite later restoration, particularly by Cardinal Baronius, the surviving church is substantially that built by Leo III. The apse arch has a mosaic of the Transfiguration, with the Annunciation on the spectator's left, and on the right the Virgin and Child with an angel at their side. On the *titulus* (originally that of Fasciola), Kirsch, 1918, 90–94; Hülsen, 388–9; Krautheimer, *Corpus* 3, 135–152; it was a deaconry by Leo III's time but the LP here is unspecific, perhaps deliberately.

98. LEO III

In St Pudentiana's *titulus* he provided a white all-silk cloth adorned all round with tyrian.

113. This blessed pontiff, after he had gloriously ruled the Roman and apostolic see 20 years 5 months and 16 days, was taken from this life and went to everlasting rest. He performed three March ordinations, 30 priests, 12 deacons; for various places 126 bishops. He was buried[203] in St Peter's on 12 June[204] in the 9th indiction [816]. The bishopric was vacant 10 days.

203 Leo I's body had been removed by Sergius I (BP 86:12; Duchesne I, 379 n. 35 with III, 97–8) to an altar in a new oratory dedicated to him. In the 12th century Mallius records that Paschal II removed the bodies of the next three popes Leo to this oratory. Consequently the original tombs of Leo II, III and IV disappeared.

204 Einhard's *Annals* give the false date 'about 25 May'.

99. STEPHEN IV (816-817)

A short pontificate, of little interest to the compiler once the incumbent was dead; hence no doubt the signs of incompleteness. The numbers and weights of the gold and silver plate provided are not given in the MSS, though the text regularly 'expects' them. Since such material was copied into the LP from the *vestiarium* registers, this suggests that even these were incomplete, at any rate when seen by our compiler. Even the date of the pope's burial is not given. Such signs of slipshod compilation, particularly in chronological data, become the norm for the next few lives.

But the record provided of this pontificate is nevertheless of value. Leo III had maintained control in Rome, with Charlemagne's support, against much opposition; this had burst out afresh after the emperor's death early in 814 and had been repressed savagely, though the compiler of Leo's life had said nothing of it. Now that Leo was dead and a new emperor was on the throne, Stephen IV aimed for reconciliation. Hence the return of the exiles. Politically this pontificate marked a crucial stage; the emperor's agreement with the papacy, worked out when Stephen visited Rheims, involved substantial concessions, even if these did not take full effect until Paschal I had succeeded Stephen; if the compiler of this life was unable to give more detail, that was because he was not privy to the higher reaches of diplomacy, not because of a lack of interest. He gives us what he can, and despite its brevity the record is nicely balanced between history and donations.

Since the compiler of the next life, that of Paschal I, shows no interest at all in political history, this is the appropriate point to consider the deal Paschal agreed with the emperor Louis (the *Ludowicianum* of the first half of 817). Einhard's Annals state that Paschal first informed Louis of his election, then sent a second embassy under the *nomenclator* Theodore to obtain and confirm the pact made with his predecessors. So this document of 817 almost certainly represents the essence of the agreement made with Stephen IV at Rheims only a few months earlier, alluded to in the present life. Furthermore, since neither Charles nor Louis seem to have made any fresh concessions of territory after 788, this text also represents Charles' agreements with Hadrian I in 781 and 787.

The documents of 816 and 817 are thought to have survived into the 12th and 13th centuries. The text now has to be reconstructed from quotations by various canonists from the late 11th century on, with the aid of the surviving text of the very similar privilege granted by the emperor Otto (the *Ottonianum* of 962). The resultant text may abbreviate the original, but as far as its territorial (as opposed to

99. STEPHEN IV

its institutional, legal and political) provisions are concerned, the only later interpolation seems to be the reference to Sicily, Sardinia and Corsica. The text (*MGH Cap* 1, 172, pp. 352–5; discussions in Hahn, 1975, and Noble, 148ff) can be summarized as follows:

Territorially, the following areas are confirmed to Paschal:

1) the city of Rome and its duchy;

2) then the cities of (Roman) Tuscia – Porto, Centumcellae, Caere, Blera, Monterano, Sutri, Nepi, Gallese, Orte, Bomarzo, Amélia, Todi, Perugia – with its three islands (in Lake Trasimene), Maggiore, Minore and Polvese – Narni, Otrícoli and all their territories;

3) then (Roman) Campania – Segni, Anagni, Ferentino, Alatri, Pátrica, Frosinone with all the borders of Campania, including Tívoli;

4) then the whole exarchate of Ravenna as Pepin and Charles had already restored it to the papacy – Ravenna and Emilia, Vobio, Césena, Forlimpopoli, Forlì, Faenza, Imola, Bologna, Ferrara, Comácchio, Adria and Gavello;

5) also the Pentapolis – Rímini, Pésaro, Fano, Senigállia, Ancona, Osimo, Numana, Iesi, Fossombrone, Montefeltro, Urbino and the territory Valvense, Cagli, Luceoli, Gubbio;

6) also the Sabine territory as Charles had given it intact, with the boundary between it and Rieti as delimited by abbots Etherius and Magenarius;

7) also in Lombard Tuscia – Castellum Felicitatis, Orvieto, Bagnorégio, Ferento, Viterbo, Nórchia (halfway between Blera and Tuscánia), Marta (at the south end of Lake Bolsena), Tuscánia, Sovana, Populonia, Roselle;

8) and the islands Corsica, Sardinia and Sicily;

9) and in the districts of Campania – Sora, Arce, Aquino, Arpino, Teano and Capua, and the patrimonies owned by the papacy,

10) as also the patrimonies of Benevento, Salerno, lower and upper Calábria, Naples and any other patrimonies under Frankish control.

11) also all the freely-given donations of Pepin and Charles, and the taxes, rents and other revenues which used annually to reach the palace of the Lombard king, both from Lombard Tuscia and the duchy of Spoleto, as agreed between Hadrian and Charles when Hadrian confirmed to Charles his precept about the duchies of Tuscia and Spoleto: the taxes should be paid annually to St Peter, without prejudice to the emperor's sovereignty over those duchies.

Louis confirms all these areas, patrimonies and revenues as transferred irrevocably, except by mutual agreement, to the pope's *potestas, dicio, ius* and *principatus*, and he guarantees he will protect papal rights. There is good reason to suppose that clauses 1 to 7 are the territorial settlement of 781, and 9 to 11 are the modifications made in 787–8; in clause 8, Corsica may be genuine, but Sicily and Sardinia seem to be interpolated, though the original might have contained a condition that the islands would be granted to St Peter if the Franks could gain control of them; the same must apply to the latter part of clause 10. In 816 the officials of pope and emperor will have extracted all relevant material from their archives to produce a coherent text. It is no surprise then that no later papal territorial claim is ever based on any earlier Carolingian document.

Some legal and institutional matters are then dealt with: refugees or criminals fleeing from papal territory to the Franks will normally be sent back unless they have escaped to gain justice against oppression by the powerful, in which case they may stay in France, or if their offences are trivial, in which case Louis reserves the right to intercede for them. There will be no Frankish or Lombard interference in papal elections; a pope freely and unanimously elected without bribery by all the Romans (in practice, no doubt, by the nobility, whose candidate Stephen had been) may be consecrated, and his envoys will afterwards inform the king, so as to maintain amity, charity and peace as under Charles (Martel), Pepin and Charlemagne. This clause had the effect of guaranteeing the freedom of papal elections from external political interference, but also of partly nullifying the election decree of 769; though the candidates would remain only those qualified under that decree (cf. 96:20). All this is confirmed on oath and a copy sent to Paschal by Theodore. In effect, autonomy was guaranteed to the papal State in matters of justice and administration, and Louis renounced any power to intervene unless called on by the pope. The pope's subjects have no right of appeal to the emperor. These matters and the territorial settlement show that Louis did not regard papal territory as part of his empire in any normal sense. The relationship had previously been constitutionally vague. Louis' pact with Stephen can be seen as part of his programme of finishing what Charles, his father, had left undone.

99. STEPHEN IV

99. 1. STEPHEN [IV; 22 June 816–24 January 817], of Roman origin, son of Marinus, held the see 7 months. From earliest youth he was brought up and educated in the Lateran patriarchate in the time of lord pope Hadrian of holy memory; sprung from noble ancestry and distinguished family,[1] when still in early youth he carefully stayed on the watch[2] to gain knowledge of sacred teaching. On the death of lord pope Hadrian of holy memory, lord pope Leo succeeded to his place. He noticed that lord Stephen's life had a character of good behaviour and humility, and promoted him to the order of the subdiaconate. When he noticed he spent more and more time on spiritual endeavours, it was by the Lord's will that he advanced him to the summit of the diaconate. From then on in various ways he was accomplished in spiritual endeavours; he bestowed enormous care not only on skilfully and lucidly evangelizing[3] the people with the message of God and the gospel, but also on putting the tradition of the church into practice; and the grace of the Holy Ghost in his heart shone so brightly that he was proved efficient and capable at everything. And so it happened that when lord pope Leo departed this life, this distinguished and holy man Stephen, loved as he was by the Roman people's burning affection, was immediately elected to the holy summit of the pontificate.[4] God's foresight ordained it that with one affection and a single love they all brought him to St Peter's and he was consecrated pope of the city.[5]

1 Stephen was a noble whose career had begun under Hadrian, also a noble, but his advancement had come from Leo III. His family would also produce Sergius II in 844 (son of Sergius and a noble mother, 104:1) and Hadrian II (108:1) in 867 (son of Talarus, bishop of Minturno by 863).

2 Perhaps *vigilare* is no more than *vacare*, but there may be an idea of burning the midnight oil, or an allusion to 1 Peter 5.8.

3 Cf. 97:3 and n. 5.

4 Most of that eulogy is based on 97:3-4, the last few lines of it word for word. No source hints at a disputed election. Following the troubles of 815, Stephen may have been a suitable reconciliation candidate, noble but also a clerical careerist.

5 Stephen's rapid consecration (this is true, even if 'immediately' in the text was copied from 97:4) shows that despite the reestablishment of the western empire, the custom of waiting for imperial confirmation of the election (from Constantinople, or the emperor's representative in Ravenna), supposedly a means of avoiding schism, was not renewed; no emperor or king had given his approbation to an election since that of Gregory III in 731. Whether Charlemagne, who had predeceased Leo, had arranged for it to happen is unknown. All that happened in 816 was that Stephen exacted an oath of loyalty to Louis from the Romans (Thegan, *Vita Ludovici Pii*, 16), and sent two envoys to Louis to inform him about it (cf. Frankish Annals). Yet the life of Louis by 'The Astronomer' does suggest (c. 26, *MGH SS* 2, 607) that the embassy was to 'satisfy' Louis as if there were some irregularity; Duchesne regarded it as less reliable for Louis' early years as it was edited after the empire had begun to claim rights in the matter. However Noble, 202-3, thinks that the aristocrats (to hasten a process likely to happen anyway)

2. Now that he was installed in the pontificate, this holy man undertook a journey to visit the pious and serene lord emperor Louis in France, to reinforce the peace and unity of God's holy church.[6] On reaching France he was welcomed by the pious prince and the people of the Franks with respect and esteem such as tongue can scarcely tell. The Lord saw fit to bestow such grace on him that he secured in full everything[7] he is known to have asked for; so much so that in his love for him, over and above all the gifts he bestowed on him, this pious prince granted from his privy purse by a written instruction a villa[8] in the territory of France to St Peter the apostle

---

had intruded into the election contrary to the decree of 769, that Stephen's journey was to satisfy the emperor of his legitimacy, and that the clause in the *Ludowicianum* opening elections to 'all the Romans' can be seen as an acceptance of the fait accompli and allowance of it for the future, but without permitting non-clerical candidates; the nobles would not find themselves facing a new Leo III, but equally the clerics would not have to face a new Constantine II.

6 Four other accounts deal with this meeting early in October 816. The Frankish Annals mention that within two months of his consecration Stephen set out by long stages to France. Louis fixed on Rheims as the meeting place, sent envoys to escort Stephen, and welcomed him there with great honour. Stephen immediately told Louis of his purpose in coming, and after mass he crowned him. Many gifts were exchanged, banquets were celebrated, and a firm friendship was established. Louis told his chancellor Helisachar to draw up a document to present to Stephen. Other opportune needs of the church were seen to, Stephen returned to Rome, and Louis to his palace at Compiègne. Further details are given in the lives of Louis by Thegan (cc. 16-18, *MGH SS* 2, 594) and The Astronomer (cc. 26-7, *ibid.*, 620-21), and Ermoldus Nigellus, *In honorem Hludowici* (ed. Faral, 1932) vv. 936ff, 1034ff. Stephen also crowned Louis' wife Irmengard; the crown used was allegedly that of Constantine(!), which Stephen had brought with him from Rome; and he anointed Louis, the first time a pope did this for an emperor. Louis had already been crowned co-emperor in 813, but coronation and unction by the pope will have been useful to Louis to consolidate his imperial dignity. His coronation by Stephen IV would 'enhance the christian characteristics' of his already existing office, much as Pepin's coronation by Stephen II had done (Noble, 302). If there was any notion that the ceremony was useful to the papacy as suggesting that without papal confirmation imperial authority was somehow incomplete, there is no awareness of this in the LP.

7 So too The Astronomer, c. 27. Except that Louis formally renewed the mutual pact of friendship and protection, the details are nowhere given. Evidently Louis allowed the return of the exiles to Rome (see below). But the *Ludowicianum* that Louis granted to Paschal I must have been worked out at this stage, since it was issued so soon after Stephen's death; see introduction. Stephen and his noble supporters had secured their State's independence of a new empire which, albeit of papal creation (that could not be undone), might prove itself as obnoxious as that of Byzantium.

8 The location of this *curtis* at Vendopera (Vandeuvre, between Troyes and Bar-sur-Aube, in the former diocese of Langres) is known from Hincmar (*Annals of St-Bertin*, a. 865, trans. J. L. Nelson p. 126) who tells how despite Louis' gift of it to St Peter it had come to be occupied by a count Wido (Guy) for many years, until with the approval of Charles the Bald it was recovered by pope Nicholas' envoy Arsenius.

in perpetual use. The sacred bishop adopted the example of our Redeemer, who for us saw fit to come down from heaven and deliver us from the devil's captivity: he brought back with him, by the church's piety, all the exiles[9] who were held captive there for their crimes and wickedness committed against the holy Roman church and lord pope Leo.

3. In St Peter's *ad vincula* he provided a silver censer, gilded over, weighing .. lb; silver bowls weighing .. lb; and .. all-silk veils with a fringe of interwoven gold. In the same church he provided a gold-studded cloth with jewels, representing St Peter; also .. gold-interwoven veils. There too in the monastery[10] he provided a gold chalice adorned with jewels, weighing .. lb, and a silver paten, gilded over, weighing .. lb; also a gold cross with jewels, weighing .. lb.

4. In St Theodore's at Sabellum[11] he provided a gold cross adorned with jewels, and a silver chalice, weighing .. lb.

In St Peter's basilica *ad vincula*[12] this venerable and distinguished pontiff provided a silver paten and chalice, gilded over, weighing .. lb; there too, a silver crown with its hangings, weighing .. lb.

In St Barbara the martyr's oratory[13] in the Subura he provided a gold-interwoven cloth. In St Helena's basilica[14] he provided a gold-interwoven cloth.

5. By God's calling he was taken from this life and went to everlasting rest. He was buried in St Peter's.[15] He performed one December ordination, 9 priests, 4 deacons; for various places 5 bishops. The bishopric was vacant 2 days.

9 Those whom Charlemagne had banished to Gaul in 800 for their part in the rebellion against Leo III (98:20, 26). The move was important for the restoration of peace at home. The other accounts omit all reference to the recall.

10 Probably of St Agapitus, close to the church concerned (so Duchesne, and Hülsen, 165); cf. 98:45 with n. 99.

11 Cf. 97:76 with n. 157.

12 Gifts to the church previously mentioned, but repeated, despite the brevity of these lists, because the source register will now have begun (perhaps with this entry) to record donations made in the new indiction, from September 816.

13 Unknown. Could it be an oratory in St Agatha's monastery in the Subura?

14 The mausoleum of Constantine's mother on the via Labicana, the ruins of which survive, was already called a church in the itineraries of the 7th and 8th centuries (*Notitia ecclesiarum* 16, 82; *de locis sanctis* 16, 86-7; *CChr* 175, 307, 318). In these and other itineraries Helena is already *sancta* or *beata*. That her real anniversary is unknown (at Constantinople she was linked with her son on 21 May; in the west she was culted, for no known reason, on 18 August) shows that her cult is not ancient.

15 The date is not given and no epitaph survives. The Frankish annals give 24 or 25 January 817; the statement of the length of the ensuing vacancy suggests that 24 January is correct, but a doubt remains.

GLOSSARY

See also the glossaries in BP, 115–141, and LNCP, 309–318.

Agareni (or Hagarenes): **91**:5, 11, 12, **93**:20; Arab enemies seen as descendants of Ishmael the son of Abraham and Hagar (Genesis 16.15 etc.); the name does not recur till the life of Leo IV, where it is a frequent synonym for Saracens. In view of Galatians 4.24 the compilers of the LP will have regarded them as servile, and if familiar with the psalms recited at nocturns on Fridays they will have seen them as conspiratorial (Ps. 83 v. 6, Vulg. 82.7).

basilica: originally an assembly hall such as might be appropriate for the emperor (βασιλεύς) to use when giving an audience; there were several such in the Lateran used for similar purposes by the popes, the most frequently mentioned being that of pope Theodore. More or less standardized architectural features (a longitudinal design with aisles and a clerestory-lit nave) which would make such an arrangement suitable for church worship, rather than thoughts of Christ as βασιλεύς, seem to have caused the christian use of the word; it then came to be used for a church building of any design. It was sometimes used to describe only those churches at Rome which were not *tituli*, but the LP is not consistent.

canister *(canistrum)*: explained by H. Leclercq (*DACL* 2, 1844–6), citing its occurrences in life 97, as a dish placed under lamps to catch drips. In the donation list of 807 some churches are given 'crowns' (*coronae*; i. e. circular lamp fittings), others canisters; we have no means of knowing why this distinction was made.

cartularius: **91**:14 (Jordanes), **96**:9 (Gratiosus), **97**:16 (Anvald); by the early eighth century, a minor military official, since his command of the army had passed to the 'duke'.

cellarer *(paracellarius)*: **93**:27; in **97**:54 the Latin word occurs three times, confusingly meaning 'cellar' twice, 'cellarer' the third time.

cemetery *(cymiterium, κοιμητήριον)*: the word refers not to an open-air burial-ground but to a basilica used for burials, generally attached to the shrines of martyrs and connected with underground galleries or catacombs (this last word was used only for the complex at S. Sebastiano).

GLOSSARY

chamberlain *(cubicularius)*: **96**:28, 32, **97**:4, 6 (all referring to Paul Afiarta), 10 (Calventzulus, Calvulus), 11 (Afiarta, Calvulus), 13-14 (Calvulus), **98**:14 (Albinus) (Chamber, *cubiculum* **94**:1). In Byzantine usage 'chamberlain' had become a title of honour. At Rome, the word was used for a group who made up the *cubiculum*; these were adolescents who were the pope's attendants, often youths of noble families being educated at the Lateran, who might be laymen or in minor orders; whereas non-nobles entered the papal court through the *schola cantorum*, for the Roman nobility the *cubiculum* was the avenue by which they gained entry to the traditional élite of the papal government; Noble, 224. But it is clear that the term is not used in the LP to refer to youths, rather to men of some distinction, presumably as a title of honour as at Constantinople. Perhaps they had entered the papal court through the *cubiculum* and later retained the title 'chamberlain'; or perhaps the word denotes the official in charge of the *cubiculum*, though Noble suggests that the chamberlains came under the *vicedominus* (who was a bishop, which the chamberlains in the LP were not).

chief men *(optimates/proceres cleri/ecclesiae)* of the church. Not the cardinal clergy but the seven major officers of papal government, whose status came from their office not from their social standing, though from the 740s most of them were probably nobles: the *primicerius* and *secundicerius notariorum*, the *primicerius defensorum*, the *sacellarius*, the *arcarius*, the *vestiarius*, the *nomenclator* (Noble, 227).

chief secretary *(proto a secreta)*: **94**:43-4 (George); the head of the imperial chancery, who put the final touches to imperial documents and also acted in some judicial cases; his close contact with the emperor made him a man of great influence, and one who was likely to be entrusted with important missions.

confessio: originally the burial-place of one who had 'confessed' Christ by martyrdom; hence the name for an area in front of an altar above a martyr's tomb, excavated to give closer access to, or sight of, the grave; some or all of the area might then be decorated with silver; eventually one could be provided for a relic of a different kind, even when there was no actual grave, e. g. for a fragment of the Cross.

consul: **92**:3, **93**:9 (Leo, Sergius, Victor and Agnellus at Ravenna), **97**:2 (Theodotus), **97**:63 (Leoninus). Originally the title for the two chief magistrates elected each year in the Roman republic; under the Roman emperors the consuls possessed little power but the system was maintained to give prestige to distinguished senators. The last consuls of this type were in the sixth century, but the title continued to be taken by emperors in the first year of their reigns, and was also bestowed as an honour, perhaps specifically for those who served in the imperial (and then papal) lawcourts; Noble, 238, Diehl, 1888, 314, Halphen, 1907, 29-31; cf. **97**:14, 16 and n. 23 for the *consularis* of Ravenna.

count *(comes*, companion): **91**:16, **97**:63 (Peter), **98**:16 (Ascheric), 20 (Helmgoth, Rottecar, Germar); a title of honour or of actual office created by Constantine;

the holder might have either civilian or military responsibilities. In areas of Italy under barbarian rule the title was used for army commanders, whether of armies on campaign or of those on garrison duties, and also for judges in some legal cases; the rank it connoted was more specific than the duties.

deaconry *(diaconia)*: a charitable institution of the church, administering the distribution of alms to the poor; see Duchesne, 1887; Lestocquoy, 1930, 261–298; cf. **97**: n. 117. By the late 11th century the 7 deacons at Rome had become 18 in number, and they were each attached to one of the 18 deaconries (**97**:81 with n. 175) rather than to one of the seven ecclesiastical regions (Duchesne, I, 364, n. 7). The deaconries are first recorded at Rome in 684/5, but Krautheimer, *Rome*, 74–77, on archaeological grounds, thinks they originated in the mid-6th century (it is possible that the actual name is later than the fact). They were staffed by monks, but were not monasteries in the strict sense (hence the expression *monasteria diaconiae*); cf. **97**:66 on the provision of bathing facilities. Cf. Noble, 232ff.

defensor: **92**:4 (Constantine, Peter), **97**:5 (Anastasius), 10–11 (Gregory), 21 (Anastasius); cf. BP 122–3, Noble, 222–3. There was one for each of the seven regions, the senior being the *primicerius,* or simply *primus* (so **97**:5), who ranked as one of the 'chief men' of the Roman church. Much as the seven deacons were concerned with the spiritual and material welfare of the poor, of widows and of orphans, the seven *defensores* concerned themselves with their legal rights, and in practice the rights of the church as well. They came to be heavily involved in the administration of the papal patrimonies and later of the papal State. Already under Gregory I they are found supervising monasteries and vacant bishoprics, dealing with testamentary affairs and contracts, judging legal cases and even protecting clerics against local bishops.

dependants *(familia)* **92**:9, **97**:7, 86 etc. *(familiaris,* **94**:16); dependent populations on a *fundus* (Bosl, 1982, 33).

duke: **91**:4 (Theodo of the Bavarians), 7 (John at Naples), 11 (Eudes the Frank), 14 (Basil, Marinus), 16 (Lombard), 17 (Italian), 18 (Exhilaratus, Peter of Rome), 19 (Lombard), 22 (Spoleto and Benevento), **92**:15 (Transamund of Spoleto), **93**:2 (Transamund, Stephen of Rome), 2–5 (Transamund), 7 (Lombard), 8 (Transamund), 11 (Agiprand of Chiusi), 12 (Stephen), 16 (Lombard), 17 (Ratchis the Lombard), **94**:4 (Hunald of Aquitania), 18, 20 (Autchar the Frank), 24 (Rothard the Frank), 48 (Desiderius the Lombard), **96**:3 (Toto of Nepi), 5 (Theodicius of Spoleto), 9 (Gratiosus of Rome), 15 (Theodicius), 25 (Maurice of Rimini), 31 (Gratiosus), **97**:2 (Theodotus of Rome), 5 (Tunno of Ivrea), 10 (John of Rome), 15 (Maurice of Venice), 20 (Stabilis the Lombard), 33 (Hildeprand of Spoleto), 35 (Lombard), 43 (Frankish), 63 (Leoninus of Rome), **98**:15 (Winichis of Spoleto). In imperial or papal territory the word denotes an army commander whose territory was a duchy; Maurice's title at Venice might, of course, be translated as *doge.* The duchy of Rome

GLOSSARY

is mentioned at **91**:14, **92**:15, **93**:2–5, 9. Among the Lombards and Franks the word may refer to an army commander subject to a king (cf. the 'vassal dukes', *duces satrapae*, of Liutprand at **93**:7) or to the military ruler of a particular territory who might achieve a measure of independence from a king.

exarch: **91**:15–17 (Paul), 19 (Paul, Eutychius), 22–3, **92**:5, **93**:12–13 (Eutychius), **97**:36; the military commander of Italy under Byzantine rule, usually resident at Ravenna.

gastald: **91**:7 (an unnamed Lombard), **93**:11 (Tacipert, Ramning); administrator of royal estates and, in practice, a local governor in germanic states such as the Lombard kingdom.

grafiones: **97**:35, 43; officers, by the end of the 8th century of equivalent rank to counts (*comites*).

hegumenos: **97**:21 (Pardus), see **97**: n. 30.

images, designs, representations: see **95**:6 for the possibility of a three-dimensional icon. The following analytical index of images etc. may be of use:

acheiropoieta, **94**:11; the Saviour **91**:23, **92**:2–3, 5, 8, **93**:18, **94**:11, 45, **95**:3, **96**:23, **97**:58, 60–61, 87, **98**:3, 5, 6, 7, 31–3, 35, 53, 57–8, 60, 84, 87–8, 105, 109–10; his birth **93**:19, **98**:4, 28–9, 48, 51, 106, 111; holy Innocents **98**:28; presentation/St Simeon **98**:4, 29, 52, 83; call of disciples from ship **98**:109; rescue of Peter from sea **98**:107; commission of Peter **98**:7; blind man given sight **98**:28; entry to Jerusalem **98**:32; passion/cross/crucifixion **98**:5, 8, 28, 33, 82, 98–9, 104, 106, 109; resurrection **98**:5, 8, 27–9, 32, 61–2, 82, 99, 101–4, 106, 108–9, 111; ascension **98**:29, 53, 106, 108–9, 111; Pentecost **98**:53, 106, 109, 111;

Cross (image), **98**:82; crosses (designs), **98**:3–4, 6–7, 10, 30, 35, 37, 40, 44, 49, 51, 83, 93, 97–8, 101–2, 104, 106; crosses (objects), **91**:22, **92**:7, 12, **94**:11, 39, **97**:36–7, **98**:9, 25, 48–50, 60, 66, 83, 86–7, 96, 110, **99**:3–4; cross-adorned silk (*stauracis*), **97**:46, 48–52, 60–61, 64–5, **98**:6, 8, 27, 29–30, 32, 34, 36–8, 40–42, 44–8, 65–6, 83, 95, 100, 102–4;

Michael **97**:58; Gabriel **97**:58; Cherubim **98**:57; angels **91**:17, **97**:60, **98**:58;

St Mary **91**:23, **92**:2–3, 5, 7–8, 10, **94**:45, **95**:3, 6, **96**:15, 23, **97**:58, 87, **98**:4, 29, 33, 51–2, 60, 110; annunciation (chaeretismos **98**:4), **98**:29, 55, 106; passing over **98**:52, assumption **97**:48; Joachim and Anne **98**:29;

Peter **97**:45, 87, **98**:5, 7, 31, 35, 39, 53–4, 61, 92, 107, 110 **99**:3; Peter's release by an angel **97**:45; passion of Peter and Paul **98**:7; Paul **97**:87, **98**:7, 31, 35, 39, 53, 61, 92, 110; Andrew **92**:11, **97**:58, 87, **98**:110; John the Evangelist **97**:58; 12 apostles **92**:2–3, 5, **95**:3, **96**:23, **98**:6, 33, 60; Laurence **97**:87, **98**:5; Petronilla **98**:110; Anastasius' passion **98**:38; saints in general **91**:17, 23, **92**:2–3, **95**:3, **96**:23;

gospels **97**:61, 87, 93; the 6 councils **91**:5; major Litany **98**:33;

birds **98**:6; elephants **98**:45; griffins **98**:7, 9, 107; world **93**:10; wheels **93**:19, **98**:6–7, 98–9, 106–7; chevrons **98**:6, 9–10, 30, 65, 83, 97;

unspecified **92**:4, **93**:18, **96**:23, **97**:83-4, 88-9, 93, **98**:4, 9-10, 32, 34, 58, 60, 64-6, 83-4, 86-8, 92-3.

indiction: a cycle of 15 years used originally for fiscal purposes but commonly used for dating documents. The indiction years began in September and were numbered serially from 1 to 15, after which the cycle began again; unfortunately the number of the cycle itself was not given. Only the context can determine that, e.g., at **98**:31 'the 9th indiction' refers to September 800 to August 801, rather than to 785-6 or 815-6 or any other year at 15-year intervals.

judges *(iudices)*: a word describing high officials of state, even if with no judicial function, and tending to be used (as at **96**:25, Ravenna) to mean the leading laymen of a city, even if they were holding no actual office.

lb: the Roman pound of 327.45 g (whereas the English pound is 453.592 g), consisting of 12 (not 16) *unciae*.

lights: the translation follows the same conventions for the various technical terms as in BP (cf. BP 128). Some additional items are dealt with in the notes; cf. above for 'canister'.

liturgical days etc.: the following are mentioned in these lives:
    Apostles' feastday **97**:46, **98**:60; Christmas **97**:46, **98**:23, 24; Easter (-tide) **97**:35, 40, 46, 59, 62, **98**:8, 34, 93; Ember Saturdays **98**:67; Epiphany **94**:26; Holy Saturday **97**:35, 37, 39; Lent **91**:9; Litany, Major **98**:11, 33; Pentecost **98**:53, 106, 109, 111; SS Abdon and Sennen's feast **96**:7; St Andrew's eve **98**:19; St Andrew's feast **98**:20; St George's feast **98**:11; St John the Evangelist's feast **98**:2; St Paul's feast **93**:17; St Peter's feast **93**:17; St Stephen's feast, **98**:2.

liturgical texts etc.: the following are referred to in these lives:
    Canon of the mass **92**:6; Creed **98**:84-5; Glory be to God (hymn), **96**:27, **98**:16; Greek chant **95**:5; Kyrie eleison **96**:20; the Peace **96**:10.

nomenclator: **96**:16 (Sergius); an official who first appears in the late seventh century, but whose original functions are obscure; he may have been master of ceremonies at the papal court, and have dealt with petitions, visitors etc.; by the 10th century he gained control of charitable services.

notary: **97**:42; Etherius was an influential clerk in the royal chancery. For the important office of the regional notaries at Rome see **97**:3 (the future Hadrian I) with n. 4.

office, papal government (*scrinium*): **97**:43; a building at the Lateran, cf. **93**:18. The *scrinium* was the office for the notaries (and perhaps for the archives) and was in the Lateran palace near the main entrance and just off the reception hall, Lauer, 60. The *scriniarii* (keepers of records, secretaries) mentioned (**96**:13, 24 Leontius; **97**:63 Agatho; cf. **96**:25-6 Michael at Ravenna) were clearly more than humble clerks.

GLOSSARY

pallium: a narrow band of white material hanging over the chest as a distinctive vestment of the pope and certain other bishops; see **94**:53 and n. 121, **96**:13 and n. 31.

patrician: **91**:15–16, 18–19 (Paul), 22 (Eutychius), **92**:4 (Sergius), **93**:2, 4, 12 (Stephen), **97**:36; formerly a title of honour, the highest class of senatorial rank, bestowed sparingly by the emperor on holders of high office; it was often held by the Duke of Rome. Patrician women from earlier times are also mentioned: **97**:53, **98**:91 (Barbara), and **98**:77, 90 (Galla). For the bestowal of the title by Stephen II on Pepin and his sons see **94**: n. 65; the LP uses it for them at **96**:16–17, 26, **97**:6, 9, 22, 26, 37, 40.

praesepe: the Manger which provided the soubriquet generally used to distinguish the basilica of S. Maria Maggiore from other basilicas dedicated to the Virgin; see **92**:8 and n. 30, also **97**:84, **98**:36, 63, 95, 98.

prefect (of Rome): see **97**: n. 20; for the *praefectorianus* Dominic see **97**: n. 125.

primicerius notariorum: **93**:12, 14, 18 (Ambrose), 26 (Agatho), **94**:5, 23–4 (Ambrose), **96**:5, 11, 15, 28 (Christopher), **97**:2 (Theodotus), 5 (Christopher), 77 (Mastalus, John), **98**:13 (Paschal); the chief secretary in the papal (and imperial) court, and as one of the seven 'chief men' of the papal court, one of the most influential dignitaries; his deputy was the *secundicerius*.

referendarius: **97**:20 (Andrew); referendary, court dignitary who received petitions and later directed the chancery; here with the Lombards.

regionary: **94**:23 (Leo and Christopher), **97**:3 (the future Hadrian I), 6 (Stephen), 10–11 (Gregory); see *defensor* and 'notary', with **94**: n. 52.

sacellarius: **91**:1 (the future Gregory II), **96**:5 (Sergius), **97**:6, 8 (Stephen), 16–17 (Gregory), **98**:13 (Campulus); paymaster or cashier (as opposed to the *arcarius* or treasurer) in the Byzantine financial machine, and thence used also in the papal court, where the incumbent was one of the seven 'chief men'; cf. **91**: n. 4. Halphen, 1907, 135–9, lists known occupants of the post. Niermeyer cites *Ordo Romanus* I (late 7th or early 8th century, ed. Andrieu, II, p. 70): 'Following the (pope's) horse, these are they that are mounted: the *vicedominus, vestiarius, nomenclator* and *sacellarius.*'

scriniarius: see 'office'.

secundicerius: **94**:23 (Boniface), **96**:5 (Sergius), 9 (Demetrius), 16, 28, **97**:5, 9–10 (Sergius), 77 (Gregory); deputy to the *primicerius*, and one of the 'chief men' of the papal court.

silentiarius: **94**:8, 17, 43 (John); one holding the office or dignity of gentleman-usher or beadle at court.

spatharius: **91**:14 (Marinus), 16, 19; a member of the imperial bodyguard, the chief dignitaries in which were often employed on important missions.

strategus: **92**:4 (Sergius); general, governor of a territory in the empire.

superista: **97**:6, 8–9 (Paul Afiarta); chief of the pope's palace guard and governor of the palace, not of the ancient imperial palace on the Palatine, but of the patriarchate (Gratian was *sacri superista patriarchii*, Benedict III 106:11); his function was evidently different from that of the *vicedominus*. Noble, 235, thinks the *superista* was the pope's official for running the militia, in place of the duke, though the latter post lasted till at least 778/81. With military involvements, he will have been a layman, but a *monachus superista* is mentioned at Grottaferrata (*Studi e documenti* VII, p. 111), which suggests that the military functions at Rome may have been secondary.

titulus: the word had come to mean a parish church, as opposed to the basilicas which did not serve the merely local community, and to the deaconries (*q. v.*) whose function was different. On the number existing at Rome see **97**: n. 115. This use of the word *titulus* is best connected with the meaning 'title-deeds', and explained as a development from the pre-Constantinian period: the Christians at Rome had already been too numerous to meet in one place and had met in private houses whose title-deeds showed them to be the property of individuals. Such properties eventually came into the possession of the church and were gradually replaced by buildings of basilical style, but for purposes of identification the name of the original owner was retained. Gradually that owner's name would be taken to be that of a saint, sometimes by confusion with a genuine martyr of the same name (e. g. Anastasia of Sirmium). New foundations in the fourth and fifth centuries were also for convenience referred to as the *titulus* of the donor (e.g. Vestina) even when the custom of dedicating the building to another saint had become normal (in Vestina's case, her foundation was dedicated to SS Gervasius and Protasius, the unknown martyrs whose relics St Ambrose had discovered, though it later came to be known by the supposed name of their father, St Vitalis, whose relics had also been discovered by St Ambrose).

tribune: **96**:14 (Gracilis), **97**:7 (Peter, Vitalian), **97**:7, 9, 17 (Julian), **97**:10–11 (Leonatius); title of a minor military official.

triclinium: **93**:18, **98**:10, 20, 27, 39. The Greek word for 'three couches' came to be used as the Latin for 'dining-room'; a main couch would be occupied by the host and the most honoured guests; others reclined at two flanking couches, so that the three couches all had equal access to a central table. A suitable architectural design for such an arrangement could be a triconch room, i. e. a room with three semicircular niches each surmounted by a half-dome, and the whole room itself might have a central dome. Further developments were clearly possible, until the word could be applied to a large hall in which banquets were served or which could be used for other purposes entirely. From **98**:10 it is clear that there were several (though the LP has mentioned only one previously) before Leo III built two more at the Lateran and one near St Peter's.

vestiarius (or *vestararius*): literally, keeper of the wardrobe; of the king of the Lombards, **97**:5 (Prandulus); at the papal court, **97**:64, 67 (Januarius). At Constantinople the official was one responsible for the emperor's treasure and private income; no doubt similarly among the Lombards. At Rome, he was a responsible official, in charge of much of the church's wealth, no longer merely of vestments and precious vessels; it will have been in his office that the register material often taken over into the LP was maintained.

vicedominus: **93**:12 (Benedict), **96**:9, 12 (Theodore), **96**:15 (Christopher); steward at the papal palace, major-domo; see Noble 223–4. At Rome the post was sometimes held by one of the nearby bishops (so Benedict and Theodore), by a priest (Ampliatus in the 6th century, BP 61:5), or by a deacon (Saiulus in 710, BP 90:4). He was perhaps in charge of the *cubiculum*.

BIBLIOGRAPHY

Amore, A., *I martiri di Roma* (1975).
Anastos, M. V., 'The transfer of Illyricum, Calabria and Sicily to the jurisdiction of the patriarchate of Constantinople in 732–33', *Studi bizantini e neoellenici* 9 (1957), 14–31.
Anastos, M. V., 'Leo III's edict against the images in the year 726–27 and Italo–Byzantine relations between 726 and 730', *Byzantinische Forschung* 3 (1968), 5–41.
Andreolli, M. P., 'Una pagina di storia langobarda: 'Re Ratchis'', *Nuova rivista storica* 50 (1966), 281–327.
Armellini, M.,*Le Chiese di Roma dal secolo IV al XIX*, ed. 2 (Rome 1891; repr. 1982).
Armellini, M., (ed. 3 by C. Cecchelli), *Le Chiese di Roma dal secolo IV al XIX*, 2 vols. (Rome, 1942).
Baumont, M., 'Le pointificat de Paul Ier (757–767)', *Mélanges de l'école française de Rome* 47 (1930), 7–24.
Bardill, J., 'A New Temple for Byzantium: Anicia Juliana, King Solomon, and the Gilded Ceiling of the Church of St Polyeuktos in Constantinople', W. Bowden, A. Gutteridge, C. Machado (eds.), *The Social and Political Archaeology of Late Antiquity*, Late Antique Archaeology 3 (Leiden, 2005).
Bavant, B., 'Le duché byzantin de Rome. Origine, durée et extension géographique', *Mélanges de l'école française de Rome, moyen âge* 91 (1979), 41–88.
Beck, H.-G., 'Die Herkunft des Papstes Leo III', *Frühmittelalterliche Studien* 3, 1969, 131–7.
Bertolini, O., 'Il primo 'periurium' di Astolfo verso la chiesa di Roma, 752–753', *Miscellanea Giovanni Mercati* 5 (Studi e Testi 125, Rome, 1946), 161–205.
Bertolini, O., 'La ricomparsa della sede episcopale di 'tres tabernae' nella seconda metà del secolo VIII e l'istituzione delle 'domuscultae'', *ASR* 75 (1952), 103–109.
Bertolini,.O., 'I papi e le relazioni politiche di Roma con i ducati longobardi di Spoleto e di Benevento. III: il secolo VIII, da Giovanni VI (701–705) a Gregorio II (715–731)', *Rivista di storia della chiesa in Italia* 9 (1955[a]), 1–57.
Bertolini, O., 'I rapporti di Zaccaria con Costantino V e con Artavasdo nel racconto del biografo del papa e nella probabile realtà storica', *ASR* 78 (1955[b]), 1–21.
Bertolini, O., 'La caduta del primicerio Cristoforo (771) nelle versioni dei contem-

poranei e le correnti antilongobarde e filolongobarde in Roma alla fine del pontificato di Stefano III (771–772)', *Rivista di storia della chiesa in Italia* 1 (1947) = *Scritti scelti* 1, 19–61.
Bertolini, O., 'Il problema delle origini del potere temporale dei papi nei suoi presuppositi teoretici iniziali: il concetto di 'restitutio' nelle prime cessioni territoriali alla Chiesa di Roma (756–757)', *Scritti scelti* 2, 485–547.
Bertolini, O., 'Sergio, arcivescovo di Ravenna', *Scritti scelti* 2, 549–91.
Bertolini, O., *Scritti scelti di storia medioevale* (ed. O. Banti, 2 vols., Leghorn, 1968).
Bertolini, O., *Roma e i longobardi* (1972).
Bosl, K., *Gesellschaftsgeschichte Italiens im Mittelalter*, Monographien zur Geschichte des Mittelalters 26 (1982).
Bouman, C. A., *Sacring and Crowning. The development of the Latin ritual for the anointing of kings and the coronation of the emperor before the eleventh century* (Groningen, 1957).
Brezzi, P., *Roma e l'impero medioevale 774–1252*, Storia di Roma X (Bologna, 1947).
Brown, T. S., 'The Church of Ravenna and the imperial administration in the seventh century', *English Historical Review* 94, 1979, 1–28.
Brown, T. S., *Gentlemen and Officers. Imperial administration and aristocratic power in Byzantine Italy, A.D. 554–800* (Bristish School at Rome, 1984)
Brühl, C., 'Chronologie und Urkunden der Herzöge von Spoleto', *Quellen und Forschungen aus italienischen Archiven und Bibliotheken* 51 (1971), 1–92.
Bury, J. B., *The imperial administrative system in the ninth century with a revised text of the Kletorologion of Philotheus* (London, 1911).
Caspar, E., 'Papst Gregor II und der Bilderstreit', *ZKG* 52 (1933), 29–89.
Caspar, E., *Pippin und die römische Kirche: Kritische Untersuchungen zum fränkisch–päpstlichen Bunde im VIII. Jahrhundert* (Berlin, 1914).
Castagnetti, A., *L'organizzazione del territorio rurale nel medioevo: circonscrizione ecclesiastiche e civile nella 'Langobardia' e nella 'Romania'* (Turin, 1979).
Cavallo, G., and others, *I Bizantini in Italia* (Milan, 1982).
Christie, N. (ed.), *Three south Etrurian Churches: Santa Cornelia, Santa Rufina and San Liberato*, British School at Rome, Archeological Monographs no. 4 (1991).
Christophilopulu, A., 'ΣΙΛΕΝΤΙΟΝ', *BZ* 44 (1951), 79–85.
Classen, P., 'Karl der Grosse, das Papsttum und Byzanz' in *Karl der Grosse: Lebenswerk und Nachleben*, I (1965), 537–608.
Collins, R., *The Arab Conquest of Spain, 710–797* (Oxford, 1989).
Collins, R., *Early Medieval Europe, 300–1000* (London 1991).
Delogu, P., 'Il regno longobardo', in *Longobardi e Bizantini*, Storia d'Italia vol. I, ed. G. Galasso (Turin, 1980), 1–216.
Diehl, C., *Etudes sur l'administration byzantine dans l'exarchat de Ravenne*

(568–751), Bibliothèque des écoles françaises d'Athènes et de Rome 53 (Paris, 1888)

Duchesne, L., 'Notes sur la topographie de Rome au moyen-âge II: Les titres presbytéraux et les diaconies', *Mélanges de l'école française de Rome* 7 (1887), 217–43 = *Scripta Minora* (Rome, 1973), 17–43.

Duchesne, L., 'Notes sur la topographie de Rome au moyen-âge VII: les légendes chrétiennes de l'Aventin', *Mélanges de l'école française de Rome* 10 (1890), 225–250 = *Scripta Minora*, 115–140.

Duchesne, L., 'Vaticana: notes sur la topographie de Rome au moyen-âge', *Mélanges de l'école française de Rome* 22 (1902), 3–22 = *Scripta Minora*, 181–200.

Duchesne, L., 'Les monastères desservants de Sainte-Marie-Majeur', *Mélanges de l'école française de Rome* 27 (1907), 479–494 = *Scripta Minora*, 329–344.

Duchesne, L., *The beginnings of the temporal sovereignty of the popes, A.D. 754–1073* (London, 1908).

Duchesne, L., 'Notes sur la topographie de Rome au moyen-âge XII: Vaticana (suite)', *Mélanges de l'école française de Rome* 34 (1914), 307–56 = *Scripta Minora*, 253–302.

Duchesne, L., *Scripta Minora, études de topographie romaine et de géographie ecclésiastique*, Collection de l'école française de Rome 13 (Rome, 1973).

Duffy, E., *Saints and Sinners, a History of the Popes* (Yale, 1997).

Ewig, E., 'The papacy's alienation from Byzantium and rapprochement with the Franks', in F. Kempf et al., *The Church in the Age of Feudalism* (vol. 3 of *Handbook of Church History*, edd. H. Jedin, J. Dolan (New York, 1969), 3–25.

Ewig, E., 'The age of Charles the Great, *op. cit.*, 54–102.

Ewig, E., 'St Chrodogang et la réforme de l'église franque', *Spätantikes und fränkisches Gallien* 2 (Munich, 1979), 232–259.

Fabre, P., 'Le patrimoine de l'église romaine dans les Alpes cottiennes', *Mélanges de l'école française de Rome* 4 (1884), 383–420.

Fasoli, G., *Carlomagno e l'Italia*, vol. 1 (Bologna 1968).

Ferrari, G., *Early Roman Monasteries. Notes for the history of the monasteries and convents at Rome from the V through the X century*, Studi di antichità cristiana XXIII (Vatican, 1957).

Folz, R., *The Coronation of Charlemagne* (London, 1974).

Fried, J., 'Ludwig der Fromme, das Papsttum und die fränkische Kirche', in Godman and Collins (1990), 221–273.

Fröhlich, H., *Studien zur langobardischen Thronfolge von den Anfängen bis zur Eroberung des italienischen Reiches durch Karl den Grossen* (2 vols., 1980).

Fürst, C. G., *Cardinalis: Prelogomena zu einer Rechtsgeschichte des römischen Kardinalskollegiums* (Munich, 1967).

Ganshof, F. L., *The Imperial Coronation of Charlemagne. Theories and Facts* (Glasgow, 1949).

Ganshof, F. L., *The Carolingians and the Frankish monarchy* (London, 1971).

Gasparri, S., *I duchi longobardi* (Istituto storico italiano per il medio evo, 109, Rome, 1978).
Geertman, H., *More Veterum, Il Liber Pontificalis e gli edifici ecclesiastici di Roma nella tarda antichità e nell'alto medioevo*, Archaeologia Traiectina 10 (Groningen, 1975, also published in Dutch).
Gero, S., *Byzantine Iconoclasm during the reign of Leo III with particular attention to the oriental sources* (Louvain, 1973).
Gibson, S., and B. Ward Perkins, 'The surviving remains of the Leonine Wall', *PBSR* 47 (1979), 30–57.
Giovenale, G. B., *La basilica di S. Maria in Cosmedin* (Rome, 1927).
Godman, P., and R. Collins, edd., *Charlemagne's Heir. New perspectives on the reign of Louis the Pious (814–840)* (Oxford, 1990).
Gouillard, J., 'Aux origines de l'iconoclasme: le témoignage de Grégoire II', *Travaux et memoires* (Centre de recherche d'histoire et de civilisation byzantines) 3 (1968), 243–307.
Grabar, A., *L'iconoclasme byzantine, dossier archéologique* (Paris, 1957).
Grierson, P., 'The coronation of Charlemagne and the coinage of pope Leo III', *Revue belge de philosophie et d'histoire* 30 (1952), 825–33.
Grierson, P., 'Carolingian Europe and the Arabs: the myth of the mancus', *RBPH* 32 (1954), 1059–74.
Griffe, E., 'Aux origines de l'état pontifical', *Bulletin de littérature ecclésiastique* (1954), 65–89.
Grotz, H., 'Beobachtungen zu den zwei Briefen Papst Gregors II an Kaiser Leo III', *Archivum Historiae Pontificiae* 18 (1980), 9–40.
Grumel, V., 'L'annexion de l'Illyricum oriental, de la Sicile et de la Calabre au patriarchat de Constantinople', *Recherches de science religieuse* 40 (1952), 191–200.
Guillou, A., *Régionalisme et indépendance dans l'empire byzantine au VIIe siècle: l'example de l'Exarchat et de la Pentapole d'Italie*. Istituto storico italiano per il medioevo, Studi storici, fasc. 75–76 (Rome, 1969).
Hahn, A., 'Das Hludowicianum', *Archiv für Diplomatik* 21 (1975), 15–135.
Hallenbeck, J. T., 'The election of pope Hadrian I', *Church History* 37 (1968), 261–270.
Hallenbeck, J. T., 'Paul Afiarta and the papacy: an analysis of politics in eighth-century Rome', *Archivum Historiae Pontificiae* 12 (1974[a]), 22–54.
Hallenbeck, J. T., 'Pope Stephen III: Why was he elected?', *Archivum Historiae Pontificiae* 12 (1974[b]), 287–99.
Hallenbeck, J. T., 'The Lombard party in eighth century Rome', *Studi Medievali* 15 (1974[c]), 951–966.
Hallenbeck, J. T., 'The Roman–Byzantine reconciliation of 728: genesis and significance', *BZ* 74 (1981), 29–41.
Hallenbeck, J. T., 'Pavia and Rome: the Lombard monarchy and the papacy in the

eighth century', *Transactions of the American Philosophical Society* vol. 72, no. 4 (Philadelphia, 1982).

Halphen, L., *Etudes sur l'administration de Rome au moyen âge 751 à 1252* (Paris, 1907).

Halphen, L., *A travers l'histoire du moyen âge* (Paris, 1950).

Halphen, L., *Charlemagne and the Carolingian Empire* (Amsterdam, 1977).

Hartmann, L. M., 'Grundherrschaft und Bureaucratie im Kirchenstaate vom 8. bis zum 10. Jahrhundert', *Vierteljahrschrift für Sozial- und Wirtschaftsgeschichte* 7, 1909, 142–158.

Herrin, J., *The formation of Christendom* (Princeton, 1987).

Hodgkin, T., *Italy and her invaders*, vol. 7, *Frankish Invasion* (Oxford, 1899).

Hülsen, C., 'Osservazioni sulla biografia di Leone III nel 'Liber Pontificalis'', *Atti della pontificia accademia Romana di Archeologia, Rendiconti* 1 (1921/23), 107–119.

Hülsen, C., *Le Chiese di Roma nel medio evo* (Florence, 1927).

Jarnut, J., 'Ludwig der Fromme, Lothar I und das Regnum Italiae' in Godman and Collins (1990), 349–362.

Kahane, A., L. M. Thriepland and J. B. Ward-Perkins, 'The Ager Veientanus north and east of Veii', *PBSR* 36 (1968).

Karl der Grosse: Lebenswerk und Nachleben; vol. 1 *Persönlichkeit und Geschichte*, ed. H. Beumann (Düsseldorf, 1965); vol. 2 *Das geistige Leben*, ed. B. Bischoff (1965); vol. 3 *Karolingische Kunst*, ed. W. Braunfels and H. Schnitzler (1965); vol. 4 *Das Nachleben*, ed. W. Braunfels and P. E. Schramm (1967).

Kehr, P., 'Die sogennante karolingische Schenkung von 774', *Historische Zeitschrift* 70 (1893), 385–441.

Kelly, J. N. D., *The Oxford Dictionary of Popes* (1986).

Kirsch, J. P., *Die römischen Titelkirchen im Altertum*, Studien zur Geschichte und Kultur des Altertums 9 (Paderborn, 1918).

Kirsch, J. P., *Der stadtrömische christliche Festkalender im Altertum*, Liturgie-geschichtliche Quellen, Heft 7/8 (Münster, 1924).

Kirschbaum, E., *The Tombs of St Peter and St Paul* (London, 1959).

Krautheimer, R., 'An oriental basilica in Rome, San Giovanni a Porta Latina', *American Journal of Archaeology* 40 (1936), 485–95.

Krautheimer, R., *Rome: Profile of a City, 312–1308* (Princeton, 1980).

Krautheimer, R., S. Corbett, W. Frankl, *Corpus Basilicarum Christianarum Romae. The Early Christian Basilicas of Rome (IV–IX Centuries)*, 5 volumes (Vatican, 1937–1977).

Kuttner, S., 'Cardinalis, the history of a canonical concept', *Traditio* 3 (1945), 129–214.

Ladner, G., *Die Papstbildnisse des Altertums und des Mittelalters* (Vatican, 1941).

Lanciani, R., 'L'aula e gli uffici del senato Romano', *Atti della reale accad. dei Lincei*, 3rd series, XI (1883), 1 ff.

Lauer, P., *Le palais du Latran, étude historique et archéologique* (Paris, 1911).
Lestocquoy, J., 'Administration de Rome et diaconies du VIIe au IXe siècles', *RAC* 7 (1930), 261–98.
Levillain, L., 'L'avènement de la dynastie carolingienne et les origines de l'état pontifical (749–757)', *Bibliothèque de l'école des chartes* 94 (1933) 225–295.
Llewellyn, P., *Rome in the Dark Ages* (London, 1971, 1993).
Loenertz, R. J., 'Constitutum Constantini. Destination, destinataires, auteur, date', *Aevum* 48 (1974), 199–245.
Löwe, H., 'Zur Vita Hadriani', *Deutsches Archiv für Erforschung des Mittelalters* 12 (1956), 493–8.
McBrien, R. P., *Lives of the Popes* (San Francisco, 1997).
McKitterick, R., *The Frankish kingdoms under the Carolingians, 751–987* (London, 1983).
Mandic, D., 'Dalmatia in the exarchate of Ravenna from the middle of the VI until the middle of the VIII century', *Byzantion* 34 (1964), 347–74.
Marcou, G. S., 'Zaccaria (679–752): l'ultimo papa greco nella storia di Roma altomedioevale', *Apollinaris* 50 (1977), 274.
Marrou, J., 'L'origine orientale des diaconies romaines', *Mélanges de l'école française de Rome* 57 (1940), 95–142.
Martin, E. J., *A History of the Iconoclastic Controversy* (London, rep. New York, 1978).
Miller, D. H., 'The Roman Revolution of the eighth century: a study of the ideological background of the papal separation from Byzantium and alliance with the Franks', *Mediaeval Studies* 36 (1974), 79–133.
Miller, D. H., 'The motivation of Pepin's Italian policy 754–768', *Studies in Medieval Culture* 4 (1973), 44–54.
Mohr, W., *Studien zur Charakteristik des karolingischen Königtums im 8. Jahrhundert* (Saarlouis, 1955).
Mohr, W., 'Karl der Grosse, Leo III und der römische Aufstand von 799', *Archivum Latinitatis Medii Aevi* 20, 1960, 39–98.
Munz, P., *The Origin of the Carolingian Empire* (Leicester, 1960).
Munz, P., 'The imperial coronation of Charlemagne' in F. L. Ganshof (1971).
Noble, T. F. X., *The Republic of St Peter, the birth of the papal state 680–825* (Philadelphia, 1984).
Noble, T. F. X., 'Louis the Pious and the frontiers of the Frankish realm', in Godman and Collins (1990), 333–347.
Ostrogorsky, G., *A History of the Byzantine State* (New Brunswick, 1969).
Partner, P., 'Notes on the lands of the Roman Church in the early middle ages', *PBSR* 34, 1966, 68–78.
Partner, P., *The Lands of St Peter* (London, 1972).
Petriaggi, R., 'Utilizzazione, decorazione e diffusione dei tessuti nei corredi delle basiliche cristiane secondo il Liber Pontificalis (514–795)', *Prospettiva, Rivista*

di storia dell'arte antica e moderna, n. 39, Settembre 1984, 37–46.

Phillips, L. E., 'A Note on the gifts of Leo III to the churches of Rome: Vestes cum storiis', *Ephemerides Liturgicae* 102 (1988), 72–8.

Platner, S. B., and T. Ashby, *A Topographical Dictionary of Ancient Rome* (Oxford, 1979)

Prandi A., 'Un iscrizione frammentaria di Leone IV recentamente scoperta', *ASR* 74 (1951), 149–159.

Ramackers, J., 'Die Werkstattheimat der Grabplatte Papst Hadrians I', *Römische Quartalschrift* 59 (1964).

Rassow, P., 'Pippin und Stephan II', *Zeitschrift für Kirchengeschichte* 36 (1916), 494–502.

Rava, A., 'S. Ciriaco in Thermis', *Roma* (1928), 160–8.

Richards, J., *The popes and the papacy in the early middle ages, 476–752* (London, 1979).

Rohault de Fleury, G., *Le Latran au moyen-âge* (Paris, 1877).

Schade, H., 'Die Libri Carolini und ihre Stellung zum Bild', *Zeitschrift für katholische Theologie* 79 (1957), 69–78.

Schäfer, A., *Die Bedeutung der Päpste Gregor II (715–731) und Gregor III (731–741) für die Gründung des Kirchenstaates* (Montjoie, 1913).

Schiefer, T., *Winfrid-Bonifatius und die christliche Grundlegung Europas* (Darmstadt, 1980).

Schmid, K., 'Zur Ablösung der Langobardenherrschaft durch den Franken', *Quellen und Forschungen aus italienischen Archiven und Bibliotheken* 52 (1972), 1–36.

Schove, D. J., and A. Fletcher, *Chronology of eclipses and comets, A.D. 1–1000* (Bury St Edmunds, 1984).

Schramm, P. E., *Die zeitgenössischen Bildnisse Karls der Grossen*, Beiträge zur Kulturgeschichte des Mittelalters und der Renaissance 29 (Leipzig, 1928).

Seston, D. S., 'Pope Hadrian I and the fall of the kingdom of the Lombards', *Catholic Historical Review* 65 (1979).

Sickel, T., *Das Privilegium Otto I für die römische Kirche von Jahre 962* (Innsbruck, 1883).

Silvestrelli, G., 'Galeria', *ASR* 40 (1917), 279.

Southern, R. W., *Western Society and the Church in the Middle Ages*, The Pelican History of the Church, Volume 2 (London, 1970).

P. Speck, P., 'Artabasdos, der rechtgläubige Vorkämpfer der göttlichen Lehren: Untersuchungen zur Revolte des Artabasdos und ihrer Darstellung in der byzantinischen Historiographie', *Poikila Byzantina* 2 (1981), 1–133.

Stein, E., 'Le période byzantine de la papauté', in his *Opera minora selecta* (Amsterdam, 1968), 501–535.

Tomassetti, G. and F., *La Campagna romana, antica, medioevale e moderna*, 4 volumes (Rome, 1913), revised edition by L. Chiumenti and F. Bilancia (Rome, 1975–6).

Topografia e urbanistica di Roma, Storia di Roma XII, 189–341 (Bologna, 1958).

Tremp, E., 'Thegan und Astronomus, die beiden Geschichtsschreiber Ludwigs des Frommen' in Godman and Collins (1990), 691–700.

Ullmann, W., *The Growth of Papal Government in the middle ages: a study in the ideological relation of clerical to lay power*, 3rd ed. (London, 1970).

Vielliard, R., *Recherches sur les origines de la Rome chrétienne* (Rome, 1959).

Wallach, L., 'Alcuin's epitaph of Hadrian', *American Journal of Philology* 72 (1951).

Wallach, L., 'The genuine and forged oath of pope Leo III', *Traditio* 11 (1955), 37–63 and in his *Diplomatic Studies in Greek and Latin Documents from the Carolingian Age* (Ithaca, 1977), 299–327.

Wallach, L., *Alcuin and Charlemagne, studies in Carolingian history and literature* (Ithaca, 1959; amended reprint New York, 1968).

Wallach, L., 'The Roman synod of December 800 and the alleged trial of Leo III', *Harvard Theological Review* 49 (1956), 123–142.

Walter, C., *L'iconographie des conciles dans la tradition byzantine*, Archives de l'orient chrétien 13 (Paris, 1970).

Ward Perkins, J. B., 'The shrine of St Peter and its twelve spiral columns', *JRS* 42 (1952), 21–33.

Whitehouse, D., 'Sedi medievali nella campagna romana: La 'domusculta' e il villagio fortificato', *Quaderni storici* 24 (1973), 861–76.

Whitehouse, D., 'The medieval pottery from S. Cornelia', *PBSR* 48 (1980), 125–156.

Wickham, C., 'Historical and topographical notes on early medieval South Etruria', *PBSR* 46 (1978), 132–179; 47 (1979), 66–95.

Wickham, C., *Early Medieval Italy* (London, 1981).

Zimmermann, H., *Papstabsetzungen des Mittelalters* (Graz, 1968).M

INDEX OF PERSONS AND PLACES

Acutiana estate, **97**:63
Adalgis, **97**:23, 31, 34
Ado bishop of Lyon, **96**:17
Ado bishop of Orte, **96**:17
Aemiliana's *titulus* (cf. SS Quattuor Coronati?), **98**:73
Africa, **93**:22
Agareni, **91**:5, 11, **93**:20
Agatho bishop of Sutri, **96**:17
Agatho primicerius, **93**:26
Agatho scriniarius, **97**:63
Agiprand duke of Chiusi, **93**:11
Agnellus consul of Ravenna, **93**:9
Agnes widow of scriniarius Agatho, **97**:63
Aistulf king, **94**:5, 18, 21–2, 30–32, 34–5, 37, 39, 41–2, 46–8
Alatri, **96**:14, 17
Albano, **96**:4, 17, 24, **97**:25, **98**:42, 107
Albinus chamberlain, **98**:14–15
Albuin (Alcuin), **97**:26
Alexandria, **91**:5
Ambrose primicerius, **93**:12, 14, 18, **94**:5, 23–4
Ambrose's monastery – see St Mary's
Amélia (Ameria), **93**:2, 11
Amiens, **96**:17
Anagni, **96**:17, **97**:10, 11
Anastasius II emperor, **91**:1, 5
Anastasius patriarch, **91**:24, **92**:4
Anastasius bishop, **92**:14
Anastasius first defensor, **97**:5, 21
Ancona, **93**:9, **97**:33
Andrew bishop of Palestrina, **96**:30, **97**:25
Andrew, Lombard referendarius, **97**:20, 23
Holy Angel's (church) at Faganum, **98**:38
Aniciorum xenodochium, **98**:81
Anna widow of primicerius Agatho, **93**:26
Ansald bishop of Narni, **96**:17
Antiqua – see St Mary's deaconry

Antoninus archbishop of Grado, **92**:3
Antoninus bishop of Cesena, **96**:17
Antoninus, bridge of, **97**:94
Anvald cartularius, **97**:16
Anzio, **93**:26
Apostles' church on Via Appia – see St Sebastian's
Apostles' basilica on Via Lata, **97**:50, 60, **98**:71, 77, 91, 102
Apostles' *titulus* – see St Peter's *titulus*
Appentinum – see St John's monastery
Appian Gate, **95**:3, **97**:76, 78
Aqua Salvia monastery – see St Mary's oratory
Aquila, **93**:13
Aquino (Aquinum), **93**:21
Aquiro – see St Mary's deaconry
Aquitania, **91**:8, **94**:4
Aratiana estate, **97**:63
Arcévia (Acerreagium), **94**:47
Archangel's basilica in Vicus Patricius – see St Euphemia's (and Archangel's)
Archangel's basilica at 7th mile, **98**:45
Archangel's deaconry, **98**:45, 75, 88, 108
Archangel's oratory in Lateran, **98**:92
Aribert king, **91**:4
Arn archbishop, **98**:20
Artavasdus usurper, **93**:20
Ascheric count, **98**:16
Asprula farm, **97**:55
Atto bishop, **98**:20
Atzuppius father of Leo III, **98**:1
Aurea Petronilla, **95**:3 (cf. St Petronilla)
Aurianos bishop of Tuscania, **96**:17
Autchar the Frank, duke, **94**:18, 20, **97**:9, 23, 25, 31, 34

Bagnorégio, **96**:17
Barbara patricia, **97**:53, **98**:91

INDEX

Basil duke, **91**:14, 15
Bavarians, **91**:4
Benedict vicedominus, **93**:12
Benevento/-tans, **91**:22, **93**:3, **97**:42
Berceto, **97**:42
Bernard bishop, **98**:20
Bernulf bishop of Würzburg, **96**:17
Blera, **91**:23, **93**:2, 11, **97**:18
Bomarzo (Polimartium), **93**:2, 11, **96**:17
Boniface (St), **91**:3
Boniface bishop of Priverno, **96**:17
Boniface secundicerius, **94**:23
Bonus bishop of Maturianum, **96**:17
Bourges, **96**:17
Buxum (El Bus near Bazzano), **91**:18

Caere (Cerveteri), **96**:17
Cagli (Cales), **94**:47, **96**:17
Calabria, **91**:2
Callinicum – see SS Sergius and Bacchus' oratory
Callistus' *titulus* – see St Mary's/Callistus' *titulus*
Calventzulus chamberlain, **97**:10
Calvisianum domusculta, **97**:55
Calvulus chamberlain, **97**:10–11, 13–14
Campania/-ians, **91**:8, 18, **92**:14, **96**:14, 17, 28, **97**:10–11, 13–14, 24, 62, 92
Campulus sacellarius, **98**:11–14, 20, 26
Campus Martius, **98**:80
Campus Neronis, **91**:22, **92**:14, **94**:39
Capracorum domusculta, **97**:54, 69
Caput Africae – see St Agatha's monastery
Carloman (d. 754), **93**:21, **94**:30
Carloman king (d. 771), **96**:16, 17, 28, **97**:5–6, 9, 23, 31, 34, 41
Castellum (Falerii Veteres, Città Castellana), **96**:17
Castellum Felicitatis (Città di Castello), **97**:33
Castrum (Acquapendente), **96**:17, **98**:41
Castrum Tiberiacum (Bagnacavallo), **94**:51
Catacumbae, **97**:76, **98**:47
Cavello (Cabellum), **94**:51
Céccano (Ciccanum), **94**:17
Cella Nova – see St Saba's monastery
Centumcellae (Civitavecchia), **92**:16, **96**:17
Césena (Caesena), **93**:12, 15–16, **94**:47, **96**:17

Ceuta, **91**:11
Charles (Martel), **92**:14, **93**:21, **94**:15
Charles (Charlemagne), **94**:25, **96**:16–17, 26, 28, **97**:6, 9, 22–3, 26–9, 34, 37–8, 40–42, 44, **98**:15–16, 23–6
Charles son of Charlemagne, **98**:16
Chiusi, **93**:11, **98**:41
Christopher regionarius, **94**:23
Christopher counsellor, primicerius **94**:49, **96**:5, 7–8, 11, 15, 28–32, **97**:5, 14
Christopher vicedominus, **96**:15
Chrodegang (arch)bishop, **94**:18, 23, 53
Citonatus bishop of Porto, **96**:4, 17
Citonatus bishop of Velletri, **96**:17
Classe, **91**:13
Claudian aqueduct, **97**:62
Clivus Scauri monastery – see St Andrew's monastery
Colosseum, **96**:14
Comacchio (Comiaclum), **94**:46, **97**:6
Conca, **94**:47
Constantine pope, **91**:1
Constantine antipope, **95**:7, **96**:3, 5–6, 9, 12–14, 16, 18–22
Constantine defensor, **92**:4
Constantine father of Stephen II and Paul, **94**:1, **95**:1
Constantine V emperor, **91**:1, 25, **92**:2, 4, **93**:20, **95**:2, **97**:15
Constantine VI emperor, **97**:88
Constantinople, **91**:2, 12, 17, 23–4, **92**:4, **93**:20, **97**:13, 15
de Corsas monastery – see St Caesarius' oratory
Corsica, **97**:42
'Cosinensis', **93**:10
Cosmedin – see St Mary's deaconry
Cottian Alps, **91**:4
Cross oratory at St Peter's, **98**:66
Cumae, **91**:7
Cunipert bishop, **98**:20

Daniel bishop of Narbonne, **96**:17
Demetrius secundicerius, **96**:9
Desiderius king, **94**:48–51, **96**:5, 25, 28–33, **97**:5–9, 15–16, 18–32, 44
Dominic praefectorius, **97**:63
Domnica – see St Mary's deaconry
Droctegang abbot, **94**:16

Dua Furna monastery – see St Agnes'
  oratory
Dulcitius' – see St Stephen's oratory

Elephantum, **97**:13
Emilia, **91**:18, **93**:12, **94**:47
Erflaic bishop-elect, **98**:20
Erlolf bishop of Langres, **96**:17
Ermenbert bishop of Worms, **96**:17
Etherius chaplain and notary, **97**:42–3
Eudes, duke, prince of Aquitania **91**:11
Eudoxia's *titulus* – see St Peter's *titulus*
Eustratius bishop of Albano, **96**:4, 17, 24,
  97:25
Eutychius exarch, **91**:19, 22, **92**:5, **93**:12–13
exarchate – see Ravenna
Exhilaratus duke, **91**:18

Faenza (Faventia), **94**:51, **96**:17, **97**:6
Faganum (Monte S. Angelo), **98**:38
Fano (Fanum), **94**:47, **96**:17
Fathers, **96**:23, **97**:1, 88
Ferentinellum territory, **97**:89
Ferentino (Ferentinum), **96**:17
Fermo, **97**:33
Ferrara, **94**:51, **97**:6
Ferrata prison, **96**:15
Ferronianum (Zenzano), **91**:18
Ficuclae (Cérvia), **96**:17
Filerad bishop of Luni, **96**:17
Firmis xenodochium, **98**:42, 70
Flaminian Gate, **91**:6, **97**:94
Florentinus bishop of Gubbio, **96**:17
Fonteiana estate, **93**:19, **98**:5
Forcona (Città di Bagno), **93**:3, **96**:7
Forlì (Forum Livii), **94**:47
Forlimpópoli (Forum Popilii), **94**:47
Formia, **93**:26
France, **91**:11, **92**:14, 18, **94**:18, 22–3, 30,
  42–3, 47, 52, 54, **96**:16, **97**:26, 34,
  41–2, 44, **98**:20, 26, **99**:2
Frank(s), **91**:11, **92**:14, **93**:21, **94**:15–16, 18,
  20, 22, 24, 27–8, 30–38, 41–7, 49–50,
  96:16–17, 26, 28, **97**:5–6, 9, 22, 25–31,
  34–44, **98**:15, 18–19, 21–2, 26, **99**:2
Fridigisus abbot, **98**:110
Frisians, **98**:19
Fulrad abbot of St Denis, **94**:24, 47, 49–50

Galeria domusculta, (**93**:26), **97**:55
Galeria II domusculta, **97**:55
Galla patricia, **98**:77, 90
Gallese, **92**:15
Gaugenus bishop of Tours, **96**:17
Gaul(s), **94**:20, **96**:17
Gemmulus deacon of Rome, **94**:23
Gemmulus subdeacon, **97**:5
George bishop of Ostia, later of Amiens,
  94:23, **96**:17, **97**:26
George bishop of Palestrina, **96**:3, 4, 6
George bishop of Senigallia, **96**:17
George priest of Rome, **92**:2
George priest of Rome, **94**:23
George byzantine official (proto a secreta),
  94:43–4
Germanus patriarch, **91**:24
Germany, **91**:3
Germar count, **98**:20
Gislebert bishop of Noyon, **96**:17
Gracilis tribune, **96**:14
Grado, **92**:3
Gratiosus cartularius, later duke, **96**:9, 11,
  14, 31
Greece, **96**:23, **97**:15
Gregory I, **93**:29
Gregory II, **91**:passim, **94**:15
Gregory III, **92**:passim, **93**:2, 4, **94**:15, **95**:1,
  96:1
Gregory bishop of Silva Candida, **96**:17, 24
Gregory priest of Urbino, **96**:17
Gregory defensor, **97**:10–11
Gregory sacellarius, **97**:16
Gregory secundicerius, **97**:77
Grimuald envoy of Liutprand, **93**:6, 11
Gubbio (Iguvium), **94**:47, **96**:17, **97**:18
Gulfard abbot and counsellor, **97**:26

Hadrian son of Exhilaratus, **91**:18
Hadrian I pope, **97**:passim, **99**:1
Hadrianium – see St Mary's deaconry at the
  Hadrianium
Helmgoth count, **98**:20
Hermenarius bishop of Bourges, **96**:17
Hesperian district, **92**:3
Hildebald archbishop, **98**:16, 20
Hildeprand king, **93**:17
Hildeprand duke, **97**:33
Hildigard queen, **97**:34

INDEX 253

Honesta mother of Gregory II, **91**:10
Honorius, pope, monastery of – see SS Andrew and Bartholomew's
Hunald duke of Aquitania, **94**:4

Iesi (Aesis), **94**:47, **97**:18
Imola, **93**:14
Innocents, Holy, **98**:28
Irene empress, **97**:88
Israel, **98**:14
Istria, **97**:42
Italy, **91**:15, 17, **92**:4, **93**:2, 17, **94**:9, 15, **96**:17, **97**:9, 41
Ivrea, **97**:5

Janiculum, **96**:8, **97**:59
Januarius vestiarius, **97**:64, 67
Jerome brother of Pepin, **94**:38
Jerome bishop of Pavia, **96**:17
Jerusalem basilica at the Sessorian, **91**:8, **97**:75, **98**:43, 72
Jerusalem monastery at St Peter's, **98**:80
Jesse bishop, **98**:20
Jews, **98**:12
John patriarch, **91**:2
John V archbishop of Ravenna, **92**:3, **93**:12
John bishop of Faenza, **96**:17
John deacon of Ravenna, **96**:17
John Lurion subdeacon of Rome, **91**:14-15
John father of Gregory III, **92**:1
John duke (of Naples), **91**:7
John duke, brother of Stephen III, **97**:10-11
John silentiary, **94**:8, 17-18, 43
John primicerius, **97**:77
Jordanes cartularius, **91**:14-15
Jordanes bishop of Segni, **96**:17, 30
Jordani cemetery – see SS Alexander etc.
Joseph bishop of Tortona, **96**:17
Jovia aqueduct, **97**:61
Julia's monastery – see St Mary's
Julian tribune, **97**:7, 9, 17
Juliana estate, **98**:77
Justinian II, **91**:1
Juvianus bishop of Cagli, **96**:17

Langres, **96**:17
Lantfred bishop of Castrum, **96**:17
Lateran bath, **97**:62; Chamber, **94**:1; grounds, **96**:15; patriarchate/office, **92**:10, 13, **93**:18, **94**:2, 12, **95**:1, **96**:1-4, 9-11, 18, 29, 32, **97**:12, 39, 40, 49, 54, 68, 70, **98**:10, 20, 39, 71, 76, 92, **99**:1; vestiarium, **96**:9, **98**:1
Latin Gate, **97**:76, 78, **98**:80
Lauretum domusculta, **93**:19
Leo III pope, **98**:passim, **99**:1-2
Leo archbishop of Ravenna, **96**:17, 25-6, **97**:7, 9, 14-17
Leo bishop of Castellum, **96**:17
Leo priest of Rome, **94**:23
Leo regionarius, **94**:23
Leo III emperor, **91**:1, 12, 25, **92**:2, 4
Leo IV emperor, **95**:2-3, **97**:15
Leo consul of Ravenna, **93**:9
Leonatius tribune, **97**:10-11
Leoninus bishop of Alatri, **96**:17
Leoninus consul and duke, **97**:63
Leontius scriniarius, **96**:13, 24
library, **91**:1, **93**:19, **97**:88
Liutprand king, **91**:4, 13, 22, **92**:14, **93**:2, 4-7, 14-15, 17
Lombard(s), **91**:7, 13, 16, 18-19, 21, **92**:14, **93**:2-4, 10-11, 14, 17, 23, **94**:4-6, 10-11, 15-18, 20-21, 23-4, 31-2, 35, 37, 41, 43-4, 46, 48, 50, **96**:5, 7-9, 15, 25, 28-33, **97**:5, 9, 15-16, 18-19, 21, 23, 25-6, 29-34, 44, **98**:15, 19
Lord's hostel at Naumachia – see St Peregrinus' oratory
Louis I emperor, **99**:2
Lucia, **97**:77
Lucioli (? Cantiano), **94**:47
Lullo bishop of Mainz, **96**:17
Luna, **91**:23
Luni, **96**:17, **97**:42
Lunisso priest, **97**:10-11
de Lutara monastery – see St Mary's oratory
Lyon, **96**:17

Magna valley, **93**:9
Mainz, **96**:17
Mantua, **97**:42
Marcellus father of Gregory II, **91**:1
Marinus bishop of Urbino, **96**:17
Marinus father of Stephen IV, **99**:1
Marinus spatharius, duke, **91**:14
Marseilles, **94**:43-4
Marsi, the, **93**:3

Marulis estate, **97**:76
Mastalus primicerius, **97**:77
Maurianus subdeacon, **96**:13
Maurice duke of Rimini, **96**:25
Maurice duke of Venice, **97**:15
Maurienne, **94**:34
Maurus bishop of Bomarzo, **96**:17
Maurus bishop of Fano, **96**:17
Maurus of Nepi, **98**:13
Meaux, **96**:17
Mediana – see St Mary's altar
Megistus Cataxanthus, **93**:25
Mentana, **94**:45
Merulana, **97**:11, **98**:94
Michael scriniarius of Ravenna, **96**:25–6
Michael's monastery – see St Mary's oratory in Michael's monastery
Milvian Bridge, **91**:6, 16, **96**:8, **97**:94, **98**:19
Mons Lucati, **94**:47
Monselice, **97**:42
Mont Cenis pass, **97**:29
Monte Celio, **97**:61, 82, **98**:47, 71, 76, 104
Montefeltro (San Leo), **94**:47, **97**:18
Monterano (Manturianum), **91**:23, **96**:17
Monteveglio (Montebellum), **91**:18
Mount Bardo, **97**:42

Naples, **91**:7, 19, **96**:19
Narbonne, **96**:17
Narni (Narnia), **91**:13, **93**:6–7, 9, **94**:41, 47, **96**:17
Naumachia, **98**:81, 90
Needle, the, **98**:27
Nepi, **96**:3, 17, **98**:13
Nicaea, **91**:5, **97**:88
Ninfa, **93**:20
Nirgotius bishop of Anagni, **96**:17
Nomentan Gate, **97**:85, **98**:80
Norma, **93**:20
Novae, **97**:35
Noyon, **96**:17
Numana, **93**:9
Olibus, **96**:1
Orfea, **97**:64, **98**:38, 75, 81, 91
Orte (Horta), **93**:2, 6, 11, **96**:17,
Orvieto, **98**:41
Osimo (Auximum), **91**:18, **93**:9, **97**:33
Ostia, **94**:23, **98**:50

Otricoli, **97**:18

Palestrina, **96**:4, 6, 30, **97**:25, 82, **98**:44, 94
Pallacinae, portico, **97**:94; see St Laurence's monastery in Pallacinis
Pammachius' *titulus* – see SS John and Paul's
Paradise, the, **95**:6
Pardus deacon of Rome, **94**:23
Pardus hegumenos, **97**:21
Paris, **94**:27
Parma, **97**:42
Paschal brother of antipope Constantine, **96**:3
Paschal bequeather of estate, **97**:77
Paschal primicerius, **98**:11–13, 20, 26
Passibus, **96**:3, 9, 12
Paul deacon/pope, **94**:5, 8, 49, **95**:passim, **96**:2, 18, **97**:3, 8, 46, 50, **98**:11, 101
Paul patrician and exarch, **91**:15–19
Paul Afiarta chamberlain and superista, **96**:28–9, 32, **97**:4, 6, 8–11, 14–17
Paunaria estate, **93**:19
Pavia-Ticinum, **96**:17; called Pavia at **94**:21, 23, 35–6, 44, 46, **97**:31, 34–5, 44; called Ticinum at **93**:13–15, **94**:20, **96**:17, **97**:16–17, 20, 44 (at **97**:44 the distinction might be Ticinum as the territory around Pavia citadel)
Penne (Pinna), **93**:3
Pentapolis/-itans, **91**:17–18, **93**:12, 16, 23, **94**:47, **97**:24
Pepin king, **94**:15, 18, 24, 27, 29–33, 36–7, 42–3, 45–6, 49, 52, **96**:16–17, **97**:6, 22, 26, 41
Pepin son of Charlemagne, **98**:16
Persiceto (Persicetum), **91**:18
Perugia, **93**:23, **96**:28, **97**:6, 20, 24, 96
Pésaro (Pisaurum), **94**:47, **96**:17
Peter bishop of Caere, **96**:17
Peter bishop of Populonia, **96**:17
Peter deacon of Pavia, **96**:17
Peter archpriest of Rome, **97**:88
Peter abbot of St Saba, **97**:88
Peter defensor, **92**:4
Peter duke (of Rome), **91**:18
Peter count, **97**:63
Peter tribune, **97**:7
Philip priest of Rome, **94**:23
Philip antipope, **96**:10–11

Philippicus emperor, **91**:5
Pinnis bishop of Tres Tabernae, **96**:17
Platana, xenodochium in (cf. St Eustace's deaconry), **94**:4
Po river, **93**:9, 14, 16, **96**:5, **97**:34
Polychronius father of Zacharias, **93**:1
Ponthion, **94**:25
Populonia, **96**:17
Porto Romano, **96**:4, 17, **97**:55, **98**:42
Portuensis Gate, **96**:31, **97**:65, 80
Potho bishop of Nepi, **96**:17
Prandulus vestiarius, **97**:5
Priverno, **96**:17
Probatus abbot, **97**:19
Pudens' *titulus* – see St Pudentiana's

Quierzy (Carisiacus), **94**:29, **97**:42

Racipert, Lombard warrior, **96**:9
Radoin bishop of Bagnoregio, **96**:17
Ramning gastald of Tuscania, **93**:11
Ratchis king, **93**:17, 23, **94**:48, 50
Ravenna/-ates, **91**:13, 16, 18, **92**:3, **93**:9, 12–17, **94**:8, 15, 17, 21, 26, 37, 44, 47, **96**:17, 19, 25–6, **97**:6, 7, 9, 14–18, 20, 22, 42, **98**:106; exarchate, **94**:15, 21, 26, 44, 47, **97**:6, 9, 18, 22, 42
Reggio (nell'Emilia), **97**:42
Remissa, **91**:6, **97**:94
Renatus' monastery – see St Lucy's oratory
Rheims, **96**:17
Rhone, **91**:11
Rieti, Reatini, **93**:3, **96**:7, **97**:32
Rimini (Ariminum), **94**:47, **96**:17, 25, **97**:9
Rothard, Frankish duke, **94**:24
Rottecar count **98**:20

Sabatius priest of Rimini, **96**:17
Sabbatina aqueduct, **97**:59, 81
Sabellum, **97**:76, **99**:4
Sabina, **93**:3, 9, **97**:19, **98**:47
St Abbacyrus' oratory in St Caecilia's domusculta, **93**:25
St Abbacyrus' oratory in xenodochium a Valeris, **98**:81
St Abbacyrus' altar at holy Archangel's deaconry, **98**:108
SS Abdon and Sennen's cemetery/basilica, **97**:65, **97**:80

St Agapitus' basilica near St Laurence outside walls, **97**:73, **98**:112
St Agapitus' basilica at Palestrina, **98**:44, 94
St Agapitus' monastery ad vincula, **98**:45, 78, **99**:3 note
St Agatha's deaconry, **98**:45, 75, 109
St Agatha's (Gregory II's) monastery/church, **91**:10
St Agatha's monastery (unclear which of the following), **96**:32
St Agatha's monastery/basilica over Subura, **98**:56, 76, 91
St Agatha's monastery in Caput Africae, **98**:79
St Agatha's oratory in Tempulus' monastery, **98**:79
St Agnes' church/monastery outside Nomentan Gate, **97**:85, **98**:46, **98**:80
St Agnes' oratory in Dua Furna monastery, **98**:78
SS Alexander, Vitalis, Martial et VII (Jordani) cemetery, **97**:80
St Anastasia's *titulus*, **98**:4, 37, 74
St Anastasius' basilica/monastery, **97**:91, **98**:38, 76
St Andrew's church at St Peter's, **92**:11, 16, **93**:26, **94**:52, **95**:3, 6, **96**:27, **97**:46, **98**:6, 35, 55, 65, 68, 71, 90, 101, 110
St Andrew cata Barbara patricia, monastery/basilica, **91**:3, **98**:91
St Andrew's monastery Massa Juliana (probably the last rather than the next), **98**:77
St Andrew's church by praesepe (probably Valila's), **98**:71
St Andrew's oratory near St Mary Antiqua, **98**:83
St Andrew's monastery by Apostles' basilica, **98**:77
St Andrew's monastery in Clivus Scauri, **96**:12, 32, **98**:30, 76
St Andrew's basilica at 30th mile on Via Appia, in silice, **97**:76, **98**:30
SS Andrew and Bartholomew's (pope Honorius') monastery, **97**:68, **98**:76
St Apollinaris' basilica/church (perhaps two of them), **97**:61, **98**:46, 72
St Apollinaris' basilica at Ravenna, **93**:13, **98**:106

SS Aquila and Prisca's *titulus* – see St Prisca's
St Aurea's church at Ostia, **98**:50
St Balbina's *titulus*, **98**:73, 91
St Barbara's oratory in Subura, **99**:4
St Basilides' in Merulana, **98**:94
St Benedict's monastery at Monte Cassino, **93**:21, **94**:7, 30
St Bibiana's monastery, **98**:78
St Boniface's church, Via Salaria, **97**:79
St Boniface's deaconry, **98**:29, 75
St Caecilia's *titulus*, **96**:1, 11, **98**:37, 74
St Caecilia's domusculta and oratory, **93**:25
St Caesarius' monastery at St Paul's, **98**:77
St Caesarius' oratory in Lateran, **96**:9
St Caesarius' oratory in monastery de Corsas, **98**:79
St Callistus' basilica, Via Aurelia, **92**:11
St Candida's basilica, **97**:80
St Cassian's monastery by St Laurence outside walls, **98**:77
St Christopher's basilica at Aquila, **93**:13
SS Chrysanthus and Daria's cemetery, Via Salaria, **97**:79
St Chrysogonus' *titulus*, **92**:8, **98**:44, 74
St Chrysogonus' monastery, **92**:9, **96**:1, **98**:77
St Clement's *titulus*/basilica, **94**:14, **97**:64, **98**:8, 73, 109
St Clement's church at Velletri, **98**:44
St Cornelius pope, relics, **97**:69
SS Cosmas and Damian's basilica/deaconry on Via Sacra at Three Fates, **97**:51, 76, 81, 96, **98**:29, 75, 91
SS Cosmas and Damian's oratory in xenodochium Tucium, **98**:81
SS Cosmas and Damian's monastery by praesepe, **91**:3, **98**:77
St Cyriac's *titulus*/basilica, **97**:70, **98**:40, 74, 108
St Cyriac's church, Via Ostiensis, **98**:109
St Cyriaca's cemetery, **97**:75
St Damasus, **97**:50
St Denis monastery, **94**:27
St Donatus' monastery by St Prisca's titulus, **98**:80
St Emerentiana's basilica, **97**:85
St Erasmus' monastery in Monte Celio, **98**:13, 30, 76

St Eugenia's basilica/monastery outside Latin Gate, **97**:78, 82, **98**:46, 80
St Euphemia (and Archangel's) basilica/monastery, **98**:47, 79
St Euplus' church, Via Ostiensis, **97**:74
St Eusebius' *titulus*/basilica, **93**:27, **97**:74, **98**:37, 74
St Eustace's deaconry (cf. xenodochium in Platana), **98**:38, 75
St Felicitas' cemetery, **97**:79
St Felix martyr and pope, relics, **97**:69
St Felix in Pincis basilica, **97**:50
St Felix's church outside Portuensis Gate, **97**:80
SS Felix and Adauctus' by St Paul's, **98**:5
St Genesius' church (Via Tiburtina), **92**:12
St George, relic, **93**:24
St George's deaconry/church at the Velabrum, **93**:24, **98**:11, 45, 75, 104
SS Gordian and Epimachus' basilica, **97**:78
St Gregory's altar at St Peter's, **98**:68, 84
St Gregory's body, **98**:35
St Gregory's oratory in Campus Martius, **98**:80
St Gregory's hostel, **97**:66
St Hadrian's basilica/deaconry, **97**:51, 73, 81, 96, **98**:45, 75
St Hadrian's (and St Laurence's) monastery by praesepe, **97**:86, **98**:77
St Hedistus' church and domusculta, Via Ardeatina, **97**:63
St Helena's basilica, **97**:50, **99**:4
SS Hermes, Protus and Hyacinth, and Basilla's basilica/cemetery, **97**:79
St Hilaria's cemetery, **97**:79
St Hippolytus' cemetery, **97**:85
St Hippolytus' basilica in Porto, **98**:42
St Hyacinth's basilica in Sabina, **98**:47
St Innocentius pope, relics, **97**:69
St Isidore's monastery, **98**:79
St Januarius' basilica outside St Laurence's Gate, **97**:65
SS Januarius, Urban, Tiburtius, Valerian and Maximus' cemetery (Via Appia) **92**:13
St John the Baptist's church/oratory by Lateran, **98**:32, 71
St John the Evangelist's church/oratory by Lateran, **98**:32, 71
SS John the Evangelist, John the Baptist, and

INDEX 257

Pancras' monastery – see St Pancras'
St John's church at the Latin Gate, **97**:76
St John's monastery in Appentinum, **98**:80
St John the Baptist's church at Maurienne, **94**:34
SS John and Paul's *titulus* (Pammachii), **97**:82, **98**:30, 73, 109
SS John and Paul's monastery, **98**:77
St Laurence's (one or both of the two following), **91**:2, **97**:60, 73-4, 85, 90, **98**:5, 29, 36, 43, 72, 77, 112
St Laurence's basilica ad corpus, **97**:49, 64, 75, 87, **98**:29
St Laurence's great basilica (cf. St Mary's basilica at St Laurence's), **97**:49, 75
St Laurence's basilica in Tivoli, **98**:47
St Laurence's *titulus* in Damaso, **97**:50, **98**:45, 73, 91
St Laurence's *titulus* in Lucina, **97**:73, **98**:11, 44, 73
St Laurence ad Formonsum/in Formonsis church, **97**:70, **98**:37, 40, 73
St Laurence ad Taurellum, **97**:50
St Laurence's above St Clement's, **94**:14
St Laurence's oratory in Lateran, **96**:4
St Laurence's monastery in domusculta Galeria, **97**:55
St Laurence's monastery in Pallacinis, **97**:71, **98**:76
St Laurence's Gate, **97**:65
St Laurence's portico, **91**:2, **97**:74
St Leo bishop, **97**:75
St Leo's oratory/altar at St Peter's, **95**:6, **98**:84, 87
St Leucius' church, Via Flaminia, **97**:77
St Lucius pope, relics **97**:69
St Lucy's deaconry in Orphea, **98**:38, 75, 91
St Lucy's deaconry in Septem Vias, **98**:38, 75
St Lucy's oratory in monastery of Renatus, **98**:38, 79
St Lucy's oratory in xenodochium Aniciorum, **98**:81
SS Marcellinus and Peter's by Lateran, **92**:13
St Marcellus' *titulus*, Via Lata, **97**:79, **98**:40, 74
St Marcellus' church at 14th mile, **98**:50
St Maria ad Grada tower at St Peter's, **95**:6

St Mark's basilica/titulus, **91**:6, **97**:2, 49, 71, 94, 96, **98**:44, 74
St Mark's basilica, Via Appia, **92**:13
St Martin's altar at St Peter's, **98**:110
St Martin's church close to St Silvester's – see St Silvester's (and/or St Martin's)
St Martin's deaconry by St Peter's, **98**:75, 90, 101
St Martin's monastery, **98**:77, 90
St Martina's altar/basilica at the Three Fates, **97**:51, 96, **98**:45, 91
St Mary (generally called God's mother; called our lady at **94**:3, **96**:23, **97**:66, **98**:5, 22, 52, 88, 95, 98, 105, 110); intercession of, **94**:3, 19, **98**:22; relics in domusculta Capracorum, **97**:69
St Mary's basilica ad praesepe (St Mary Major), **91**:3, **92**:8, 13, 16, **94**:3, 11, 13, 45, **97**:11, 40, 48, 74, 84, 86-7, 89 **98**:4, 5, 25, 29, 36, 43, 50-2, 62-3, 69, 71, 77, 83, 86, 88, 95, 98, 105, 110, 112
St Mary's church ad martyres (Pantheon), **92**:12, **93**:11, **94**:14, **96**:15, **97**:60, 96, **98**:29, 70, 99
St Mary's altar/oratory called Mediana at St Peter's, **98**:55, 101
St Mary's basilica at St Laurence's outside walls, **97**:49(unnamed), 64
St Mary's/Callistus' *titulus* in Trastevere, **97**:79, 84, **98**:29, 36, 40, 62, 69, 83
St Mary's church in Fonteiana estate, **98**:5
St Mary's deaconry in Cosmedin, **97**:72, **98**:29, 70, 99
St Mary's deaconry at the Hadrianium, **97**:66, **98**:70
St Mary's deaconry outside St Peter's Gate, **94**:4, **97**:66, **98**:70
St Mary's deaconry Antiqua, **98**:45, 52, 70, 83
St Mary's deaconry in Aquiro, **92**:12, **98**:45, 70
St Mary's deaconry Domnica, **98**:29, 52, 62, 70, 98
St Mary's deaconry, Via Lata, **98**:45, 70
St Mary's monastery called Ambrose's, **98**:77
St Mary's monastery called Julia's, **98**:77
St Mary's monastery in Sabina (Farfa), **97**:19

St Mary's (pope Paul's) chapel/oratory at St Peter's, **95**:6, **98**:101
St Mary's oratory in Michael's monastery, **98**:79
St Mary's oratory in monastery of Aqua Salvia, **98**:80
St Mary's oratory in monastery de Lutara, **98**:80
St Mary's oratory in xenodochium Firmis, **98**:42, 70
St Maurice's monastery (at Agaune), **94**:24
St Mennas' basilica, **98**:5
SS Nereus and Achilleus' deaconry, **98**:29, 75, 111–112
St Nicomedes' church, **97**:85
St Pancras' basilica outside walls, **97**:49, 61, 73, **98**:29, 36, 72, 77
St Pancras' basilica at Albano, **98**:107
St Pancras' monastery by Saviour's basilica, **92**:10, **97**:68, **98**:56, 76
St Pancras' Gate, **96**:3, 8
St Paul, donation to **91**:21, grave ad Catacumbas **98**:47, intercession of **98**:16
St Paul's basilica, **91**:2, 3, **92**:13, 16, **93**:19, **94**:13, **95**:7, **96**:2, 27, **97**:24, 40, 47, 60, 67, 70, 74, 84–5, 89–90, **98**:4–6, 8, 24, 28, 31, 35, 43, 49, 56, 58, 61, 68, 71, 77, 85, 88, 93, 97, 110
St Paul's church Conventus in territory of Orvieto, **98**:41
St Paul's Gate, **97**:74
St Peregrinus' oratory in Lord's hostel at Naumachia, **98**:81
St Peter, bounty of, **98**:69, donation to, property of **91**:21, **93**:9, 25–6, **94**:41, 45–6, **97**:6, 19–20, 22–3, 27, 33, 41–3, 63, 69, 77, **98**:17, **99**:2, choice of pope by **96**:10, grave ad Catacumbas **98**:47, honour of, **98**:106, inscription by **95**:3, intercession of **93**:13, **94**:19, 44, **97**:24, **98**:13, 16, 22–3, loyalty/devotion to **94**:31, 45 **97**:33, 56–7, **98**:15, promises/oath to/by **94**:42–3, **97**:5, 26, 33, 41, rights of **96**:28–30, **97**:8, 22, 26, 30, see of **95**:2, service of, **97**:32, treaty on behalf of **94**:26, vicar of, **97**:19, 41, 43
St Peter's basilica, **91**:4, 25, **92**:3, 5, 8–11, 13–14, 16–18, **93**:8, 11, 19, 21, 23, 26, 29, **94**:4, 13, 19, 40, 47, 52, 54, **95**:2–3, 6–7, **96**:4, 13, 24, 27–33, **97**:14, 24, 32, 37–41, 43, 45–8, 53, 57, 59, 61, 64, 67, 70, 72, 74, 78, 81, 83–4, 87, 89, 93, 96–7, **98**:1, 6–8, 14–15, 19, 21–4, 27, 33, 39, 47–8, 53, 57, 64, 66–8, 71, 72, 75–7, 80, 84, 86, 89–90, 93, 96, 100, 105, 110, 112–3, **99**:1, 5
St Peter's basilica at Marulis estate, **97**:76
St Peter's Gate, **91**:6, **96**:8, **97**:66, 94, **98**:70, 99
St Peter's oratory in Lateran patriarchate, **91**:9
St Peter's hospice and church at Naumachia, **98**:90
St Peter's (ad vincula, Apostles', Eudoxia's) *titulus*, **97**:75, 89, **98**:7, 37, 71, 78, **99**:3, 4
St Peter's basilica at Albano, **98**:42, 107
St Peter's basilica at Pavia, **93**:14
SS Peter and Marcellinus' cemetery, **97**:50
SS Peter and Paul's church, Via Sacra, **95**:6
St Petronilla, relics, inscription, **95**:3
St Petronilla's cemetery, **92**:13
St Petronilla's mausoleum/altar at St Peter's, **94**:52, **95**:3, 6, **97**:78, **98**:8, 35, 55, 60, 68, 72, 86, 101, 110
St Praxedes' *titulus*, **97**:78, **98**:37, 74
SS Primus and Felician, bodies, **98**:47
St Prisca's *titulus*, **97**:51, **98**:10, 73, 80
SS Processus and Martinian's basilica, **92**:11
St Pudentiana's (Pudens') *titulus*, **97**:76, **98**:37, 74, 79, 112
SS Quattuor Coronati *titulus* (cf. Aemiliana's *titulus*?), **97**:89, **98**:40
St Rufina (Buxum, now Boccea), **97**:55
SS Rufina and Secunda's basilica at Silva Candida, **97**:76
St Saba's (Cella Nova) monastery, **96**:12, 14, **97**:21, 88, **98**:76
St Sabina's *titulus*, **98**:4, 29, 40, 42–3, 73, 81, 85, 103
St Sabina's church in territory of Ferentinellum, **97**:89
St Saturninus' basilica, **97**:79
St Sebastian's/SS Apostles on Via Appia at Catacumbae, **97**:76, **98**:47
St Secundinus' basilica at Palestrina, **97**:82
St Sergius' monastery, **98**:79

INDEX

SS Sergius and Bacchus' deaconry at St Peter's, **92**:13
SS Sergius and Bacchus' deaconry inside Rome, **97**:90, **98**:38, 75
SS Sergius and Bacchus' oratory in Callinicum, **98**:78
St Silanus' church, **97**:79
St Silvester's (and/or St Martin's) basilica/titulus/deaconry in Orfea, **97**:64, 73, **98**:45, 75, 81
St Silvester's deaconry by St Peter's, **94**:4, **97**:66, **98**:75
St Silvester's oratory at Lateran, **93**:18
St Silvester's cemetery, Via Salaria, **97**:80
St Silvester's (pope Paul's) monastery, **95**:5, **96**:12, **98**:11, 13, 38, 76
SS Simplicius, Servilian, Quartus, Quintus and Sophia's cemetery/church, **97**:78
St Soteris' cemetery, **94**:14
St Stephen's basilica/church on Monte Celio, **97**:61, 82, **98**:47, 71, 104
St Stephen's basilica, Via Latina, **98**:94
St Stephen's church by St Hippolytus' cemetery, **97**:85
St Stephen's church by St Laurence's basilica, **97**:75
St Stephen's monastery by Lateran, **98**:76
St Stephen's monastery by St Laurence outside walls, **98**:77
St Stephen's monastery at St Paul's, **98**:77
St Stephen's monastery (minor) by St Peter's, **94**:40, **98**:76
St Stephen's monastery (major) by St Peter's, cata Barbara/Galla patricia, **97**:53, **98**:47, 77, 90
St Stephen Vagauda monastery, **97**:71
St Stephen's oratory in Dulcitius', **98**:78
SS Stephen, Laurence and Chrysogonus' monastery – see St Chrysogonus'
SS Stephen and Silvester's monastery – see St Silvester's monastery
St Susanna's *titulus* ad duas domus, **97**:70, **98**:9, 74, 103
St Symmetrius' monastery, **98**:80
St Tertullinus' cemetery outside Latin Gate, **97**:78
St Theodore's deaconry, **98**:45, 75
St Theodore's basilica in Sabellum, **97**:76, **99**:4

St Thomas' (church), Via Appia, **97**:76
SS Tiburtius, Valerian and Maximus' church outside Appian Gate, **97**:78
St Tiburtius', Via Labicana, **97**:50
SS Urban, Felicissimus and Agapitus, Januarius and Cyrinus' cemetery, **97**:78
St Valentine's basilica outside walls, **97**:49, 61, **98**:29, 72, 91
St Valentine's basilica at Terni, **93**:7, 10
St Venantius' church/altar by Lateran baptistery, **96**:9, **98**:32
St Victor's monastery at St Pancras' basilica, **97**:73, **98**:77
St Vincent's monastery (al Volturno), **94**:7
St Vitalis' *titulus*, **98**:5, 37, 74, 108
St Vitus' deaconry, **98**:45, 75
St Vitus' oratory/monastery de Sardas, **96**:10, **98**:78
St Xystus' *titulus*, **97**:73, **98**:45, 73
St Xystus' (and St Cornelius') cemetery on Via Appia, **98**:5, 40
St Zeno's basilica outside Appian Gate, **97**:78
St Zoticus' cemetery, Via Labicana, **98**:5
Salarian Bridge, **96**:7
San Marino (Castellum S. Marini), **94**:47
Saracens, **91**:11–12
Sardas monastery – see St Vitus' oratory
Saviour, altar in St Genesius' church, **92**:12
Saviour, relics in domusculta Capracorum, **97**:69
Saviour's/Constantinian basilica, **92**:10, 16, **94**:3, **96**:9–10, 13, 18, **97**:39, 49, 68, 70, 84, 87, **98**:4, 6, 8, 25, 32, 39, 43, 51, 56, 69, 76, 82, 88, 95; baptistery, **97**:62
Saviour's oratory at St Peter's, **92**:6, **93**:8
Saviour's monastery (near Rieti), **96**:5
Saxon(s), **98**:9, 19
Segni, **96**:17, 30
Senate, **97**:69
Senigállia (Sena Gallica), **94**:47, **96**:17, **97**:18
Sens, **96**:17
Septem Viae, **98**:38, 75
Sergius I pope, **91**:1
Sergius archbishop of Ravenna, **96**:19, 25
Sergius bishop of Ferentino, **96**:17
Sergius bishop of Ficuclae, **96**:17

Sergius priest of Rome, **92**:14
Sergius secundicerius and nomenclator, **96**:5, 7–8–10, 16–17, 28–32
Sergius patrician and strategus, **92**:4
Sergius consul of Ravenna (same as the archbishop?), **93**:9
Serra, **94**:47
Sessorian – see Jerusalem basilica
Sicily, **92**:2, 4, **96**:1
Silva Candida, **96**:17, 24, **97**:76
Sori, **97**:42
Sovana, **98**:41
Spain, **91**:11
Spoletines, **91**:16
Spoleto, **91**:22, **92**:15, **93**:2–8, **94**:47, **96**:5, 7, 15, **97**:5, 32–3, 42, **98**:15
Stabilis bishop of Pesaro, **96**:17
Stabilis, Lombard duke, **97**:20
Stephen II pope, **94**:passim, **95**:1, 3, **96**:2, **97**:8, 41
Stephen pope-elect, **94**:2
Stephen III pope, **96**:passim, **97**:8
Stephen IV pope, **99**:passim
Stephen bishop of Centumcellae, **96**:17
Stephen bishop of Naples, **96**:19
Stephen notary and sacellarius, **97**:6, 8
Stephen priest of Rome, **93**:14
Stephen priest (perhaps the future Stephen III), **94**:23, 50
Stephen patrician and duke, **93**:2, 12
Subura, **98**:56, 76, 91, **99**:4
Sulpiciana domusculta, **97**:76
Sussubium, **94**:47
Sutri, **91**:21, **93**:9, 11, **96**:17
Syrian, **92**:1

Tacipert gastald, **93**:11
Temple of Rome, **95**:6
Tempulus' monastery – see St Agatha's oratory
Terni, **93**:6–7
Theodicius duke of Spoleto, **96**:5, 15, **97**:5
Theodimus subdeacon, **91**:7
Theodo duke of the Bavarians, **91**:4
Theodore pope, basilica of, **93**:18, **96**:29
Theodore bishop, vicedominus, **96**:9, 12
Theodore archpriest of Pavia-Ticinum, **96**:17
Theodore father of Hadrian I, **97**:1

Theodore son of Megistus, **93**:25
Theodosius bishop of Tivoli, **96**:17, 24, **97**:25
Theodosius III emperor, **91**:1, 5
Theodota widow, **97**:63
Theodotus consul and duke, **97**:2
Theophylact archdeacon, **94**:23, **95**:1
Three Fates, **96**:11, **97**:51, 76, **98**:91
Three Sickles arch, **97**:94
Tiber river, **91**:6, **95**:7, **97**:94
Tiberius bishop of Rimini, **96**:17
Tiberius Petasius usurper, **91**:23
Ticinum – see Pavia
Tilpin bishop of Rheims, **96**:17
Tivoli, **96**:17, 24, **97**:25, **98**:47
Tortona, **96**:17
Toto of Nepi, **96**:3, 9
Tours, **96**:17
Transalpine armies, **94**:48
Transamund duke of Spoleto, **92**:15, **93**:2–5, 8
Trastevere, **97**:79, 84
Tres Tabernae, **96**:17
Trevi, **96**:17
Tucium xenodochium, **98**:81
Tunno duke of Ivrea, **97**:5
Tuscánia (ancient Tuscana), **93**:11, **98**:41
Tuscánia (Toscanella), **96**:17
Tuscia, **91**:23, **93**:9, 11, 26, **94**:48–9, **96**:3, 14, 17, 28, **97**:18, 24, 35, 92
Urbino (Urbinum), **94**:47, **96**:17, **97**:18

Vagauda – see St Stephen Vagauda
Valentine priest of Ravenna, **96**:17
Valeran bishop of Trevi, **96**:17
Valerius/a Valeris, xenodochium of, **96**:15, **98**:81
Valva, **93**:3
Veii, **97**:54
Velabrum – see St George's deaconry
Velletri, **96**:17, **98**:44
Venetiae, **91**:17, **97**:15, 42
Venetians, **93**:22
Verabulum, **91**:18
Verona, **97**:31, 34
vestiarium (St Anastasius'), **97**:91; see Lateran
Via Appia, **92**:13, **97**:76, 78, **98**:5, 30, 40, 47
Via Ardeatina, **97**:55, 63

INDEX

Via Aurelia, **97**:55
Via Flaminia, **97**:77, **98**:91
Via Labicana, **97**:50, **98**:5
Via Lata, **91**:6, **95**:6, **97**:1, 50, 60, 79, 94–5, **98**:45, 70, 71, 74, 91, 102
Via Latina, **98**:94
Via Ostiensis, **98**:109
Via Portuensis, **97**:55
Via Sacra, **95**:6, **98**:91
Via Salaria, **97**:79, 80
Via Tiburtina, **93**:25
Victor consul of Ravenna, **93**:9
Vicus Patricius, **98**:47
Vienne, **92**:18
Vincula – see St Agapitus' monastery, and St Peter's *titulus*
Virgo aqueduct, **97**:65
Vitalian tribune, **97**:7

Viterbo, **93**:11, **97**:25
Vobio (? Sarsina), **94**:47

Waldipert priest, **96**:7, 8, 10, 15
walled towns round Rome, **94**:6, 17
Warnehar religious man, **94**:42
Wilchar bishop of Mentana, **94**:23 Wilchar of Sens, archbishop of the Gauls (same as last?), **96**:17
Wilchar of Vienne, archbishop of the districts of France, **92**:18
Winichis duke of Spoleto, **98**:15
Worms, **96**:17
Wulfram bishop of Meaux, **96**:17
Würzburg, **96**:17

Zacharias pope, **93**:passim, **94**:2, 15, **95**:1, **96**:1

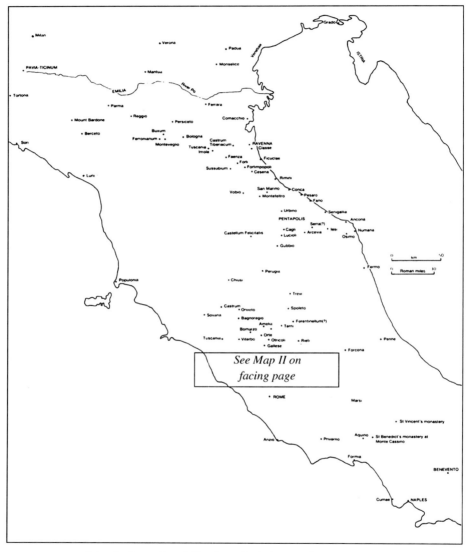

Map I Central and Northern Italy in the Eighth Century

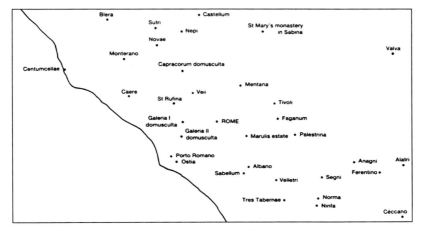

Rome and Surrounding Areas *(see Map 1 on facing page)*

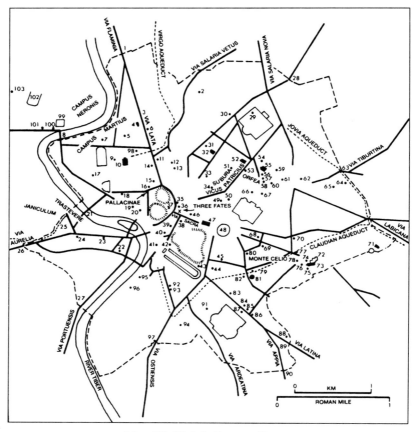

Map III Eighth-Century Rome

Key

1 Flaminian Gate
2 St Felix in pincis basilica
3 Three Sickles arch
4 St Laurence's titulus in Lucirla
5 St Gregory's oratory in Campus Martius
6 St Silvester's (pope Paul's) monastery
7 St Apollinaris' basilica/church (inside Rome)
8 St Peter's Gate
9 St Eustace's deaconry (xenodochium in Platana)

10 St Mary's church ad martyres
11 St Marcellus' titulus
12 Apostles' basilica
13 St Andrew's monastery by Apostles' basilica
14 St Mary's deaconry on Via Lata
15 St Mark's titulus
16 St Laurence's monastery in Pallacinis
17 St Laurence's titulus in Damaso
18 St Mary's (Julia's) monastery
19 St Mary's (Ambrose's) monastery
20 Archangel's deaconry with St Abbacyrus' altar
21 Antoninus, bridge of
22 St Caecilia's titulus
23 St Chrysogonus' titulus and monastery
24 St Mary's (Callistus') titulus in Trastevere
25 Sabbatina Aqueduct
26 St Pancras' Gate
27 Portuensis Gate
28 Nomentan Gate
29 St Cyriac's titulus
30 St Susanna's titulus
31 St Agatha's deaconry
32 St Vitalist titulus
33 St Agatha's monastery/basilica over Subura
34 SS Sergius and Bacchus' oratory in Callinicum
35 St Martina's altar/basilica
36 St Hadrian's deaconry
37 SS Sergius and Bacchus' deaconry inside Rome
38 St Mary's deaconry Antiqua
39 St Theodore's deaconry
40 St George's deacorry at the Velabrum
41 St Mary's deaconry in Cosmedin
42 St Anastasia's titulus
43 St Lucy's deaconry in Septem Vias
44 St Andrew's monastery in Clivus Scauri
45 SS John and Paul's (Pammachius') titulus
46 SS Cosmas and Damian's deaconry on Via Sacra
47 Temple of Rome
48 Colosseum
49 St Agapitus' monastery ad vincula
50 St Peter's ad vincula (Apostles', Eudoxia's) titulus
51 St Laurence ad Formonsum church
52 St Pudentiana's (Pudens') titulus
53 St Euphemia's (and Archangel's) basilica/monastery
54 S8 Cosmas and Damian's monastery by praesepe
55 St Mary's basilica ad praesepe
56 St Hadrian's (and St Laurence's) monastery

57 Dua Furna monastery with St Agnes' oratory
58 St Praxedes' titulus
59 St Andrew's church by the praesepe
60 St Andrew's monastery Massa Juliana (cata Barbara patricia)
61 St Vitus' deaconry
62 St Eusebius' basilica
63 St Laurence's Gate
64 St Isidore's monastery
65 St Bibiana's monastery
66 St Lucy's deaconry in Orfea
67 St Silvester's (and/or St Martin's) titulus/deaconry
68 St Clement's titulus
69 SS Quattuor Coronati (Aemiliana's) titulus
70 SS Marcellinus and Peter's by the Lateran
71 Jerusalem basilica at the Sessorian
72 Lateran patriarchate
73 Saviour's/Constantinian basilica
74 St Stephen's monastery by Lateran
75 St Pancras' monastery by Lateran
76 Constantinian baptistery
77 St Sergius' monastery
78 SS Andrew and Bartholomew's (pope Honorius') monastery
79 St Erasmus' monastery in Monte Celio
80 St Agatha's monastery in Caput Africae
81 St Stephen's basilica on Monte Celio
82 St Mary's deaconry Domnica
83 Tempulus' monastery with St Agatha's oratory
84 St Xystus' titulus
85 Monastery de Corsas with St Caesarius' oratory
86 St Symmetrius' monastery
87 SS Nereus and Achilleus' deaconry
88 St John's church at the Latin Gate
89 Latin Gate
90 Appian Gate
91 St Balbina's titulus
92 St Donatus' monastery
93 St Prisca's titulus
94 St Saba's (Cella Nova) monastery
95 St Sabina's titulus
96 St Boniface's deaconry
97 St Paul's Gate
98 St Mary's deaconry in Aquiro
99 Hadrianium
100 St Mary's deaconry at Hadrianium
101 St Mary's deaconry outside St Peter's Gate
102 Naumachia
103 St Peregrinus' in Lord's Hospital